EXECUTIVE COMPENSATION— A TOTAL PAY PERSPECTIVE

Bruce R. Ellig

McGRAW-HILL BOOK COMPANY

New York   St. Louis   San Francisco   Auckland   Bogotá
Hamburg   Johannesburg   London   Madrid   Mexico
Montreal   New Delhi   Panama   Paris   São Paulo
Singapore   Sydney   Tokyo   Toronto

Library of Congress Cataloging in Publication Data

Ellig, Bruce R.
  Executive compensation—a total pay perspective

  Includes index.
  1.Executives—Salaries, pensions, etc.
2.Compensation management. I.Title.
HD4965.2.E44   658.4'072   80-28873

1234567890   DODO   8987654321

ISBN 0-07-019144-1

The editors for this book were William R. Newton and Esther Gelatt, the designer was Mary Ann Felice, and the production supervisor was Teresa F. Leaden. It was set in Garamond by University Graphics.

Printed and bound by R. R. Donnelley & Sons Company.

Contents

Preface   vii

1. The Problem   1
2. The Compensation Elements   9
3. Executive's Perception of Pay   19
4. Salary   39
5. Employee Benefits   87
6. Perquisites   141
7. Short-Term Incentives   185
8. Long-Term Incentives   219
9. Deferred Compensation   267
10. The Compensation Committee   285
11. Plan Objectives   305
12. Conclusion   317

Index   323

About the Author

Bruce R. Ellig, a Phi Beta Kappa graduate of the University of Wisconsin, has a B.B.A., an M.B.A., and over fifteen years of compensation experience. He is Vice President of Compensation and Benefits, Corporate Personnel Division, Pfizer Inc., and is also responsible for the personnel portion of the company's computerized data system.

Among Mr. Ellig's professional activities are membership in the Conference Board's Council on Compensation and in NAM's Employee Benefits and Compensation Policy Committee. He is also Charter President of the New York Association of Compensation Administrators, Charter President of the Eastern Region of the American Compensation Association, and a past president of the New York Personnel Management Association. In 1976 Mr. Ellig participated in the Presidential Quadrennial Pay Commission study of employee benefit programs for top federal employees. In 1977 he served in a similar capacity for the city of New York, reviewing the pay of top elected and appointed officials. In 1980 he was chairman of a pay commission with a similar assignment. In addition, he has worked with the federal Council on Wage and Price Stability in establishing pay standards and with the U.S. Civil Service Commission in implementing the Civil Service Reform Act.

Mr. Ellig is a frequent speaker at personnel workshops, seminars, and conferences throughout the United States. He has taught at New York University and the New School for Continuing Education, has published articles in his areas of responsibility, has had his opinions widely quoted, and is coauthor of a book, *Compensation and Benefits: Analytical Strategies*, published by the American Compensation Association. He was a contributing author to McGraw-Hill's *Encyclopedia of Professional Management* and is now serving as consulting editor for AMACOM's *Compensation Review*.

The American Compensation Association has officially recognized Mr. Ellig as one of the country's leading compensation experts. He has also been awarded the Accredited Personal Diplomate certificate (APD)—the American Society for Personnel Administration's highest level of recognition for a compensation and benefits specialist.

Preface

This book differs from others in that it attempts to cover all aspects of executive compensation. Some books focus on incentive pay, some on employee benefits. Others cover total compensation for all levels of an organization and therefore spend little time on the unique nature of executive pay. This book was written to fill what is perceived to be a specific void: the lack of information about total executive compensation.

Five basic elements of executive pay are examined: salary, short-term incentives, long-term incentives, employee benefits, and perquisites. The analysis points out the characteristics, strengths, and weaknesses of each element and shows how it can be combined with other elements to shape a total pay package.

The book is intended for three separate and distinct audiences: those designing executive pay programs, those responsible for the approval and maintenance of such plans, and those receiving executive pay—namely, the executives themselves.

In covering the subject of executive pay, the approach is multifaceted: clear definitions are given and each element of executive pay is examined in terms of tax, accounting, and SEC treatment. Furthermore, the elements of pay are viewed in relation to executive needs and company objectives; the role of the compensation committee in designing and administering the pay program is also discussed.

The material is presented in a manner that attempts to make a very "heavy" subject interesting. Where possible, definitions are supplemented with examples and charts. Tables are used liberally to help each reader apply the material to his or her own specific situation.

An impartial analytical style has been the intent throughout the book. Readers are cautioned that the book is *not* intended to advise and that, because of the technical and changing nature of tax, accounting, and SEC issues, specific situations should be reviewed by counsel before an action is taken. Also, all examples and specifics, unless otherwise noted, are fictional in nature. Any resemblance to actual companies, individuals, reports, or situations is purely coincidental.

The author is especially indebted to Mr. Donald C. Lum, Pfizer's Vice President of Personnel, for establishing an environment in which these and other ideas could be nurtured and developed. However, the comments and views in this book are solely those of the author and in no way imply a position of Pfizer Inc. or its management. And a very special "thank you" to Dolores Poindexter. Without her assistance the book would not have been possible; she cheerfully deciphered illegible writing and turned it into type-written prose.

Bruce R. Ellig

The Problem

The plethora of articles and reports on the subject of executive compensation does more to confuse than to enlighten those who are not hip deep in the mainstream of compensation planning and administration. Each piece focuses on one aspect of top management pay with little attempt to place this aspect in proper perspective to the whole.

Not too surprisingly, some chief executive officers (CEOs) have thrown up their hands in disgust and adopted a plan one of their counterparts discussed across the luncheon table—or perhaps picked what appeared to be the best features of several plans.

This never ceases to amaze me. Each company proudly points to the results of its research function, its own marketing strategies, and its production process improvements but is willing to accept an incentive plan used by another company with little or no attempt to determine its appropriateness.

The basic objective should be to produce pay delivery systems which will result in compensation that is internally equitable (given assigned level of responsibility and degree of success in attaining it) and externally competitive (thus neither overpaying and misusing capital nor paying too little to attract and retain needed level of performer).

The procedures which ensure realization of the objective must be cost effective. Having nothing committed to writing is as bad as a bureaucratic function that is more interested in ensuring its own continuance (by developing increasingly precise rules which only it can interpret) than in optimizing the production of a viable pay delivery system.

In addition, the record-keeping ability of the company must be sufficient to allow it to produce data at a time and in a manner which enables one to make periodic assessments of the degree to which the pay objective (internally and externally) is being met. A computerized personnel data bank is the optimum, but admittedly for some organizations it may not be cost effective.

PAY COMPRESSION

The compensation program is a dependent, not independent, component of the organization. Its structure must be consistent with the organizational objectives and should facilitate their attainment and penalize their degree of failure. Usually this is a philosophy agreed to in principle but largely ignored (especially the aspect dealing with failure) in practice.

The problem is further complicated by the impact of collective bargaining agreements and increasing starting salaries for college graduates. They result in significant pressure to increase the lower end of the exempt salary structure. Conversely, public pressure on visible compensation for the five or so highest-paid executives serves to retard growth in the upper portion of the structure. This is illustrated in Figure 1-1. While the absolute increases are probably still greater at the upper portion than the lower end, the percentage increases are higher at the bottom of the structure. This results in a flattening or compressing of the salary curve (a perfectly flat curve would be parallel to the X axis) and a diminishing in the amount of pay differentials for greater responsibility (i.e., job value). This is the effect called *pay compression*. Since this is a reduction of the differential between organizational levels, it is a phenomenon that can only be measured at two or more intervals in time. An additional factor contributing to compression is the introduction of additional layers of management, thus lessening the differential between organizational levels.

Many companies further compound the inequity by stretching out the salary review period to 15 months, 18 months, or even 2 years at the top of the compensation structure. While the increase given is larger than for annual reviews, rarely is it proportionately larger. In other words, instead of giving 18 percent after 18 months versus 12 percent after 12 months (for a given level of performance), the company is more likely to give

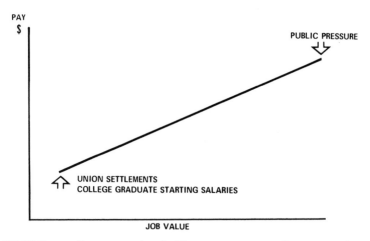

FIGURE 1-1 Pay compression (public pressure versus college-union adjustments).

2

TABLE 1-1 Ordinary versus Personal Service Income

Taxable income	Ordinary income		Personal service income	
	Taxes	After tax	Taxes	After tax
$ 50,000	$ 14,778	$ 35,222	$ 14,778	$ 35,222
100,000	41,998	58,002	39,678	60,322
150,000	74,868	75,132	64,678	85,322
200,000	108,772	91,228	89,678	110,322
250,000	143,740	106,260	114,678	135,322
500,000	318,740	181,260	239,678	260,322

15 percent after 18 months. One could argue that because the individual had to wait 6 months longer (a period during which another person already was enjoying the 12 percent increase) the increase should be somewhat greater than 18 percent, certainly not less.

Since little can be done to slow the growth at the bottom of the structure (as it would mean insufficient differentials between first-line supervisors and the union employees they supervise), compensation planners focus on devising less visible forms of pay for the senior executive (e.g., benefits and perquisites) and those which relate directly to performance (e.g., short- and long-term incentives) and where high payments can be explained in terms of specific performance.

This book therefore will deal not simply with the salary structure but also with the other four elements (i.e., benefits, perquisites, short- and long-term incentives). Each element will be defined and described. Emphasis will be not on a textbook definition but rather on how various forms relate in different manners to individual and organizational needs.

TAX CONSIDERATIONS

In describing various forms of the five elements and how they may be employed, the tax treatment will be discussed, when the income is something other than straight personal service income (which is currently taxed at a maximum of 50 percent beginning at about $60,000 for a married person filing a joint return). This is not intended to be a book on taxation of executive compensation; therefore, the discussions will be supportive and illustrative rather than primary and exhaustive. However, the importance of considering taxes is demonstrated in Table 1-1, which reports the federal income tax (and after-tax income) at selected levels of taxable income, under the 1978 Revenue Act, for both ordinary and personal service income.

The pessimist at the $500,000 level cries about the $239,678 tax liability; the optimist rejoices over the $260,322 after taxes. Regardless of the perspective, one thing is clear: it is better now than it was previously. Namely, in 1964 the top marginal rate was reduced from 91 to 77 percent, the following year it was lowered to 70 percent, and in

3

TABLE 1-2 Federal After-Tax Cost to Company

	Status of $1.00 paid to executive		
	No expense or tax credit	Tax deductible	Nondeductible
Company cost	0	$0.54*	$1.00

*Assumes 46 percent tax rate.

1969 the 50 percent maximum tax for wages was introduced. Furthermore, many countries abroad have tax rates more confiscatory than even our earlier policies.

In examining tax impact, it is appropriate to consider what is left after taxes. This after-tax examination can be done for both the executive and the company: the first is *after-tax value*, while the second is *after-tax cost*. Dividing the former by the latter, we achieve a numerical expression of *after-tax effectiveness*. Namely, to the extent the executive's after-tax value increases or the company's after-tax cost decreases, one has improved the after-tax effectiveness.

As shown in Table 1-2, the company essentially has three situations with regard to a compensation expense: no expense or tax credit, tax deductible, and non–tax deductible. The first says either there is no out-of-pocket expense or the expense is a tax credit and therefore reduces dollar-for-dollar its tax liability (truly a no-cost expense since the federal government is paying the full charge). If it is tax deductible, it reduces the company income before taxes dollar-for-dollar (here the federal government is a partner in paying the expenses). The worst situation is when the expense is nondeductible for tax purposes and the company therefore receives no tax assistance and bears the full expense of the payment.

The executive's after-tax value is dependent on the manner in which the expense is taxed. In the best situation it either is not taxed or, if taxable, is fully tax deductible and therefore cancels itself out (i.e., the amount is entered as income but income is then reduced by the amount of the deduction). The next best situation is long-term capital

TABLE 1-3 Federal After-Tax Value by Type of Income

	Net (after-tax) value of $1.00			
Executive's taxable earnings	Nontaxable or taxable, but fully deductible	Long-term capital gains	Personal service income	Short-term capital gains or ordinary income
$250,000	$1.00	$0.720	$0.50	$0.30
200,000	1.00	0.728	0.50	0.32
150,000	1.00	0.744	0.50	0.36
100,000	1.00	0.764	0.50	0.41
50,000	1.00	0.804	0.50	0.51

gains (i.e., property held longer than a year), where 60 percent of the gain is excluded and the remainder taxed as ordinary income. Short-term capital gains (i.e., income on property held 1 year or less), ordinary income, and personal service income are taxed exactly the same, except that personal service income has a maximum rate of 50 percent. This becomes important for a married person filing jointly with taxable earnings above $60,000, a single person with taxable income above $41,500, and a married person filing a separate return with taxable earnings above $30,000. Table 1-3 indicates the federal after-tax value of $1.00 for these different tax situations at selected income levels. State income tax, where appropriate, would further reduce the values.

Tax Effectiveness

As indicated earlier, dividing the executive's after-tax value by the company's after-tax cost gives one a measurement of the tax effectiveness of the form of payment. The higher the value, the more tax effective the payment.

$$\text{Tax effectiveness} = \frac{\text{executive's after-tax value}}{\text{company's after-tax cost}}$$

By combining the three possibilities for net company cost with the four possibilities of net executive income at $250,000, it is possible to construct the matrix shown in Table 1-4. While similar matrices could be constructed for $50,000, $100,000, $150,000, and $200,000, they would be identical for the first and third columns. Throughout this report the values from the matrix in Table 1-2 will be used to illustrate tax impact. It should be remembered that if long-term capital gains or ordinary income are involved, a more precise measurement can be obtained by returning to Table 1-1.

The normal value is 0.93. This reflects a 50 percent personal service income tax for such payments as salary and bonuses with a corporate tax rate of 46 percent. Thus $0.50 after-tax value divided by a $0.54 after-tax cost equals 0.93. A low value for a $250,000 executive would be 0.30 such as would be derived from stock dividends since they are taxed as ordinary income to the executive and are not tax deductible to the company. The importance of salary not being a non−tax deductible dividend to a small company executive-shareholder is quite apparent. Even if successfully identified as personal service

TABLE 1-4 After-Tax—Company Cost versus Employee Value

Company's after-tax cost	Executive's after-tax value of $1.00			
	Nontaxable or taxable but fully deductible	Long-term capital gains	Personal service income	Short-term capital gains or ordinary income
No expense	∞	∞	∞	∞
Deductible	$1.85	$1.33	$ .93	$0.56
Nondeductible	1.00	0.72	0.50	0.30

income, it is important that it not be deemed unreasonable compensation by the Internal Revenue Service (IRS), for it would then move from a 0.93 (i.e., $0.50 divided by $0.54) to a 0.30 for a highly paid executive (i.e., $0.30 ordinary income divided by $1.00 since unreasonable compensation is not tax deductible).

The maximum value is infinity, determined by dividing $1.00, $0.72, $0.50, or $0.30 by zero cost. However, very few items are both income to the executive and no cost to the company. One example is when an executive travels on a company plane for pleasure by merely taking an empty seat on a business trip to the same location; certainly there is no additional out-of-pocket expense to the company, yet there is a definite after-tax value to the individual.

In addition to direct pay (or fair market value for such things as stock awards), executives must be familiar with several taxable situations, namely constructive receipt, economic benefit, and imputed income.

Constructive receipt occurs when the executive had the right to take the pay currently but chose to defer it or to accept it in some other form. Simply turning one's back on the offered compensation is not sufficient to avoid constructive receipt (i.e., being taxed as if it were received). A more detailed explanation of this principle is found in Chapter 9, Deferred Compensation. *Economic benefit* is closely allied with the doctrine of constructive receipt. The former is usually invoked when the company funds a future payment to the executive through an insurance contract or trust. In these situations the individual will be taxed on the annual value of the employer contributions even though the principle of constructive receipt was not invoked. This point is also covered in more detail in Chapter 9. *Imputed income* occurs when the value of a service is estimated (e.g., personal use of corporate aircraft). The value may be the actual cost to the company or, in some instances, the value of a comparable service through other means (e.g, the cost of first-class commercial air fare). The impact of imputed income is discussed in some detail in Chapter 6, Perquisites.

SEC DISCLOSURE REQUIREMENTS

In addition to being familiar with the tax aspects of various forms of compensation, it is important to be aware of the Securities Exchange Commission (SEC) requirements of disclosure. Currently these apply individually to the five highest-paid executive officers or directors earning more than $50,000 per annum, as well as to the officers and directors as a group. The requirements for the remuneration table are identified by columns:

Column A: Name of individual or number of persons in group

Column B: Capacity in which persons served

Column C: Cash and cash-equivalent forms of remuneration

Column C_1:   Salaries, fees, commissions, and bonuses

Column C$_2$:   Securities or property vested or received, insurance benefits or reimbursement, and other personal benefits

Column D: Aggregate of contingent forms of remuneration

Thus it can be seen that columns C and D are the compensation columns. The determining factor of where an item is reported is whether or not a contingency exists as to payment. If so, it is reportable in column D. If no contingency exists, regardless of whether received or not, it is reportable in column C. Thus, vested and deferred compensation with no forfeiture features is reportable in column C. Compensation previously reported in column D logically would not be reported in column C when actually received. Also, the cost of perquisites should be included in column C unless the value cannot be obtained without reasonable effort and expense, the cost is not greater than $10,000 per individual, and omission is not misleading.

Beginning with the 1981 proxy season, the SEC decided that stock options and stock appreciation rights should be described in separate tables, rather than being included in columns C$_2$ and D of the remuneration table. In addition, a separate table is required for defined benefit plans whose amounts are not included in the remuneration table.

WHO IS AN EXECUTIVE?

It's important to clarify that definition quickly since this is a book on executive compensation. On one hand we have the definition of executive provided by the Fair Labor Standards Act, which specifies those jobs exempt from overtime pay. Its requirements, supervising at least two full-time subordinates in a position customarily requiring the exercise of independent judgment and discretion, could be assumed to mean that any supervisor earning approximately $15,000 or more would be an executive. Conversely, some insist that the definition applies only to corporate officers. Both positions are extremes. Certainly a significant portion of this book is directed solely to divisional officers and even higher ranks, but in most organizations many aspects of the pay discussion will be applicable several layers below these levels.

An "executive" for purposes of this book is any individual in a managerial position within the organization who is probably in the highest-paid 2 to 3 percent of the company's total employee population or the highest-paid 5 percent of the exempt portion of the work force.

The Compensation Elements

There are five basic compensation elements: salary, employee benefits, short-term incentives, long-term incentives, and perquisites. As shown in Figure 2-1 only salary and employee benefits are a factor at the lower portion of most organizations; however, all five are present at the CEO level—each of the other three being phased in at different points in the organization.

The objective of the *salary* element is to reflect extent of experience and sustained level of performance for a job of a particular level in importance to the organization. It is also the basis on which the other four elements are based. For many, salary is the income level which will allow the executive to meet many but not all of his or her lifestyle objectives. For that, the individual must also successfully meet short- and long-range incentive objectives (and resulting payouts). The latter keeps the executive "at risk." However, since incentives are essentially nonexistent in some industries and in nonprofit organizations, the salary program takes on added importance in adequately reflecting short- and long-range contributions to the organization.

The *employee benefits* element deals with providing time off with pay, employee services, nonperformance awards, health care, survivor protection, and retirement coverage to all employees in the organization. The extent of coverage is determined by years of service and/or level of pay.

The *short-term incentives* are designed to reward the extent of accomplishment of a short (normally yearly) target. Typically, the amount of payment goes up and down each year in relation to performance.

The *long-term incentive* is similar to the short in objective except it is multiyear (typically 3 to 5). The incentive award by definition means the executive has a portion of pay placed "at risk" with degree of attainment of objectives. Not meeting the expected target calls for no bonus or low bonus, a form of punishment short of termination of employment.

Perquisites are employee benefits which are designed only

Chapter
2

9

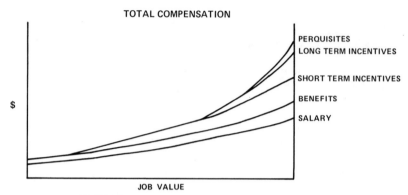

TOTAL COMPENSATION

PERQUISITES
LONG TERM INCENTIVES

SHORT TERM INCENTIVES

BENEFITS

$

SALARY

JOB VALUE

FIGURE 2-1 Total compensation (five element curves).

to apply to executives. In some instances, they merely supplement employee benefit coverage, in other instances they provide coverage which does not exist in the employee benefit program.

As depicted in Figure 1-1 the progression on pay is nonlinear. The pyramidal structure of the company means an arithmetic increase in responsibility (a promotion) and a geometric decrease in the probability of receiving an additional one. Thus sufficient room must be allowed in the pay for the job to reflect longer "rest intervals" at each succeeding grade. By definition when the person has been promoted to CEO the individual has exhausted his or her career potential in that company! The structure must take into account and provide sufficient stretch for compensation growth for performance.

As seen in Figure 2-1, but perhaps more clearly in Table 2-1, these elements of compensation take on different emphasis at different levels in the organization. For example, at the $50,000 total compensation level, 65 percent (i.e., $32,500) might be in salary, 10 percent (i.e., $5000) in short-term incentives, 2.5 percent (i.e., $1250) in long-term incentives (maybe all in a stock option), and 22.5 percent (i.e., $11,250) in employee benefits.

TABLE 2-1 Possible Compensation Distribution of Five Elements

	Total compensation				
	$50,000	$100,000	$250,000	$500,000	$1,000,000
Salary	65 %	60%	50 %	40%	30 %
Short-term incentive	10	15	20	20	20
Long-term incentive	2.5	5	10	20	30
Employee benefits	22.5	20	17.5	15	12.5
Perquisites	—	—	2.5	5	7.5
Total	100 %	100%	100 %	100%	100 %

Moving up the five levels of total compensation, decreasing emphasis is applied to salary and benefits, whereas there is an increasing emphasis given to short-term incentives, long-term incentives, and perquisites.

The reason for the decreasing emphasis of salary at the expense of short- and long-term incentives is that it is more advantageous to the company to relate reward to performance and, in many cases, it is more advantageous to the individual to receive the award in a form other than cash.

The limitations imposed on many benefit plans (e.g., maximum pension) and the non–income-related programs (e.g., medical and dental insurance) account for the decreasing percentage of total compensation as that figure grows. In many situations, however, this decrease is offset by the extent of perquisites (e.g., chauffeured limousine, extensive medical exam plans, and supplementary pensions).

The relative importance of each element at the different income levels would, of course, vary from industry to industry and even within a given industry from company to company.

MARKET CYCLE IMPACT

The importance of each of these elements is conditioned on the stage in the market cycle for both the company and the industry. Shown in Figure 2-2 are the four classical stages: threshold, growth, maturity, and decline.

Threshold

During this stage the company probably has a limited range of closely related products. Distribution of these products may be primarily in a regional area, the company may have attained a position of dominance in a small industry, sales are probably under $50 million, and managers are exploring new markets for products.

Decisions are made by individuals, often with little thought or delay and usually on intuition. Relative duties and responsibilities of individuals have not been clearly identified, and a high degree of overlap in apparent responsibilities exists among a number of jobs. There is no depth of management.

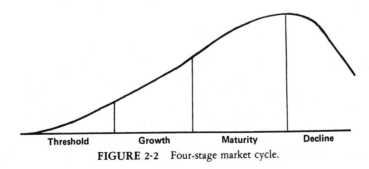

| Threshold | Growth | Maturity | Decline |

FIGURE 2-2 Four-stage market cycle.

The tone is casual with everyone on a first-name basis, and the dress code emphasizes comfort rather than appearance. Survival of the products has the full attention of everyone. Cash is scarce and cash flow problems periodically occur, with management often deferring their own salary payments to ease the crunch.

Growth

This phase marks the period of tremendous growth as the threshold company emerges with strong success in new venture areas as well as becoming a national influence by challenging the established leaders in market share. The increase in product lines probably has increased the diversity and complexity of related management processes. The number of employees increases along with sales, and management may shift from the original owners into the hands of professional managers as the company must cope with different problems brought on by apparent success. Coordination needs are greater and communication more formalized to ensure consistent interpretation; relative priorities need major review to ensure optimal success. Return on shareholder equity is very strong and increasing significantly during this phase.

During this period the company is likely to state its nature of business too broadly, venturing into product lines for which it lacks expertise. This often results in a level of performance far short of expectations; however, success in main lines overcompensates.

Cash and available time both seem to be in short supply as full energy is directed to maximizing product success. Little time exists for formalizing job descriptions, although individual responsibilities are better understood as greater specialization is required. The depth of management is very thin; however, some replacements or new positions can be staffed internally by juggling. Decision making has become more formalized, and alternatives are viewed in light of precedents set during the threshold stage. White shirts, rolled up at the sleeves, have replaced sport shirts; however, the tone is still informal and essentially on a first-name basis.

To stay in the "growth" phase, the company must continually find new uses for existing products and/or introduce new products. This requires a careful analysis of available capital for manufacturing and marketing to optimize the return on investment.

Maturity

This phase is marked by little change in market position (possibly some slippage is offset by new products—mainly interpolating or minor extrapolation of existing products rather than new breakthroughs). Emphasis is probably on maintaining current market penetration and servicing existing customers rather than adding new customers. Market share is more likely to gain by lowering prices than by increased investment. Administrative expenses become an increasing percentage of total costs as productivity improvements chip away at direct expenses. However, staff functions are increasing faster than the reductions in direct labor.

Job descriptions and organization charts have appeared, as have management succession charts to ensure adequate depth of management to meet organization needs. Corporate policies have been written to cover the full gambit of business issues, and an extensive financial record-keeping system has been developed. Managers find their freedom to act restrained by both. Due to policy limitations or dollar ceilings the manager must now recommend, rather than decide. Such recommendations require considerable time to prepare the justification. Committees have become popular during this phase and are often part of the decision-making process, resulting in both a slowdown of the decision-making process and a diffusing of individual responsibility.

Companies in a mature stage often undergo a "consolidation" whereby they trim their management ranks and narrow their marketing focus. Usually the latter is focused on their high-profit product lines in a more concentrated area. Product areas where the company sees little hope for increasing low profit margins are abandoned or spun off. Many conglomerates in the mature stage return to the businesses in which they have excelled. Others expand in acquired business lines. The need to develop new products or find new markets for existing products has surfaced.

Decline

This phase is the period during which market share is falling and/or the market itself is disappearing due to technological obsolescence. Cost improvement programs take on strong importance, many times in the form of amputation of unprofitable operations. The need to develop new products or find new markets for existing products is now critical.

Procedural manuals exist on almost every topic, specifying the preparation of forms to get approval on everything from a dozen pencils to a multimillion dollar capital investment. Form has become more important than substance. Commitment to the process has replaced commitment to results.

The organization is more formal in tone than in earlier phases, and first names are rarely used, regardless of how well known the person. Individuals are oblique and obtuse in their statements, and the manner of presentation has become more important than the substance. Although the *Titanic* is listing badly, some crew members are methodically rearranging the deck chairs, oblivious to the fact that the ship is sinking!

Paradoxically, cash is more likely to be available during this phase than most others, due to cutbacks in research and marketing expenses or the sale of part of the business. In capital-intensive companies the strong cash position could be the result of depreciation allowances which have not been reinvested in newer equipment. Also, the book value of the stock may very well exceed its market value. Or even more dramatically, net working capital (assets less all liabilities including preferred stock) may exceed the aggregate market value for the company market stock.

In this stage many companies will be forced to diversify simply by nature of their product line. Mining, oil, and gas companies facing a dwindling natural resource must look to supplementary business lines. The projected exhaustion point can be set back by new discoveries, but they delay rather than alter the inevitable result. For some this will mean other forms of geological exploration (such as minerals); for others it will mean entering businesses where its product is an essential part of business (such as chemicals). Others may reach outside of the related business worlds and enter a completely new field. The decision to leave the energy business may not be related to demand, but rather to supply.

The problem with food companies is the reverse, one of leveling demand (related to population). Here the desire to diversify within the field leads some to different, higher-profit product lines or alternative preparations (such as fast-food outlets). For others, vertical expansion to include growing, breeding, and shipping may be a more logical approach.

STRATEGIC PLANNING

Many consultants are engaged to assist in strategic planning, one aspect of which is to help identify the market phase by product. Some have used a matrix to assist in this identification process. A simple version of this is shown in Figure 2-3. As can be seen, the two criteria are "dollar return" and "market performance."

Obviously the grid could be more refined; however, even this simple version shows where certain combinations call for certain actions:

Combination A: Ideal situation, prime candidate for additional investment, assuming industry in threshold or growth stage.

Combination B: Investment needs are directed to improving strength of market performance. However, this must be assessed in terms of probable success; investment without improved market performance may turn this into a D combination.

Combination C: Probably not likely to be a candidate for additional investment; probably a source of capital for other projects.

Combination D: Prime candidate to be deleted; continuance is based on the extent to which deletion would adversely affect the product line and/or extensive overhead charges now absorbed would lower other products to C or D combinations.

MARKET PHASE MATRIX

$ RETURN	HIGH	B	A
	LOW	D	C
		WEAK	STRONG
		MARKET PERFORMANCE	

FIGURE 2-3   Market phase—dollar return versus market performance.

TABLE 2-2 Compensation Element versus Market Stage

	Emphasis by market stage			
Compensation element	Threshold	Growth	Maturity	Decline
Salary	Low	Moderate	High	High
Employee benefits	Low	Moderate	Moderate	High
Perquisites	Low	Low	Moderate	High
Short-term incentives	Low	Moderate	High	Moderate
Long-term incentives	High	High	Moderate	Low

This type of analysis is very helpful as it places each product in perspective, but it does not create any new products, merely aids the decision-making process regarding the current product line. In addition, it must be recognized that a particular company may have units in different phases of the market cycle. Thus while it may be possible to generalize on the whole as to the stage of the market cycle for the company, there are different needs for different parts. For this, different divisional pay programs may need to be developed.

As compared with company plans, however, divisional incentive plans suffer from a great disadvantage: lack of financial identity. Only rarely is a common stock traded on the market for a subsidiary; by financial definition there is no common stock for a division.

Even a true profit is often difficult to ascertain for a division or subsidiary (due to decisions made by corporate, not divisional, management on cross-divisional pricing, assigned products, and assessments). Thus, the range of design possibilities for long-term divisional incentives is severely limited—often so greatly that a corporate plan is the de facto decision.

MARKET CYCLE AND COMPENSATION ELEMENTS

Determination of market phase is also an important frame of reference for viewing the importance of each of the compensation elements as shown in the matrix in Table 2-2.

As Table 2-2 shows, the most important element in the *threshold* phase is the long-term incentive, essentially for two reasons. First, the need to reinvest earnings for marketing and production requirements places a heavy curtailment on direct cash outlays. Second, the belief that the company is about to emerge into the growth stage should mean significant improvement in earnings, and the company needs something to retain its top people. The latter is a strong case for use of stock options.

During the *growth* stage capital investment needs are still strong, but the company is in a good position to improve salaries and benefits (especially profit sharing) and set up some type of annual incentive plan. Long-term incentive plans, however, still have the major emphasis, as there is a strong interest in capital income programs tied to

15

company growth. The period is identifiable as one during which pay plans become more structured and complex.

By the time the company shifts into the *maturity* stage, short-term incentives have replaced long-term incentives as the major item; emphasis on cost containment as a major way to improve earnings becomes important. Long-term incentives start to shift from stock market to nonmarket valuation techniques as price earnings multiples start to slide. Perquisites start to increase in importance as psychic income becomes a partial trade-off for real income through the incentive plans. There is increased emphasis on salaries, leading to increased importance of wider structural ranges because promotional opportunities (and their big pay increases) are less likely and thus executives remain in job grades longer.

During the *decline* phase, fixed expenses such as salary, benefits, and perquisites become extremely important, although short-term cost reduction plans and long-term book (or other internal) value plans have some impact.

A comparison of the growth of product innovations in different decades readily shows that many more products and companies were in the development and growth stage in the 1950s and 1960s than today. One could logically argue that this is also reflected in the sluggish stock market. If price is really the present value of future earnings, it is easy to see why for many companies stock prices are not higher. Projections of the future based on past company performance are subject to significant error since the rate of growth is likely to be greater or less than the past. This degree of miscalculation is compounded by the number of years used in the projection.

Recognizing that a number of factors outside the company's control can and do significantly affect the market value of its stock, some might argue that the relationship of stock prices to book value (i.e., shareholder equity divided by number of shares issued and outstanding) is as shown in Figure 2-4. Note that during the growth stage market price significantly exceeds book, during maturity the spread diminishes and finally disappears, and finally during decline book starts to pull away from market value.

Given the difference between company and industry in terms of stage in market cycle, more emphasis should be placed on industry. Thus if the company is in the maturity phase while the industry is in the growth stage, the latter should be the primary

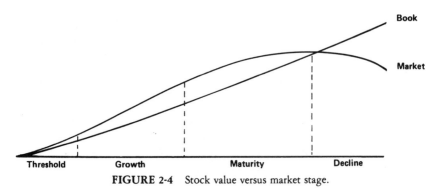

FIGURE 2-4   Stock value versus market stage.

reference since the company should be able to realize new crests (due to established market position) as the industry reaches maturity. Conversely if the company is in the growth stage and the industry in the maturity phase, it will be more difficult for the company to improve its current level of success.

SUMMARY AND CONCLUSIONS

It is important that the compensation elements be examined in terms of their characteristics and how such traits relate to the differing needs of each phase in the company's product cycle. Simply performing this basic analysis will significantly increase the probability of structuring a viable pay delivery system.

Executive's Perception of Pay

An additional consideration in the relative importance of the compensation elements is their impact on attracting, retaining, and motivating the executive—the basic requirements of a positive pay package. Shown in Table 3-1 are the five elements in terms of these three requirements.

Salary is very important in attracting and retaining executives but of little value in motivating them since salary adjustments are usually modest even for top performers. The salary associated with a promotion, however, is believed to be a positive factor. Thus, while the promotional pay increase may be motivational, it is doubtful that the normal merit pay policy serves as an inspiration.

A good employee benefit and perquisite program usually will have little impact on attracting (although poor ones may make it more difficult to interest wanted executives) and motivating the executive, but may have at least a moderate retention effect. Some factors, such as a final pay pension plan, may have a considerable holding impact if the executive has not attained a 100 percent vested level.

Short-term incentives can be very attractive and motivational to a top performer, especially if the payout is based on individual rather than group achievement. However, for incentive plans to work, the executive must have a positive attitude toward them and must believe that differences in performance will result in comparable differences in reward. In addition, the required level of performance must be considered not only attainable but cost effective (i.e., what is received must be deemed worth the time expended).

Long-term incentives, on the other hand, do have some positive aspects in attracting and motivating, but their main strength is usually in retaining the executive, due to the future-payout-on-current-performance definition. Long-term incentives are separated in time from performance and thus do not have strong motivational appeal.

It is believed that even if the pay packages do not attract, retain, and motivate as desired, their form and level of reward

19

TABLE 3-1 Impact of Five Compensation Elements on Executives

Compensation elements	Impact on individual executive		
	Attract	Retain	Motivate
Salary	High	High	Moderate
Employee benefits	Low	Moderate	Low
Perquisites	Low	Moderate	Low
Short-term incentives	High	Moderate	High
Long-term incentives	Moderate	High	Moderate

do serve as reinforcement vehicles to attract and retain a particular type of executive. As an example, a company with a high emphasis on salary (therefore by definition low on incentives) is likely to retain a steady performer but not the high risk accepter who wishes to be appropriately rewarded for success.

ATTRACTING EXECUTIVE TALENT

While companies usually express a desire to retain solid performers, they often do not pay them as well as new people they hire for comparable jobs. The latter receive a premium to leave a known and move to an unknown: increases of 25 percent or more are not uncommon. The greater the need and the more risky the position, the greater the premium expected. Thus the individual who has moved every 4 or 5 years is invariably ahead in compensation, after 15 or 20 years, of the individual who stayed with one organization—even though both started out on the same job at the same pay and both now have the same responsibilities. Twenty years ago individuals who had made several job changes were considered suspect, but today the individual who has stayed with the same company is considered the oddity.

Organization structure can have a significant impact on the type of executive needed for a particular job. With some companies the group executive is a significant position essentially responsible for organizational changes and allocating capital to the appropriate division (based on assessment of need and potential return on assets or ROA) and possibly defining markets and sales strategies for the group. In other situations the group executive is essentially a high-priced liaison between the CEO and a number of autonomous divisions. Needless to say these two jobs call for different personality makeups and compensation packages.

Reportedly some companies, in an attempt to minimize being raided, employ all the major executive search firms on a regular basis. Since ethical conduct prohibits search firms from raiding clients, the company thus purchases additional insurance against losing key executives—insurance which can be very important as more and more companies use search firms to seek out underutilized and underrewarded executives. Sick companies especially are in search of an executive with instant healing powers. Rather than simply the capable problem solver, they want the individual who is able to turn around a crisis situation. Typically this means controlling costs and increasing productivity in order to turn a losing venture into a profitable operation.

Not only do many individuals look for a 25 percent or greater increase in total pay for making the jump to a new job, but an increasing number also look for a front-end bonus. This is used to buy out, at least in part, forfeited benefits and deferred pay at the former company. Thus it becomes necessary to project a reasonable payout level under the former company plan and then discount to present cash value equivalency. Also of interest is the pay contract going beyond the normal 2- to 5-year employment agreement. This longer-term agreement stipulates a pay level (usually considerably lower than the salary) until retirement.

Management should recognize that its pay philosophy in large part determines the type of talent it will attract and keep. For example, a company that says its salary plus bonus is competitive with salary plus bonus of other companies is more likely to attract a risk taker than a company who says its salary is competitive with salary plus bonus of other companies. In the first instance if the company does cut back bonuses for ineffective performance while giving very handsome awards for top performance, it is likely to get more than its share of results-oriented individuals and less than its share of security-oriented individuals. Conversely, if the company rarely reduces bonuses or gives significant increases (it is difficult to do the latter without doing the former simply because the individual may not consistently be a super-star performer) then it is more likely to attract and retain the steady but unspectacular performer.

Million dollar packages are often extended only as lures to those who perceive a small increase in power and responsibility and/or a significantly greater risk of failure (and loss of job). Due to the low birth rate during the Great Depression there is increasing competition for the talented executive aged from the mid-forties to early fifties. For some companies this means having to stay a little longer with executives who should retire or reaching further down in the ranks for a less seasoned individual in the early career phase.

RETAINING EXECUTIVES

Once executives are inside the organization, the next objective is to keep the better performers. Executives not only expect to be properly paid for their performance and to receive promotions when they have demonstrated ability to assume greater responsibilities, they also expect formal recognition. While pay is a form of recognition, many individuals also need oral and written communication officially recognizing the level of accomplishments. To the extent this is communicated to the individual's peer group it may disrupt needed teamwork. Nonetheless, such recognition is extremely important to some individuals. If it is not given, the person may be unhappy although very well paid.

Lavishing praise for a job well done is a lot less expensive to the company than increasing the compensation. While few would accept official recognition in lieu of a pay change, for many the amount of the pay change could be reduced if proportionately offset by an increase in recognition.

Many executives reach a level in the organization where they are comfortable with their responsibility and reward. They have little interest in competing for greater responsibility because for them the effort and stress is not worth the compensation. For them the recognition is very important. This may be accomplished in part with a few perquisites (e.g., larger office, more impressive title, and access to the executive health spa). However, further recognition may also be needed, ranging from the simple "Nice job, Sandy" to a story in the company magazine.

EXTRINSIC VERSUS INTRINSIC COMPENSATION

It may be easier to think of pay as a form of *extrinsic compensation* while work environment, type of work, and extent of recognition form *intrinsic compensation,* often called *psychic income.* Other forms of intrinsic compensation include autonomy and power.

Organizations that are visiby successful may be providing some intrinsic compensation to their executives (i.e., a pride in membership). Since such organizations usually are also able to pay at least competitively, the intrinsic pay reinforces the retention capability of direct pay. Conversely, less successful organizations which may also be unable to afford fully competitive pay may be placing additional pressure on the pay package since there may be actually negative, if not low, intrinsic compensation which must be offset to retain the individual.

As shown in Figure 3-1 all jobs have a combination of intrinsic and extrinsic compensation. It is personally believed that to the extent the job does not have a desired level of intrinsic compensation, an offsetting level of extrinsic compensation is required. This could explain why garbage collectors earn almost as much pay as some college

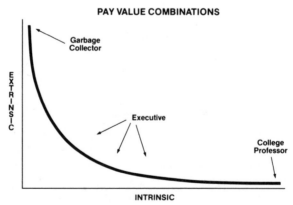

FIGURE 3-1 Pay value combinations.

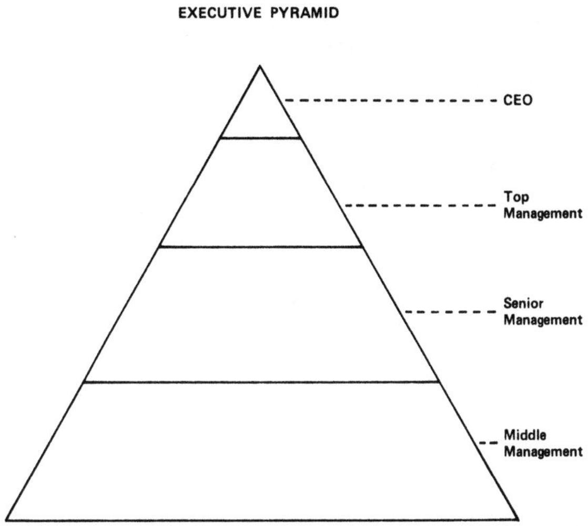

EXECUTIVE PYRAMID

FIGURE 3-2   Executive pyramid.

professors. No one will ever mistake the garbage collection for a job with high levels of intrinsic compensation. Conversely, the intrinsic appeal of being a college professor or a prominent politician (e.g., U.S. Senator) explains why extrinsic pay seems low as compared with other jobs.

Executives are believed to be somewhere in the middle of the curve, either shedding intrinsic needs due to positive pay-performance situations or increasing searches for high intrinsic compensation because the direct pay-performance link is not sufficiently strong.

In addition to seeking a position which has sufficient extrinsic compensation to meet ego and other needs, most are looking for work which is high in intrinsic compensation—personally meaningful and satisfying. Executives more than others in the corporation usually have sufficient flexibility in organizational issues to be able to organize their work, at least in part to meet their intrinsic needs; however, their accountability may be in areas of low interest.

Another important factor many companies overlook is ensuring that the executive who is likely to figure in a future promotion understands the situation. Many individuals leave because they do not know what the company has planned. A number of companies either believe executives are mind readers or expect them to "trust" the organization. Thus, companies sometimes lose top executives for modest compensation increases simply because someone else provides a well-laid-out plan for career advancement. For talented executives, the golden handcuffs of long-term incentive plans and/or deferred compensation have less retention value than open communication about advancement opportunities. Level of pay, while important, is secondary to relative rate of movement upward through the executive pyramid illustrated in Figure 3-2. It has been estimated by some that two-thirds or more of executives' pay comes from promotional adjustments with the remainder from merit increases.

It should be remembered also that incentive compensation is a two-edged sword. It should reward executives handsomely during very successful years and thereby increase the likelihood of retention, but in bad years it may make a company vulnerable to loss of top executive talent by withholding a portion of total pay. This is especially true where the company places a high value on the portion of incentive pay to total compensation. While the company should probably prune off some deadwood during the poor years, it probably has a greater need than ever to ensure it loses no top-caliber executives—for these individuals may be the ones who will help the company again rise to the ranks of the successful.

MOTIVATING EXECUTIVES

The basic motivational model indicates that effort times ability leads to outcome or performance. Thus, a shortfall in one factor can be offset by a higher value in the other. Many individuals compensate for average ability with a very high level of effort. The amount of energy the individual will expend in a given area is a function of the desirability of the expected outcome versus alternative outcomes from efforts directed toward other areas. In any event, most analysts would probably agree that there is not a constant relationship between level of effort and performance. Above a certain level of effort, there is a decreasing rate of return.

Traditionally, the motivation of pay is explained by two formulas, equity and expectancy. The *equity theory* states that the individual will increase level of performance if level of pay is believed greater than output and conversely will decrease performance if level of pay is believed below current performance. Most people will argue that the latter alternative is more plausible than the former. Of course, the executive who believed his or her performance exceeded the level of pay would first attempt to obtain a pay increase; only if this effort failed would the individual lower performance or, more drastically, leave to accept another job.

Expectancy Theory

Expectancy theory suggests that an individual will increase output in the expectation of receiving an increase in pay. This could be an increase in pay for performing current responsibilities or a promotional increase commensurate with a job reclassification. If the individual does not receive an increase consistent with the level of performance, the person is again likely to reduce performance or seek a different job.

However, the level of pay can be either a "carrot" or a "stick." The carrot symbolizes higher pay, held out to motivate the individual to work harder. The stick, on the other hand, is a negative symbol meaning "Do it right or we'll find someone else." Logically the carrot works best until the individual's compensation has risen to a level where

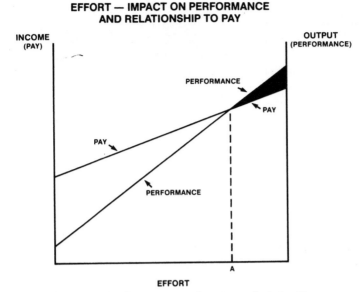

**EFFORT — IMPACT ON PERFORMANCE
AND RELATIONSHIP TO PAY**

FIGURE 3-3   Effort—impact on performance and relationship to pay.

additional pay no longer has the same motivation, and then the stick takes over. The executive is thus encouraged to continue a high level of performance in order to keep the job and the high level of pay.

Executives typically wear the hats of both subordinate and superior. As subordinates, they are very vocal about the need to equitably link pay and performance; as superiors, they often become defensive and describe the problems of adequately relating pay to performance.

Obviously, this dual standard is inappropriate. Part of the problem is that executives are often poorly trained in identifying and discussing performance problems with subordinates. The result? To avoid unpleasant discussions many performance ratings are artificially raised. No wonder the pay delivery system is failing. Those responsible for training and development have not kept up with pay program designs. The latter are usually more sophisticated than the ability of the users due to inadequate training.

Importance of Effort

As indicated earlier, the classic performance model indicates that effort times ability will equal outcome or performance. Thus, a lower value in one can be offset by a higher factor in the other. For example, a person with average ability could become very successful by expending great amounts of effort. The amount of effort expended is a function of the desirability of the outcome and the capacity for effort.

This may be illustrated in Figure 3-3. In this example the two curves are straight

25

lines; however, either or both could be curves of varying slopes dependent upon the structure of the reward system and the nature of the work. It is believed with some forms that there is an increasing efficiency; with others, a decreasing efficiency and with still others, a combination or S curve. In this model the executive receives a decreasing rate of return on effort (although the variance is positive) up to point A. After that point, although the individual continues to receive more pay, the return for effort is not equitable. Thus, if there were competing opportunities, the individual would probably shift to those after point A. This shift can be offset if the organization increases the slope of the payline and moves the intersection point farther to the right.

Obviously it is much easier to demonstrate this type of relationship clinically with a set of curves than for the executive to quantify it personally. However, although the measurements may not be as precise, it is believed they nonetheless are made and are used as the basis for altering behavior.

Achievement versus Pay

While the objective of a sound compensation program is to pay correctly in relation to performance, there are repeated examples of pay not being in concert with achievement—even for those companies that strive diligently to administer in an equitable manner. This can be demonstrated with the matrix in Table 3-2 which compares level of pay with level of achievement. Setting aside the legal issues of equal pay for equal work, there are a number of interesting observations that can be made.

While the correctly paid column is the pay program's objective, obviously the company should be pleased if it has more overachievers than underachievers in this situation. Level of achievement here is defined as the quantity as well as the quality of accomplishment. Three different individuals could have the same level of quality, but one could produce 80 percent of expected quantity, the second 100 percent, and the third 120 percent. Conversely, all three could produce the same quantity of work but one could do so in a truly outstanding manner, the second at a fully satisfactory level, and the third in a less than satisfactory fashion. Most performance evaluation programs can deal with the second situation more easily than with the first; however, the level of output can be built into the performance program. Assume three individuals perform at a 3.0 level of performance (using the university 4.0 system). For the overachiever the

TABLE 3-2   Achievement versus Pay

Level of achievement	Level of pay		
	Underpaid	Correctly paid	Overpaid
Underachievement	1	2	3
Desired achievement	4	5	6
Overachievement	7	8	9

adjusted rating is 3.6 (i.e., 3.0 × 120 ÷ 100). The individual attaining the desired level of performance retains the 3.0 rating (i.e., 3.0 × 100 ÷ 100), while the underachiever's rating drops to 2.4 (i.e., 3.0 × 80 ÷ 100). Admittedly the concept is easier to describe than to apply; nonetheless, it is a workable concept.

But let's look at some of the other interesting combinations and see what they represent:

- A 1 (underpaid, underachievement) is an individual who is paid even less than the poor performance warrants. This appears to be the result of some form of discrimination or recrimination, perhaps for past failures. It may be a management message to the individual: "You are not wanted. Why not leave?" Such an action would obviate the need for a messy company-initiated severance.

- A 4 (underpaid, desired achievement) is similar to 1 except not as flagrant. Some companies may knowingly or otherwise allow this to happen to some of their older executives, feeling they are unlikely to leave due to all the accrued advantages of long service (e.g., pensions, deferred bonuses, and long vacations). Withholding a portion of pay increases from such executives means more merit dollars are available for other seemingly more deserving persons.

- A 7 (underpaid, overachievement) is usually not likely to remain that way for long. Either the company will correct the inequity or the individual will correct it (by lowering performance, by directing efforts to other interests outside of the company, or by simply leaving). Classically, this situation exists in companies that make little effort to truly reward performance. Such a company or division, when faced with an 8 percent merit budget, gives adjustments ranging from 7 percent to 10 percent (placing greater emphasis on restoring lost purchasing power to marginal performers than on adequately compensating the overachiever).

- A 3 (overpaid, underachievement) may develop out of a 5 or 8 whose performance drops but whose bonus does not, or out of a 4 or 7 who reaps a bonanza in pay but does not keep performance high enough to become a 5 or 8 (some believe many professional sports stars playing under long-term contracts meet this description). Lack of adequate downside risk in pay programs causes development of many 3's.

- A 6 (overpaid, desired achievement) is less dramatic but similar in nature and development to the 3.

- A 9 (overpaid, overachievement) is probably an individual who has been demoted. This overachiever may remain an overachiever in the new position but may have had little or no reduction in pay and thus may be overpaid in relation to the new level of responsibilities.

This analysis provides a way of describing level of pay and performance in relative terms and also shows (contrary to the belief of some) that pay versus performance can be a fluid and changing relationship. Too many pay technicians are content to simply fall back on their merit guide charts without trying to ascertain the dynamics of particular situations.

Pay-for-Performance Problems

An ineffective pay-for-performance program not only does not send the proper signals for good performance but probably also reinforces poor performance because it does not withhold sufficient pay. This is especially true for companies that have little or no incentive pay, since salaries are rarely reduced. A zero bonus is only a punishment when a minimal level of bonus is needed simply to make pay levels competitive.

Not only must differences in pay relate to differences in performance but the executives must believe that the company is administering the program on this basis. A lack of consistency in administration will have a debilitating effect on the most efficacious pay plan. Invariably, in such situations managers will blame the pay system rather than the ability (desirability) of differentiating. If the pay system provides the basis for significant differences in individual pay, including reducing pay (by lowering incentive payments) when performance drops, the system is not at fault. It is the manager who makes the recommendations and the person who approves the proposal who are failing to make the necessary differentiation.

When pressed many managers will indicate they need more objective measurements by which to differentiate pay adjustments. Obviously these are desirable; unfortunately (or fortunately) the costs of developing, installing, and maintaining sophisticated measuring devices to judge the value of a particular report, decision, or activity are usually prohibitive. The pay-for-performance concept is difficult to effectively administer, but consider the alternative. Not to vary compensation in relation to an objective assessment of performance is de facto to reward mediocrity and to penalize the better performing executive. Thus either managers work hard to use what is available to make pay differentiations or they must accept pay for seniority or on some other basis. In either event they should stop blaming the system when in fact the system provides the opportunity but they lack the ability.

Incentives work best where the individual has a clearly defined measurable objective to accomplish—either an objective with few external impacting factors or an objective with factors that can be easily measured. The company must be careful to ensure that incentive plans are not so attractive that they encourage individuals to violate the corporation's standards of business conduct, much less commit illegal acts. Not only must falsifying records to show increased production or sales or reduced expense be formally forbidden, but also necessary control procedures must be adopted to officially enforce the rules. In addition, plans must be structured to serve the financial interests of the shareholders, not simply the well-being of the professional manager; otherwise, beneficial mergers or acquisitions might be thwarted.

A logical way to motivate the professional manager to take more personal interest in the success and well-being of the company is to make that individual a part owner. This has been the main rationale behind the use of stock options and stock awards.

Importance of Pay

Pay is admittedly not of equal importance to all executives. As indicated earlier, some have achieved a level that is satisfactory in meeting financial needs. For others the need is greater, either for direct use of pay or simply as recognition of their importance.

The importance of pay in altering or reinforcing performance is strongly influenced by several factors, including background and current economic status. For those who grew up in an affluent environment and currently have sufficient money, pay has little impact. Conversely, for someone who did not grow up with money and still doesn't have it but does have high economic desires, pay is very important.

Some have questioned how much the individual is motivated by greed rather than simply need. Envy of the level of pay of others is often a factor, but dissatisfaction with one's own level of pay relative to others is often based on perception rather than facts. Since most people probably overestimate the pay of others and also overestimate their own level of contribution, it is not surprising that many are unhappy with their pay programs, regardless of how lucrative. Therefore, it is critical to attempt to demonstrate that the pay program is competitive with what other organizations are paying for comparable performance and responsibility.

COMMUNICATION OF PAY

Increasingly executives want to know how the pay program works. The honor of being singled out to participate in the incentive program or receive a particular perquisite is often not enough. The executive is not as inclined as in years past to simply trust the company; the individual wants to understand the basic features of the plan. Perhaps this is due to prior failures on the part of the plan to deliver when the executive performed well, but more likely it is simply a desire to minimize effort expended in nonproductive areas.

Information needs seem to be highest when trust is low. The executive's trust of superiors is typically based on a combination of personal characteristics (e.g., integrity, openness, and consistency) with performance and professional competence. If the executive believes something to be true, simple assurances by the superior that it is not are insufficient, especially when trust is low. The perception of reality is more important than reality itself. This is especially troublesome since it has been suggested that most employees underestimate the contribution of others (at comparable organizational levels) and also overestimate their level of pay. A completely open pay communication system might eliminate the latter misconceptions, but it would be very difficult to alter the former. Also, the more open the system, the more likely supervisors are to minimize pay differentials for variances in performance, since they would have to defend deviations. Thus, one must question whether open pay systems and pay for performance are complementary or conflicting objectives.

Nonetheless, the executive must receive enough information to believe the compensation program to be a logical system that pays in relation to performance. While it is personally believed unnecessary for the individual to know exactly how the system functions, there should be sufficient knowledge to remove any feelings that it is all black magic. If pay is to have any motivational aspects, the executive must perceive a definite link between performance and pay.

Therefore it is logical for an executive to know the amount that can be expected in compensation for doing a commendable or outstanding job, especially in incentive pay. This is much easier when the incentive plan is formalized than when subjective judgment is an important factor. Whether or not the individual should know his or her own salary range is a matter of debate, but certainly the process should be carefully explained. For many the knowledge that the pay delivery system is logical and systematic is sufficient.

Personally the author believes that communicating information about the program can be very beneficial, as shown in Figure 3-4. However, to the extent that this communication becomes specific about the pay of others, it is believed that this communication can then become a demotivating factor. This is simply because the executive has

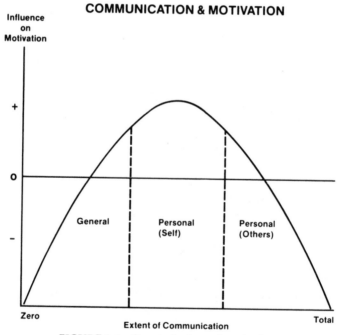

FIGURE 3-4 Communication and motivation.

TABLE 3-3 Stock Option Status Notice

On this date	You were granted an option which now has this many outstanding shares	And this many appreciation rights	At this price	You can exercise your option on or after	And on or before
Oct. 15, 1977	2,500	0	$47.50	Oct. 15, 1978	Oct. 14, 1987
Sept. 16, 1978	5,000	500	53.50	Sept. 16, 1979	Sept. 15, 1988
Oct. 6, 1979	7,500	0	58.75	Oct. 6, 1980	Oct. 5, 1989
June 27, 1980	9,000	2,000	61.50	June 27, 1981	June 26, 1990

a higher regard usually for his or her own level of contribution than for that of others in the peer group.

Communication of the total package to the executive takes the forms of: letters and booklets explaining plans in general, personalized calculations identifying value in terms of time frame (such as the computer-produced benefit statement), and verbal communications (with individuals or small groups) to permit questions and answers about plan features. The various communication approaches are often structured to include the executive's spouse and financial adviser. Inclusion of the adviser is especially important to avoid possible liability action. The company should explain the package clearly but should avoid giving advice.

In examining the extent of information to be communicated, it is possible to construct plateaus or levels. For example, in communicating information about the executive's participation in the stock option plan, the first plateau would be listing the outstanding options with price and appropriate dates (as shown in Table 3-3, for example).

The second plateau is to indicate possible value (perhaps using assumptions on growth and discount, as described in Chapter 8, Long-Term Incentives). Finally a complete history of all prior transactions of the executive, showing exercise and forfeitures, is included.

EXECUTIVE QUALITIES

What personal qualities are likely to make an executive effective? Fortunately there is no one model which can be used to clone replacements. Variances in positions, companies, industries, and stage of the market cycle demand different profiles. Nonetheless there are certain qualities which seem to exist to some extent in many situations.

If asked, most executives would probably indicate that they got where they are through their own efforts rather than because of whom they knew. Long work hours have probably kept the individual away from the family more than he or she wanted, but a genuine interest in the job has made this a rational trade-off. The executive's results-oriented philosophy is reinforced by a desire for greater responsibility and balanced by a high level of integrity. While pay-for-performance-oriented, the executive has a higher degree of loyalty than he or she would probably admit. Probably no other employee group is as stereotyped as are "executives" as being believers in the work ethic: "Work hard, do a good job, and you will be appropriately rewarded."

Although professional or technical competence is highly regarded, the executive probably attributes success more to level of effort than to ability. The executive also probably believes that personal strengths lie in problem-solving situations, circumstances requiring creativity, and/or being able to effectively lead others.

There is a conviction that the job of the executive today is tougher than it has ever been. Government intervention, shareholder dialogue, and visibility of executive compensation are all becoming more evident. Executives realize they must continually prioritize the events impacting upon them—taking only as much time to analyze the data as is cost effective given the problems facing them. Furthermore, they must be prepared to modify each decision or alter its impact as events and additional data make the earlier action inappropriate. Many must continually fight with themselves not to overindulge in an area of their own interest and expertise at the expense of less attractive but more significant issues.

For most executives there is diminishing time to relax. In spite of how successful they have been in the past, the worry is about the present and the future. There is always pressure. Being successful is difficult enough, but continuing to be successful without experiencing a setback is both an impossibility and a requirement. The euphoria of success contrasts with the humiliation of failure.

The ultimate humiliation is being fired. This is especially traumatic to those in mid-career since it may be difficult for them to get another job with commensurate pay and responsibilities. The higher placed the individual, the fewer the opportunities. Executives who are fired late in their careers may be able to simply retire (depending on the largess of the separation agreement); those in early career usually have a number of other opportunities available and don't have to fight middle-age discrimination (ADEA notwithstanding).

Many successful executives are apparently motivated by fear of failure. This drive to ensure that their present work is always considered good, or preferably better than their earlier work, drives them to spend whatever hours are necessary to reduce the risks of failure. As indicated, the ultimate failure is being fired. The worst part of being fired is not so much the economic repercussion (since an alternative job elsewhere is probably available) as the humiliation of defeat. The threat of failure hangs like the sword of Damocles over the heads of successful executives.

For individuals with tremendous drive and a desire to prove to themselves (even more than to others) that they have the ability to overcome virtually impossible obstacles, the objective of the pay delivery system logically is to channel these efforts by rewarding the individual for doing those things which the corporation thinks best.

Peer pressure is another factor; many employee directors of the board track their pay progress versus their counterparts in other organizations. At the minimum they consider it necessary to stay even with such individuals, but they desire even more to have their pay progress at a faster rate. Such views are tempered by the extent to which the person believes his or her own responsibilities to be less or greater than the contemporaries' responsibilities.

Furthermore, the executive typically believes that his or her own standards of performance exceed the expectations of the organization. Thriving under pressure, the individual is capable of both planning and paying attention to detail, as well as successfully executing a decision that is personally not agreeable.

The problem many organizations have with such an executive is not how to motivate the individual to achieve better performance but rather how to avoid establishing demotivating conditions. Successful recruitment of such an executive by another company will probably be due to the promise of new challenges (with commensurate pay) rather than simply a significant increase in compensation.

Identification with Superiors

To be successful the executive must deal effectively with three levels in the organization: above, the same, and below. The executive must remember that the superiors control the pay increases and promotions. Therefore, being an effective subordinate is probably as important as being an effective manager. Interestingly enough, the emphasis in personal development programs is on the latter. Yet probably as many effective managers are fired because they are poor subordinates as vice versa. To be an effective subordinate the executive must identify with the company philosophy, which can range from a family atmosphere to one of intense competition and little loyalty. The superior's management style is also important. One of the first facts to determine is whether the boss wants a written memo or a verbal briefing. Some are readers, others are listeners. The readers are handled by sending the memo and following it up with a meeting; the listeners are best approached by having a meeting and then leaving a memo.

Ideally, the executive will both like and professionally respect the superior, although it is more often one or the other. It is doubtful whether the relationship will last if both ingredients are missing, unless the executive is prepared to be a very good actor—and the executive who receives unsatisfactory pay and recognition will probably not be able to keep up the act.

Being too good can be almost as bad as being a poor performer if the superior lacks self-confidence. A possible indicator of this is when the executive's work is signed by the superior and then discussed with others at meetings to which the executive received no invitation. Executives must assess carefully the likelihood of their being given proper recognition in such situations. In addition, some superiors require a certain amount of stroking by their subordinates, perhaps to compensate for the lack of such recognition coming from their own peers and superiors. In such situations the executive must recognize it is important to acknowledge the superior's accomplishments and to show respect for the superior's rank.

A successful relationship is often typified as one where the executive brings to the superior solutions, not simply problems—especially after the toothpaste is out of the tube. Preferably, the solutions proposed should be ones that can be implemented smoothly without upsetting others. Few executives (including superiors) openly seek confrontations. In addition, it is important that the executive keep superiors informed of events, including possible significant problems. Many superiors abhor surprises, even pleasant ones. It is important, however, to be well-organized in effectively utilizing the superior's time. Time is a finite quality in short supply for all executives. Showing superiors that one is well-organized in this respect is very important.

In some situations it is also very important for the executive to "look the part." Here the old adage "Clothes don't make the man" is not completely true. Some executives spend considerable time and money working with image consultants who focus on speech, mannerisms, and weight as well as wardrobe. It is not always the most effective executive who gets the promotion or the big bonus. Unfortunately in some situations it is the executive who looks good and sounds persuasive.

Interacting with Peers

Peer relationships are difficult because it is important to be both competitive and cooperative. The successful executive must be competitive because superiors are examining performance not simply on the job but also relative to others in the peer group. It is important to be cooperative because considerable interaction takes place among those on the same organizational level. Invariably it is important to earn the respect of peers for one's functional knowledge and effectiveness. Some executives are more concerned with self-perpetuation than with meeting their assigned responsibilities, a few to the point where they have become legends in their own minds. Others suffer from foot-in-mouth disease, engaging vocal cords while their brain is in neutral. Still others are gunslingers who shoot from the lip: they may be wrong, but they are never in doubt. Needless to say, such individuals are not very highly respected by their peers.

Relating to Subordinates

How many executives treat their subordinates as they want to be treated by their superiors? Probably many fewer than profess to meet this common standard. There is a difference between correcting and humiliating subordinates, which some executives either have not learned or for some particular reason choose to ignore. Some apparently thrive on keeping their subordinates in a continual state of anxiety and fear. Others seem to ignore subordinates, allowing them to function completely on their own. A common complaint of the subordinate is that the superior does not spend sufficient time with the individual discussing objectives and performance.

Typically, as an executive rises in the organization, less and less time is available for his or her own work, and more and more time must be directed to the work of others, especially within the unit. This places an inordinate demand on the executive's time. It is thus essential that the executive be able to use time effectively. For most this means identifying and prioritizing tasks daily, examining the monthly requirements weekly, assessing the yearly commitments monthly, and examining the long-range needs at least yearly. This continual assessment of priorities to ensure proper focus is as important as the expenditure of effort in completing the tasks.

Every executive must maximize the capabilities of subordinates while limiting their exposure to their limitations. However, in areas of strength it is important that they be afforded the opportunity to fail! This means rewarding success and punishing for failure. However, the risk of failure should be commensurate with the subordinate's ability and the ability of the unit to accept failure of that particular task.

Some executives are completely "open" with their subordinates, others are more obtuse. Some are very objective, others more subjective. Some are directive, others more participative. The effectiveness of the executive in executing a particular style is probably more important than the style itself. Furthermore, each subordinate must be counseled on performance, and the assessment must be based on current work, not past successes or failures. It is also important not to confuse pronouncements by subordinates with performance.

Subordinates should believe they are not "being used" by the executive simply to further his or her own career. Subordinates can more effectively sabotage an executive's career growth than the peer group because it is the subordinate's work for which the executive takes credit or blame.

Impact of Stress

Stress is a part of most executives' lives. Engineers talk of stress in terms of the amount of weight a substance can support before it collapses; executives talk in terms of the amount of pressure to perform that can be absorbed without having a breakdown.

In previous centuries people were placed in situations of stress when their physical safety was threatened by physical harm or lack of food. Today executive stress is on a much higher plane; most of the back stabbers threaten job success rather than physical well-being. The desire to at least retain, if not improve, corporate position and pay is threatened by both change in the work place and other competitors.

Some argue that a little stress is good. It elevates the blood pressure and apparently provides the adrenalin needed to move quickly through difficult situations. However, it may also impair the individual's ability to carefully examine alternative courses of action. In addition, stress may cause physical and mental health problems, probably the most common being ulcers and depression.

For some executives the absence of stress may lower mental acuity. For them, stress is the vitamin providing the energy needed to be a high achiever. This is one reason, it has been argued, that a number of corporations have their headquarters in major metropolitan areas. The hassle of the commute gets the blood pumping and the adrenalin flowing. The office routine takes on an accelerated pace, one that might not be achieved in the idyllic forest setting of the suburbs.

The Workaholic

Just as the alcoholic is a person who can no longer control the role of alcohol, the workaholic can no longer keep work in perspective. The workaholic is a person obsessed with the good old American work ethic. The individual focuses on one half of the cliché "Work hard and play hard." The person works hard and makes up for not playing hard by working harder!

Long hours of work do not make the executive a workaholic; a true workaholic does not know how to relax. The work effort takes on a meaning of its own rather than being simply a means of achieving results. This lack of perspective may result in less than optimum performance as well as alienating peers and superiors. Individuals who have lost sight of the true reason for work usually are not good planners or very creative; they don't have the time to devote to such activities. In addition, the workaholic is probably not a believer in delegation, choosing rather to do the work personally.

Few companies really want workaholics. Rather, they want executives capable of expending a great amount of energy but able to work under control and keep perspective. However, many jealous peers maliciously label a hardworking overachiever as a workaholic in order to minimize some of the competitive threat. It is believed that only a small percentage of those labeled workaholics meet the basically negative definition.

Mid-career Crisis

The mid-career crisis usually occurs some time after 40 as the executive begins to doubt that he or she will attain the level of success earlier dreamed. Some feel trapped within a particular industry due to their particular skills. This would seem more likely to occur to those in line than staff positions, due to the latters' abilities often to cross industry lines.

By definition, this trauma is greatest for those who had high expectations but are still a significant way from top management with no apparent shortcuts in sight. Those who identified their strengths and interests earlier in developing career paths, and have made the necessary adjustments to stay on course, probably have less of a crisis with which to cope.

For those with very significant difficulties, alcohol and emotional concerns may be sufficient to require counseling. Unfortunately, although the facilities exist in many organizations to handle such situations, executives are often concerned that their problems may not be treated in complete secrecy. They may fear that discussions with a counselor will be revealed and used to minimize future promotions. Therefore they often do not use the facilities available.

Burnout

A problem similar to mid-career crisis is "burnout." Both problems result in significantly lowered job performance. Whereas mid-career crisis is associated with lack of promotion, burnout is typified by lack of interest in present position. Individuals have lost their enthusiasm for continuing their duties. Reasons cited include disillusionment as to job importance and loss of new ideas. The job not only is no longer "fun," it is a depressive form of punishment.

INDIVIDUAL PREFERENCES ON PAY

Although it appears on the surface that perceived value and after-tax value should correlate closely, some analysts have advanced the hypothesis that recipients assign a higher value to deferrals and noncash forms of payment than to other forms of pay. Such a valuation would presumably be lessened during inflationary periods. It is important to consider executive preferences in developing the pay package, but it should be recognized that such preferences may not be optimally appropriate. For example, many companies persisted with qualified stock options for their highest-paid people long after the net cost–net value analysis had relegated them to a secondary position. In part this was due to the fact that executives wanted qualified options. In addition, many executives place a low value on stock options when the market is depressed and listless; yet many financial people would counter that such times are precisely when options should be used in order to benefit from a subsequent rally.

There are many problems in considering individual preferences, namely developing the appropriate possibilities, determining after-tax cost and value for each executive, avoiding IRS problems of constructive receipt, and maintaining the necessary records. In addition, as suggested above the executive's perception may be misplaced, and it will be necessary to subsequently do a little handholding.

The Incorporated Executive

A relatively recent development is the incorporated executive. More specifically, the executive takes the necessary legal steps to incorporate. Usually this is prompted by the lack of adequate employee benefit programs within the employing company. By forming a personal service corporation, the executive not only is able to provide these benefits to himself or herself, but typically is able to pay less taxes as well, because of the lower taxes to corporations than to individual taxpayers. Any individual seriously considering such an action should review the situation very carefully as the IRS has not looked favorably on such a move to avoid taxes. For example, Rev. Rul. 80-231 indicates that even if the payment for an individual's services is made to a trust, the employer is subject to FICA taxes and withholding requirements.

37

SUMMARY AND CONCLUSIONS

Ideally the entire compensation program is designed, developed, and administered in a manner which will motivate the executive to work harder, faster, and smarter. It is therefore important that the program be examined to determine the extent to which this is true and, just as important, whether the executives perceive that it is designed in this manner.

Although many executives believe they are worth every penny of the hundreds of thousands of dollars they are paid, their view is not shared by all. The dissidents range from shareholders to lawmakers. With million-dollar-plus compensation packages becoming more common, public resentment may initiate confiscatory tax rates for the super-paid.

It is important to reward executives for taking appropriate business risks. Professional managers do not have the same motivation as owner-managers. Many will agree that no successful company has gone through the perils of the threshold stage without taking the calculated risk on an innovative product. Few professional managers are successful entrepreneurs, and few successful entrepreneurs are successful administrators. Participation and sense of ownership are therefore essential to properly channel the work efforts of the professional manager.

Establishing a perfect reward-for-accomplishment system is a virtual impossibility, since we are dealing with imperfect measurements. Nonetheless it is imperative to make the system as good as it can possibly be. There aren't so many talented, self-motivated individuals with a strong need to exceed that a company can afford to mishandle their pay program.

The entire premise behind well-designed compensation programs is to modify executives' behavior until it is considered optimal by the organization and then to reinforce continuation of that level of performance. Unless executives are properly compensated, the organization will have a very difficult time in successfully attracting, motivating, and retaining top-quality executives.

Salary

We have all heard the statement "He's worth his weight in gold," but how many recall hearing "She's worth her weight in salt?" (except perhaps in reference to Lot's wife). Yet, in ancient days salt was a form of barter and payment, at least as valuable as gold, due to its preservative qualities. In fact, one view is that the word salary is derived from the Latin word *sal* for salt.

Today, salary is the cornerstone of the compensation program, for it is upon this element that the other four are layered. Typically, the amount of salary an executive is paid is a function of the value of the individual's work to the organization and how well the individual is discharging these responsibilities. The value of the individual's work is typically determined by job analysis, job evaluation, salary surveys, and the resulting salary structure adjustments. Individual pay actions result from promotion and how well the executive performs the assigned tasks.

JOB ANALYSIS

The objective of job analysis is to obtain information about the job and summarize it in a manner which sets it apart from other jobs within the organization. Typically, such information is obtained through an interview with the executive, or the job incumbent completes a questionnaire. The focus at this point is on the reporting relationships within the organizational structure as well as on the principal responsibilities. Therefore, it is important to obtain information on the extent of planning required, the degree of involvement and responsibility for specified tasks, and the type and extent of contacts within and outside the organization. A *task* is a separate definable portion of the job, it is the most basic simplified portion—the element. Following this analogy, the job is a compound consisting of various elements existing in varying degrees.

The supervisor, the job incumbent, and/or the personnel representative will write the *job description*. Technically, a distinction can be made between a job and a position. A job is performed by more than one person, whereas a position is filled by only one individual. Thus the distinction between a job description and a *position description*. However, in this book the two will be used interchangeably.

39

In writing the job description, the tasks are listed either in a logical work sequence or in descending order of frequency of occurrence. If listed in work flow sequence, typically the percentage of time spent on each task is shown at the end of each statement. From these statements a summary of one or two sentences is constructed and placed at the beginning of the description to give the reader a quick synopsis. And finally a *job title* is selected (if one does not already exist). It should be only several words in length but should indicate the basic nature of the work as well as the organizational level (e.g., vice president—corporate personnel).

It is important that jobs be carefully and accurately described, because they form the basis for the subsequent evaluation of the job's relative worth. Rater bias coupled with organizational politics will otherwise distort valid comparisons.

Few organizations undertake job analysis at all levels of the organization. Typically, it includes those below group or division president level; few position descriptions exist for company presidents. After all, if the president does not want a job description, who is going to say one must be prepared? The rationale for sidestepping job analysis is that it is not necessary above a certain organizational level. Anyhow, we all know what a company president does, don't we? Interestingly, many who express such confidence are the same individuals who question whether or not survey data is for comparable jobs when only a job title can be used for purpose of match-ups.

JOB EVALUATION

The objective of job evaluation is to array the jobs described in the job analysis phase in a manner which will best reflect their value to the organization and their relationship to similar jobs in other companies.

There are literally thousands of different job evaluation plans in existence throughout the country at the executive level. Probably no two companies have exactly the same job evaluation program. However, these many plans can be categorized into essentially five types: ranking, classification, point factor, maturity, and market pricing.

Whatever system is used, it must correlate strongly with what the company perceives as important; otherwise it will surely fail. Also, it must be viewed as being valid by the executives being evaluated; otherwise it will similarly fail. Thus to be workable, it must be acceptable to both the evaluator and the evaluatee.

Ranking

The ranking approach is by far the simplest; it is a nonquantitative method of arraying jobs in order of importance. This array is accomplished by comparing two jobs with one another and determining which is the more important. The third job is compared with the first two, and its position with respect to the first two is determined. The process is repeated until all jobs have been slotted into the array.

The type of difficulty encountered in such a plan is whether a group executive with four different divisions (each with $50 million in sales) should be worth more than a division head with $200 million of business. The argument "for" focuses on the additional layer of management in a centrally managed company; the argument "against" says the real value rests with the division managers in a decentralized organization.

The simplicity of the ranking approach to job evaluation is its greatest virtue: little preparation is required and it works well when not too many jobs are involved. Unfortunately, simplicity is also its greatest drawback. Many find it difficult to think in terms of the whole job. Therefore, there is a natural tendency to rate each job on the basis of its dominant characteristic(s). Such an approach will definitely affect the resulting hierarchy.

Another drawback of the ranking method is that the array reflects absolute rather than relative differences. In other words, there is no way of knowing whether the difference between the vice president of personnel and the director of compensation and benefits is equal to, greater than, or less than the difference between the director of compensation and benefits and the manager of compensation. Ranking will simply report the sequence in the ascending hierarchy—not the relative differences between the various jobs.

Classification

Whereas the ranking method requires comparing jobs directly with each other, the classification method calls for comparing each job with a set of written standards. For example, if 20 grades were in effect for executive-level positions, each grade would have a set of standards describing the type of job that should be classified in that grade.

The advantage of this approach is that the grade levels have been established, and identifying the grade for the job simply requires matching the most appropriate descriptors. Unfortunately, this also means a significant investment of time and effort in developing these standards, which must be sufficiently generic to be relatable to any type of job and yet sufficiently specific to allow direct comparison with a particular position. Obviously, the greater the number of grades, the greater the difficulty in separating and identifying distinctions.

Another problem with the classification method is its inflexibility (i.e., the number of grades). As the organization matures and more levels of management are introduced, it may not be possible to adequately reflect organizational differences. This may mean adding additional grades and completely rewriting the standards. Too few organizational levels exist when insufficient compensation growth (i.e., too small a number of grades) exists between levels. A practical test of this hypothesis is to determine when the differences in compensation midpoints no longer adequately reflect promotional growth.

Point Factors

Point factor plans are similar to the classification method in that they require the comparison of the job to an impartial measuring stick rather than directly with other jobs.

TABLE 4-1 Point Factor Example of Educational
Requirements

Amount of experience needed	Job points
Under 3 months	25
At least 3 but less than 6 months	50
At least 6 but less than 12 months	75
At least 1 but less than 2 years	100
At least 2 but less than 4 years	125
At least 4 but less than 8 years	150
At least 8 but less than 15 years	175
15 years or more	200

However, rather than develop a composite standard for each grade level, the point factors begin at the opposite end of the spectrum. They indicate the separate factors that make up the composite and identify degree statements describing various levels of requirement, assigning each degree statement a number of points. Thus, if work experience needed to satisfactorily learn the job is one factor, it might be broken down into the various degree statements shown in Table 4-1. Therefore, a job requiring 6 months to learn would be given 75 points, while a job requiring 5 years would receive 150 points.

Most factor plans focus on responsibilities and the knowledge needed to perform the tasks. Within these two major categories, a number of separate factors can be constructed (e.g., separate factors of responsibility for sales, profit, equipment, and employees). Such plans typically have from 5 to 10 factors. The more factors, the more suspect the evaluation plan, as it is very likely that several factors are measuring the same value in only a slightly different manner.

Developing the Structure By examining the job factor by factor and assigning the correct number of points to the most appropriate degree statement within the factor, it is possible to sum the points assigned and array the jobs on their point totals. These point totals along with the current pay of each person in that job are typically displayed in a *scattergram* using an X (job points) and a Y (pay) axis as shown in Figure 4-1.

This data is then converted into grades by first identifying the cutoffs on the X axis which would seem consistent given any clustering of similarly valued jobs, as shown in Figure 4-2.

Next, a *regression analysis* is performed on the data to describe the line of best fit. This may be either a linear formula (which will force a straight line regardless of the format) or a nonlinear formula (which will describe the simple curve best reflecting the data). A nonlinear formula will result in a straight line only if all the plots truly describe a straight line. We will not take the time to perform the necessary calculations; the specific methodology for calculating the line (or curve) may be found in almost any statistics book. However, it is important to know the formula values.

The formula for a linear regression analysis is $Y = a + bX$. The a is the value on

**PAY AND JOB VALUE
SCATTERGRAM**

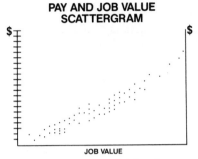

FIGURE 4-1 Pay and job value scattergram.

CONVERSION TO JOB GRADES

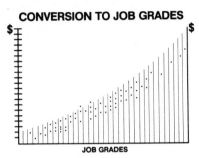

FIGURE 4-2 Job value conversion to job grades.

the vertical or Y axis when X equals zero. The b describes the slope of the curve, namely the extent of increase in Y axis (e.g., compensation) resulting from a stated change in value of the X axis (in this case job points).

The nonlinear formula is $Y = a + bX + cX^2$. The value c indicates the rate of change in the slope of the curve. A positive value indicates an increasing rate of change; a negative or minus c value indicates a decreasing rate of change.

The difference between the plot points and the curve is measured vertically and is identified as the *deviation*. The line of best fit will, by definition, minimize the degree of deviations existing.

Employing the nonlinear formula to test for the presence of a curve in our example results in the line shown in Figure 4-3—a curve with a positive slope.

By establishing the line value as the midpoint for each grade, it is possible to construct the salary ranges shown in Figure 4-4. Typically, these range widths increase as one progresses through the structure. This is a simple reflection of decreasing promotional opportunities due to the organization's pyramid shape. Thus ranges must be wide enough to accommodate longer periods of residence.

Therefore, while ranges of plus and minus 15 percent from the midpoint might be

**NON LINEAR PAY CURVE
WITH GRADES**

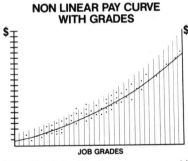

FIGURE 4-3 Nonlinear pay curve with job grades.

SALARY STRUCTURE

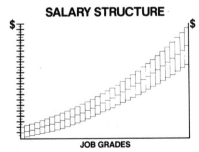

FIGURE 4-4 Job grades with pay ranges.

43

TABLE 4-2 Plus-Minus Midpoint Adjustment versus Maximum-Minimum Ranges

Plus-minus adjustment to range midpoint of, percent	Equals the following maximum over minimum spread, percent
50.0	200.0
40.0	133.3
33.3	100.0
30.0	85.7
25.0	66.7
20.0	50.0
18.4	45.0
16.7	40.0
15.0	35.3

appropriate to construct the range minimum and maximum at the bottom of the structure, ranges of plus or minus 25 percent may be appropriate at the top. Ranges of plus and minus 33.3 percent or more may be necessary in the absence of short- and long-term incentives. Table 4-2 shows the relationship of plus and minus deviations from the midpoints to the normal manner in which ranges are described, namely spread between minimum and maximum of the range. Thus, a plus and minus deviation from the midpoint of 16.7 percent will construct a range with a maximum over minimum spread of 40.0 percent.

An example of a salary schedule for the salaried exempt jobs in an organization is shown in Table 4-3. Note that this schedule has positive slope to the curve with the increase in midpoints beginning at 5 percent at the bottom and progressing in an arithmetic progression to 12 percent at the very top. In addition, the range spread (maximum over minimum) increases also in a progression beginning with 40 percent at grade 1 and increasing to 65 percent for grade 40. If there were few or no incentives, however, these ranges might typically range from 50 to over 100 percent.

Grades versus Curves The problem with the typical grade structure is that it does not consistently result in increased pay for increased job points. Shown in Figure 4-5 are three jobs: A, B, and C. Note that the difference between A and B is much greater than the difference between B and C, and yet A and B are in the same grade, whereas C is in the next higher grade.

Therefore some companies, namely those who really believe in the efficacy of their factor point plans, do not establish arbitrary point cutoffs to form grades. Rather, the maximum and minimum are, like the original midpoint value, a set of curves. As shown in Figure 4-6, the pay relationship of jobs A, B, and C is essentially the same as their job value. While this may be a more accurate basis for establishing pay, it must be remembered that the addition of even one point will result in a higher pay range, and thus there may be numerous requests by management to review the points assigned to

TABLE 4-3 Forty-Grade Salary Schedule

Grade	Minimum	Lower one-third	Upper one-third	Maximum	Midpoint
40	$211,800	$257,700	$303,500	$349,400	$280,600
39	190,300	230,900	271,500	312,100	251,200
38	171,300	207,300	243,300	279,300	225,300
37	154,400	186,300	218,300	250,200	202,300
36	139,500	167,800	196,200	224,500	182,000
35	126,200	151,400	176,600	201,800	164,000
34	114,300	136,800	159,200	181,700	148,000
33	103,700	123,800	143,800	163,900	133,800
32	94,300	112,200	130,200	148,100	121,200
31	85,900	102,000	118,000	134,100	110,000
30	78,100	92,700	107,300	121,900	100,000
29	71,700	84,600	97,400	110,300	91,000
28	65,600	77,200	88,800	100,400	83,000
27	60,300	70,800	81,200	91,700	76,000
26	55,800	65,300	74,700	84,200	70,000
25	51,600	60,200	68,800	77,400	64,500
24	47,600	55,500	63,500	71,400	59,500
23	43,900	51,200	58,600	65,900	54,900
22	40,600	47,300	54,100	60,800	50,700
21	37,500	43,800	50,000	56,300	46,900
20	34,700	40,500	46,300	52,100	43,400
19	32,200	37,600	43,000	48,400	40,300
18	29,900	34,900	39,900	44,900	37,400
17	27,800	32,500	37,100	41,800	34,800
16	26,000	30,300	34,700	39,000	32,500
15	24,300	28,400	32,400	36,500	30,400
14	22,800	26,600	30,400	34,200	28,500
13	21,400	24,900	28,500	32,000	26,700
12	20,100	23,400	26,800	30,100	25,100
11	18,900	22,000	25,200	28,300	23,600
10	17,800	20,800	23,800	26,800	22,300
9	16,900	19,700	22,500	25,300	21,100
8	16,100	18,700	21,300	23,900	20,000
7	15,400	17,800	20,200	22,600	19,000
6	14,700	17,000	19,200	21,500	18,100
5	14,000	16,100	18,300	20,400	17,200
4	13,400	15,400	17,400	19,400	16,400
3	12,800	14,700	16,500	18,400	15,600
2	12,300	14,000	15,800	17,500	14,900
1	11,800	13,400	15,000	16,600	14,200

GRADES

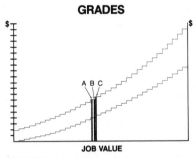

FIGURE 4-5   Job grade inequity (three-job comparison).

CURVE

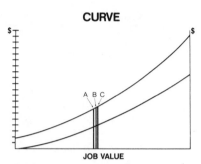

FIGURE 4-6   Pay ranges without grades (three-job comparison).

the jobs. Conversely, under the grading approach such requests will essentially be limited to those jobs which are close to the point cutoff for the next higher grade.

Maturity Data

The maturity method of job evaluation is similar to the point factor approach, except that instead of establishing points for separate factors only one measurement of job value is used—time. Thus, the X axis is defined as time (e.g., years since B.S., years of experience, or age). This method of job evaluation is rarely used for executives since by definition its greatest appeal is in those instances where there are a large number of employees who are performing essentially the same work and it is almost impossible to draw lines of distinction establishing separate jobs. Frequently this method is used, therefore, for engineers and chemists, with separate curves for each discipline as well as separate curves for supervisors and nonsupervisors.

As shown in Figure 4-7, individuals automatically move up one notch on the X axis each year rather than await a reevaluation as under the more traditional point factor method of evaluation. Note that the curve has a descending slope rather than the ascending one shown earlier. This occurs for at least two reasons: (1) pay increases are usually more pronounced during the first years of assignment, following a typical learn-

MATURITY DATA

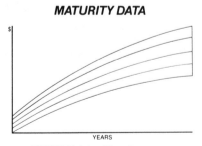

FIGURE 4-7   Maturity curves.

ing curve pattern, and (2) many of the top performers have left the job after a number of years (e.g., either they were promoted or they quit to accept a better job elsewhere).

Note that the maturity data shown has 4 bands or ranges within the minimum and maximum values. These could be used to distinguish between levels of performance on the job.

Market Pricing

The traditional methods of job evaluation begin with an establishment of job value based on some method of internal equity. This hierarchy is then measured in terms of survey data to determine the competitive level of pay for comparable positions, in order to establish external equity. The problem is that any attempt to measure items using two different methods stands a very good chance of reaching dissimilar conclusions from every other attempt. Invariably the survey results will suggest that several jobs are either overgraded or undergraded by one or more levels under the internally oriented job evaluation plan. This places the company in the uncomfortable position of knowingly either underpaying or overpaying certain jobs in relation to the market, or overriding the job evaluation plan based on the market results.

The market pricing method of job evaluation begins with the labor market as the basis for evaluating the jobs. Jobs for which no survey data exists are then evaluated by the ranking method. For example, as illustrated in Table 4-4, if the president of the Brucell Division is assigned grade 30, the vice president of sales and marketing grade 27, and the plant manager grade 24—all based on survey data—the vice president of production (for which no survey data exists) is probably grade 26, 27, or 28, depending on the perceived internal value in relation to the vice president of sales and marketing.

Many will argue that it is possible to be more precise and accurate in classifying jobs using the market pricing method at the lower end of the structure where there is a greater likelihood of similar jobs existing in other companies. The difficulty in market pricing the executive positions is that, with the possible exception of functional division heads, there is a great divergence of differences in specific responsibilities. While this

TABLE 4-4   Market Pricing Example

Grade	Salary midpoint	Job	Survey Data	Grade
30	$100,000	Division president	$98,600	30
29	91,000			29
28	83,000			28
27	76,000	VP sales and marketing	74,500	27
26	70,000			26
25	64,500			25
24	59,500	Plant manager	60,200	24

TABLE 4-5   Market Pricing Principles

1. In using survey data, consideration will be given not only to measures of central tendency (simple or adjusted for scope measurement) but also to raw data where available (viewing its dispersion from reported measurement of central tendency). Other reported compensation correlates will be examined (e.g., total compensation and 5-year average return on investment) where appropriate and believed significant.

2. Survey results will be factored up or discounted to the extent it is believed the position is heavier or lighter than the position surveyed.

3. Market data will also be tempered by the lack of necessity of replacing the job incumbent from a particular industry (i.e., sales and marketing positions would relate very strongly to industry survey data, whereas staff positions would primarily be based on cross-divisional data and internal factors).

4. With a market-oriented compensation program, in structuring the grade for a job it can always be placed higher than market dictates (in order to preserve internal relationships), but it cannot be placed lower without running the risk of turnover.

5. When survey data older than 1 year is used in ranking jobs, a factor will be added to equate it with other data used.

6. Survey problems (i.e., small sample and significant dispersion from reported averages) will require a closer look at internal job relationships.

7. In viewing relative positions of jobs, at least a two-grade differential is needed in order to talk of a significant difference (i.e., a likely promotion). Furthermore, at least a two- or three-grade difference would normally be expected when talking of reporting relationships.

8. Market data on average compensation paid for the position dictate the job grade. The performance of the individual within the job determines the position within the range.

9. Staff and line positions are both sensitive to size of unit served (as a general indicator of extent of responsibility); however, staff positions are much more sensitive to the individual in the position. There is, therefore, usually a greater range on competitive compensation data for staff positions.

10. When evaluating a position, it is important to determine how jobs with similar responsibilities interact with the one in question. Decentralization causes some duplication; it is important to determine to what extent this affects the rating of a particular job.

11. Structural compensation (i.e., range and midpoint), when available, is a helpful aid in pricing jobs inasmuch as actual compensation is a product of the maturity of the job incumbent. One would expect, for example, a person with more job experience to be paid more.

12. The best way to rank jobs relative to market data and assure comparability is to "lock in" on job comparability for the lowest and highest levels and then to work toward the middle.

13. A practical test of overstructuring in an organization is to determine when the differences in compensation midpoints no longer adequately reflect a normal promotional increase.

14. To ensure compensation adequate to attract and retain qualified persons, the primary equity must be with the marketplace. Therefore, when there are two jobs considered to be equal by internal standards but unequal by external standards (compensation surveys), the latter should prevail unless there are unusual circumstances.

may make job matching more suspect, it may be possible to obtain meaningful data through multiple regression studies as will be discussed subsequently.

After the initial structuring, the need for extensive surveys is minimized since the structure is adjusted periodically on an assessment of the rate of compensation growth over the previous period. Therefore, only those jobs which have not moved at the same rate would be graded, probably by not more than a grade.

A listing of market pricing principles that might be appropriate is shown in Table 4-5.

SALARY SURVEYS

Whether market pricing is used to evaluate the jobs or the more traditional method of internal equity followed by selectively pricing the structure is employed, information on what other companies are paying executives in comparable jobs is needed.

While a plethora of executive compensation surveys exist today, this is a rather recent development. Even as recently as 1960 such studies were uncommon and in 1950 they were nonexistent. Early efforts were directed to reviewing the data submitted to the Securities and Exchange Commission on the three highest-paid executives; today such data is available through a number of studies conducted by associations, consulting firms, and other companies.

Indeed, if there is a problem today, it is that there are too many surveys, each drawing on its own sample of a defined population. Considering the costly inefficiencies of generating and maintaining separate data banks, the amount of duplication of efforts is appalling.

Defining the Community

Before undertaking a survey or examining existing studies, it is important to first define the survey community appropriate to this company. Typically, companies will look to companies in the same or similar industries which are approximately the same size. The larger the company, the greater the problem in this respect since there are only a limited number of companies of comparable size.

An industry analysis is especially appropriate for jobs which are industry-sensitive, namely sales and marketing and to some extent production and research. However, functions such as finance, legal, and personnel are less industry-sensitive, and it is appropriate to look across industry lines to determine the competitive level of pay for executives in these functions. Whether intra- or interindustry it is important that the companies selected be looking for comparable-level people. For example, perhaps there are only five companies within a particular industry that consistently look to hire only those individuals in the 90th percentile of qualified candidates.

49

Selecting the Jobs

Unfortunately, not all jobs can be surveyed (due to a combination of magnitude of effort and lack of comparability). However, a careful attempt should be made to ensure that the survey has a good balance of horizontal and vertical representation. Horizontal representation requires the inclusion of the various organizational functions (e.g., research, production, marketing, sales, finance, legal, and personnel). The vertical requirement focuses on promotional career paths within a particular function (e.g., plant manager to general production manager to vice president of production). The number of jobs to be surveyed is a function of availability (and extent of cooperation of the surveyed companies) as well as the method of evaluation. Point factor plans require surveying only a few key jobs representing the various levels, whereas market pricing requires surveying as many jobs as possible, perhaps 25 percent or more.

Job Comparability

Before obtaining any data, it is important to determine the manner in which the surveyed companies will be reporting on comparable jobs. Essentially, there are three methods: job matching, job evaluation, and multiple regression.

Job Matching Job matching is the most common method of ensuring comparability of data. It requires matching jobs to ensure that similar responsibilities exist. This is important because job content can vary significantly between two organizations, even though the job may have the same title. For this reason, organization charts showing reporting relationships along with job descriptions are included to maximize the attaining of good job matches.

Nonetheless, it becomes increasingly difficult to find companies with similar positions at senior levels. In many instances the differences in job content for the same job title in different companies are as great as if not greater than those for jobs with dissimilar titles.

Further, the implicit assumption is that like responsibilities will be valued comparably by other organizations. Unfortunately, there are too many instances where this is simply not true. Be it a formal job evaluation plan or a simple ranking program, different companies come up with different perceptions of the importance of different disciplines. Thus, even if two jobs in two different companies were identical, the pay practices of the companies would differ if they placed different values on the position.

Another difficulty many companies have is trying to match up with a company with either fewer or more management levels. For example, assume a survey has data on the top functional heads at the corporate, group, and division levels. How does a company with four levels—corporate, business, multidivision, and division—relate to this data? The answer: by matching first those most comparable (namely corporate and division) and then interpolating (e.g., between corporate and group for business and between group and division for multidivision). Obviously, less confidence should be placed in data which has to be massaged in this manner than in data which matches well.

TABLE 4-6   Survey Leveling

Degree of comparability	Data weighting
Noticeably heavier	0.5
Slightly heavier	0.8
Good match	1.0
Slightly lighter	0.8
Noticeably heavier	0.5

Another technique that may be employed in job matching is adjusting for degree of deviation. For example, the data received from each company could be weighted based on degree of closeness of fit with the survey job. Therefore, as shown in Table 4-6, a company which had a job either noticeably heavier or lighter would be given a weighting of 0.5 whereas those which were only slightly different would be given a weighting of 0.8. This technique is typically called *leveling*.

A technique which may be employed to test the possible existence of lack of comparability is the *survey ratio*. This is simply the division of the lowest salary reported for a position into the highest (after the data has been arrayed high to low). If this value is much above 1.5, it is appropriate to examine the data more closely since it indicates that there is over a 50 percent difference in the amount being paid to individuals allegedly performing the same job.

Another refinement in job matching is to stratify the data based on a meaningful measurement of scope such as that shown in Table 4-7 for plant managers. Whenever this is done it is important to be certain the measurement is essentially meaningful. Size of work force for plant managers would not be very useful if the survey data consisted of a mixture of capital-intensive and labor-intensive operations.

An extension of the stratified example is where the actual data (e.g., the number of employees in the plant) are given along with the compensation data. As will be seen in the later section on analysis of survey data (page 53), this infomation can be displayed on a scattergram and run through a regression analysis in a manner similar to the techniques used to develop salary ranges.

TABLE 4-7   Survey Job Match Based on Number of Employees in Plan

Number of employees in plant	Report for plant manager, job number
5,000 and up	6
2,500 to 5,000	5
1,000 to 2,500	4
500 to 1,000	3
100 to 500	2
Under 100	1

Job Evaluation A variation to determining what companies pay for comparable jobs is to determine what they would pay *if* they had jobs similar to the ones in the survey. This requires identifying those positions most similar to the survey for each company and then evaluating these positions using a common job evaluation plan, probably a version of the point factor plan. It can be seen that this is essentially simply a more refined version of the leveling process described in job matching. However, it requires an extensive effort in time to collate and evaluate the appropriate job data.

Multiple Regression The power of the computer has made possible the multiple regression analysis. Instead of simply comparing compensation to one independent variable, it is possible to compare two or more. While single regression results can be plotted using the typical X and Y axes, it is not possible to plot three or more. It is even difficult attempting to visualize more than a three-dimensional chart; nonetheless the analysis is possible.

By employing a *step-progression analysis,* the computer orders the independent variables studied (e.g., sales, assets, profits, age, and length of service of job incumbent) in terms of single regression analysis values and picks the one which when combined with the first analysis will produce the highest two-measurement prediction. This is not simply the single regression analysis with the second highest value, since it could be accounting essentially for the same values as the first if they are strongly related (e.g., age and years of experience). Thus, sales might account for 55 percent of the variance in pay within the community for the CEO position, but when combined with incumbent's years of service the total might be 75 percent. Then a third variable is combined with the first two, and so on.

Some suspect that this approach brings a level of analysis to the issue far greater than the data warrants, or than the executive is interested in attempting to absorb. Nonetheless, it is a device which enables a refined method of job matching.

What to Survey

Having determined what to survey and what jobs to include, it is next important to determine what questions to ask. At the minimum this would include: number of incumbents, salary structure, average actual salary, short-term incentive maximum, average actual short-term incentive pay, and total salary and short-term incentive. It may also be appropriate to include questions on long-term incentive plans, although as will be seen in Chapter 8, it is not as easy to place a value on such plans. While inclusion of perquisites may be appropriate for very senior positions, it will usually be found that these are common to certain levels of positions. Thus, if several division president positions were surveyed, it would not be surprising to find they were all eligible for essentially the same perquisites. A study of employee benefits limited to retirement and survivor protection may be helpful in identifying companies significantly above or below the average in level of coverage.

For those interested solely in the highest-paid five executives within an organization, the company proxy statement may be sufficient, although one should read the footnotes very carefully as well as obtain at least the previous year's copy due to the relationship of columns C (paid or vested) and D (contingent). It may be recalled that compensation reported earlier in column D need not be reported subsequently when actually received.

It is important to remember that if a company has few or no incentives, it will be establishing a position less than competitive if it compares its salaries only with the salaries of other companies. It must attempt to include total salary and incentive pay of the community in order to be competitive. Since incentive-paying companies typically pay more than nonincentive companies (one would hope especially during profitable years), it may be more logical to average the short- and long-term incentives paid in the community over a period of time to reduce the fluctuations.

Plan payout periods are important to know in long-term incentive plans since one company may pay interim awards annually while another pays only after 3 full years. In 2 of the 3 years the first company will appear to be paying more than the second; in the third year the second company will appear to be paying significantly more than the first company.

If a regression analysis (single or multiple) is going to be performed, the appropriate data is also required. As indicated earlier, this might include sales, assets, profits, stockholder equity, number of employees, age, and length of service for the job incumbent.

How to Analyze

Essentially, there are two basic approaches to analyzing the data: average pay only or average pay in relation to one or more independent variables. Shown in Table 4-8 is an example of average pay only. In this hypothetical study for a CEO we see that the average total compensation for the community is $662,100 versus $626,000 for the Brucell Company. Note in this example that Brucell would be even further below the average except for its long-term incentive plan.

All in all, not too bad. But note the wide range in total compensation reported. Is the average really meaningful? Let's examine the same data in relation to sales volume. As shown in Figure 4-8, a significant amount of this variation is explained by the relative sizes of the organizations. Brucell is identified by a star.

Since such an approach can result in literally hundreds of pages of graphs, a logical way to summarize the results is shown in Table 4-9. This hypothetical table is for the division level of positions. Similar tables could be constructed for multidivision, multibusiness, and corporate levels. The numbers in the matrix reflect grades appropriate for the Brucell Corporation. These were calculated from the compensation reading at the appropriate sales level by identifying the grade midpoint which was closest to the survey data. This midpoint would be either salary or total compensation, depending on what the survey reported.

Problems with the Independent Variables Sales is probably the most common independent variable used in regression analysis studies of compensation. Probably for

TABLE 4-8   Survey Pay Data for CEO, Thousands

Rank	Company code	Salary	Incentive pay Short-term	Incentive pay Long-term	Total
1	J	$410.5	$217.0	$197.6	$825.1
2	M	275.0	384.1	152.4	811.5
3	B	378.0	267.5	155.5	801.0
4	Q	550.0	232.4	0	782.4
5	E	437.5	219.6	110.2	767.3
6	H	482.2	267.0	0	749.2
7	A	393.0	181.2	167.3	741.5
8	M	409.1	262.0	65.0	736.1
9	R	420.0	172.5	137.5	730.0
10	D	386.0	203.0	134.6	723.6
11	G	365.2	233.8	113.0	712.0
12	T	319.3	260.7	101.0	681.0
13	C	331.0	331.0	0	662.0
15	I	380.0	175.0	61.0	616.0
16	S	265.0	148.0	126.0	539.0
17	P	293.0	162.3	57.7	513.0
18	F	310.0	177.0	0	487.0
19	L	338.3	134.7	0	473.0
20	O	460.0	0	0	460.0
21	K	432.0	0	0	432.0
Survey average		$381.8	$199.6	80.7	$662.1
Brucell (14th)		$350.0	$151.0	$125.0	$626.0

this reason more than any other, it also usually has the highest correlation with compensation. The reason is simple: because many companies are using it to set their pay policies, individual executives are having their rate of salary change slowed if they are high relative to the regression value (at their sales volume) or accelerated if they are low. It could be argued, therefore, that the primary emphasis is on increasing sales rather than increasing profits within an organization. It is dubious how many shareholders would agree with such an objective.

Similarly, surveys that include number of employees supervised and number of organizational levels reporting to the position reward bureaucratic empire building. They penalize the top-performing executive who is accomplishing the same results with a smaller organization! Unfortunately, short of a massive organizational study with significant value judgments, this variance cannot be explained away. Thus, while its impact cannot be fully assessed, its existence cannot be completely ignored.

Another example of a questionable correlation is one that compares size of research

SURVEY PAY DATA FOR CEO

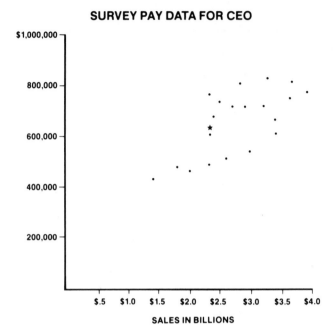

FIGURE 4-8   Scattergram survey pay for CEO.

budget with pay of the research head. The obvious message here is to justify a larger budget in order to get a pay increase! Completely lacking is a measurement of performance.

Impact of Rate of Change on Independent and Dependent Variables   How often have there been surveys describing the rate of compensation change (dependent variable) in terms of a constant independent variable (e.g., sales) over a period of time?

TABLE 4-9   Survey-Suggested Divisional Grades

Sales, millions	Vice president Marketing	Sales	President
$500	24	22	30
250	22	20	28
150	21	20	27
100	20	19	26
75	19	19	25
50	18	18	24
25	17	17	23
10	15	15	21
5	13	13	19

55

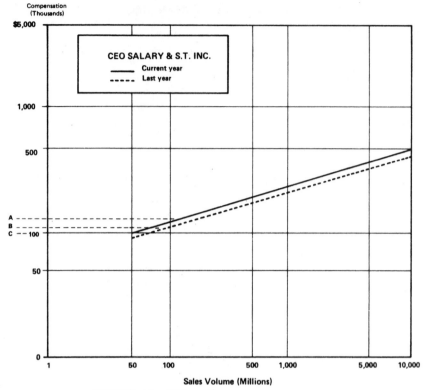

FIGURE 4-9   CEO pay last year versus current year.

As suggested in Figure 4-9, this would suggest the increase in CEO pay at the $100 million sales level as the difference of A minus B. This assumes the same sales volume of surveyed companies in successive years: a very questionable assumption. If, for example, the average increase in sales was 10 percent, then the comparison should really be between $91 million and $100 million (points A and C)—obviously a much more significant increase.

Therefore, in evaluating compensation in terms of an independent variable, it is essential to understand the impact of the rate of change of each. There are three situations: (1) compensation and sales increase at the same rate, (2) compensation increases faster than the rate of sales, and (3) compensation increases slower than the rate of sales. Each of these situations is described below.

1. As shown in Figure 4-10, if compensation and sales increase at the *same rate*, the slope and Y intercept of the curve are *unchanged* over time. (Assume the average pay for presidents of $100 million divisions is $100,000 and both sales and pay increase 10 percent for the year. While the average pay for $110 million divisions

56

will be $110,000, so too will the average pay be $100,000 at $100 million for division presidents who the previous year were paid $91,000 for running $91 million divisions. Thus, the $100,000/$100 million coordinate is unchanged.) The abbreviations TY and LY represent "this year" and "last year," respectively.

2. If rate of compensation increases *faster* than the rate of increase in sales, the curve *rises:*

   a. *Without change* in slope if rate of compensation increase is the same at all levels. For example, if the average rate of increase in sales is 10 percent and the average increase in compensation is 15 percent, the $100 million in sales last year is worth $110 million this year, but the $100,000 level of pay last year has increased to $115,000. Similarly, last year's $91 million division increased to $100 million this year, while average pay increased from $91,000 to $105,000. Thus, the reading at $100 million sales increased from $100,000 to $105,000, as shown in Figure 4-11.

   b. And slope *increases* if pay rate changes are greater relative to sales growth as sales volume increases. For example, if the average rate of increase in sales ranges from 10 percent at the low end to 5 percent at the upper end of the curve and the average increase in compensation is 15 percent, the result described in item 2a above is repeated at the $100 million level of sales, but the increase in com-

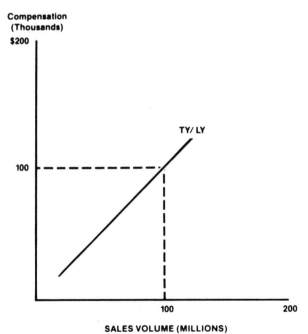

FIGURE 4-10 Sales versus compensation—same curve.

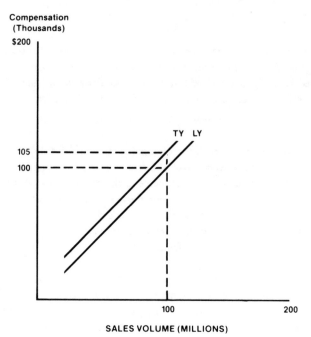

FIGURE 4-11   Sales versus compensation—same slope but TY higher.

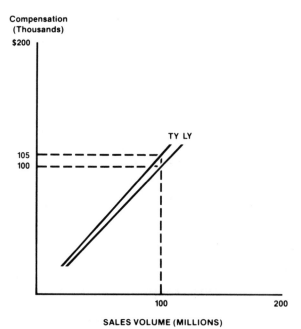

FIGURE 4-12   Sales versus compensation—TY higher and ascending.

pensation becomes more dramatic with increases in sales volume. This is high-lighted in Figure 4-12. A similar result is attained if sales increase at a constant percentage but the rate of compensation increases faster than sales.

c. And slope *decreases* if pay rate changes are lower relative to sales growth as sales volume increases. Therefore, if the average rate of increase in sales ranged from 5 percent at the low end to 10 percent at the upper end of the curve and the average increase in compensation was 15 percent, then the result described in items 2a and 2b might be repeated; however, the increase in compensation would be slowed with further increases in sales volume. This is highlighted in Figure 4-13. A similar result is attained if sales increase at a constant percentage but the rate of compensation increase drops with increases in sales.

3. If compensation increases at a rate *slower* than the increase in sales, the curve is *lowered:*

a. *Without change* in slope if rate of compensation increase is the same at all levels. Thus, if the average sales increase at all volumes is 15 percent versus a 10 percent average increase in compensation, the $100 million division increases to $115 million and the average pay for division presidents at this level increases to $110,000. Similarly, the $91 million division increases to $105 million and the average pay for division presidents increases from $91,000 to $100,000. Thus,

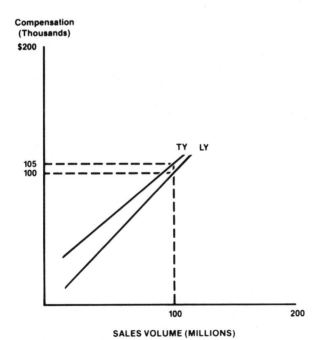

FIGURE 4-13   Sales versus compensation—TY higher but descending.

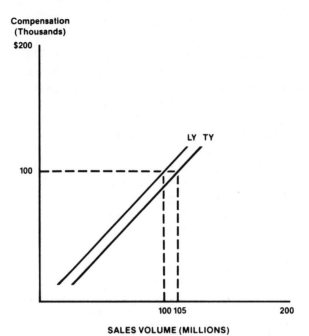

FIGURE 4-14   Sales versus compensation—same slope but TY lower.

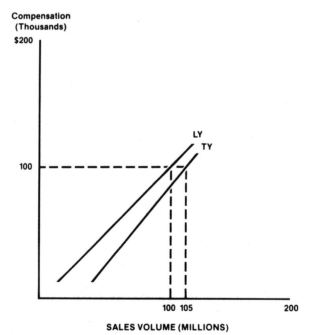

FIGURE 4-15   Sales versus compensation—TY lower but ascending.

the $100,000 reference has been increased from $100 million to $105 million, reflecting a lowering of the compensation curve as shown in Figure 4-14.

b. Slope *increases* if rate of sales growth *decreases* as sales volume increases. Therefore, if the average level of pay increases 10 percent at all levels but the increases in sales range from 25 percent at the low end to 5 percent at the high end of the curve, it may mean that last year's $91 million increased 20 percent to $109 million while the $100 million increased 15 percent to $115 million. The result is a lower but more sharply rising compensation curve, this year versus last. This is reflected in Figure 4-15. A similar result is attained if sales increase at a constant percentage but the rate of compensation increases with an increase in sales.

c. Slope *decreases* if rate of sales growth *increases* as sales volume increases. Thus, if the average level of pay increased 10 percent at all levels of sales but the increase in sales ranged from 15 percent at the low end to 25 percent at the upper end of the curve, it might mean that last year's $91 million increased 15 percent to $105 million while the $100 million increased 20 percent to $120 million. The result is a lower and flatter compensation curve, this year versus last year, as shown in Figure 4-16. A similar result would be obtained if the growth in sales was constant but the increase in compensation decreased with an increase in sales.

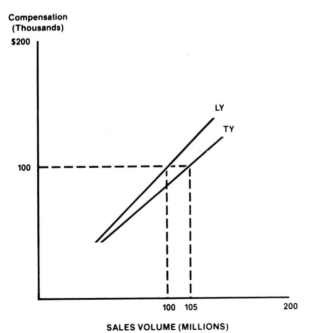

FIGURE 4-16 Sales versus compensation—TY lower and descending.

TABLE 4-10   Probability of Regrading Based on Sales and Pay Changes

Sales increase in relation to survey community	Structure increase in relation to survey community		
	Less than	Equal to	Greater than
Less than	No change	Possible lowering	Probable lowering
Equal to	Possible increase	No change	Possible lowering
Greater than	Probable increase	Possible increase	No change

The above-described changes in slope and position of the compensation curve from one year to another for the survey community must be examined in relation to one's own increase in sales and structural midpoint to determine the probability of having to regrade the position. The matrix in Table 4-10 identifies the probable result, recognizing that the degree of difference in the rate of change increases or decreases the likelihood of regrading.

Multifactor Analysis   The simple regression analysis illustrated in Figure 4-8 and Table 4-9 explained away a significant portion of the variation found in Table 4-8. If other data had been collected, it would be possible to rerun a multiple regression analysis which might explain 90 percent or more of the variances in pay.

Thus, studies can determine the level of competitive pay, given a host of financial factors. The results, however, express various levels of success in terms of significantly different risks. Without carefully examining the strategies of each company over the previous years and quantifying on a common scale these risk variances (a practical impossibility), it is not possible to include risk analysis in a study of competitive pay. However, it is possible to measure company size and success.

Company size can be measured in *absolute* terms (e.g., sales, net profits, total assets, stockholders equity, and total number of employees). Company success can also be expressed in *relative* terms (e.g., return on investment, return on shareholder equity, and net income as a percentage of sales). Measurements can be for 1 year or compound averages for 2 or more years.

Personal factors of the executives (e.g., age, education, years in position or related positions, and years of service) can be examined in relation to themselves and to the company financial factors by use of multiple regression analysis, thus permitting an important quantification of each of the pay elements.

TABLE 4-11   Indexing Pay of Highest-Paid Three

	Company A		Company B		Average	
	Pay	Index	Pay	Index	Pay	Index
Highest paid	$500,000	100	$400,000	100	$450,000	100
Second highest paid	350,000	70	325,000	81	337,000	75
Third highest paid	197,000	39	295,000	74	247,000	55

TABLE 4-12 Indexing Pay of Highest-Paid Three—
Company C versus Survey

	Company C		Survey	
	Pay	Index	Pay	Index
Highest paid	$400,000	100	$440,000	100
Second highest paid	330,000	83	330,000	75
Third highest paid	242,000	61	242,000	55

In short, given the appropriate data, the analytical techniques available are capable of making very sophisticated measurements of the interaction of pay determinants. In fact, these measurements are probably more sophisticated than most people are really comfortable with in analyzing the data.

Indexing Pay Relationships

A frequently employed survey reporting format is the percentage relationship of pay for the top three executives. Setting the pay of the highest compensation as 100, the second and lowest paid are expressed in numbers such as 75 and 55, as shown in Table 4-11.

What is the value of this format in viewing the competitiveness of these three executives? Not very much if only the index values are reported, since they can mask very significant differences! Note the variance between the two companies on the third highest paid. The index value of 55 may be statistically accurate, but it is certainly not representative.

Furthermore, these numbers only express pay relationships; they do not indicate anything about level of pay unless the actual pay values are also reported. For example, assume that company C's second and third highest-paid executives receive 83 percent and 61 percent, respectively, as much as the highest paid. Versus survey averages of 75 and 55, one might be tempted to conclude that these two executives are overpaid versus the market. Not true! As seen in Table 4-12, it is the CEO who is underpaid while the other two are paid at the competitive level. Thus, if the absolute pay levels are not known, the relative percentage relationships are of little value. Furthermore, remember that it is also unlikely that the second and third highest positions are the same jobs in the survey community. This is an excellent example of an attempt to compare apples and oranges.

Updating the Survey Data

Since survey data is actual as of a point in time, it is by definition historical in nature and at least several months old. This raises the question of whether or not to update the information and if so to what point in time using what factors?

Breaking this question down, the problem is whether to project the survey data to the date of intended adjustment and, if so, how much further the projection should be extended. For example, assume the survey used for determining job grading has an effective date of March, it is now September, and the individual pay increases using these new ranges will take place in January (and will not be reviewed again until the following January).

It seems logical to first project the survey community to January 1. If it is assumed that the survey community will be increasing pay at an annual rate of 10 percent, then it is logical to add 7.5 percent to the reported rate (i.e., 10 percent times ¾ year). If it is also assumed that pay increases next year for the survey community will be increasing at a 10 percent annual rate, there are essentially three choices: (1) make no additional projection recognizing that pay will begin to slip competitively shortly after January 1 and will be trailing 10 percent by the following January, (2) increase the survey data an additional 10 percent (on top of the 7.5 percent adjustment) thereby placing the company theoretically 10 percent ahead of the survey on the date of adjustment, recognizing that this will deteriorate and by next January will approximate community pay, and (3) take a compromise position between "no increase" and "full increase" (e.g., use 5 percent, recognizing that this will place the company 5 percent ahead of the community on the date of adjustment, equal to the community average at midyear, and 5 percent behind the community by the following January). Which of these three positions to take is a matter of company philosophy regarding competitive position in the marketplace.

STRUCTURAL ADJUSTMENTS

Most companies use the survey data to adjust their structures, usually annually, although more frequent updates (e.g., quarterly) could be argued for companies which use individual review dates (e.g., anniversary date of employment) rather than a common date for all. If the structure is not updated at least annually, the company must be prepared to face the pressure to increase the grades of most jobs in response to the increase in pay in the marketplace.

The adjustment to the structure reflects the company's decision on what it believes the increase to be at varying job levels in the marketplace. For some, this is a simple action of adjusting the structure by a specific percentage (e.g., 8 percent) based on what the nonexempt employees have received in the way of increases. For most, it is a more sophisticated analysis.

Assume the company last adjusted its structure September 1. Further assume that all the survey data suggests that lower management jobs have increased at the rate of about 9 percent, whereas top management has increased by 7 percent. One could stop at this point and develop a new schedule, with increases of 9 percent at the bottom tapering consistently down to a 7 percent adjustment at the top. While such an action per se probably will not cause any problems, continual movement of this type will continue to compress or reduce the relative differential between executives and their subordinates as

STRUCTURAL CHANGE

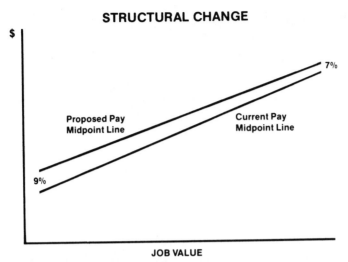

FIGURE 4-17   Structural change in midpoints.

shown in Figure 4-17. The impact of such a result is that the pay incentive to accept promotions is reduced.

Thus, flattening the curve and introducing compression must be examined whenever the structure is adjusted. Empirically, it seems that differentials of 20 to 25 percent are needed between supervisor and subordinate to provide sufficient financial incentive for a subordinate to accept the responsibilities of supervisor. Such evidence has been seen in production operations—line supervisor and skilled operator. One could argue that because of the progressive tax structure and the increased visibility (and resulting risk of failure) of higher-level positions, this relationship should increase progressively through the pay structure, and there is some evidence at very senior levels of management to support this hypothesis.

Position versus Survey Community

In developing the structural adjustment it is also important to consider where the company wants to be positioned competitively, and at what point in time. Many companies simply indicate they want to be competitive (or about equal to the average) with the companies in their surveys. Others will take a more aggressive posture such as in the 75th or 90th percentile. In either event, it is very important to identify the surveyed community. For example, in three different survey communities the same company might be at the median, the 75th, or the 90th percentile.

The impact of the timing reference can be illustrated with a brief example. Assume that the company is 7 percent behind at all pay levels in its defined survey community. Further assume that all indicators are that pay at all levels will increase by 8 percent over the next 12 months. If the company wishes to be about equal to the survey community, how much should it increase its salary ranges? The obvious answers are 7 percent or 15 percent, depending on *when* the company wishes to be competitive. Another choice is to increase the ranges now by 7 percent and then by 0.67 percent every month for the next year. However, this does not seem realistic since the community average is probably not increasing in a straight-line progression during the coming year.

Increasingly companies are answering the timing issue by compromising between adjusting only for the immediate lag and including the full year's growth. In our example, this would mean an 11 percent adjustment. The large jump versus market data occurs only the first time this action is taken. To illustrate, assume that 1 year later we found our foresight was 20–20 and pay did increase by 8 percent—thus placing us currently about 4 percent behind the market. Assuming pay is estimated to increase at the rate of 8 percent during the coming year, we should increase the schedule by 8 percent to retain the same relationship. In other words, after the first adjustment for projecting pay for the community, the schedule is subsequently adjusted simply by the full amount of the estimated future community growth plus or minus adjustments to the extent the previous estimate was less or more than actually occurred. This is illustrated in Table 4-13 using index numbers for comparative purposes.

If the first year actual for the survey community was 9 percent instead of the estimated 8 percent, then the company would adjust the ranges by 9 percent the following year (8 percent for the estimated future growth and 1 percent for the adjustment to last year's estimate). If the actual proved to be 7 percent, then the new adjustment would be 7 percent using the same logic.

Are Grades Necessary?

Formal minimums and maximums for jobs are more likely to be found in the mature organizations than those in the threshold or emerging stage. However, even some mature organizations have no official grades for their very senior executives. Their position is usually that grades at that level have no meaning since compensation is very personalized. Perhaps. But compensation committees (as will be discussed in a later chapter) are showing increasing interest in knowing whether such individuals are overpaid or underpaid in relation to the market. Once the job has been placed in a grade based on a study

TABLE 4-13   Structural Change—Company versus Survey Community

		1 year later				1 year later		
	Current	Est. increase	Actual	New rate		Est. increase	New rate	
Survey	107	8%	8%	115.6		8%	124.8	
					4.1%			4.1%
Company	100	11	11	111.0		8	119.9	

of competitive level of compensation, such a concern is rather easily resolved. However, those totally flexible ungraded situations are much more difficult for compensation committees to address. Furthermore, the lack of grades is totally inconsistent with a philosophy of adjusting individual pay in relation to performance and competitive pay levels. Without a grade reference the latter is not readily apparent. Therefore, lacking a formal structure which is updated for market conditions, the pay of individual executives is more likely to be adjusted in relation to the average increases reported in the marketplace than on the basis of individual contributions. In such instances an executive's level of pay is more likely to be a function of length of service than degree of accomplishments.

Use of Average Increases in Pay Many are confused by apparent conflicts in average increases in executive salaries as reported by different surveys. For example, three different studies might report figures of 8, 9, and 10 percent and yet be completely compatible.

Taking them in reverse order, the last study may have examined the average increases only of those who received adjustments, whereas the second might have examined the average increase in all salaries. Thus if 90 percent received an average increase of 10 percent, the data would be comparable to the 10 percent number reported by the first. Finally, the first study might have been looking at the increase in payroll after 1 year. This is similar to the second study except that it is "net" of all additions and terminations to payroll as well as measuring the promotional adjustments. To the extent replacements are hired at rates less than those being replaced and/or the work force is being expanded at a pay level below the average payroll (i.e., total payroll divided by number of employees), this will not only offset promotional increases but may offset a portion of the average increase in salaries as well.

Therefore, it is very important in examining survey data reporting average increases in pay to know the definition(s) used. In the above illustrations the results were comparable; however, different company mix, timing of study, and poor survey techniques might have resulted in widely divergent data in apparently comparable studies.

Communicating Grades Admittedly having grades and ranges sometimes is an apparent disadvantage. For example, it makes it easier for executives to judge the appropriateness of offered promotions, assuming grades are known. In addition, executives may want to know their position in the range. However, such questions often come from executives who are "flattening out" in career growth and know it, and/or from individuals who have not been treated properly. Those who believe they are essentially being compensated properly (most identify this as a point slightly below true value) are more interested in being assured the pay delivery system is logical and systematic in its approach and recognized individual performance contributions. Not having ranges does not remove the concern of these executives who believe they have been "had" but simply makes it more difficult for the individual to make a very definitive appraisal.

67

Must All Grades Have Jobs?

Some are troubled when they examine the pay structure and find grades with no positions. Their immediate response is to request that the structure be collapsed to eliminate these situations. Most, however, recognize that the job grades have been developed with either a constant increase in midpoint (e.g., 10 percent) or a progression (e.g., 5.0 percent, 5.1 percent, 5.2 percent, etc.). The latter approach partially takes into consideration the need for fewer grades at the upper executive levels since they may be 10 percent or more apart, while allowing for more fine tuning at the lower exempt levels, where job comparisons with survey data are more dependable and less subject to validity questioning.

Geographic Differentials

Some surveys demontrate a definite difference in level of pay for comparable positions in different parts of the country. Therefore, to ensure the organization is not overpaying in lower pay areas or underpaying in higher pay areas, some companies have adopted area pay differential policies. It should, however, be noted that while such differences admittedly still exist, the degree of difference seems to be dropping (a reason holding back a number of companies from adopting such a policy). The main reason for adopting such a policy, however, is that there is usually insufficient data on level of pay in different areas to adopt geographic differentials, and therefore the company must switch from a level-of-pay basis to a cost-of-living basis. While this works on the presumption that level of pay will follow and be dependent on cost of living, it brings into prime focus cost of living—a difficult point for those working hard to sever any linkage of their pay program with the cost of living.

It is important to take a moment and indicate that contrary to popular opinion, the consumer price index (CPI) is not a measurement of cost of living but is merely the weighted change in the movement of prices. While the weighting is based on total United States usage, it does not apply to any one family. The family of four used by the Department of Labor describes a "typical," perfect, average family which does not exist. How can it? The CPI includes conflicting situations such as both the cost of renting and the cost buying a home. Furthermore, it does not include changes in the quality of the product, merely its price. Therefore, to the extent price increase is partially offset by quality improvement, the CPI is overstated. We are obsessed with movements in the CPI. Why? Because there is always a desire to seek a simple answer to complex issues—even when it is shown to be wrong. But back to the issue of geographic differentials. Essentially, there are two approaches: develop separate salary structures or pay separate premiums.

Separate Salary Structures This might result in two or more different schedules to cover communities ranging from New York City to Manitowoc, Wisconsin. The structure might bear a consistent percentage difference (e.g., schedule B is 90 percent of schedule A, schedule C is 80 percent of schedule A, etc.) or some other mathematical basis consistent with the intent of recognizing differences in pay levels. Therefore, a person who moves from the area C schedule to the area A schedule is able to receive a significant promotional increase due to the more liberal structure. Unfortunately, it similarly means that moving from area A to area C will mean little salary growth, if not an actual reduction in pay. One way to minimize these issues is to keep the portion of the salary that reflects geographical differential in a separate check. This practice does not remove the problem, but it does keep the differential payment very visible.

Separate Pay Premiums Some companies take a simpler view of area differentials and simply structure premium percentages by area or city (e.g., New York 10 percent, Chicago 5 percent, etc.). This seems more prevalent in companies headquartered outside the highest premium percentage markets. As with separate schedules the adjustment can be folded directly into salary, or more logically kept as a separate monthly payment. An additional advantage of the percentage approach is that it can be phased out. In other words, if the rationale for paying the premium is to help the individual get adjusted, then the payment could be structured to phase out over a period of time (e.g., fifteen percent the first year, 10 percent the second, 5 percent the third, and zero thereafter).

Where geographic differentials exist they normally do not apply fully to executives. This is accomplished by either completely excluding those above a certain salary level (e.g., $75,000) or applying the differential to only a certain portion of pay (e.g., 10 percent on the first $50,000 of salary, thereby effectively giving a 5 percent premium to an executive earning a $100,000 salary). It should also be remembered that differentials apply only to salary, and thus a company with a high short- and long-term incentive opportunity would have a higher percentage differential than a company with little or no short- and long-term incentive plans, assuming both were paying approximately the same in total compensation.

INDIVIDUAL PAY ACTIONS

Job analysis, job evaluation, salary surveys, and structural adjustments are all keyed to determining how much to pay a particular job. The individual pay actions are determined within this set of determinations. Typically, pay of individuals is determined in relation to the executive's performance over a period of time and position within the salary range. An indication of how these two interrelate is illustrated in Figure 4-18. Note the reference to "compa-ratio"; this is simply actual pay divided by structural control point (midpoint of range for most companies). Thus, a person earning a $90,000 salary in a grade with a $100,000 control point has a compa-ratio of 0.90. The compa-ratio enables the reviewer to relate position in range of one executive to another, as well as a grade-by-grade analysis.

As can be seen, the width of the structural compensation compa-ratio increases with management level. This is consistent with our earlier discussion that ranges might be 50

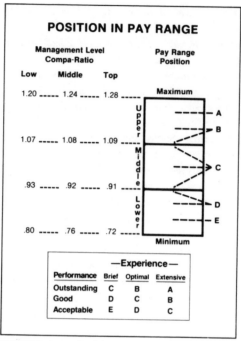

FIGURE 4-18 Position in pay range—experience and peformance.

TABLE 4-14 Performance Matrix—Quality versus Timeliness

	Final completion date				
Quality	Not finished	Very significantly late	Significantly late	Slightly late	On or ahead of schedule
Perfect	1.0	2.0	2.8	3.7	4.0
Outstanding	0.7	1.7	2.5	3.3	3.8
Superior	0.4	1.4	2.2	2.9	3.4
Very good	0.1	1.1	1.8	2.5	3.0
Good	0.0	0.8	1.4	2.0	2.5
Acceptable	0.0	0.5	1.0	1.5	2.0
Marginal	0.0	0.2	0.6	1.0	1.5
Very marginal	0.0	0.1	0.3	0.5	1.0
Unacceptable	0.0	0.0	0.1	0.2	0.5

percent (maximum over minimum) at the low end of the structure but would increase with management level.

As seen in Figure 4-18, executives with only "brief" experience and "acceptable" levels of performance (combination E) should be low in the lower one-third of the range. Conversely, only individuals with "extensive" experience who have been consistently judged as "outstanding" performers (combination A) should be paid near or at the range maximum.

The middle one-third of the range is appropriate for those individuals who have the "optimal" experience and have been consistently rated as "good" (combination C). However, experience and performance levels can offset each other. Combination C can also reflect an executive with "extensive" experience who has been consistently judged as "acceptable" or an individual with only brief experience who is rated as "outstanding." Additional experience and performance combinations suggest positions in the range shown by the letters D and B.

Performance Appraisals

Differentiating pay by performance means by definition it is necessary to evaluate the executive's performance. While this may be nothing more than a 5-minute reflection by the manager in some instances, most organizations are more formalized in their appraisals. However, small threshold companies are likely to have a greater degree of informality than the larger, more mature organizations. In some instances, formality can retard the growth of an organization as the bureaucracy of the process takes on a goal of its own.

Not uncommon is the lack of formal performance appraisals at the very senior levels of management. The common reply is that the individuals know how they are doing simply be examining their unit's performance versus the operating plan for the period. Admittedly that indicates how the unit is doing, but is the executive aiding or hindering the level of performance?

Interestingly, a number of executives hold two divergent views about performance appraisal. They don't believe appraisals are necessary for people who report immediately to them (as there is enough interaction and data to make structured appraisal unnecessary); however, they want to have their own performance reviewed by their superior! Under such circumstances the most satisfied individual is the one receiving a performance appraisal (hopefully positive) who is not required to formally review the performance of his or her own subordinates. Conversely, the most frustrated executive is the one who is told to have formal review sessions with subordinates but is not given a session by a superior. It is believed a large number of executives today fall into the latter category.

Type Appraisals The appraisals essentially range from a simple checklist allowing the rater to identify the most descriptive statement to a rather detailed point grid used to evaluate each goal in terms of timeliness and quality (see Table 4-14).

71

TABLE 4-15 Goal-Oriented Performance Appraisal Program

1. Identification and written description of specific goals to be accomplished (including timetable and basis of measurement) by supervisor.

2. Vertical linkage of individual with group goals is carried out.

3. The subordinate makes a commitment to meeting the objectives

4. Horizontal balance must be assured by the supervisor to ensure equal stretch by subordinates in achieving goals.

5. Real-time assessments and feedback are given to the subordinate by the supervisor, assessing the degree of accomplishments in relation to the stated objectives.

6. Closure at year-end measures the extent of achievement on each goal and aggregates these component parts for the job as a whole.

7. The overall appraisal is "leveled" by adjusting for rater strictness or leniency, and is then expressed in numerical or key work form for the purpose of determining the appropriate size of pay adjustment.

A brief description of an objective or goal-oriented performance appraisal program is shown in Table 4-15.

By multiplying the rating by the assigned weighting for each objective and dividing by the total number of points, it is possible to calculate an overall performance rating. Typically, such a system would use the university-based 4.0 system shown in Table 4-14. The results may be summarized in a verbal manner as shown in Table 4-16. Note that any score between 2.6 and 3.5 would be considered "superior." This rating might be further subdivided so that 2.6 to 3.0 was "very good" while 3.1 to 3.5 would be "superior." However, the difficulty in identifying key words which clearly describe differences in levels of performance has caused some people to simply stay with the numerical results.

How Much Detail? Performance appraisals should be sufficiently detailed to minimize disagreement between supervisee and supervisor on the level of performance. This requires being specific. However, such information can take the form of several well-chosen paragraphs describing the performance, or it can be a listing of objectives for the year and the extent to which they have been accomplished and are in accord with the timetable. Many programs fail because they require either too little or too much detail. The optimum program would balance simplicity with validity to attain an acceptable compromised position.

When Shall Appraisals Be Conducted? Performance appraisals that are conducted shortly prior to an anniversary merit review are subject to great pressure to be sufficiently positive to justify an appropriate compensation action. Where anniversary dates of review exist it is probably appropriate therefore to have two reviews: one on a common review date for all employees and the second prior to the adjustment. The first is needed to minimize heaving skewing to the top performance levels, and the second is required to jusify the compensation action. The two should be reasonably close in

outcome; if they are not, it would be appropriate to have a discussion with the super-
It may be more logical to have a common merit review date and thus only one performance review, which would have the advantage of placing the compensation actions
directly within a prescribed merit budget.

Who Is Involved?   The extent of interaction and participation is a function of how
closely the supervisee and supervisor see eye to eye on the performance level. To the
extent there is an appreciable difference (invariably the supervisor having the lower opinion), frequent discussions during the year on specific project performance are necessary.
When the year-end wrap-up session is held, there is little opportunity for the individual
to be "surprised" by the supervisor's rating. Another technique that is useful is requesting
the ratee to prepare and give to the rater a self-appraisal before the review session.

At the minimum, it is believed appropriate that the supervisor's manager see the
performance write-up (along with the individual's self-assessment if one is prepared),
preferably before and after the review with the individual. By showing the write-up to
the manager before the meeting, the supervisor has an opportunity to obtain the manager's agreement: nothing is worse than to have the manager later agree with the ratee
that the rater was incorrect in the rating. It is also logical for the manager to review it
after the performance review session, especially when the individual is allowed to add
written comments to the appraisal. This session forms the basis for ensuring that an
appropriate follow-up course of action is agreed upon.

Distribution of Performance Ratings   Some companies believe it appropriate to
"force" the distribution into a prescribed pattern (e.g., a bell-shaped normal distribution
curve). Others suggest such a distribution but do not force it; for these the distribution
of performance ratings is skewed negatively as shown in Figure 4-19, reflecting a "drift"
to higher performance ratings. The normal distribution is shown as a dotted curve.

It is not possible to force distribution by grade because of the few individuals
involved; however, it it possible to develop bands of management as indicated in the
table in Figure 4-20, and to attempt to obtain some type of normalcy in ratings except
to the extent unit performance legitimately suggests overall higher or lower ratings.

Ideally, performance distributions comparing one division to another should reflect
differences in performance rather than differences in raters. In many cases, however,
what the distributions really show is a range from the "softie" to the "hard marker."

TABLE 4-16   Key Word versus
Numerical Performance Ratings

Descriptor	Rating
Outstanding	3.6–4.0
Superior	2.6–3.5
Good	1.6–2.5
Marginal	0.6–1.5
Unacceptable	0.0–0.5

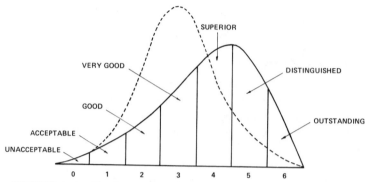

FIGURE 4-19 Distribution of performance ratings—normal versus skewed.

While an objective performance appraisal can help to minimize such differences, it can never completely eliminate them.

In addition to attempting to achieve an overall rational distribution of performance within a division, it is important to watch for the "high grade/high performance" syndrome. This is evidenced when the top performance ratings are awarded to the executives in the highest job grades, forcing lower rankings to those in the lower grades (as illustrated in Figure 4-21. This is a manifestation of the "my best people are in those top grades" philosophy. Some find it difficult to accept that while this statement is assumed to be true, it is not pertinent. The top-graded jobs have greater responsibility for which they have been rewarded with a higher salary range. The issue is whether or not the individuals are meeting these higher standards.

Another way of stating it is that an individual may be a grade 20 and yet, because he or she is exceeding the standards of the position, be judged to be a "distinguished"

DISTRIBUTION OF PERFORMANCE RATINGS

	0	1	2	3	4	5	6
TOP MGT	4	8	16	44	16	8	4
SENIOR MGT	4	8	16	44	16	8	4
MIDDLE MGT	4	8	16	44	16	8	4
LOWER MGT	4	8	16	44	16	8	4
COMPANYWIDE	4	8	16	44	16	8	4

FIGURE 4-20 Distribution of performance ratings—management bands.

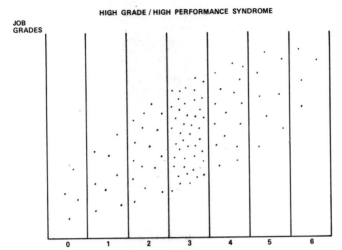

HIGH GRADE / HIGH PERFORMANCE SYNDROME

JOB
GRADES

0   1   2   3   4   5   6

FIGURE 4-21   High-grade/high-performance syndrome.

performer. After due deliberation, management may decide to incorporate these higher standards into the job and make them the normal requirements. The position then merits grade 23 rather than 20, and unless performance is further elevated, the individual should not be judged any higher than "very good," because he or she is simply meeting, not exceeding, the new and higher job standards. Assuming a base salary of $43,000, the individual would be eligible for an 11 percent salary increase, either as a "distinguished" performer in the middle one-third of grade 20 or as a "very good" performer below minimum in grade 23. See Table 4-17 and Table 4-3, page 45.

Note that no pay increase is normally expected to be given to a person above the range maximum. However, after 1 or 2 years with no adjustment most such individuals fall back within the range, simply as a result of the annual structural adjustments. These overmaximums, typically identified as *red circles*, are the result of individuals having been demoted from higher-graded responsibilities.

TABLE 4-17   Merit Pay Matrix—Performance versus Position in Range

Performance level		Percentage increase based on position in range				
Alpha	Numeric	Below minimum	Lower ⅓	Middle ⅓	Upper ⅓	Above maximum
Outstanding	6	21	16	13	11	0
Distinguished	5	17	13	11	9	0
Superior	4	14	11	9	7	0
Very good	3	11	9	7	5	0
Good	2	8	6	5	4	0
Acceptable	1	6	4	3	2	0
Unacceptable	0	0	0	0	0	0

Timing of Salary Action

In many companies the pay review is related to the anniversary of employment, but in some it occurs at a common time during the year. Different portions of the company may have reviews on their own separate dates, or the entire company may have a common adjustment date.

The advantages of a common review date include: (1) maximum utilization of management time in the review process, (2) a minimal need for separate budgetary controls, (3) easy adjustment to economic conditions, and (4) promotion of internal equity. The disadvantages are that such a system is less personalized in nature, and it enables individuals to make easier comparisons on how well they did.

The advantages and disadvantages of distributed adjustments are essentially the mirror image of the common date system. The advantages are that management can be more personalized in deciding and communicating adjustments, and that the making of pay comparisons is diffused. The disadvantages include: (1) the demands on management time are greater since the manager must "come up to speed" on each situation; (2) budgetary game playing (namely, deferring the increase to later in the year in order to be able to give a bigger percentage without incurring more expense for the year) is made possible; (3) it is more difficult to respond equitably to rapidly changing economic situations (consider those who just missed versus got caught by the last set of federal pay guidelines); and (4) it is more difficult to ensure equitable pay treatment throughout the organization.

Frequency of Salary Reviews

Some companies vary the time interval between salary reviews, normally stretching out the period for upper-level positions. Thus, while entry-level positions might be reviewed every 6 months for the first several years of employment, middle management positions

PERFORMANCE	POSITION IN SALARY RANGE				
	BELOW MIN.	LOWER 1/3	MIDDLE 1/3	UPPER 1/3	ABOVE MAX.
OUTSTANDING	20% / 4-8 mos.	16% / 6-9 mos.	13% / 8-12 mos.	10% / 12-18 mos.	5% / 18-24 mos.
DISTINGUISHED	17% / 5-10 mos.	13% / 7-12 mos.	11% / 9-15 mos.	8% / 15-21 mos.	3% / 24-36 mos.
SUPERIOR	14% / 6-12 mos.	11% / 8-15 mos.	9% / 10-18 mos.	6% / 18-24 mos.	
VERY GOOD	11% / 7-14 mos.	9% / 9-18 mos.	7% / 11-21 mos.		
GOOD	8% / 8-16 mos.	6% / 10-21 mos.	5% / 12-24 mos.		
ACCEPTABLE	6% / 9-18 mos.	4% / 12-24 mos.			
UNACCEPTABLE					

FIGURE 4-22   Merit pay matrix—amount versus timing.

TABLE 4-18 Frequency of Review Varied by
Performance—Common Adjustment

Performance	Frequency of adjustment, months	Annualized effect of 8 percent increase
Outstanding	3–4	24–32%
Distinguished	5–8	12–19
Superior	9–12	8–11
Very good	12–18	5–8
Good	18–24	4–5
Acceptable	24–30	3–4

would be on an annual or 18-month basis and the very senior executives on a biennial review.

These longer intervals mask the slowing down in compensation (e.g., a 10 percent pay increase after 18 months is really just a little more than a 6 percent annual adjustment). Furthermore, increasing the time interval for a stated percentage adjustment as one moves further up the organization automatically contributes to the compression problem (i.e., lack of sufficient pay differential between supervisor and subordinates).

Another approach is to increase the normal time interval as the executive progresses within the salary range. An example of this is found in Figure 4-22. The percentages are the annual target amounts; thus an "outstanding" performer below range minimum might receive anything from about 7 percent 4 months after the last change to about 13 percent after 8 months with the target being 10 percent after 6 months. Figure 4-22 also illustrates the type of merit program that establishes ceilings within the range. Note that an "acceptable" performer is not expected to move above the lower one-third, and "good" and "very good" performers are held to the middle one-third of the range. Only "superior," "distinguished, " and "outstanding" performers are permitted to reach the full range maximum. Furthermore, the highest two performance ratings permit token increases for those above range maximum, but on less than a yearly basis.

Another possibility is to hold the percentage increase constant and simply vary the performance, although no instance is known where this is done. This possibility is illustrated in Table 4-18, with an 8 percent adjustment. Actually the amount is higher when compounding is considered.

Developing the Merit Budget

For companies using a common review date it is a simple matter to model the population in terms of position in range and a desired performance population against a merit grid (such as the one in Table 4-17) to develop salary increase funds of pools. For those units which distribute increases throughout the year, the same principle is involved, but the data must be time-weighted in relation to the anticipated date of adjustment.

There are several approaches available for developing the control total, including: (1) projection of most recent actual performance by individual, (2) weighting individual performance in accord with desired performance distribution, and (3) using the described average performance rating.

Using the Most Recent Performance Rating   Projection of the most recent actual performance rating assumes that each individual will have the same rating as last year. Thus, if Brett was "outstanding" last year and a current salary of $60,000 placed the individual in the middle one-third of grade 24, a 13 percent increase, or $7800, is used. Repeating the process for all employees generates a total (which can be increased or decreased by top management in accord with willingness and ability to pay). The problems with this approach are (1) its static nature, assuming neither an increase nor a decrease in performance one year to the next, (2) the lack of a previous rating for newly hired individuals, and (3) the questionable use of a rating at a lower grade for a recently promoted person.

Weighting Based on Desired Distribution   The second approach in developing the control total is assigning probable performance weights to each individual in accord with a desired distribution of performance. This is illustrated in Table 4-19, again using the same Brett example. Note that the 6.96 percent increase would generate a $4176 increase. Repeating the same process for the other employees and summing the dollar increases would generate a raw control total.

Using the Average Performance Rating   The third method of developing a control total is an extension of the second. However, rather than assign probable weightings to each performance rating, the expected mean value is used. Following this approach, one might conclude that "very good" is the average performance rating and that therefore all individuals below their salary grade minimum would, using Table 4-17, be projected for an 11 percent increase, those in the lower one-third for 9 percent, those in the middle one-third for 7 percent, and those in the upper one-third for 5 percent. By

TABLE 4-19   Weighting Performance Based on Desired Distribution

Performance	Raw percentage	Assigned weighting, percent	Adjusted percentage
Outstanding	13	4	0.52
Distinguished	11	8	0.88
Superior	9	16	1.44
Very good	7	44	3.08
Good	5	16	0.80
Acceptable	3	8	0.24
Unacceptable	0	4	0.00
Total		100	6.96

TABLE 4-20 Adjusting for Unit Performance and Position in Range

	Below minimum	Lower one-third	Middle one-third	Upper one-third	Above minimum
Outstanding	2.25%	1.88%	1.5%	1.13%	0.0%
Distinguished	1.50	1.25	1.0	0.75	0.0
Superior	0.75	0.63	0.5	0.38	0.0
Very good	0.00	0.00	0.0	0.00	0.0
Good	−0.75	−0.63	−0.5	−0.38	0.0
Acceptable	−1.50	−1.25	−1.0	−0.75	0.0
Unacceptable	−2.25	−1.88	−1.5	−1.13	0.0

identifying the appropriate percentage based on the executive's position within range and then summing the results, a control total is calculated.

Adjusting for Unit Performance

It is possible to adjust for division performance by identifying a division's performance and adding the value on that line of the grid to the basic simulation, as illustrated in Table 4-20. Thus, using the simple average performance rating approach, if the division's performance were adjudged "superior," the "below minimum" guideline percent for everyone in that division would be increased 0.75 percent to 11.75 percent, the "lower one-third" would move up 0.63 percent to 9.63 percent, the "middle one-third" would be incremented by 0.5 percent to 7.5 percent, and those in the "upper one-third" would have a 0.38 percent higher amount, or 5.38 percent.

A simpler approach but one which does not take into consideration position in range is plus or minus a stated amount from the "very good" performance as shown in Table 4-21. After the basic simulation, if a division had a weighted average allowable increase of 7.4 percent but a performance of "superior," it would be allowed a merit pool average of 7.9 percent.

TABLE 4-21 Adjusting only for Unit Performance

	Percent
Outstanding	Plus 1.5
Distinguished	Plus 1.0
Superior	Plus 0.5
Very good	No adjustment
Good	Minus 0.5
Acceptable	Minus 1.0
Unacceptable	Minus 1.5

Adjusting the Merit Increase Guidelines

Many companies work very hard to disassociate the size of their merit budget from the assigned level of inflation by indicating they set the budget in relation to ability and willingness to pay versus the assumed growth in compensation levels in other companies.

An empirical observation of the relation to merit budgets in the United States and abroad essentially reflects this as shown in Figure 4-23. Except in those situations where government controls artificially restrict the average pay increase for exempt employees, the "merit budget," while normally at least equal to the annual rate of inflation, provides decreasing opportunity to reward meritorious performance as inflation increases.

Thus, while a company may set a merit budget of 8 percent with a 5 percent inflation assumption, it may also set an 18 percent budget with a 15 percent increase in the CPI. While the absolute difference is identical (i.e., three percentage points) the relative difference has been reduced from a 60 percent increase (i.e., 8 percent/5 percent) to a 20 percent increase (i.e., 18 percent/15 percent). Thus, the opportunity to truly differentiate in pay levels has been lessened.

Needless to say, this places great pressure on pay planners devising effective pay delivery systems to maximize the utilization of available dollars in times of high inflation. During inflationary periods there is likely to be increased pressure to restrain the growth in executive pay, since holding their increases to slightly below the average allows a

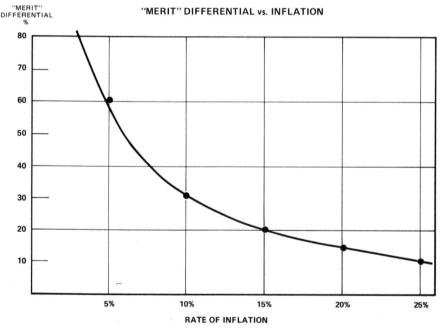

FIGURE 4-23   Merit pay versus rate of inflation.

TABLE 4-22 Position in Range After Merit Adjustment (Mid ⅓ = 0.90 — 1.10)—82 Percent Spread

Year	Range minimum	Performance rating							Range maximum
		0	1	2	3	4	5	6	
0	0.71	0.71	0.71	0.71	0.71	0.71	0.71	0.71	1.29
1	0.71	0.67	0.71	0.72	0.74	0.76	0.78	0.81	1.29
2	0.71	0.63	0.71	0.74	0.78	0.80	0.84	0.89	1.29
3	0.71	0.60	0.71	0.75	0.80	0.84	0.89	0.97	1.29
4	0.71	0.56	0.71	0.76	0.82	0.88	0.95	1.03	1.29
5	0.71	0.53	0.71	0.76	0.85	0.92	0.99	1.10—	1.29
6	0.71	0.50	0.71	0.76	0.87	0.96	1.04	1.15	1.29
7	0.71	0.47	0.71	0.76	0.90—	0.99	1.09	1.21	1.29
8	0.71	0.45	0.71	0.76	0.92	1.02	1.14	1.27	1.29
9	0.71	0.42	0.71	0.76	0.95	1.05	1.17	1.29	1.29
10	0.71	0.40	0.71	0.76	0.96	1.08	1.21	1.29	1.29

Performance rating	Below minimum	Lower one-third	Middle one-third	Upper one-third	Above maximum
6	21%	16%	13%	11%	0
5	17	13	11	9	0
4	14	11	9	7	0
3	11	9	7	5	0
2	8	6	5	4	0
1	6	4	3	2	0
0	0	0	0	0	0

greater proportion of the remaining exempt employees to receive higher percentage increases, because the executives have by definition a higher absolute base.

Each year, therefore, the matrix has to be reexamined in terms of appropriateness. The matrix in Table 4-17 reflects the position that a "very good" performer should keep pace with the increase in competitive pay in the marketplace (here assumed to be 7 percent). The remaining matrix is expanded on the double premise that (1) those lower in the range should move faster than those higher and (2) increase should vary directly with performance. After the matrix is constructed, it has to be tested under varying structural increase assumptions to track the rate in which different level performers move through the salary range.

Table 4-22 shows an example of how this type of simulation can be performed. The seven performance ratings have been expressed in numerical form (6 high and 0 low). In this illustration, a range of $71,000 to $129,000 is tested for a 6 percent annual structural increase for 10 years. The issue is how quickly a person currently at the minimum ($71,000) will progress within the structure if it is adjusted annually by 6 percent, given each of the seven possible performance categories.

Note that performance rating 0 drops progressively further below minimum; however, since such a performance rating probably reflects an unacceptable performer who will probably be terminated within a year or two, this effect is academic. Rating 1 just stays even with the minimum, whereas rating 2 achieves a very limited growth. Rating 3 does not move to the middle one-third until the seventh year, whereas rating 4 reaches this level in the fifth year, rating 5 in the fourth year, and rating 6 in the third year. Only ratings 5 and 6 move into the upper one-third—the former after 8 years and the latter after 5 years.

These progressions must be examined in terms of what appears reasonable. Assuming the norm is performance rating 3, is it defensible that such an executive would take 7 years to move to the middle one-third (i.e., to perform in a fully satisfactory manner all aspects of the job)? Probably not. It may be concluded that for this particular level, 4 or 5 years is more logical.

As indicated earlier, there is another reason salary ranges get wider as one progresses through the organization: recognition that it will take the person longer to attain a level of fully satisfactory performance. There are four ways to improve this rate of progression: (1) lower the structural increase percentage, (2) increase the merit percentage amounts, (3) narrow the range, (4) shorten the interval between increases.

Assuming the structural increase is a reasonable assessment of market increase in pay, it is not logical to lower the estimated structural increase. The merit increase amounts which reflect the company's willingness (ability) to pay in relation to market movements may have to be increased, although this may be a troublesome precedent (i.e., if it is believed the amount will be less the following year). The compromise is a strategy allowing the desirable position to be attained over several years and thereby minimizing significant up-down repercussions.

Narrowing the range can have a significant impact. In the earlier example the maximum-over-minimum spread was 82 percent; by lowering this to 50 percent (and thereby

TABLE 4-23 Position in Range After Merit Adjustment (Mid ⅓ = 0.93 − 1.07)—50 Percent Spread

Year	Range minimum	Performance rating							Range maximum
		0	1	2	3	4	5	6	
0	0.80	0.80	0.80	0.80	0.80	0.80	0.80	0.80	1.20
1	0.80	0.75	0.80	0.82	0.84	0.86	0.88	0.91	1.20
2	0.80	0.71	0.80	0.83	0.83	0.90	0.94	1.00	1.20
3	0.80	0.67	0.80	0.85	0.90	0.94	1.00	┌1.07─	1.20
4	0.80	0.63	0.80	0.86	┌0.93┘	0.99	1.05	1.14	1.20
5	0.80	0.60	0.80	0.86	0.95	1.03	1.10	1.19	1.20
6	0.80	0.56	0.80	0.86	0.98	1.06	1.15	1.20	1.20
7	0.80	0.53	0.80	0.86	1.01	1.09	1.19	1.20	1.20
8	0.80	0.50	0.80	0.86	1.02	1.13	1.20	1.20	1.20
9	0.80	0.47	0.80	0.86	1.03	1.16	1.20	1.20	1.20
10	0.80	0.45	0.80	0.86	1.04	1.17	1.20	1.20	1.20

TABLE 4-24 Position in Range After Six-Month Merit Adjustment (Mid ⅓ = 0.90 − 1.10)—82 Percent Spread

Year	Range minimum	Performance rating 0	1	2	3	4	5	6	Range maximum
0	0.71	0.71	0.71	0.71	0.71	0.71	0.71	0.71	1.29
1	0.71	0.67	0.74	0.77	0.81	0.85	0.89	0.94	1.29
2	0.71	0.63	0.77	0.81	0.85	0.89	0.94	1.00	1.29
3	0.71	0.60	0.78	0.86	0.93	0.93	0.99	1.07	1.29
4	0.71	0.56	0.80	0.91	0.94	0.96	1.04	1.14	1.29
5	0.71	0.53	0.82	0.91	0.95	0.98	1.08	1.19	1.29
6	0.71	0.50	0.83	0.91	0.96	1.01	1.14	1.25	1.29
7	0.71	0.47	0.85	0.91	0.97	1.04	1.17	1.29	1.29
8	0.71	0.45	0.87	0.91	0.98	1.07	1.20	1.29	1.29
9	0.71	0.42	0.88	0.91	0.99	1.10	1.24	1.29	1.29
10	0.71	0.40	0.90	0.91	1.00	1.13	1.27	1.29	1.29

starting our hypothetical employee closer to the midpoint) the impact is noticeable as shown in Table 4-23. Note that for most performance classifications it has meant movement into the middle and upper portions of the range several years sooner.

Shortening the time interval between adjustments also means faster movement through the structure. This ranges from lowering the norm by 1 or more months (e.g., 10 months instead of a year) to significant changes (e.g., reviewing everyone in the lower one-third every 6 months as long as they are in that portion of the range). The latter approach has a very dramatic impact as seen in the table in Table 4-24, which again has an 82 percent maximum-over-minimum spread. Note that performance rating 3 moves to the middle one-third in 3 years versus 7 in the first grid (using only annual increases), and rating 6 (the top performer) gets into the middle one-third in 1 year and the upper one-third in 4 years.

Table 4-25 reflects the compound effect of reducing the range spread from 82 percent to 50 percent and reviewing pay every 6 months for those in the lower one-third of the structure. Rating 3 is now in the middle one-third after 2 years, the same time frame it takes rating 6 to move into the upper one-third. The optimum construction of range spread, merit matrix, and review frequency is one that is logical, given management philosophy.

Promotion Increases

In addition to examining the appropriateness of the merit increase policy, it is also important to review the promotional increase guidelines. Few companies structure their pay programs to properly compensate the promoted individual. Too often there is a flat percentage (e.g., 10 percent) available in such event, and yet the same logic which applies to performance and position in range for merit increases also applies to promotional

TABLE 4-25 Position in Range After 6-Month Adjustment (Mid ⅓ = 0.93 — 1.07)—50 Percent Spread

| Year | Range minimum | Performance rating | | | | | | | Range maximum |
		0	1	2	3	4	5	6	
0	0.80	0.80	0.80	0.80	0.80	0.80	0.80	0.80	1.20
1	0.80	0.75	0.83	0.86	0.91	0.96	1.00	1.06	1.20
2	0.80	0.71	0.87	0.92	0.94	1.00	1.04	1.13	1.20
3	0.80	0.67	0.88	0.97	0.97	1.03	1.09	1.20	1.20
4	0.80	0.63	0.90	0.97	0.99	1.06	1.15	1.20	1.20
5	0.80	0.60	0.92	0.97	1.00	1.09	1.18	1.20	1.20
6	0.80	0.58	0.94	0.97	1.01	1.12	1.20	1.20	1.20
7	0.80	0.53	0.96	0.97	1.02	1.15	1.20	1.20	1.20
8	0.80	0.50	0.94	0.97	1.03	1.16	1.20	1.20	1.20
9	0.80	0.47	0.94	0.97	1.04	1.17	1.20	1.20	1.20
10	0.80	0.45	0.94	0.97	1.05	1.18	1.20	1.20	1.20

adjustments. For an individual receiving a significant increase in responsibilities, a 10 percent increase may still be far short of the new job's pay minimum; conversely it may be a modest organizational change and therefore 10 percent would be overly generous (e.g., pay is already well within the middle one-third of the new job's pay grade). Remember that position in grade is the company's best assessment of the individual's worth vis-á-vis the marketplace and other individuals within the company (in relation to their position within grade). Following such a logic, a guide could be constructed such as the one shown in Table 4-26, with varying percentages of increase depending on position in the new job's salary structure.

As a test of the efficacy of the adjustment, one could ask "What could I offer this individual to accept this job if he or she came from another company?" Under such an examination most internal promotional pay actions pale by comparison. Too often, the additude exists that the individual must earn the new money, and after all the person might fail. True! But if this is really a significant risk, it also says something about the state of management development and organization planning within the organization, and the need to address it rather than to waffle in the administration of the salary program.

A well-thought-out promotional pay policy is essential to retaining internal equity, not to mention its value during the period of federal pay controls when promotional increases are usually easier to accomplish than merit adjustments.

TABLE 4-26 Promotion Guidelines, Percent

Below minimum	Lower one-third	Middle one-third
25	15	5

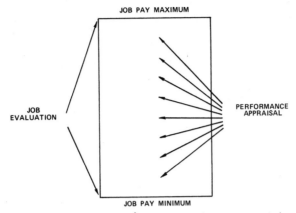

FIGURE 4-24   Job evaluation versus performance appraisal.

SUMMARY AND CONCLUSIONS

Unlike the other four elements, the tax aspect and SEC requirements for salary are quite simple and straightforward. The tax effectiveness of the salary is 0.93—tax deductible to the company and reportable as personal service income to the individual. Proxy disclosure is equally straightforward: column C_1 for payments as well as unconditional deferrals and column D for conditional deferral amounts.

Many express concern that executive pay in the last several years has gone up faster than during the early seventies or sixties. Even after netting out CPI impact this should not be so surprising. Up until 1964 we had a marginal tax rate of 91 percent for income in excess of $400,000 (married person filing joint return); only after 1969 did this drop from 70 percent to 50 percent for earned income (or personal service income as it is now called, namely salary and bonus). Also, we had wage controls from 1971 to 1974. In addition, the attractiveness of stock market–related plans waned because of performance and the tax impact on qualified options. It is not surprising that direct pay started to take on more emphasis.

Typically, companies will set a range of pay appropriate for a particular job based on job evaluation and competitive level of pay for comparable jobs. The employee's performance combined with experience is the basis for determining the rate of movement through this structure, as shown in Figure 4-24.

Unless the salary of the individual is both externally competitive and internally equitable, these inequities will be further compounded and magnified after the impact of the other four elements (short- and long-term incentives, employee benefits, and perquisites) has been added on.

Employee Benefits

Until rather recently this element was identified as "fringe benefits"—a term denoting peripheral importance. With many companies today expending over a third of their payroll on this element, it is certainly no longer an item of peripheral importance.

Although some forms of benefits can be traced back a hundred or so years, due to their limited application, employee benefits truly were "fringe" in nature until World War II. The Stablization Act of 1942 froze wages and salaries but allowed limited benefit improvements; needless to say there were almost limitless "limited benefit improvements." Then after the war the U.S. Supreme Court ruled that pension plans were negotiable items for collective bargaining agreements. Shortly thereafter the Defense Production Act of 1950 came into being because of inflationary pressures caused by the Korean conflict; again "limited benefit improvements" were allowed. Thus within 10 years "fringe benefits" exploded into "employee benefits."

Before proceeding any further it is important to indicate that one must be careful in citing benefit costs as a percent of pay due to the varying definitions of numerator and denominator. While there are numerous variations dependent on what is and what is not a benefit, essentially there are three major definitions.

1. *Total costs for all benefits (numerator) divided by gross pay or W-2 (denominator).* On the surface this appears sound and logical. Its problem is simply that a number of benefits are cash benefits which are reflected in the W-2, and thus some items are in both numerator and denominator. By increasing such benefits (e.g., vacation pay) it is possible to show less of an increase in benefit costs than for non-W-2 items. To illustrate: assuming total benefit costs of $30 million and total payroll of $100 million, if a benefit improvement of $1 million is implemented for a non-W-2 item the total benefit cost is 31 percent (i.e., $31 million ÷ $100 million). However for improvements also counted in the denominator the final tally is 30.7 percent (i.e., $31 million ÷ $101 million).

2. *Total costs for all benefits (numerator) divided by base pay for time actually worked (denominator)*. The numerator is the same as the earlier definition, but the denominator consists only of the base pay for the time actually worked. This is probably the optimal formula, for all items are accounted for and only once.

3. *Benefits costs except for time off with pay (numerator) divided by gross pay (denominator)*. Of the three this approach is going to reflect the lowest benefit percentage, simply because it has the highest denominator and lowest numerator. It occurs in companies which lack payroll records indicating lost time with pay when it occurs— invariably for those on the monthly payroll.

The various benefit programs can be classified under one of six categories: time off with pay, employee services, nonperformance awards, health care, survivor protection, and retirement. These categories and the specific plans range in importance to the executive from limited to very significant, as will be seen in this chapter.

TIME OFF WITH PAY

As the phrase implies this is payment for time not worked. It ranges from coffee breaks and meal periods on one extreme to sabbaticals and termination pay on the other.

The executive, like everyone else in the company, is eligible to take a specified number of *paid holidays*. For most companies these holidays are the equivalent of between 2 and 3 weeks (i.e., 10 to 15 days). In addition to the basic six of New Year's Day, Memorial Day, Fourth of July, Labor Day, Thanksgiving, and Christmas, common additions include: President's Birthday, Good Friday, Columbus Day, Veteran's Day, Election Day, and employee's birthday. Additional floaters are often employed to make longer weekends (e.g., Friday after Thanksgiving). Sometimes these are welcome respites, but more often they simply mean the executive works at home instead of in the office those days. As such, holidays are not very significant to executives.

More important is the *vacation allowance*. Not atypical is an allowance of 2 weeks after the first year of work, 3 weeks after 5 years, 4 weeks after 12 (or 15) years, 5 weeks after 20 (or 25) years, and 6 weeks after 30 years of service. Such a schedule is probably reasonable for the executive who has been with the company 10 or more years. However, even if they are workaholics and unlikely to take the full allowance, not many newly hired executives are going to be content with 2 weeks vacation. To resolve such situations some companies adopt a minimum age as an alternative eligibility criteria. For example, regardless of years of service a person of age 40 to 49 will receive four weeks, 50 to 59 will receive 5 weeks, and 60 or more will receive 6 weeks. Alternatively a program of 4 weeks' vacation for all corporate or divisional officers could be adopted.

Funeral leave (or bereavement pay) and *court leave* (for jury or witness duty) are of little importance to the executive since it is assumed that the company will cover such absences.

Accident or illness is covered by *worker's compensation* if occupationally caused or *disability pay* plans if nonoccupational in nature. Although there have been instances of suits for worker's compensation coverage in cases of heart attack (on the grounds that it was caused by work stress), executives are more concerned about disability plan benefits than worker's compensation. Disability plans are usually of two types: short-term and long-term, depending on the length of absence. Normally the short-term plan will cover the first 6 (maybe 12) months of absence at full pay. Long-term disability (LTD) benefits begin when short-term expire. Unlike short-term they are typically integrated with social security benefits (in other words LTD benefits are added to social security payments to reach a specific pay target such as two-thirds of pay). In addition, they may be offset by other statutory benefits and other plans in which the employer pays all or a portion of the expense. However, LTD benefits typically are not offset by any insurance benefits paid under a contract paid for solely by the employee.

Normally plan benefits run for 2 years if the individual is unable to return to the same work he had previously, and after that payments are contingent upon ability to work in any field of suitable employment. Social security payments are tax-free, as are LTD payments from a plan paid for by the individual. Some companies may thus have decided to allow the executive to pay the LTD premium but then reimburse the individual at the end of the year with a separate bonus check.

Since a significant portion of plan benefits may be after-tax, while gross pay is pretax, plan benefits rarely exceed about two-thirds of gross pay. Also, a number of expenses associated with work (e.g., transportation) no longer continue, reducing further the needed income replacement level. From the company's viewpoint it is important that benefits not be high enough to be a disincentive to return to work.

Typically, such plans discriminate against higher-paid employees in two ways: (1) incentive pay is often excluded as a definition of pay, and thus the formula becomes two-thirds of salary rather than two-thirds of earnings, and (2) there is a maximum monthly benefit (e.g., $3500), and thus as shown in Table 5-1, the percentage of pay that is replaced becomes progressively smaller at upper income levels.

The executive who does not perform satisfactorily may receive another form of pay for time not worked—*severance* pay. Conceptually, such pay is given in lieu of notice.

TABLE 5-1 LTD Benefit versus Salary

Salary		LTD benefit	Percentage of pay
Annual	Monthly		
$ 50,000	$ 4,166.67	$2,791.67	66.7
75,000	6,250.00	3,500.00	56.0
100,000	8,333.33	3,500.00	42.0
150,000	12,500.00	3,500.00	28.0
200,000	16,666.67	3,500.00	21.0
300,000	25,000.00	3,500.00	14.0
400,000	33,333.33	3,500.00	10.5
500,000	42,666.67	3,500.00	8.4

This is in addition to unemployment compensation provided by the state (in conjunction with the federal government). Previously these state benefits were not subject to income taxes; however, beginning with the year 1979 they are no longer completely excludable. Such benefits plus any other gross income during the year are added together. This amount is reduced by $25,000 for married individuals and $20,000 for singles and tax is paid on either one-half the difference or the total amount of unemployment compensation benefits, whichever is lower. For executives this essentially means including their unemployment benefits as taxable income. For example, if an executive had $65,000 in compensation and $5000 in unemployment benefits, the total of $70,000 would be reduced by $25,000 (assuming marriage), leaving $45,000. Since one-half of this ($22,500) is greater than the $5000 unemployment benefits, the latter is taxable income.

A typical severance plan might be 2 weeks pay plus 1 week for every year of service; thus an individual with 10 years' service would receive approximately 3 months' pay. Some companies distinguish between individual and group decisions. Thus they may give 2 weeks plus a half-week of pay for every year of service for an individual whose performance is no longer acceptable, but will give 2 weeks plus 1 week for every year of service when an installation is being closed or a department within a site phased out. Such payments of course occur only after all attempts to otherwise place the affected employees elsewhere within the company have failed.

Executives are terminated for failures in performance and/or ability to have their personality mesh with the decision makers. As a matter of fact, some speculate that the less-than-competent executive will be retained if he or she is personally acceptable to those responsible for making the termination decision, whereas a topflight performer will be terminated for making waves (and thus being seen as a personal challenge to the authority of others). Thus, in spite of many of the teachings of results-oriented management, what matters in some organizations is not how well one performs but the extent to which one's personality is completely compatible with others.

In addition, companies that have little variation in pay for performance are more likely to have "sweat-through" performance problems. A company that uses its bonus plan to acknowledge performance can tell a manager very clearly about poor performance simply by cutting back or completely eliminating the bonus. In such companies it would be unlikely that a person would have 2 zero-bonus years and still be around. In companies with modest variation in compensation adjustments there is a greater requirement to have a face-to-face discussion to indicate to the executive that performance needs improvement. This is unlikely to happen since it is this same inability to face problem cases that causes the modest compensation adjustment! Thus, what happens is the situation deteriorates until finally they fire the person—or convince him or her to retire if that is a reasonable option.

While severance pay is given for ineffective performance of duties, typically it is not given for violation of company rules (e.g., gambling or drinking on the job). In addition, companies may not give severance payments to performance failures due to insubordination.

EMPLOYEE SERVICES

There is a wide range of items which can be provided to the employee at little or no cost, ranging from recreation programs to discounts on company products.

Relatively new on the benefit scene are mass-merchandised insurance programs for automobiles and homeowners. Usually the company provides little more than the payroll deduction (and perhaps some office space); in return the employee receives a reduced rate. While this could result in an annual savings of a couple of hundred dollars, it is not looked on by executives as a significant benefit. However, it is important for the executive to be sure the protection is adequate.

Until recently, most *auto insurance* protection was based on determining negligence (namely the negligent party and the insurance company should pay the injured innocent party). Now no-fault protection is more the norm than the exception. This has eliminated the need for a number of lawsuits where negligence was contested.

Initially only protection against loss resulting from fire was insurable under *home-owner's insurance*. Then protection from loss from snow, ice, hail, and windstorm was available along with human-related events (e.g., vandalism, malicious mischief, riots, civil commotion) and man-created objects (e.g., falling aircraft and damage from other vehicles). Essentially, the homeowner's policy has become an all-risk coverage for the property. However, even an apparent all-risk policy has exclusions and it is important that the executive know what they are and whether he or she wishes to accept the risk of such loss or seek insurance to cover the risk. For example, the policy value for personal property may be determined to be inadequate. Therefore, an additional personal property floater is purchased, listing the additional major items (e.g., mink coat, diamond ring, or original artwork) along with the insured value.

Legal services can be provided under an insurance contract or direct company payment. They take the form of either a closed panel (a specific list of attorneys is provided) or an open panel (allowing the executive to choose an attorney). The former is an easy plan to administer for cost control purposes, whereas the latter provides the employee more flexibility. While most plans are limited to routine work (e.g., adoptions, property closings, wills, and divorces), some offer a full range of covered services (including criminal defense).

Until recently such plans had no favorable tax feature, but the Tax Reform Act of 1976 provided that benefits to the employee (and family) under a qualified plan (no discrimination in favor of higher-paid executives) would not be considered income for tax purposes. Section 120 of the Internal Revenue Code further indicates that employee-shareholders or owners with more than a 5 percent interest in the company may be included in the plan; *however*, company costs for this group cannot exceed 25 percent of the total plan costs. This effectively eliminates the possibility of this benefit for very small organizations.

Thus it can be expected that such plans will increase in popularity in coming years, assuming the expiration of this tax treatment after 1981 is extended. Some argue that these plans will give the middle class the same benefit now enjoyed by the affluent (who can afford top legal advice) and the indigent poor (who have such services provided at no cost through legal aid programs).

In some companies *credit unions* are available to cover employee needs for loans, in other instances the company will establish a *loan policy* to cover such items as relocation (initiated by the company) and education of dependents. In addition, loans from savings and investment plans are sometimes adopted, although it is difficult to rationalize charging less in interest than the fund managers are able to realize through investment.

Preretirement counseling is considered by many to be a worthwhile program. Executives and other employees nearing retirement are invited to attend seminars addressing such issues as how to utilize increased leisure time, the company benefit program upon retirement, and what the individual can expect in the way of social security and medicare benefits. The meetings are supplemented by magazines, reports, and individual sessions with company representatives as needed. While such sessions are of value to the executive, much of the material has been covered in financial counseling sessions (an item we will discuss among perquisites).

NONPERFORMANCE AWARDS

These are awards in cash or equivalent upon the attainment of a certain event, not for failing to meet performance expectations as the name might imply. By their nonperformance nature, they by definition should be of limited scope to executives.

While hourly and weekly employees might be eligible for *attendance* bonuses (for specified period of perfect attendance) or *length of service* bonuses (for each additional year of company service), executive participation is normally limited to such programs as the *service award*. Thus for achieving milestones (normally in 5-year multiples), the employee receives a pin or other item reflecting the degree of such service. In addition, 25 or more years of service usually means induction into a quarter-century club.

For those interested in additional education some form of *educational assistance* is usually available. Such a program might pay for 75 percent or more of the tuition and related expenses; for the executive this could be combined with a fully paid sabbatical for a year to obtain an M.B.A. or complete the Ph.D. requirements. Sometimes special programs are established in conjunction with preretirement counseling programs to encourage the individual to adopt new interests.

This benefit was significantly enhanced by the 1978 Revenue Act. Prior to its enactment, individuals could avoid imputed income for company-reimbursed educational expenses only if the study was work-related (namely was needed to maintain or improve skills used in one's present job). To the extent the employer did not provide reimbursement, the employee could deduct these expenses from income for tax purposes. However, educational expenses incurred to prepare for a new job would not be a qualified expense.

Now, while the same rules regarding deduction apply to the individual, the company may reimburse for education unrelated to the present job without resulting in additional compensation to the employee. Thus, this is an extremely cost effective benefit as the corporation receives a tax deduction for the expense while the employee has no income liability for the reimbursement. Although the 1978 change only applies through 1983, one could conclude that it has a reasonable chance of being extended.

To qualify for this favored tax treatment, the company must show that it has a plan—one that does not discriminate in favor of higher-paid executives (although greater use by this segment of the employee population apparently would not upset the benefits). Also the plan cannot offer employees the option of choosing benefit coverage instead of other benefits which are taxable.

Children of employees have the opportunity to further their education at company expense through *scholarships* provided by the company. Although such programs are usually open to all employees, it seems that a high portion of executives' children usually are winners. Since selection is usually made on the basis of competitive test scores monitored by an independent agency, this in no way implies any "hanky-panky." Rather, for whatever reason or combination of reasons, executive offspring rank high among the intellectually able. When such programs are widely based in eligibility, the company receives a tax deduction while neither the executive nor the child has income tax consequences.

A very popular nonperformance program with executives is the *matching gifts plan* in which the contribution made by the employee to a college or university (charitable institutions are normally not included due to cost and administrative problems) is equaled by the company. Thus an executive who sends a check for $1000 to his or her alma mater knows the company will send a matching $1000 check. Thus the executive gets the recognition of a $2000 contribution at a $500 cost (assuming a 50 percent marginal tax bracket). The company's $1000 contribution is also tax deductible. While typically such programs are open to all employees, the greatest degree of utilization is by the executives because of their visibility to solicitors and their higher tax bracket.

When the company wishes an employee to relocate to another area, it is customary to reimburse the individual for a significant portion of the *relocation expense*. In addition to paying for the cost of moving the employee's possessions, many companies will pay for all or a portion of the selling costs (this would include any loss the individual might incur in selling below the appraised value of the house), travel and lodging accommodations while searching for a new home (and waiting for it to be vacated), carrying charges (e.g., mortgage payments and utilities) on the old house, as well as low-cost or no-cost loans until such house is sold. In addition, a flat payment (e.g., 1 month's pay) may be given to cover miscellaneous related expenses. Also, when the executive must accept a higher mortgage interest on the new home than for the previous residence, some companies will make up all or a portion of the difference for a limited period of time. All such expenses paid by the company are tax deductible; however, the executive has a limited tax-free benefit. First, in order to receive any tax-free reimbursement, the

93

individual must be relocated to a company operation which is at least 35 miles farther from the current home than was the previous operation. Then the individual has no tax liability on the first $3000 of reimbursement. Of this the maximum allowable for temporary living expense and travel to locate new quarters is $1500, and the remainder is available to cover closing costs. Costs in excess of these amounts as well as such non-covered items as preoccupancy carrying charges, loss on sale of house, visits to former location, and incidental expenses are not deductible. To the extent the company reimburses any of those items, the individual will have income. Thus it is rather common for companies to gross up any relocation expense payments by the amount of federal (and in many instances state) tax liability.

An approach followed by some companies is to buy the house from the employee at the appraised price and thereby apparently remove any tax consequences to the employee on this portion of the relocation policy. Others have a relocation firm purchase the house to effect the same result. Under the earlier identified guarantee approach, if the individual sold the house at $125,000 and it was appraised at $135,000, the employee would receive the $10,000 difference from the company—an amount taxable under the above stated conditions. Conversely if the company or its agent purchased the house at $135,000 and subsequently sold it at $125,000, the employee might have no tax consequences.

While such moving expense policies apply to all employees, they usually are of greatest value to the executive due to the expense associated with moving and the extent of investment in current housing.

Similar to relocation expense reimbursement is the *assignment* policy. Under such a policy a portion of the relocation policy is given to newly hired employees who must relocate in order to join the company. At lower levels this may simply be the cost of moving the possessions and the family; at the executive level this could mean the entire relocation policy including guaranteed selling price and loan. The tax situation to both company and employee is the same as under the relocation policy.

Paying for *travel and entertainment expenses* incurred on behalf of the company due to business responsibilities is a traditional benefit. While hypothetically this is applicable at all organizational levels, it probably has its greatest application at sales and executive levels. The IRS and Congress continue to peck away at this benefit in the belief that all executives have three-martini lunches (including an expensive exquisite meal) and charge it off as a business expense. For the expense to be tax deductible by the corporation and not an income item for the employee, the individual must be able to demonstrate that it was incurred while conducting business. Furthermore an expense while on the road, as well as for anything in excess of $25, requires a receipt indicating date, who was in attendance, the business purpose of the expense, the nature and amount of the expense, and where the expense was incurred. When the reimbursed employee owns more than 10 percent of the company stock, additional documentation is needed. There may be no such thing as a free lunch, but a lunch properly documented as business-related is at least tax deductible.

HEALTH CARE

Certainly one of the most cost-effective benefits is reimbursement for medical expenses, for it is tax deductible by the company and the recipient has no income tax liability. Such plans can be provided by an insurance company under a contract covering a specified group of employees or self-insured by the company on a pay-as-you-go basis. Under the former it is the insurance company which is obligated to pay all covered expenses, even if such claims payment coupled with taxes, commissions, and administrative expenses leaves no profit—although it is logical to assume the following year the carrier will be seeking higher premiums. Under a self-insured plan it is the company which is responsible for determining the efficacy of the claim and making the payments. Since some companies find it unpalatable to personally deny a claim, they engage insurance companies for "administrative services only" to determine the appropriateness of the claim with the company then making the payment.

In addition to insurance companies there are the prominent *Blue Cross* and *Blue Shield* forms of protection. These nonprofit membership corporations provide reimbursement for hospital charges and surgical and other forms of medical care, respectively.

Even before the individual is covered by the company medical program the person has probably received a medical benefit—the *preemployment physical*. In addition to wanting to know the health status of potential employees, a number of companies have ongoing physical examination programs. In many cases, due to cost, such programs are limited to multiphasic screening with emphasis on urine and blood samples. Depending on nature of work, chest x-rays and gastrointestinal studies may also be undertaken.

For individuals with particular medical problems, wallet-size cards listing allergies, blood type, and medications required may be appropriate. For some, a bracelet or necklace identifying a particular problem (e.g., allergy to penicillin) could be very helpful in case of an accident or serious injury. Others have microfilmed their medical history highlights and carry this in their wallet.

Health care maintenance organizations (i.e., HMOs) are community-rated health care plans which for a fixed monthly charge provide the employee and his or her family with health care at no additional cost. Under such a program there is a financial incentive to diagnose and treat the patient quickly rather than delaying until it becomes more serious and more costly. Under the Health Maintenance Act of 1973 companies are required to allow HMOs which meet federal requirements to be selected by employees in lieu of other types of protection. The employer is obligated to pay the HMO up to the same amount it currently is expending in health care; the employee must make up the difference. Such forms of medical care are quite attractive when the employee's place of residence and work site are both within easy commuting distance of the HMO center, although some are not pleased with what they consider as the less personal nature of treatment than that provided by a family doctor.

Also, many executives are not eager to relinquish the ability to make a free and independent decision on the provider of needed medical service. In spite of the fact that the HMO is virtually assuring the individual that the needed services will be available when needed, many executives want to be certain that the doctor, especially in cases of surgery, is the best in the field—not simply one capable of adequate care! While a number of very qualified surgeons are in HMOs by definition, not all of the established, top names are affiliated with such organizations.

Insurance contracts provide coverage under either a *"comprehensive"* or a *"schedule"* plan. Under the first there are three separate parts: the portion paid by the plan, the portion paid by the employee, and the portion in which expenses are paid by both. As an example, the employee may be liable for the first $100 of covered expenses during the year, the plan will pay the next $500 in full, and thereafter the plan will pick up 80 percent of the expense with the employee paying for the remaining 20 percent.

Under a scheduled plan, each covered expense is identified and a maximum dollar reimbursement assigned to each. Typically such plans also have an extended medical reimbursement feature which will pay a specified percentage (e.g., 80 percent) of all covered expenses beyond the schedule after an annual deductible (e.g., $100) is fully paid by the employee. As can be seen, there is a high degree of similarity between the two plans. However, the scheduled plan will reimburse a higher percentage of medical costs in communities with a lower cost for health services; also, such a plan requires periodic update to increase the schedules to appropriate levels of reimbursement.

Where the company has enough employees these plans are experience-related, which means that the premium charged by the insurance company is determined by the claims experience only of this unit. Conversely, the HMOs described earlier are community-rated—meaning that premiums will be determined by the experience of the full community of users, not simply the users from a particular company. The third approach is a pool experience, in which a group of employees is placed in a unit consisting of other groups; the premium is based on the experience of the entire pool.

Factors impacting on the premium charged include (1) plan changes, (2) prices of services, (3) size of unit covered, and (4) utilization of the plan. To the extent these increase, one can expect the premium to increase, and conversely to the extent these decrease, one should expect a reduction in premium. Usually the result is a combination of different rates of increase among the four items.

When the insurance carrier and the employer differ significantly on the amount of premium for the following year, quite often they agree to write a *retrospective premium adjustment*, or "retro," into the contract. The carrier agrees to accept a lower premium than it wanted in exchange for the agreement by the employer to reimburse at the end of the year up to a predetermined limit. The employer can improve its cash flow during the year in exchange for an increased level of financial risk by year-end.

Another way companies control expenses is by entering into a *minimum premium arrangement* with the insurance company. As the term implies, this will reduce the premium to perhaps 10 percent of its former size, because the company agrees to deposit into a bank account an amount believed sufficient in size to probably cover normal claim experience. The carrier agrees to pay any and all claims beyond the amount deposited by the company. The premium paid by the company is to ensure this excess protection. This approach results in savings to the company in two ways: (1) a reduction of proportionate amount (e.g., 90 percent) in premium taxes due the state and (2) significant reduction in reserves (i.e., company money held by the carrier) to cover *open and unreported claims* (commonly called "O and U")—namely claims that are incurred during the year the contract is in force but not paid until the following year (when the contract may no longer be in force) because they were either not reported or reported but not paid as of the end of the contract year.

The final step is when the company takes all financial risk for claims; namely it *self-insures*. This may be either on a "pay-as-you-go" basis or by establishing reserves to level out payments. If the company establishes a trust in conformance with Section 501 (c)(9) of the Internal Revenue Code, it is able to take a deduction for the amount contributed to the trust. Additionally, earnings of the trust are not subject to taxes, thus making contributions very cost effective. While the trust is constructed to hypothetically meet all claim expenses, it is possible that unusual circumstances could completely exhaust all the funds in the trust without paying them completely. Rather than face this possibility, some companies purchase stop-loss protection from an insurance company which stipulates at what point the carrier will assume responsibility for losses.

Another manner in which companies use insurance carriers when self-insured is to purchase claim review and processing. This *administrative services only* (or ASO) approach enables the company to place a third party between itself and its employees on difficult claim reviews, as well as purchase the expertise of the carrier in being able to ensure reasonable and customary amounts are being charged for services performed.

Prescription drugs are usually covered only while in a hospital (or after satisfying the extended medical reimbursement deductible under most medical insurance programs. It is not surprising therefore that a number of companies have developed plans to reimburse expense (normally after a modest per-prescription deductible of a dollar or so). Obviously the incentive under such a plan is to get a bigger prescription and thereby reduce the number and cost of refills.

A shortcoming of most medical insurance plans is the limited degree of expense reimbursement for dental problems; it is not atypical for a plan to cover only repair necessitated by an accident. In recent years this void has been filled by the rapid acceptance of *dental insurance*. Like medical insurance such policies are either scheduled or comprehensive type plans. Many plans pay the full cost of normal checkups, x-rays, and cleaning to encourage early detection of problems, believing this to be a cost effective manner of keeping costs within control since, unlike medical care, the individual has a high degree of choice in dental care. Thus, early diagnosis and treatment should result in less utilization of expensive restoration care necessitated by years of neglect. Usually covered as a separate item is orthodontia—an increasingly utilized procedure, expecially for the employee's children who have ill-formed teeth.

There have been some instances of *vision care* insurance to reimburse all or a portion of examinations and resulting eyeglasses. *Audio care* is a similar health care item dealing with the hearing and necessary corrective devices. To date neither has become very popular, perhaps due to a combination of tolerable expense in one instance and infrequent utilization in the other.

While health care protection and some form of company cost reimbursement is important to all employees, it can be especially attractive to executives. Since the cost of medical care can only be deducted to the extent that it exceeds 3 percent of adjusted income, an individual with taxable income of $100,000 must earn $6000 to pay $3000 of nonreimbursed medical costs; the other $3000 is for federal income tax on the $6000. Any expense beyond $3000 in this example will allow the individual to split the cost with the federal government in the form of a tax deduction.

SURVIVOR PROTECTION

As the words imply, this category of benefits is intended to address the financial needs of the employee's family after the individual dies. It is designed to preserve the executive's estate assets by providing sufficient liquidity to pay the federal estate and state inheritance taxes, as well as perhaps meet longer-term income liabilities for the beneficiaries. It can be very tax effective since life insurance proceeds incur no income tax liability and the federal estate tax and state inheritance tax can be avoided.

Most people probably buy life insurance for protection rather than investment. This is important because even policies which return a dividend to either build cash value or reduce premiums probably have a rate of return below many other investments. Also, if the face value of the contract is fixed (i.e., does not appreciate over the years in relation to some formula), it will suffer much as bonds do during periods of inflation. A $100,000 policy today is worth $50,000 seven years from now if annual inflation is 10 percent.

The most basic form of life insurance is *whole life*, which denotes the period of protection and, under an *ordinary life policy* (also called straight life), the period during which premiums are paid. A limited period payment is expressed either in the number of years during which premiums are required (e.g., Twenty Payment Life to denote 20 years of premiums after which the policy is paid up) or the age at which the policy will be considered paid in full (e.g., Age 65 Life).

Each year a portion of the premium is credited to a reserve created to meet the financial obligation incurred by the insurance company. This amount (less an amount to meet other claims) is invested by the carrier, oftentimes in mortgages. Another portion is credited to a reserve for the policyholder, usually beginning several years after the policy has been purchased. This cash value is available to the policyholder during the period of insurance protection in the form of a loan against the value of the policy. The rate of interest is specified in the contract. For many these rates are significantly below what the individual would have to pay a bank. Furthermore, there is usually no prescribed payment date, and even unpaid interest is simply added to the loan. However, when the insured dies, the cash value is not an additional amount but is included in the face amount on the policy; furthermore, the value of the outstanding loan will be subtracted from the face value of the policy at the time of the insured's death.

Term insurance specifies the term during which the value of the policy is in force (e.g., Twenty Year Term means the policy is only good for the first 20 years; if the insured lives beyond that point in time, the policy has no value). The cost of term insurance is very low, especially if purchased while in the twenties or early thirties. However, it increases with age. By the time one has reached the sixties, the amount has increased very dramatically.

Some policies are "renewable"; this means that the policy may be continued for another prescribed period of time (at a higher premium) without having to undergo a medical examination. In addition, the term policy may be "convertible" which means before its expiration the insured may switch over to another form of insurance (e.g., whole life or endowment). One should expect that contracts with such provisions cost more than straight term since they do guarantee coverage beyond the normal term even if health is poor. In addition, the employer pays a one-time conversion charge (e.g., $25 for every $1000 of group term insurance converted).

Term is the typical form of insurance provided by companies to its employees. Called *group term*, it identifies a group of eligible employees and provides insurance coverage, typically until (1) the employee leaves or (2) the contract expires (traditionally the contract is renewed annually), whichever occurs first.

It is advantageous to have the definition of "group" acceptable to the IRS, for that will mean the first $50,000 of coverage incurs no income tax liability. Typically this means: (1) eligibility is defined in terms of age, years of service, level of pay, organizational level, or some other clearly measurable criteria, (2) at least ten employees are covered, and (3) eligibility is not restricted to shareholder employees. Furthermore, to qualify under Section 79 of the Code, the amount of insurance must be determined by a formula which precludes individual variation.

An *endowment* policy is similar to term insurance in one respect, the period during which payment for death of the insured is limited. However, if death does not occur during that period, then the face value is paid to the insured, either in a lump sum or an annual annuity. Since the face value of the policy has to be paid not later than the end of the endowment period (e.g., 20 years), the premiums are higher than whole life.

Many indicate that term insurance is the true form of life insurance. Other forms, including whole life, have some form of investment consideration in addition to insuring the risk. Some advise purchase of term insurance for the amount of protection needed and investment of the difference in cost versus a whole life policy. However, when considering investing the difference between term and whole life or some other form of insurance with cash value buildups, there are a number of considerations. Is the individual willing to have no insurance beyond the period in which term will expire? What is the rate of return on the alternative investment(s)? How secure is the investment? What is the risk on rate of return? On invested principle? Will the individual stay with the investment plan?

Rather than view term and whole life as competing forms of insurance, they should be viewed as complementary—each with different characteristics that must be evaluated in terms of individual requirements.

Company Coverage

It is rather common to give each employee an insurance amount equal to two times pay. Alternatively the contract could provide a specified amount of coverage for everyone (e.g., $50,000); however this might mean overinsurance at the low earnings level and significant underinsurance at the executive level. Company coverage is most probably 1-year renewable term insurance purchased from a life insurance company. Being term, it has no cash surrender value and is in effect on a year-to-year contract basis with the insurance company.

A number of companies provide a *survivor benefit* in addition to or in lieu of the basic life insurance program. This benefit typically provides a stated percentage of the employee's earnings at time of death (e.g., 25 percent) to the spouse (possibly higher benefits if dependent children are also involved) either for life or a stated number of years (e.g., until the deceased's 65th birthday). The advantage of such a feature is that the spouse does not have to convert a significant portion of the lump sum benefits into long-term annuity payments to meet ongoing income needs. In addition, if the beneficiary died before all payments had been made, the unpaid remainder would become part of the beneficiary's estate.

The amount could be constant (e.g., $2000 a month) or adjusted based on certain milestones (e.g., $2500 a month until children are no longer dependents, then $2000 a month). Or it could be adjusted based on age (e.g., $2000 a month until age 65, then $1000 a month); such a program might be tied to certain assumptions about social security benefits. Sometimes such programs give executives a false sense of security, as they fail to assess the possible impact of inflation upon a constant payment. For example, inflation of 7 percent would halve the purchasing power of the payments in approximately 10 years. Thus, while such a program is very helpful, it may need to be supplemented, especially for the executive with a young spouse. It is also important to determine whether such plans permit the survivor to *commute* or convert the unpaid installments into a lump sum.

In addition to payment of the prescribed amount at death, a number of policies include an additional amount if death was *accidental*. Although some policies include such coverage only working on the job, it is more common to have 24-hour protection. Thus it would not be uncommon to have a basic coverage of two times pay plus an additional two times pay for accidental death. Due to the limited conditions under which payment will be made, this amount is not charged against the $50,000 tax-free exclusion which will be described below and is usually paid for by the company.

The *basic life insurance* may be either fully paid by the company, or a portion of the expense may be absorbed by the employee. Where the latter is true, it is common to have a waiver of premium (while continuing coverage) if the employee becomes disabled. While the company receives a deduction on its premium expense, the individual receives the first $50,000 of coverage purchased by the company free of income tax liability. After that point income is imputed in accordance with rates prescribed by the IRS. Usually these rates are less than charged by the insurance company and, therefore, advantageous to the executive. However, if the actual premium paid is less than the IRS table, logically one should be able to argue that the lower premium rates be used instead in determining the imputed income tax. However, the IRS may view this from the economic benefit perspective, rather than in terms of actual cost.

Shown in Table 5-2 is a worksheet indicating how this calculation is made. Note that in this example the executive is paying more than the minimum required by the IRS tax table, and therefore there is no tax liability. However, increase the age to 57 and the individual has a $2030 imputed income figure (i.e., $2640 — $610). Even at the 50 percent marginal tax bracket, this is a bargain since the executive would pay $1015 tax rather than a total premium of $2640 (an increase of $2030 to avoid the imputed

TABLE 5-2 Imputed Income Worksheet

Analysis of group life insurance imputed income, for federal income tax purposes, for	John Jones
Age as of December 31 of taxable year	42
Employee contribution for group life insurance for taxable year	$ 610
Gross amount of group life insurance	$250,000
Annual exemption from gross coverage	−50,000
Net taxable coverage	$200,000
Uniform premium rate, selected from the table below for employee's age (2.76) times net taxable coverage (200) equals value of company contribution per IRS table	$ 552
Minus employee annual contribution	− 610
Equals imputed income subject to tax	$ 0

Uniform Premium Rate Table (per each $1000 of insurance)

Age class	Annual rate
Under 30	$ 0.96
30 to 34	1.20
35 to 39	1.68
40 to 44	2.76
45 to 49	4.80
50 to 54	8.16
55 to 59	13.20
60 and over	19.56

income). Actually, it is a bargain only if the executive wants the insurance; an executive who does not want it will only look at the additional $1015 tax liability.

Additional insurance can be provided through a supplementary employee pay-all program. Such a plan would allow the individual to purchase insurance in specified dollar multiples (e.g., $50,000) or in multiples of pay (e.g., one, two, or three) to a stated dollar maximum (e.g., $500,000). The advantage of the latter approach is that insurance protection is automatically increased with each compensation increase. This can be an important factor since it is common for such plans to have an open enrollment period at time adopted, or within a short period of employment (e.g., 30 days); after that period enrollment or increases in dollar protection often require successfully passing a medical examination. This medical exam requirement for increased insurance can be overcome by using the multiple-of-pay approach, since the increase in protection is automatic.

Since the $50,000 free insurance limitation can only be used once each year, it normally is applied to the bargain portion of the basic plan. Thus, for the supplementary insurance to escape imputed income aspects, the cost to the employee must be equal to or in excess of the Section 79 rates.

How Much Life Insurance?

In determining how much life insurance the executive should have, the individual either estimates what is needed to replace future net income or the amount needed to meet the needs of the survivors. Let's examine these two approaches.

Net Income   Under this approach the income loss is determined by taking the executive's current gross compensation (e.g., $100,000) and subtracting taxes (since life insurance proceeds are not subject to income tax), own maintenance, and investments (e.g., $70,000). The remainder (e.g., $30,000) is either held constant or increased by an assumed growth in compensation and projected for the remaining working years of the insured's life. Thus, while $600,000 is adequate if no compensation increases are assumed over a period of 20 additional working years, as shown in Table 5-3 over $1.7 million is required if an annual 10 percent increase in compensation is assumed. However, as can be seen, this amount assumes no investment growth, whereas if the net investment were assumed equal to the 10 percent increase in compensation, $600,000 is adequate if death is assumed in the first year. Note, however, that this amount rises over the first 10 years because the decrease in number of years of payment (e.g., 5 percent when dropping from 20 to 19) is less than the increase in compensation (e.g., a constant 10 percent in this example). Thus, it is very important in estimating lost income to adequately estimate future compensation growth and assumed rate of investment on the death benefit once received. To the extent the compensation growth is underestimated and the investment increase overestimated, one will be underinsured; to the extent the compensation increase is overestimated and the investment growth underestimated, one will be overinsured.

While many individuals making these estimates will only project the number of years

TABLE 5-3 Insurance Required by Year

	By year	Insurance requirement by year*	
		0.0 percent interest	10.0 percent interest
Now	$ 30,000	$1,718,250	$600,000
1 year later	33,000	1,688,250	627,000
2 years later	36,300	1,655,250	653,400
3 years later	39,930	1,618,950	678,810
4 years later	43,923	1,579,020	702,768
5 years later	48,315	1,535,097	724,725
6 years later	53,147	1,486,782	744,058
7 years later	58,462	1,433,635	760,006
8 years later	64,308	1,375,173	771,696
9 years later	70,738	1,310,865	778,118
10 years later	77,812	1,240,127	778,120
11 years later	85,594	1,162,915	770,346
12 years later	94,153	1,076,721	753,224
13 years later	103,568	982,568	724,976
14 years later	113,925	879,000	683,550
15 years later	125,317	765,075	626,585
16 years later	137,849	639,758	551,396
17 years later	151,634	501,909	454,902
18 years later	166,798	350,275	333,596
19 years later	183,477	183,477	183,477

*Assumes amount paid at beginning of year.

of their working life, it is important to also estimate the amount of retirement income and the point in time at which it is estimated to begin. Thus, in the above example the individual might estimate that beginning in the 21st year a net pension of $70,000 will be received. This amount would be projected for the remaining lifetime (with either a constant or an increased value) and the insurance values reworked.

As the table indicates, this type of analysis would suggest some combination of decreasing term and permanent insurance to meet the lost income needs. There are many, however, who indicate that the lost income approach results in either overinsuring or underinsuring, since the needs of the dependents are not examined.

Income Needs   Under this approach the expenses rather than the income are estimated. These can be identified and arranged in order of priority. First, there are settlement expenses: the amount needed to cover the decedent's expenses (e.g., burial costs, payment of outstanding loans, and probate costs) and the estate taxes (especially important when large capital income programs, including nonqualified deferred compensation, exist for the survivors). Next there is survivor income. This can be separated into: initial adjustment period (usually several years at 75 percent or more of deceased's net annual income), the family period (e.g., until children reach age 18 or, more liberally, age 22 assuming college education) and the surviving spouse period. In addition, amounts can be established for: a mortgage fund (or a separate term insurance policy can be purchased), educational expenses of dependents, and an emergency fund to cover unexpected financial liabilities.

These expenses can be separated into essentially stable and declining need categories. For example, settlement expenses, emergency fund, and adjustment period income are essentially stable. However, the mortgage coverage and income for dependent children by definition are declining needs. Thus, one could argue for some amount of permanent life insurance and another piece of term insurance to meet the 10 to 12 times pay while the children are young (and the executive is in the mid-thirties) versus the 2 to 4 times pay immediately prior to retirement. In addition, as was done in the case of estimating income loss, some estimate of the impact of inflation on the dependent needs and the possible investment growth opportunities on the paid death benefit need to be taken into consideration to estimate the needed amount of insurance.

Identifying such expenses by year (including some assumption for impact of inflation) and then calculating a present value (using a reasonable but conservative investment rate assumption) makes it possible to calculate an amount, which after netting out the value of current capital investments indicates the amount needed for life insurance. This approach assumes the last dollar has been spent the minute before all the above needs have been met. If an inheritance for children is also intended, its value must be factored in as well.

For many this will mean purchasing whole life insurance to provide dollar protection needed for the entire life, and some form of term insurance to meet those needs which do not cover the entire life (e.g., period of dependent children). For some, whole life insurance is one of the few ways in which they can actually accumulate some savings and then use this cash value to increase their net worth by borrowing against it. The reason this is attractive is that the interest rate charged is significantly less than that available through commercial banking institutions. Thus, it may be possible to borrow an amount equal to the cash value at 5 percent interest and invest in short- or medium-term United States obligations at 8 percent or more. Thus a person with a $100,000 face value policy and a cash surrender value of $50,000 would be able to increase gross earnings $500 a year for every 1 percent point that interest earned exceeds interest paid. Furthermore, the level of protection remains the same at $100,000. This consists of $50,000 life insurance (i.e., $100,000 less $50,000 loan) and $50,000 in investments. However, it should be remembered that interest is not subject to the 50 percent personal service income maximum.

In addition some borrow against the cash surrender value to pay the premiums. While there are some restrictions on how much can be borrowed for this purpose and when it can be borrowed, this feature is very attractive to some. Of course, still others take the increase in cash surrender value to purchase additional life insurance.

Obviously the longer the executive lives and provides the needed income, the less is needed in the amount of insurance. Without adequate planning, the coverage (especially

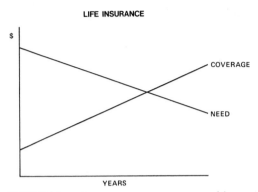

FIGURE 5-1   Insurance coverage versus need by age.

that provided by the basic company formula of a multiple of pay) either exceeds or falls short of need. This is illustrated in Figure 5-1 in the situation all too typical for many individuals, underinsured early in life and overinsured in latter years.

Company Response to Executive Life Insurance Needs

One way companies can minimize this type of disparity is by adjusting the multiple based on age: the highest multiple for the younger and the lowest multiple for the older employees. The example in Table 5-4 begins with a multiple of five for employees under age 25 and then decreases uniformly each year to a final value of 0.1 at age 74 (with perhaps a minimum of $2500 of insurance). Such a plan would have to be reviewed carefully in light of the Age Discrimination in Employment Act.

An additional advantage of this type of program is that it reduces the amount of imputed income, as described earlier, in the later years when the tables are very high. Conversely a disadvantage is that it might reduce the protection faster than the executives need and, therefore, force them to supplement this protection with additional coverage. In addition, it is important to remember in analyzing insurance needs versus coverage that company programs are by definition only in effect during the period of employment. Thus very attractive insurance protection at one employer may not be available at the next, and the executive must plan accordingly.

Important to executives leaving the company who are not in the best of health is the *conversion privilege* which, within a specified period of time such as 30 days, allows the insured to convert the group term protection to an individual policy of permanent protection without having to pass a medical examination. Typically companies are assessed a charge per $1000 of converted coverage, in large part to offset the higher risk the carrier is assuming without receiving a higher premium. In many instances, the premium paid by the executive is higher than that charged for low-risk protection for insured persons who are in excellent health.

TABLE 5-4   Insurance Coverage by Age

Age	Multiple	Age	Multiple
Under 25	5.00	50	2.50
26	4.90	51	2.40
27	4.80	52	2.30
28	4.70	53	2.20
29	4.60	54	2.10
30	4.50	55	2.00
31	4.40	56	1.90
32	4.30	57	1.80
33	4.20	58	1.70
34	4.10	59	1.60
35	4.00	60	1.50
36	3.90	61	1.40
37	3.80	62	1.30
38	3.70	63	1.20
39	3.60	64	1.10
40	3.50	65	1.00
41	3.40	66	0.90
42	3.30	67	0.80
43	3.20	68	0.70
44	3.10	69	0.60
45	3.00	70	0.50
46	2.90	71	0.40
47	2.80	72	0.30
48	2.70	73	0.20
49	2.60	74 and over	0.10

Definition of Pay for Insurance   While both basic and supplementary plans were traditionally applied only to salary for determining the amount of coverage, it is now rather common to use salary plus short-term incentives in determining the amount of insurance protection. This is logical where a bonus is a significant and rather stable percentage of salary; however, where the bonus can swing dramatically it may not be attractive to the executive as he or she fluctuates between an overinsured and an underinsured position. In such situations applying higher multiples to salary can accomplish the same degree of desired protection. To illustrate: company A allows one, two, or three times salary plus bonus while company B permits enrollment for one, two, three, or four times salary. Shown in Table 5-5 are salary and bonus figures for an executive and the amount of insurance protection under the two company plans.

Recognizing that protection needs change depending on age of children (and their degree of financial dependency), monetary needs of spouse, and liquidity requirements for estate taxes, assume that these have not significantly changed during this 3-year period. Three times coverage under company A might mean being slightly underinsured in years 1 and 3 or, if these amounts are consistent with need, being overinsured in year 2. Which of these two conditions was true would determine whether three or four times salary under company B would be more appropriate.

After Retirement   Typically the coverage cuts back quickly and significantly. One approach is to reduce coverage over several annual installments to a final death claim of $5000 or less within 5 years of retirement, regardless of the amount of protection while active. Some plans provide for one times protection until death; however, this can be a very costly benefit and it is not very common. A middle position is a plan which reduces by equal installments over a 10-year period after retirement to some minimum death benefit amount. Regardless of the plan, the executive must determine whether the postretirement insurance will be sufficient and, if not, begin to prepare for it well before retirement. One advantage of retiree life insurance provided by the company is that it is not subject to imputed income. Therefore, the $50,000 restraint for active employees is not an issue for retirees.

Taxation of Proceeds   Life insurance proceeds are not subject to income tax, but they are considered part of the deceased's estate and therefore subject to estate taxes. An exception to this is where the policy has been irrevocably *assigned* by the employee to another person, either a trust or the individual intended to be the beneficiary. The assignee now owns the policy, names himself or herself as beneficiary, and is responsible for paying any premiums due. Assuming such assignment meets the legal test (some argue that group term insurance can never be irrevocably assigned since it is essentially 1-year term insurance) and is made at least 3 years prior to the executive's death, the proceeds probably will not be considered part of the estate. However, the imputed value

TABLE 5-5   Insurance versus Salary and Total Compensation

	Year 1	Year 2	Year 3
Salary	$ 75,000	$ 80,000	$ 85,000
Bonus	5,000	25,000	10,000
Total	$ 80,000	$105,000	$ 95,000
Company A			
One times salary plus bonus	$ 80,000	$105,000	$ 95,000
Two times salary plus bonus	160,000	210,000	190,000
Three times salary plus bonus	240,000	315,000	285,000
Company B			
One times salary	$ 75,000	$ 80,000	$ 85,000
Two times salary	150,000	160,000	170,000
Three times salary	225,000	240,000	255,000
Four times salary	300,000	320,000	340,000

of the insurance will be considered a gift, and while no tax payment is required at the time, it will be charged against the allowable lifetime exclusion (Revenue Ruling 79-47).

To meet the assignment test, all incidents of ownership must be completely relinquished. Even the ability to borrow a limited amount of money on the policy may be sufficient for the entire policy (not simply the borrowable amount) to be considered part of the estate for taxation.

For those concerned about a possible subsequent divorce which might place the insurance in the wrong hands, the policy could be assigned to a trust rather than directly to the spouse. The trust in turn would name the "wife" or "husband" (whichever is appropriate) as the beneficiary, carefully avoiding a specific name.

The assignment should not be affected by the employer changing insurance carriers (Rev. Rul. 80-239) as long as the two contracts are identical in all relevant aspects. This ruling reversed a position in Rev. Rul. 79-231 which stated that such an action by the employee would begin a new 3-year waiting period before the assignment was considered effective.

Business Travel Accident Insurance

This kind of policy provides life insurance if the executive is killed accidentally while traveling on company business. In some plans, due to cost concerns, salespersons are excluded while driving in their own territory; others establish a maximum payoff for a common accident (e.g., $1 million). Such plans normally have high multiples (e.g., five times pay) but the individual maximum (e.g., $500,000) often significantly lowers this multiple for higher-paid executives. Others may structure level of benefit by job category (e.g., corporate officers, $250,000; division heads, $200,000; assistant division heads, $150,000; department heads, $100,000; and all others, $50,000). Though the large multiple is impressive, it simply means the executive may be overinsured for one type of death and underinsured for the others.

Invariably the premium for business travel accident insurance is paid by the company as a tax deductible expense. Due to the limited conditions under which payment is made, it is not subject to the $50,000 income tax–free insurance restriction. However, the earlier outlined impact of income and estate taxes (including assignment) also applies here.

Form of Settlement

While the normal form of payout from the above-described policies is a lump sum amount, some policies could be structured to provide annuity payments. Annuities have a certain appeal as they resemble the regularity of the paycheck which is no longer arriving.

A prime source for the annuity is the company pension plan, which we will discuss in more detail in the next section. The important point is that the pension plan can be constructed to pay the surviving spouse an annuity if the employee died while actively employed but was eligible for retirement. In such instances the plan will calculate a joint and survivor benefit as if the employee retired the day before death. This is more liberal coverage than prescribed in the 1974 Employee Retirement Income Security Act. This type of benefit in the pension plan has increasing significance as the employee's creditable earnings and service accumulate; however, it is of little or no help for a younger executive.

In addition to insuring the life of the employee some companies provide *dependents life insurance*. Due to heavy restrictions in many states as to the amount of such coverage for spouse versus dependent child, this type coverage is not very common. Furthermore, the IRS will allow free coverage for spouse and dependent children up to $2000 insurance each. Any coverage in excess of that amount and the full value of the policy will be given an imputed income value, not simply that portion in excess of $2000.

RETIREMENT

Whereas pension plans were earlier considered to be a gratuitous gift by the company to employees reaching an age at which they were no longer able to perform their tasks, current thinking of many employees is that such payments are an earned right—an involuntary form of deferred compensation. The view has to a large extent been reinforced by the earlier mentioned ERISA, which requires the employer to "vest" or bestow an earned right to a portion of the benefits after a specified period of time or age and service has been attained. More specifically: (1) 100 percent vesting after 10 years of service, (2) 50 percent vesting after 10 years, with an additional 10 percent each of the next 5 years for 100 percent vesting after 15 years, or (3) 50 percent vesting after age and service equal 45 (minimum 5 years' service), with 10 percent additional vesting for each additional year, for a total of 100 percent vesting when age and service equal 50. The choice of vesting formula remains with the company, but one of these three must be adopted in order to establish a qualified retirement plan. Stringent vesting provisions (1) encourage individuals to stay to meet the minimum vesting requirements and (2) reduce plan costs to the extent nonvested individuals terminate employment.

Basis for Benefit

Little has been done to develop retirement benefits based on what is needed by the retiree. Rather, most planning focuses on what is competitive. While this seems at first a logical extension of the pay program for active employees, there is a minor flaw. Employees can always leave for a better-paying opportunity; retirees cannot leave for a better pension (by definition they waited too long). Needs analysis would focus first on after-tax income immediately prior to retirement and then adjust for the new lifestyle (no business-related expenses of clothes, lunches, and transportation). For many retirees this will mean a significant reduction in expenses (including dropping the second car).

The next step is more difficult; what else is subtracted (reflecting lowering of lifestyle) or added (because of more leisure time to incur expenses)? This issue is especially important at the senior executive level; while most shareholders and lower-paid employees, even if begrudgingly, tolerate $500,000 pay while executives are working, they do not understand why such people are unhappy with pensions of only $100,000 (which is probably multiples of what blue-collar types made while working). Therefore, while pension plans could be developed from the perspective of needs analysis, it is easier and more advantageous for communication to talk of comparable percentage benefits based on pay while working—in essence, to assume that the pension benefit is part of deferred pay.

A qualified retirement plan has several very attractive features. Namely the company is able to make currently tax deductible contributions on behalf of an active employee to ensure a pension is ready when the employee retires, but the employee has no income tax liability until actually receiving these payments, nor are earnings on invested funds taxable to either the company or the employee. To qualify, the plan cannot discriminate in favor of highly paid employees (discriminating *against* such employees is all right). Also either 70 percent of all employees (excluding those in short service permitted under ERISA and those covered by collectively bargained plans) must be covered by the plan, or 70 percent or more of all employees must be eligible and at least 80 percent of these must be covered. Failing both of these alternatives, the employer must demonstrate to the satisfaction of the IRS that plan eligibility does not discriminate in favor of higher-paid employees. Additional requirements include: (1) the plan must be written, (2) covered employees must be informed of the key aspects of the plan in accord with ERISA disclosure requirements, (3) contributions must be to a trust or other third party, and they cannot be made to the employee on a pay-as-you-go arrangement, (4) the plan must be intended to be a permanent program, and (5) unique to the defined benefit plan, forfeitures must be used to reduce company contributions, not to increase benefits of any retirees.

Types of Plans

Retirement plans are of two types: *defined benefit* and *defined contribution*. The former specifies the amount of annuity that the employee will receive after attaining certain age and/or service requirements, and the contribution is determined annually to meet this annuity amount. The latter specifies the amount of money to be set aside each year, and the value of such money at the time of retirement will be a factor of the market value of the investments made. In other words, in one instance you know how much you are going to get but the ultimate cost is unknown until the assets are valued, whereas in the other instance you know how much is being set aside each year but don't know how much it will be worth when you retire.

Since the benefit is known under a defined benefit plan, the unknown is the amount the company should contribute. To make this estimate, the actuary would logically make an assumption about the investment performance of the trust. The better the performance, the lower the company contribution. A rough rule of thumb used by some is that the cost can be reduced by 4 percent for every ¼ percent improvement in the investment performance.

If the plan benefits are related to pay received by the employee, an assumption must be made as to the level of future pay increases (this is more critical for final pay than career earnings plans since the former affects all years of prior service). If the plan is integrated with social security, future increases in social security benefits must be estimated but only to time of estimated retirement. It is not permissible to reduce benefits after retirement because of increases in social security payments. In addition, assumptions must be made about how many people will leave before becoming vested, when the vested employees will leave and begin drawing benefits, and how long they will live (and continue receiving benefits). Finally, any administrative expenses that will be charged to the plan must be estimated.

While qualified plans cannot be designed to discriminate in favor of executives, too often the plans do not take full advantage of permissible provisions and in fact discriminate against higher-paid individuals. A classic example is when the defined benefit plan is not integrated with social security. The result is that a higher benefit is created for lower-paid employees and a lower benefit for higher-paid employees, than would be permissible.

Defined Benefit Plans

Defined benefit plans fall into three categories: *career service* (e.g., $16 a month for every year of service), *career earnings* (e.g., 1.4 percent per year for every $1000 in earnings from the company over the full career of employment), and *final pay* (e.g., 1.0 percent per year for every $1000 of average earned income during the highest-paid 5 out of the last 10 years of employment prior to retirement, multiplied by all years of service with the company).

Career service plans essentially are limited to hourly blue-collar workers and are typically negotiated by unions. Career earnings plans were very common 20 years ago; today they have been outdated by the rapid increase in inflation (and employee pay). Therefore, most of the career earnings plans still remaining effect "updates" and in so doing take on an appearance similar to final pay plans, although without the heavy cost impact of future service liability—thereby making them very attractive to financial people. For example, every several years the company will update all earnings prior to 5 years ago to that figure. For an employee with 20 years of service now earning $100,000, this would mean updating the first 15 years of pay to that earned 5 years ago. Assume the latter was $68,500 and he started at $32,500; as shown in Table 5-6, this would mean an increase in creditable earnings of $314,500.

Assuming a pension formula of 1.4 percent career earnings, this $314,500 increase in creditable career earnings means an increase in the annual annuity of $4403—from $16,030 to $20,433.

Final pay plans are more popular with employees than career service plans due to

TABLE 5-6 Creditable Pension Earnings—Career versus Career Updated

Year	Actual	Adjusted
20 (current)	$ 100,000	$ 100,000
19	92,500	92,500
18	87,500	87,500
17	79,500	79,500
16	72,500	72,500
15	68,500	68,500
14	65,500	68,500
13	61,000	68,500
12	56,500	68,500
11	53,000	68,500
10	50,500	68,500
9	48,000	68,500
8	45,500	68,500
7	43,500	68,500
6	41,500	68,500
5	39,500	68,500
4	37,500	68,500
3	36,000	68,500
2	34,000	68,500
1	32,500	68,500
Total—actual	$1,145,000	
Total—adjusted		$1,459,500
Difference		$ 314,500

their emphasis on most recent earnings. Even updated career earnings plans have a drawback to employees inasmuch as there is no guarantee that the company will continue such actions, and without them the pension will be significantly smaller. However, corporate financial people will typically prefer a career earnings updated plan over a final pay plan due to the current cost impact. Under the latter both prior and future service will be affected by future earnings; under the former only future service is affected by future earnings.

Using the same example as above, a 1 percent average of the highest consecutive 5 out of the last 10 years' earnings would generate an annual annuity of $17,280 (i.e., $432,000/5 $\times$ 0.01 $\times$ 20 = $17,280). Though highest 5 out of 10 is the most prevalent approach, there are plans that use the highest 3 out of 5. Anything less will have problems in passing the IRS review for qualified plan status. Using the average highest consecutive 3 out of 5 in our example would result in an annuity of $18,667, or 8 percent higher than the best 5 out of 10 formula. Thus, as expected, as one lowers the average period, the benefit rate can also be lowered to meet a targeted payout level.

Other things being equal, the executive receiving large percentage pay increases is more interested in lowering the years used in calculating the average than a person receiving more modest pay increases. Table 5-7 shows the impact of using the highest 3-, 5-, or 10-year earnings averages versus full career earnings average, assuming pay increase of 5, 10, or 15 percent over 15, 25, and 35 years of service. For example, using a 3-year average for a person with 25 years of service who consistently received 10 percent increases would mean earnings for pension purposes would be approximately 128 percent more than if a simple career average were used. As would be expected, the greatest variance is at the highest compound pay increase (15 percent), the most years of service (35), and the fewest number of years in the average (3). Thus, the higher the "number of years" used to define earnings, the higher the needed formula percentage and vice versa.

As everyone knows, in addition to the company pension, a retired employee is usually eligible for social securiy benefits. Started in the mid-thirties as a modest benefit, social security has, especially in recent years, been continually improved and no longer can be ignored in pension planning. Whereas the company plan of either career earnings or final pay will produce the same percentage of final years of earnings (assuming same percentage of pay increases and years of service) for both clerk and executive, when added to social security benefits it produces a total retirement curve similar to the one shown in Figure 5-2. This is because the executive probably qualifies for the maximum social security benefit while the clerk earns a lower benefit. Nonetheless, because the benefit represents a very significant percentage of the clerk's final earnings and a very

TABLE 5-7 Years of Service versus Pay Increase for Final Pay and Career Earnings Plans

	Three	Five	Ten
	Number of years used to calculate average		
35 years of service			
15% pay increase	303%	255%	166%
10% pay increase	201	175	123
5% pay increase	94	85	65
25 years of service			
15% pay increase	194	159	94
10% pay increase	128	109	69
5% pay increase	61	54	37
15 years of service			
15% pay increase	95	72	29
10% pay increase	64	50	21
5% pay increase	31	25	12

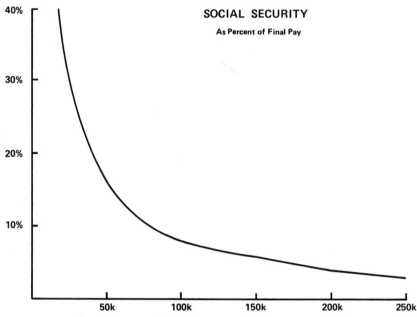

FIGURE 5-2   Social security as a percentage of final pay.

small portion of the executive's final pay, we have the decreasing percentage curve shown. The X values will change depending on the increase in social security benefits, but the curve is likely to retain the same shape.

Given the impact of social security benefits, it is virtually impossible to set the company formula to pay off an appropriate amount at the executive level without placing the clerk's combined pension at or above the final year's pay. It should also be remembered that social security payments are not subject to income tax, and thus they represent an even higher percentage of net than gross pay.

Integration

Therefore many companies integrate their pension plan benefits with social security to try to smooth out the percentage curve. To maintain qualified plan status, the plan must integrate in a manner acceptable to the IRS; essentially this provides two approaches: step-up and offset.

Step-Up   This approach is also called the "carve-out" plan and is more common with career average than final pay plans. It applies one benefit rate for all earnings up to the social security tax base and another higher figure for earnings above that base. Shown in Table 5-8 are the taxable earnings bases; it should be recognized that Congress periodically adjusts these on a prospective basis. Note the continued growth in the maximum tax. After no increase through the forties, fifties and sixties saw approximately

114

10 percent compound increases, while the seventies were jolted with a 14 percent compound average hike. For most employees the increase in social security taxes outpaced their increase in compensation.

Therefore although current law prescribes that $29,700 be the maximum taxable earnings base for 1981, it is subject to change. The tax rates shown by year are the FICA taxes the employee pays on all earnings up to the maximum taxable earnings base. This is the same amount the company must pay for that employee.

To illustrate the application of the step-up formula, assume the existence of a plan crediting 1 percent and 1.5 percent. Applying this to our earlier $100,000 executive and assuming 1981 is the 20th year of work results in an annual annuity of $15,981.50 as

TABLE 5-8 Social Security Taxes

Years	Maximum taxable earnings base	Tax rate expressed as percent			Maximum tax dollars	Percent increase
		OASDI	Medicare	Total		
1937–49	$ 3,000	1.0	—	1.0	$ 30.00	—
1950	3,000	1.5	—	1.5	45.00	50.0
1951–53	3,600	1.5	—	1.5	54.00	20.0
1954	3,600	2.0	—	2.0	72.00	33.3
1955–56	4,200	2.0	—	2.0	84.00	16.7
1957–58	4,200	2.25	—	2.25	94.50	12.5
1959	4,800	2.5	—	2.5	120.00	27.0
1960–61	4,800	3.0	—	3.0	144.00	20.0
1962	4,800	3.25	—	3.25	156.00	8.3
1963–65	4,800	3.625	—	3.625	174.00	11.5
1966	6,600	3.85	0.35	4.20	277.20	59.3
1967	6,600	3.90	0.50	4.40	290.40	4.8
1968	7,800	3.80	0.60	4.40	343.20	18.2
1969–70	7,800	4.20	0.60	4.80	374.40	9.1
1971	7,800	4.60	0.60	5.20	405.60	8.3
1972	9,000	4.60	0.60	5.20	468.00	15.4
1973	10,800	4.85	1.00	5.85	631.80	35.0
1974	13,200	4.95	0.90	5.85	772.20	22.2
1975	14,100	4.95	0.90	5.85	82485	6.8
1976	15,300	4.95	0.90	5.85	895.05	8.5
1977	16,500	4.95	0.90	5.85	965.25	7.8
1978	17,700	5.05	1.00	6.05	1,070.85	10.9
1979	22,900	5.08	1.05	6.13	1,403.77	31.1
1980	25,900	5.08	1.05	6.13	1,587.67	13.1
1981	29,700	5.35	1.30	6.65	1,975.05	24.4
1982–84	*	5.40	1.30	6.70	*	
1985	*	5.70	1.35	7.05	*	
1986–89	*	5.70	1.45	7.15	*	
1990 and after	*	6.20	1.45	7.65	*	

*Automatic adjustment in wage base related to changes in average covered earnings.

TABLE 5-9 Step-Up Pension Example

Year	Earnings	Social security taxable base maximum		At 1 percent	Excess		At 1.5 percent
20	$100,000	$29,000	=	$297.00	$70,300	=	$1,054.50
19	92,500	25,900	=	259.00	66,600	=	999.00
18	87,500	22,900	=	229.00	64,600	=	969.00
17	79,500	17,700	=	177.00	61,800	=	927.00
16	72,500	16,500	=	165.00	56,000	=	840.00
15	68,500	15,300	=	153.00	53,200	=	798.00
14	65,500	14,100	=	141.00	51,400	=	771.00
13	61,000	13,200	=	132.00	47,800	=	717.00
12	56,500	10,800	=	108.00	45,700	=	685.50
11	53,000	9,000	=	90.00	44,000	=	660.00
10	50,500	7,800	=	78.00	42,700	=	640.50
9	48,000	7,800	=	78.00	40,200	=	603.00
8	45,500	7,800	=	78.00	37,700	=	565.50
7	43,500	7,800	=	78.00	35,700	=	535.50
6	41,500	6,600	=	66.00	34,900	=	523.50
5	39,500	6,600	=	66.00	32,900	=	493.50
4	37,500	4,800	=	48.00	32,700	=	490.50
3	36,000	4,800	=	48.00	31,200	=	468.00
2	34,000	4,800	=	48.00	29,200	=	438.00
1	32,500	4,800	=	48.00	27,700	=	415.50
Total				$2,387.00			$13,594.50
Combined							$15,981.50

shown in Table 5-9. Using the same methodology but the updated earnings history of $68,500 would result in an annuity of $20,699.

The step-up form of integration has the advantage of being easier to communicate to employees; however, it has the following disadvantages:

- This form of integration does not make it clear to employees that the company's real objective is to supplement social security up to a certain overall benefit level.

- Although a step-up plan can be structured to take into consideration adjustments in the wage base, it offers no built-in cost-containing features for legislated social security changes. Accordingly, major design changes in the pension formula could be necessary each time a new social security law is passed.

- It does not appear logical to relate benefits in a retirement plan to movements in the social security taxable wage base, particularly when the objective is to integrate benefits from both sources to provide an appropriate amount of total retirement income.

Offset This second basic approach is more common with final pay than career earnings plans. It employs one percentage for all earnings and then another percentage (equal to or lower than the first) which is applied to the social security benefit. To illustrate, let's use the following formula: 1.5 percent of average earnings − 1.25 percent of primary social security benefit. The resulting amount will be multiplied by the years of creditable service. Assume that average earnings is equal to the highest consecutive 5-year average (which in our earlier example was $86,400) and that primary social security equals $6000. The annual annuity is therefore $24,420 [i.e., 1.5% ($86,400) − 1.25% ($6000) × 20 years].

The rationale of this form of integration is that the company has contributed to the employee's social security benefit and therefore it should be entitled to reduce pension benefits by a portion of the social security benefit. With this type of plan formula, the company can develop a total retirement income objective (plan benefits plus primary social security) based on the employee's length of service (e.g., 70 percent for 35 years of service). The offset method of integration is considered to have the following advantages:

- The offset can be designed to adjust automatically to increasing social security benefits. Therefore, this type of integration can provide a company with some protection against spiraling benefits and costs.

- Offset integration provides a more direct approach to achieving benefit objectives (i.e., more equitable distribution of plan benefits to higher-paid employees).

- The offset approach meshes logically with benefit formulas based on earnings close to retirement. Social security benefits are wage-indexed, and therefore an offset is a logical approach to utilize in order to ensure a more equitable distribution of plan benefits.

The disadvantage of offset plans is that they are not easy to communicate to employees; furthermore, having to indicate that the company pension is reduced by a portion of social security is a disadvantage both in fact and in the employee's mind. However, it is possible to minimize this negative aspect if both formula values are the same (e.g., 1.5 percent − 1.5 percent) by employing some basic algebra as shown in Figure 5-3.

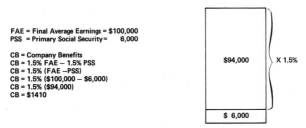

FAE = Final Average Earnings = $100,000
PSS = Primary Social Security =   6,000

CB = Company Benefits
CB = 1.5% FAE − 1.5% PSS
CB = 1.5% (FAE −PSS)
CB = 1.5% ($100,000 − $6,000)
CB = 1.5% ($94,000)
CB = $1410

$94,000   ⎱ X 1.5%

$ 6,000

FIGURE 5-3   Final pay example.

117

TABLE 5-10 Pension Survey Example*

		To 65		65				
Rank	Company	Company	Percent FE	Rank	Company	Percent FE	Including SS	Percent FE
1	C	0	0.0	1	48,834	48.8	54,845	54.8
2	L	0	0.0	2	44,927	44.9	50,938	50.9
3	R	0	0.0	3	43,516	43.5	49,527	49.5
4	D	0	0.0	4	41,357	41.4	47,368	47.4
5	H	0	0.0	5	39,295	39.3	45,306	45.3
6	J	0	0.0	6	38,994	39.0	45,005	45.0
7	E	0	0.0	7	38,785	38.8	44,796	44.8
8	G	0	0.0	8	38,209	38.2	44,220	44.2
9	B	0	0.0	9	37,423	37.4	43,434	43.4
10	M	0	0.0	10	37,170	37.2	43,181	43.2
11	F	0	0.0	11	36,625	36.6	42,636	42.6
12	I	0	0.0	12	36,175	36.2	42,186	42.2
13	Q	0	0.0	13	35,672	35.7	41,683	41.7

Rank	Company	To 65		65				
		Company	Percent FE	Rank	Company	Percent FE	Including SS	Percent FE
14	K	0	0.0	14	34,578	34.6	40,589	40.6
15	A	0	0.0	15	29,872	29.9	35,883	35.9
16	P	0	0.0	16	27,303	27.3	33,314	33.3
17	Brucell	0	0.0	17	27,262	27.3	33,273	33.3
18	N	0	0.0	18	26,455	26.5	32,466	32.5
19	O	0	0.0	19	25,920	25.9	31,931	31.9
Averages (excluding Brucell)		0	0.0		36,728	36.7	42,739	42.7
2	FP 2-2 35	0	0.0	2	48,233	48.2	54,244	54.2
1	FP 2-1.5 35	0	0.0	1	49,135	49.1	55,146	55.1
4	FP 1.75-1.5 35	0	0.0	4	42,655	42.7	48,666	48.7
4	FP 1.75-1.25 40	0	0.0	4	43,105	43.1	49,116	49.1
5	FP 1.67-1.67 30	0	0.0	5	40,194	40.2	46,205	46.2
13	FP 1.5-1.5 35	0	0.0	13	36,175	36.2	42,186	42.2
12	FP 1.5-1.25 40	0	0.0	12	36,625	36.6	42,636	42.6

*Final earnings (FE), $100,000; age at retirement, 65; years of service, 30.

Stated another way, using the above example, the company could say "We will pro-vide a pension equal to 1.5 percent (times years of service) of that portion of your final average earnings that is not 100 percent replaced by primary social security."

In summary the main difference between step-up and offset is that the former inte-grates on the taxable earnings base, the latter directly with the benefit level. For many the latter is believed to be the more logical approach.

Determining Competitiveness of Benefit In reviewing the appropriateness of the company pension plan, it is logical to determine its competitiveness vis-à-vis the same companies used in evaluating current pay. By obtaining copies of their pension plans and constructing model earnings examples (e.g., $15,000, $25,000, $35,000, $50,000, $100,000, $250,000, and $500,000), it is possible to determine competitive position at selected points along the earnings continuum. A format illustrating this type of com-parison is shown in Table 5-10 for a $100,000 executive with 30 years of service retiring at age 65.

Note that Brucell currently ranks 17th; however, we are able to determine its new rank by substituting alternative model plan formulas. While these calculations can be done by hand, it may be more appropriate to program them given the number of com-binations involved. For example, in addition to testing the seven earnings examples at age 65 with 30 years, it may be desirable to test also for 35 and 25 years. At age 60 earnings histories of 30, 25, and 20 might be appropriate, whereas at 55, service of 15, 20, and 25 could be appropriate. Combined, this would mean 63 worksheets, and this is before considering possible changes in the discount schedule for early retirement.

In analyzing the data it is logical to ascertain competitive position in terms other than the simple average of the survey data. Shown in Figure 5-4 is a company's nonin-tegrated 1.0 percent final pay (average of highest 10 years) stated in terms of the survey's 50th, 75th, and 90th percentile (for an employee age 65 with 30 years of service). After selecting the desired competitive position, it is possible to work backward into a for-mula. For example, if a final pay formula (highest average 5 years) offset with social security were desired, a little trial and error with values might reveal that: 2 percent — 2 percent might equate to the 90th percentile, 1.75 percent — 1.5 percent would approximate the 75th percentile, and 1.5 percent — 1.25 percent would come closest to the 50th percentile.

In addition to analyzing the competitive position of the company retirement plan at a normal retirement age (e.g., 65), we should also examine it for payout levels at early retirement. Typical is a plan that will permit retirement on or after age 55 with a specified number of years of service (e.g., 10). Leaving prior to that age but meeting the vesting requirement will mean a "vested" or earned right in an annuity to begin not earlier than earliest retirement age.

When an employee decides to retire early (versus staying another year), the pension benefit is reduced in three ways: (1) there is one less year of service, (2) there is one less year of earnings, and (3) there is a greater discount of the annuity. Thus final pay plans will show a greater spread than career average, and plans with actuarial discounts will

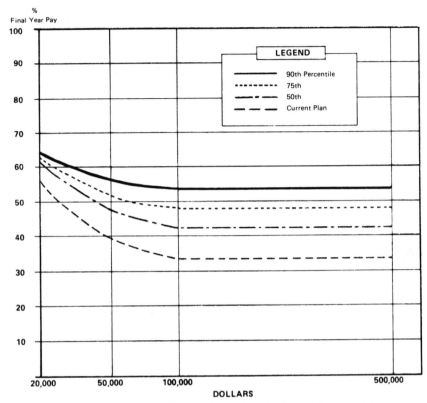

FIGURE 5-4 Competitive pension position (50th to 90th percentile).

generate a larger difference than those with more modest reductions. In addition, integrated plans that apply the discount at time of retirement will be less attractive to an early retiree than one that applies it at age 65.

Therefore it is necessary for the company to determine its desired competitive position under specified conditions of early retirement just as it did for a normal retirement at age 65 with 30 years of service. Logically a company that wants a stronger competitive position encourages early retirements; conversely a company that does not want to lose its experienced employees will adopt a more conservative posture.

During times of high inflation, executives are likely to defer plans for early retirement, thereby building up additional years of credit for pension payments. This will be especially true when the company does not periodically improve the annuities of retired employees. Since social security payments, which are adjusted annually in terms of increases in the consumer price index, represent a greater portion of the pension of lower-paid employees, such individuals are less affected by the company's unwillingness to improve annuities of retirees than the executive whose major portion of pension is from the company plan, not social security.

Besides testing hypothetical examples, it might be appropriate to input actual data for specific key executives, thus being able to answer specific as well as general questions about the plan's competitiveness. Such an approach would also allow calculating the normal form required by ERISA (i.e., joint and survivor annuity with 50 percent of the benefit continuing to the spouse after the retiree's death), since the spouse's age could be entered into the calculations.

It should be noted that this joint and survivor form can also be included as a pre-retirement benefit. In other words when the executive dies while actively employed but eligible for retirement, the surviving spouse will be given a benefit equal to the 50 percent survivor benefit if the employee had retired the day before his or her death. While this is a logical benefit to include in the basic plan, it should certainly be considered for executives if not adopted broadly.

A number of plans will pay a pension after a specified number of years (e.g., 10); however, this is not optimal to the executive. Rather the company should ensure adequate long-term disability plan benefits and continue the employee in the pension plan (thereby accruing plan credits). Thus, when LTD benefits terminate at 65 or some other age, the individual will have a reasonable pension.

Early Retirement   Companies should recognize the difference between a person seeking early retirement for health, family, and other reason versus a person seeking another job (whose pay will be supplemented by the current employer's early retirement

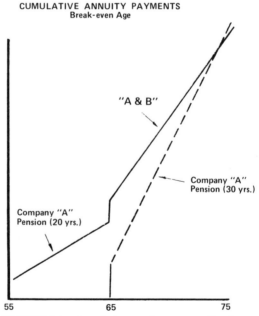

FIGURE 5-5   Cumulative annuity payments (break-even age).

TABLE 5-11   Years of Service versus Remuneration for Estimating Pension Benefits

Remuneration	Years of service			
	10	20	30	40
$ 50,000	$ 9,250	$ 18,500	$ 27,750	$ 37,000
100,000	18,000	36,000	54,000	72,000
150,000	26,250	52,500	78,750	105,000
200,000	34,000	68,000	102,000	136,000
250,000	41,250	82,500	123,750	165,000
300,000	48,000	96,000	144,000	192,000
400,000	60,000	120,000	180,000	240,000
500,000	70,000	140,000	210,000	280,000

pension). The economics are such that the latter usually does best leaving a company with fully vested benefits in a final pay plan and joining a company with a career earnings formula. However, the mathematics are such that if the individual has many more years of life ahead, it usually means the person should not leave the first employer, for the heavily discounted pension from company A plus a small one from company B (due to shortness of service) is less than the pension at 65 the person would have been eligible to receive from company A. The chart in Figure 5-5 shows how the alternative choices can be projected to a break-even age (i.e., the life expectancy age beyond which it would have been advantageous to not leave company A for another job). In this illustration joining company B at age 55 and drawing a discounted pension from company A for 20 years of service would mean greater cumulative benefits until age 75 than staying with company A and receiving a nondiscounted 30-year pension.

Furthermore, when the early retirement annuity is more generous than a mortality actuarial discount and/or the interest rate assumption is less than offered by insurance companies, it encourages the executive to request a lump sum payment and either purchase an annuity (after paying tax on 10-year averaging) from an insurance company, beginning immediately, or, if the executive can live by other means, roll over tax-free into an IRA and start to draw down at age 70.

In addition to integrating pension benefits with social security, Revenue Ruling 68-243 allows pension plan benefits to be reduced by workers' compensation benefits, although some have challenged the appropriateness of this reduction in the benefit program.

The SEC requires that annual benefits from pension plans be disclosed in the proxy in a manner similar to Table 5-11. The reported benefits are to include any supplementary or excess payments and are to be based on a straight life annuity (even though joint and survivor payments are available). In addition, the company is to describe the remuneration covered by the plan and whether benefits are subject to social security benefit deductions. These changes, effective January 1, 1981, are believed to be a signficant improvement over previous rules in that pension benefits can be compared, one company with another. However, the best way to make a valid comparison is to obtain a copy of the plan and make an analysis similar to that shown in Table 5-10.

Defined Contribution Plans

In addition to the defined benefit plan, many companies have a defined contribution plan taking the form of either a savings or a profit sharing plan. Under a *savings plan* the employee authorizes a specific deduction from his or her paycheck (e.g., 5 percent) which is to some degree matched by the company (e.g., 50 cents on the dollar), whereas under a *profit sharing plan*, the individual makes no contribution and the company payment is in relation to profit.

Savings Plan Normally the company contribution is in the form of company stock or dollars to purchase company stock, whereas employees normally have several choices about how their dollars will be invested (e.g., fixed income fund, common stocks excluding own company, and company stock). In addition, it is becoming more common to allow the individual to contribute additional monies (e.g., up to an additional 5 percent) which are not matched by the company.

Furthermore, unlike the defined benefit plans, forfeitures of company contributions (caused by employees leaving with less than 100 percent vesting) can be allocated to the remaining participants. Thus, an employee in a plan which is experiencing high employee turnover may be receiving significantly more than the amount of the company match. This is not a required feature, and some plans take the same approach required of

TABLE 5-12 Defined Contribution Example (Years of Service versus Pay Increase)

Pay increase, percent	Annual compound growth		
	5 percent	10 percent	15 percent
30 years			
15	$2,436,912	$4,022,896	$7,448,824
10	1,033,788	1,963,058	4,205,755
5	466,219	1,083,016	2,668,999
20 years			
15%	$ 539,959	$ 795,221	$1,227,490
10	320,844	504,563	831,367
5	198,997	336,122	591,384
10 years			
15%	$ 95,156	$ 119,775	$ 151,709
10	75,982	97,265	125,219
5	61,084	79,600	104,219

defined benefit plans, namely to use the value of the forfeitures to offset the amount of the company contribution.

The advantage to employees is that, although their contribution is made in after-tax dollars, the tax on company contribution plus any appreciation on the company and own investments is deferred until the time of retirement. Under some situations it may be possible to defer tax liabilities on unrealized capital gains even further if at the time of withdrawal the amount is taken in company stock.

The chart in Table 5-12 shows the impact of a 5 percent employee contribution with a 50 percent company match for an individual currently earning $50,000. Assume the individual received 10 percent annual pay increases for 20 years and the contributions set aside grew at the annual rate of 10 percent. At the end of that time the individual would have a fund value of $504,563, but his or her compensation would be $336,375 (i.e., $50,000 increased annually at 10 percent for 20 years). The breakdown of contributions and growth is not shown in Table 5-12, but in this situation it is:

	Amount	Percent of total
Employee contributions	$143,188	28.4
Company contributions	71,594	14.2
Investment growth	289,781	57.4

This example illustrates several points regarding such plans: (1) the higher the company contribution and investment rate of return, the more attractive such plans are, and (2) the projected amount at a specified date in the future looks very awesome in terms of current pay level, but it must more realistically be expressed in relation to projected pay (i.e., in this illustration $504,563 versus $336,375).

Where rate of return has been dependent on stock market performance, few if any plans have been able to sustain double digit growth for prolonged time intervals. In some instances due to poor investment results, some executives have redirected their investments to some form of *guaranteed income contracts* (or GICs), in which an insurance company or other institution guarantees a specified rate of return for a specified number of years. Typically, the funds are invested in the general assets of the carrier. Another group contract written by insurance carriers is the *immediate participation guarantee* which, like the GIC, may be invested in the general assets of the carrier or placed in separate accounts. Unlike the GIC it does not guarantee a minimum rate of return. Thus, the payout could be greater or less than under the GIC.

Many plans have self-imposed dollar maximums on the amount of contributions that the employee may make; however, there has been an apparent trend away from such features other than to the extent required by ERISA. Under this law the company portion plus any forfeitures credited to the employee cannot exceed $25,000 per annum— an amount which is increased annually by the change in the consumer price index. While this would affect very few plans, another feature of ERISA called the 1.4 Rule can dramatically reduce this amount if the company has both a defined benefit and a defined contribution plan. Using the earlier identified $75,000* (defined benefit) and $25,000* (defined contribution) maximums, it simply means that you do not have $100,000 under combined plans. Rather, the percentages of these individual maximums used cannot exceed 140 percent. To illustrate, if the company used the full $75,000 defined benefit amount (i.e., 100 percent), it could only use $10,000 (i.e., 40 percent) of the $25,000 defined contribution maximum. Conversely, if the full $25,000 defined contribution were used (i.e., 100 percent), only $30,000 (i.e., 40 percent) of the $75,000 defined benefit maximum could be used.

A number of people looking at these two extremes assume it is better to take the full 100 percent on the defined benefit maximum because they then have an annual allowance of $85,000, whereas by taking the full 100 percent on the defined contribution they would have only a $55,000 annual allowance. Others have concluded it is better to take the maximum on the defined contribution because ERISA permits unfunded executive pensions. Following this approach the executive would receive a $25,000 defined contribution credit, $30,000 under the qualified defined benefit plan, and a $45,000 allowance under a nonfunded executive pension plan.

Conversely the company could credit the individual toward the full $75,000 in the defined benefit plan and $10,000 in the qualifed defined contribution plan, and could invest $15,000 in a separate investment plan. The tax aspects of this latter amount are more suspect, but it probably could be structured in such a way as to be treated as a company-imposed deferred compensation plan which currently has no tax liability to the individual until received. However, the company also cannot claim a tax deduction until paid. Thus, if it actually invests the dollars, it has an adverse cash flow; if it uses a book reserve method of tracking progress, the executive may have no capital gains opportunity.

Thus, after such an analysis a number of companies apparently have concluded to take the full allowance needed on the defined contribution and make up the lost portion of the defined benefit plan through an unfunded executive pension plan.

While employees are, of course, 100 percent vested in the market value of their contributions, the vesting of the company contribution takes several forms. Within the same vesting rules of ERISA described under pension plans, savings plans either take a class year or a total plan participation approach to vesting.

Class year vesting is a limited period rollover. Typically, the employee has the option of removing money from the plan or leaving it in for investment; this money is the value of the company's earlier contribution (e.g., 3 years previous). In other words, the individual has zero vesting in the company contribution until the third year, at which time the person is 100 percent vested in that value. Under such a plan the individual always has 2 years of employee contribution "at risk."

The *total plan participation* approach is one that counts all years of participation in

---

*The maximums set forth in the Employee Retirement Income Act of 1974 are adjusted annually in relation to the increase in consumer price index. Normally these increased limits are identified sometime during the first quarter of each year.

the plan against one of the ERISA vesting schedules. One possibility is to step-vest (e.g., 10 percent a year so that the participant is 100 percent vested in the value of all employer contributions—past and future—after 10 years). In contrasting this approach with class vesting, several differences can be noted: (1) the class vest always has several years at risk, but the total participation approach only places at risk the earlier years of participation, and (2) the class vest plan annually provides the employee with a choice of withdrawing or keeping in the plan a portion of the plan assets, whereas the total plan approach provides this opportunity at any time (although it probably places restrictions on continued participation).

Plans that make it very difficult to get money out of the plan probably have lower levels of participation than plans which have liberal withdrawal provisions. For some, withdrawal privileges may be as important as a higher percentage company match.

Typically, the employee has several options in taking out the money. The individual who is still an employee usually can make either a partial or a full withdrawal. As the terms imply, the difference lies in whether all or only a portion of the money is removed.

Depending on the objective of the plan, withdrawals are either reasonably easy to accomplish (within the requirements prescribed by the Internal Revenue Code and interpreted by the IRS to avoid constructive receipt of employer contributions) or more difficult (consistent with a plan intended to be a supplement to the defined benefit pension plan). Plan penalties set the period of suspension from the plan, the frequency in which withdrawals may be made, and in the case of partial withdrawals, the amount withdrawn. The rules may be different for partial versus full withdrawals.

However, many plans make an exception for *hardship withdrawals* (i.e., amounts needed to meet a financial crisis). Typically, this might include college expenses for children, purchase of a primary residence, or significant medical expenses not covered by the health care program. Under such provisions the normal penalties for withdrawals are suspended or made less punitive.

Partial withdrawals have an advantage in that the IRS applies the familiar FIFO (first-in–first-out) accounting rule. Namely, no tax liability is incurred until the withdrawals exceed the amount of employee money invested; in other words, no taxable investment growth is acknowledged until all the nontaxable principal has been withdrawn. Meanwhile the investment growth remains in the fund to form the basis for future growth.

However, when an annuity payment is elected a portion of each payment is considered return of principal and the remainder investment growth. The annual exclusion for return of principal is determined by dividing the employee aggregated contribution by the expected years of payment. The exception to this is if the entire value of the executive's contribution has been returned within 3 years, in which case all amounts received shall be excluded as income until the amount received is equal to the value of the contribution: Section 72(d) of the Code.

If the employee was a plan participant for at least 5 full years, then the portion of gain that is attributable to pre-1974 is eligible for capital gains tax treatment, while that portion attributable to post-1973 is considered as ordinary income. The latter, however,

127

may be taxed under the *10-year forward averaging* rules [(Section 402(e) of the Code]. Namely, the total value of the distribution is reduced by the employee's aggregate contributions, the remainder is divided by 10 (there are more liberal steps for net sums under $70,000), the tax is identified on the single taxpayer's table, and the tax is multiplied by 10. This amount is multiplied by the percentage of plan participation after 1973. Alternatively, the total distribution can be afforded 10-year averaging.

It should, however, be noted that to receive this favorable tax treatment, there must have been a lump sum distribution, not simply a lump sum payout. If it is not a lump sum distribution and/or the 5-year participation rule has not been met, then the payment is subject to ordinary income tax rules (unless it is rolled over into an Individual Retirement Account, which will be discussed shortly), although 5-year income averaging may be applied.

Furthermore, it is possible to have a tax-free rollover and favorable 10-year averaging if the individual is covered under both a defined benefit and a defined contribution plan. To receive this favorable treatment, the distribution must be in separate taxable years. Thus, the pension plan lump sum could be rolled over and the savings plan lump sum accorded 10-year averaging or vice versa.

Another point to recognize is that utilization of unisex tables will probably penalize the male employee wishing to buy a single life annuity (say at age 65) from a defined contribution plan and reward him for taking a lump sum under a defined benefit plan. To illustrate: the cost of a $1000 single life annuity might be $9300 at 65 for a male, but a unisex table might charge $9700. Thus, with an account balance of $9300 in the defined contribution plan, the male executive will not be able to buy the $1000 annuity but rather can only buy a lesser amount, using the unisex table. Conversely, taking a lump sum from the defined benefit plan would mean receiving $9300 under a male discount schedule versus $9700 under a unisex schedule. The reverse would, of course, be true for a female.

Lump Sum Payout versus Lump Sum Distribution   All lump sum distributions are lump sum payouts, but not all lump sum payouts are lump sum distributions. Since lump sum distributions receive favorable tax treatment (as described above), it is important to know what constitutes a "distribution." It is payment within one taxable year of the full amount the employee is eligible to receive, and that amount is paid under one of the following conditions: (1) the employee is at least age 59½, (2) the employee retires or otherwise separates from employment, or (3) the employee dies. Thus, only an active employee at least age 59½ may qualify.

An additional complication arises if the employee is in several qualified plans and wishes to receive a lump sum distribution from one and installment payments from another. This can be accomplished only if they are different types of plans (e.g., one is a defined benefit and the other a defined contribution plan). Similar types of plans will be treated as one plan for purpose of tax distribution of payout (e.g., a profit sharing plan and a money purchase pension plan would probably be treated as a single plan, and therefore it would not be possible to receive annuity payments from one and a lump sum distribution, or a lump sum payment, from the other). Even if they are different types of plans, it is preferable to receive payment in separate taxable years.

Mandatory versus Voluntary Employee Contributions   The IRS has generally held that mandatory contributions by employees to defined benefit or contribution plans in total that do not exceed 6 percent of pay will not be discriminatory. Voluntary contributions in total should not exceed 10 percent of pay (plus the unused portion of 10 percent for all previous years in which the full 10 percent was not taken). Therefore, assuming both maximums were employed, employees could contribute up to 16 percent of pay. Though numbers in excess of these might be acceptable to the IRS, the burden of proof would be upon the company to demonstrate that the contributions were not so burdensome as to only enable highly compensated employees to take full advantage of the plan(s).

Revenue Ruling 80-350 apparently reinforced the above position. Previously some considered that matched amounts in excess of the minimum contribution required for participation were considered voluntary contributions and were included in the 10 percent limitation. Thus, a company which permitted contributions of 2, 3, 4, 5, or 6 percent of pay assumed that the total allowable would be 12 percent (rather than 16 percent).

Profit Sharing   In this very popular form of defined contribution plan, the employee typically makes no contribution (although a number either permit or require employee contributions), and the amount of company contribution is usually based on company profits. To qualify, the plan must defer payment for at least 2 years. While the amounts may accumulate tax-free during this period, the company is allowed to take a deduction for compensation expense for the year in which the expense was incurred. Since the maximum that may be deducted by the company in any one year is an amount equal to 15 percent of participating payroll, it is not too surprising that assuming earnings are up, the common payout maximum in any year is 15 percent of earnings. However, if the employer chooses, it may utilize a carry-over rule by contributing more than 15 percent in one year and "carrying over" the excess for charge to a subsequent year when the formula would provide a lesser amount.

Plans are of two types: short-term and long-term. The short-term plan pays out all the employer's contribution after a minimum time period, such as 2 years (similar to the class year vesting savings plans described above). This period may be waived for employees who have been plan participants for 5 years or more. Unfortunately, some employees adjust their standard of living on the expectation of a certain level of payment and then experience cash flow problems when the company has one or two less successful years.

Others prefer to make all or a portion of the profit sharing plan a long-term investment. This is the cash-deferred type of profit sharing plan, in which all or a portion of the company contribution is deferred to a later date. While lower-paid employees may be interested in receiving a significant portion in cash due to other financial obligations, higher-paid employees see the attractiveness of deferring receipt on a tax-sheltered basis.

The Revenue Act of 1978 added three requirements to those that exist for basic profit sharing plans: (1) the amount deferred cannot be distributed in relation to a formula identified with the simple passage of time (e.g., payment 3 years later); instead, distribution should be due to attainment of age 59½ or separation from service (including retirement or death); (2) the deferred amount that could have been taken in cash must be 100 percent vested; and (3) the use of deferrals must not be discriminatory in favor of highly paid employees.

The first two requirements are straightforward, but the nondiscriminatory rule is a little more complicated. There are three tests and the plan must meet at least one. First, the requirement is satisfied if all income levels have the same deferral requirement and that amount is not less than two-thirds of the company contribution. Second, where company contribution is less than 9 percent, a slightly larger percentage may be elected as immediate cash payment, using Table 5-13 (again the percentage must be the same for all employees).

The third is a year-by-year test which specifies the relationship of deferrals for the highest-paid one-third of employees versus the lowest-paid two-thirds. This test is a factor only when the top one-third is deferring a higher percentage of pay than the lower two-thirds. Since this is a year-by-year situation, it is possible to initially make the test but then fail in a subsequent year. Thus, many companies have concluded it is appropriate to adopt one of the first two rules and not risk administration problems. Others feel the year-to-year test gives employees more flexibility and the result of failing the test is merely the inclusion of excess amounts of deferral in W-2 income of the highly paid.

It should be noted that such cash-deferred plans might also take the form of investment (and deferral) in company stock. In such instances the investment experience is a function of growth in the stock price coupled with dividends paid. Also, the formula can be integrated with social security on the basis of pay in excess of that subject to social security tax. The maximum difference between the amount allowed on that portion subject to social security tax and the excess is 7 percent. Thus, a formula of 5 percent on earnings up to social security taxable earnings base and 12 percent on earnings in excess of that base would qualify, but 4 percent and 12 percent would not. Also, if another plan (e.g., defined benefit pension plan) is integrated with social security, a more complicated requirement of determining the allowable spread is required.

TABLE 5-13   Current versus Deferred
Payments under Profit Sharing

Company contribution as percent of pay	Maximum cash percent
9 and more	33.3
8	37.5
7	42
6	50
5 and less	60

While many profit sharing plans are self-standing, some are combined with pension plans in an either-or situation. Typically, the pension plan (defined benefit) prescribes the minimum benefit using one of the formula approaches described earlier. The profit sharing plan stands alongside of the pension plan and the employee will receive whichever produces the greater benefit. Pension plan liabilities are thus reduced when the company has sustained periods of high contributions to the profit sharing plan. The employee still sees a very visible accumulation of assets which form the minimum payout at time of separation from service. Furthermore, this approach combines the advantages of both while canceling several basic disadvantages. More specifically, defined benefit plans favor the older employees, as plan improvements extend not only to future but also past service. Defined contribution plans are by definition always fully funded programs which provide younger employees many years in which to build up plan values.

Combination Plan When a defined benefit plan is combined with a defined contribution plan to guarantee a minimum benefit, the company has established a combination defined benefit–defined contribution plan. Such plans were developed by several companies which had relied on profit sharing (defined contribution) plans to provide pension benefits. Unfortunately, several years of bad market experience resulted in employees going out with smaller pensions than they would have been eligible to receive years earlier. Attaching a defined benefit plan on the bottom of the defined contribution plan provides a floor or stop-loss guarantee for the employees.

ESOP Another form of defined contribution, which has become more popular in recent years, is the *employee stock ownership plan* (ESOP). Originally more applicable to smaller companies, it was used by many as a basis for gaining financing and passing a portion of ownership on to the employees. The company would make a contribution of company stock to an ESOT (employee stock ownership trust). The trust in turn would use stock to obtain a loan, the proceeds of which it would give to the corporation. The corporation would then pay off the loan through the trust and gain a tax deduction on the principal (as an employee benefit) and the interest (as a normal business expense).

ESOPs can be very attractive to individuals who own a large portion of company stock, especially a privately held business. Death, disability, and retirement often create significant problems dealing with liquidity and keeping control of the business in friendly hands. By selling their stock to an ESOP, owners are able to get needed cash and their companies obtain a tax deduction for the employee benefit. In addition, by taking out key employee insurance on majority shareholders, it is possible for the trust to use the proceeds to purchase the deceased's stock from the estate, thereby providing liquidity and keeping control of the business in friendly hands. However, these attributes are more important for smaller organizations (than their larger counterparts) due to problems associated with determining the value of the stock and obtaining a buyer both willing to purchase at fair market value and acceptable to the other owners. These plans are also known as LESOPs (leveraged employee stock ownership plans), although the Technical Corrections Act of 1979 officially identifies them as ESOPs.

In recent years, ESOPs have been adopted by larger companies in the form of a

TRAESOP (Tax Reduction Act form of employee stock ownership plan). As the name implies, this is an ESOP provided by a tax reform act (more specifically the Tax Reform Act of 1975). The Technical Corrections Act of 1979 officially identifies such plans as tax credit employee stock ownership plans. The rules affecting TRAESOPs have already been amended several times and appear to be candidates for more shaping; therefore the specifics may change, but the concept has to do with a tax credit versus a tax deduction. Compensation and benefit expenses usually qualify for a tax deduction, which simply means the government will underwrite a portion of the expense (i.e., the applicable tax rate). Under a tax credit the government underwrites the full cost of the plan since the deduction is applied to the taxes due rather than the company income! Needless to say, this is a more attractive form of benefit "expense" to the company— especially since it increases corporate cash flow by the amount of the "expense." Unfortunately, to date the allowable TRAESOP amounts are very meager on a per-employee basis. While all employees are to share proportionately in the amount of the credit, most recent law places a $100,000 ceiling on this feature. In other words, anyone earning above $100,000 will receive the same dollar benefit as a person earning $100,000. Furthermore, while contributions are immediately 100 percent vested, they cannot be distributed before 7 years, except in cases of separation from service (including disability, retirement, and death). Some companies choose to make payments only under such conditions, barring distribution to active employees. In any event there are likely to be small accumulations except in cases of long service at high earnings for a capital-intensive company (which has a high credit and a small employee population).

Stock Purchase Plans   Stock purchase plans can also be used to supplement other sources of retirement income. Section 423(b)(1) through (9) of the Internal Revenue Code cites the nine requirements that must be met:

1. Only employees of the company and its subsidiary corporations are eligible.

2. Approval of the shareholders is required within 12 months of the date of the plan adoption by the granting corporation.

3. Employees owning more than 5 percent of the voting stock of the company are not eligible. See Section 425(d) for rules of stock ownership.

4. Options to purchase must be given on a nondiscriminatory basis, although it is permissible to exclude: (a) those with less than 2 years of service, (b) those working 20 hours or less a week, (c) those working not more than 5 months a year, and (d) officers and other highly compensated employees.

5. Participating employees must have the same rights and privileges, except it would be possible to allow the amount of stock available to employees to vary directly with their compensation. Furthermore, a maximum amount of stock available under the grant can be established.

6. The purchase price cannot be less than the lower of 85 percent of fair market value (FMV) at (a) time of grant or (b) time of purchase or exercise.

7. The purchase period may not exceed 27 months. However, where the grant is only set at not less than 85 percent FMV at date of exercise, the purchase period may run as long as 5 years.

8. No employee may be granted an option which exceeds an accrual rate of $25,000 of fair market value for each calendar year in which the option is outstanding.

9. The option is not transferrable by the employee other than by will or the laws of descent and distribution, and is exercisable only by the employee during his or her lifetime.

Under such a plan the employee agrees to purchase a specified number of shares or invest a specified number of dollars (e.g., up to 5 percent of pay) to purchase company stock on an installment basis. By terms of the agreement the percentage discount is prescribed and as indicated above may be as low as 85 percent.

If the employee purchases the stock while an active employee or within 3 months of termination of employment in accord with plan terms and does not dispose of the stock within (a) 2 years from date of grant and (b) 1 year after purchase, then under Section 423 the employee has no income at time of purchase and the gain from FMV at time of purchase to that realized upon sale will be considered long-term capital gains. If these requirements are not met while the tax liability is still deferred until the individual sells the stock, at that time the discount below fair market value at time of purchase is taxed as ordinary income. Any appreciation above FMV at time of purchase is subject to short- or long-term capital gains depending on length of time held. If the stock is held less than 2 years, the company may take a tax deduction on the discount portion.

Such plans have been used by some companies in lieu of an across-the-board stock option plan, giving options only to executives. When the latter is the case and the executives are also prohibited from participating in the stock purchase plan, the company may have a problem if the stock is "flat" for several years because the stock purchase participants are realizing a bigger benefit than the executives.

Some of the differences between a stock purchase plan and a stock option plan are: (1) stock option plans allow the company to pick and choose participants, but stock purchase plans require that essentially all employees be eligible to participate; (2) stock option plans usually set the price as of grant date, but some stock purchase plans set the price at time of purchase; (3) stock option plans provide the opportunity to purchase at any point along a prescribed time period, whereas stock purchase plans stipulate the intervals at which the stock is to be purchased; (4) stock option plans allow the company to determine the number of shares to be optioned by individual, but stock purchase plans require that all participants be eligible for a number determined by a common formula.

Individual Retirement Accounts (IRA)   As indicated earlier, one way in which taxation of a lump sum distribution may be postponed is by transferring it within 60 days of receipt of payment into an Individual Retirement Account or IRA. This postpones the tax until withdrawn.

For example, an employee may transfer to an IRA via lump sum distribution from the plan that is being terminated, or from the proceeds of a previous employer's plan. While the executive cannot make additional contributions to the IRA while being covered by the employer's defined benefit or contribution plan (without being subject to a 6 percent annual penalty tax on such amounts), the individual may be allowed to maintain the IRA (and benefit from investment growth). Similarly, while the employee is covered by an employer plan, no tax deduction may be taken for a contribution to the IRA.

Should the individual want to remove the money from the IRA before age 59½, he or she would be subject to an additional penalty tax equal to 10 percent of the distribution. Moreover, at the time of withdrawal, the amount will be taxed as ordinary income; it is not eligible for the special 10-year averaging method. Therefore, before proceeding individuals should fully examine rollovers into IRAs in light of tax and alternative investment opportunities.

Furthermore, it is not possible to establish an IRA (without benefit of a rollover) if the individual is an active participant in a defined benefit or contribution plan, without invoking the above-described tax penalties.

But, it may be possible to establish an IRA beginning at age 65 while continuing to work *if* the company pension plan provides no additional credit for service beyond age 65. Stated another way, if the actuarial equivalent when the person retires is the same as would have been received if retiring at 65, the individual may be able to contribute to an IRA until the age 70½ cutoff.

Conditions under which IRAs might be logical include: (1) joining a company without a defined benefit or defined contribution plan, (2) becoming self-employed, or (3) retiring on other income.

In addition to setting up the plan, it is possible to make annual contributions equal to 15 percent of income or $1500, whichever is less. Such amounts may be contributed up to the time the federal income tax is filed for the year in question. There is a tax advantage to such contributions since they are tax deductible to the individual regardless of whether the person itemizes or takes the standard deduction. Furthermore, the appreciation accumulates tax-free until distribution. Then 5-year income averaging rules may be applied; the 10-year averaging rule discussed earlier and capital gains treatment are *not* available for IRA payments. However, for some this will still have been advantageous since the compound growth on the pretax rollover may still net more after tax than the company growth on the after-tax lump sum equivalent (assuming taxation at favorable rates at time of receipt).

Distributions from IRAs may begin as early as age 59½ and must begin no later than age 70½. Significant tax penalties are imposed for withdrawals earlier than permitted or later than required. The withdrawals may be either in a lump sum or in some form of annuity.

A disadvantage of making a contribution to an IRA established via rollover is that it will prevent a future rollover to a qualified defined benefit or contribution plan should the individual again become covered by such a plan. However, the IRA could continue in such a case, but the individual would be barred from making any additional contributions to the IRA during the period of participation in the other plans.

Some companies, interestingly enough, express a reluctance to allow an employee to waive rights to defined benefit or contribution plan in order to set up an individual IRA but permit the employee to waive such rights to enjoy the extra $250 for a full marital deduction of a plan established by the spouse. But where is the logic? It can't be because of allowing the individual to potentially discriminate against self since a total marital deduction is only $1750 per year whereas two separate IRAs would permit $3000 per year.

Keogh Plans Another popular retirement plan is the Keogh plan. Similar to the IRA in many respects, a key difference is that the contribution applies to net earnings (excluding investment income) from self-employment, even if also covered by an employer's pension plan. Essentially, this benefits the executive who "moonlights" (e.g., serves as a member of the board of directors for one or more firms).

In addition, while the allowable contribution of 15 percent is the same for both Keoghs and IRAs, the annual dollar maximum is $1500 for an IRA versus $7500 for a Keogh. Effectively this means only the first $10,000 is available for an IRA (at the maximum deduction) versus the first $50,000 under a Keogh. Actually it is possible to exceed this dollar amount if the individual is prepared to adopt a more definitive defined benefit type Keogh plan which will provide an annuity at 65 equal to a stated percentage (maximum 15 percent) of current compensation (maximum $50,000). However, such a plan has more restrictive requirements regarding accumulation of investments. More specifically, if the investments are doing very well, future contributions will have to be reduced to prevent overfunding of the maximum allowable annuity.

The earlier described conditions and rules of IRA including premature or late withdrawal, overfunding, and the 59½ to 70½ period are virtually the same. However, a key difference is that you can't set up a Keogh only for yourself if you have employees; those with 3 or more years of service must be included. Also, IRA by definition is an individual retirement plan. Another key difference is that lump sum payment under a Keogh may qualify for the special lump sum distribution taxation discussed earlier; lump sum payments from an IRA do not qualify for such treatment.

A hybrid IRA and Keogh plan is the *Simplified Employee Pension* or SEP introduced by the Revenue Act of 1978 which permits the employer to contribute even though the plan was established by the individual. Its appeal is to younger employees given the allowable annual contribution of a Keogh plan but the relative simplicity of an IRA. Small businesses find the SEP attractive since many of the reporting requirements of other plans do not apply.

Some of the highlights include:

- The IRA percentage maximum of 15 percent applies, but so does the Keogh dollar maximum of $7500.

- Only the first $100,000 of earnings is eligible.

135

- Employer contributions can be made, and they can vary year to year, however they must be in accord with a written formula and cannot discriminate in favor of higher-paid employees. Any year they are below 15 percent, the individual can make up the difference with a tax deductible contribution.

- All employer contributions are vested 100 percent immediately (thus this is not a holding device).

- Unlike Keogh plans, voluntary tax deductible contributions beyond the limit are not allowed.

- All employees meeting service period requirements must be included in the plan, and there must be a separate account for each covered employee.

- Employees can have other pension plans, but their benefits reduce the amount available for contribution under SEP.

Value of the House in Retirement Planning   Another contribution to a financially secure retirement is afforded by the Revenue Act of 1978, which allows an individual age 55 or older to ignore the first $100,000 of capital gains from the sale of primary residence (i.e., net selling price less purchase price and capital improvements). This is attractive not only to the individual who has lived in only one house, but also to the executive who has moved frequently, since the profit on each sale was deferred (as long as the proceeds were used within 18 months to purchase another home at least as expensive). Thus, while such a person might not have $100,000 capital gains on the current house, the delayed capital gains on all previous homes is probably well over $100,000.

By selling, the individual is able to purchase a smaller home, since the children assumedly have grown up, and thereby not only set aside a portion of the sale for investment but also cut down on such direct living expenses as utility bills and property taxes. Since this exclusion can only be used once, it is important that the executive carefully consider the timing.

SUMMARY AND CONCLUSIONS

Employee benefits are pay for membership, not pay for performance except to the extent they are directly related to those elements of pay which are performance-related (e.g., salary and incentives). The value to the recipient may either be current or deferred, and may be in the form of cash, stock, or other tangible goods to offset expenditures for certain expenses or provide additional income. Additional savings can be effected through group rather than individual rates and/or preferred tax treatment. The costs to the employee for employee benefits take the form of payroll deductions, noncovered expenses, and/or additional income taxes. When the employee pays a portion of the cost of the program through a payroll deduction, the plan is said to be *contributory;* when the company requires no payroll deduction for coverage, the plan is said to be *noncontributory.*

Expenses not reimbursed by the benefit are of three types: the deductible (the amount the employee must pay before the plan will pay anything), coinsurance (the plan will pay a specified percentage of covered expenses but the employee must pay the rest), and noncovered expenses (these are expenses outside the scope of the plan, such as cosmetic surgery in many medical plans).

Additional income tax liabilities come through either a direct compensation expense (e.g., a nonperformance/noncash bonus) or an imputed income benefit (e.g., free insurance beyond $50,000). Under such conditions it is important that the individual want the benefit because the tax must be paid from other income rather than from the benefit itself (unless it was paid in cash or something easily convertible to stock).

Normally the company is able to take a tax deduction on a compensation expense at the time it becomes taxable as income to the recipient. Qualified pension and profit sharing plans are exceptions to this basic principle, as are medical reimbursement plans. In the former the company takes a deduction in advance of the time it is taxable to the recipient, and in the latter the recipient never has a tax liability. A summary of the after-tax effectiveness for the major benefit plans is shown in Table 5-14. As discussed in Chapter 1, these values are determined by dividing executive after-tax value by company after-tax cost.

Proxy disclosure of employee benefits is fairly simple since all the "time off with pay" benefits are part of salary (which is reported in C_1), and all nondiscriminatory health care and survivor protection plans need not be reported. Since nondiscriminatory coverage is part of our definition of "employee benefits," this leaves only the reporting of retirement plans. As was indicated in the chapter material a table, showing annual benefits based on representative combinations of remuneration and years of service, is to be included, along with a description of definitions for defined benefit plans.

Defined contribution plan costs by the company should be separated between column C_2 for the vested portion of that payment and column D for the unvested portion. Typically, this would cover profit sharing plans, thrift plans, and employee stock ownership plans. The TRAESOP contribution would appear only in column C_2 since it is 100 percent vested. A summary of the proxy disclosure of employee benefits is shown in Table 5-15.

The extent of an individual's participation in the benefit package is normally based on longevity with the company and level of salary. It is rarely related to performance. Therefore, while it is a part of executive compensation, it is a portion which merely must be recognized as being an extension of what is in effect essentially at all salary levels. Furthermore since the extent of coverage is not varied with performance, it is not part of the incentive plan design.

A number of companies are now investigating *customized benefit packages*, where the employee is given an opportunity to tailor-make his or her own program. The Revenue Act of 1978 requires that company contributions for such programs be considered income to the highly compensated employee *unless* the plan meets nondiscriminatory standards in coverage and eligibility. Essentially, these are of two types of programs: add-on or plus and minus adjustments. Add-on benefit programs either begin with the

TABLE 5-14 Employee Benefits Summary of After-Tax Treatment

	Unattractive	Attractive	Very attractive
Time off with pay			
Holidays		0.93	
Vacation		0.93	
Funeral leave		0.93	
Court leave		0.93	
Workers' compensation		0.93	
Disability		0.93	
Severance pay		0.93	
Employee Services			
Automobile insurance			∞
Homeowner's insurance			∞
Legal services		1.85	
Credit unions		1.85	∞
Loan			∞
Preretirement counseling		1.85	
Nonperformance awards			
Attendance bonus		0.93	
Length-of-service bonus		0.93	
Service award		1.85	∞
Educational assistance		1.85	∞
Scholarships		1.85	∞
Matching gifts plan		1.85	∞
Relocation expense		0.93 1.85	
Assignment expense		0.93	
Travel and entertainment expense		1.85	
Healthcare			
Preemployment physical		1.85	
Medical insurance		1.85	
Prescription drugs		1.85	
Dental insurance		1.85	
Visioncare		1.85	
Audiocare		1.85	
Survivor Protection			
Employee's life insurance		0.93	∞
Business travel accident			∞
Dependent's life insurance			
Retirement			
Defined benefit pension*		0.93	
Defined contribution pension*		0.93 1.33	
IRA			∞
Keogh			∞
Simplified employee pension			∞

*Tax rate could be even more advantageous when 10-year averaging of lump sum distributions is permitted.

TABLE 5-15 Employee Benefits Proxy Treatment

Time off with pay
    Holidays — Part of C_1 salary
    Vacation — Part of C_1 salary
    Funeral leave — Part of C_1 salary
    Court leave — Part of C_1 salary
    Workers' compensation — Part of C_1 (statutory benefits excluded)
    Disability — Part of C_1 (statutory benefits excluded)
    Severance pay — C_1

Employee services*
    Automobile insurance — Nothing
    Homeowner's insurance — Nothing
    Legal services — Nothing
    Credit unions — Nothing
    Loan — Nothing
    Preretirement counseling — Nothing

Nonperformance awards*
    Attendance bonus — C_1
    Length of service bonus — C_1
    Service award — Nothing
    Educational assistance — Nothing
    Scholarships — Nothing
    Matching gifts plan — Nothing
    Relocation expense — Plan description probably appropriate
    Assignment expense — Plan description probably appropriate
    Travel and entertainment expense — Nothing

Healthcare*
    Preemployment physical — Nothing
    Medical insurace — Nothing
    Prescription drugs — Nothing
    Dental insurance — Nothing
    Visioncare — Nothing
    Audiocare — Nothing

Survivor protection*
    Employee's life insurance — Nothing
    Business travel accident — Nothing
    Dependent's life insurance — Nothing

Retirement
    Defined benefit pension — Table of estimated annual benefits
    Defined contribution pension — C_2 for vested portion; D for nonvested portion
    IRA — Description of the plan
    Keogh — Description of the plan
    Simplified Employee Pension — Description of the plan

*Nondiscriminatory benefit plans, healthcare, and survivor protection need not be reported.

existing benefits or these programs are scaled back to form a new minimum. Employees are then given a number of benefit dollars which they may use to purchase increased benefit coverage. Normally such choices are already packaged (e.g., four levels of medical coverage, two levels of dental insurance, and three levels of life insurance). To minimize selecting against the plan (e.g., buying dental insurance for 6 months to get the teeth fixed up and then shifting to medical for another 6 months to take care of elective surgery), there are various time periods of minimum coverage (e.g., 2 years for dental). The plus and minus approach to customized benefit design begins with the existing benefit plans but provides opportunities for employees to reduce the existing level of coverage in some areas in order to gain more in others.

Customized benefit programs are attractive to executives in that they may be able to shed unnecessary life insurance in order to pick up additional health care coverage or place additional monies in a defined benefit plan where the investment growth will be sheltered from taxes while in the plan. The ability to make such selections was enhanced by the Miscellaneous Revenue Act of 1980. It permits the executive to make three-way trade-offs among cash, benefits, and deferred compensation. However, to avoid taxes the program must be nondiscriminatory in nature and not simply used by executives. Because this method of flexible compensation is a cost-effective device, allowing the company to provide individuals with additional benefit coverage without incurring increased cost, it is expected this will become an increasingly popular feature of the employee benefit program.

Perquisites

Perquisites (perks for short) begin where employee benefits leave off. They are benefits extended on a very selective basis. They are given to only a select few executives based on organizational level (and perhaps to some extent, past performance). However, like benefits they have a low risk factor because degree of participation is not varied with performance. Also, once given they are rarely taken away.

Many perks simply supplement the basic benefit program by lifting or completely removing dollar maximums. This essentially applies to disability, retirement, and survivor protection plans.

A prime advantage of such supplemental plans is that the company can be selective in determining participation, extent of coverage, forfeiture and vesting provisions, and period of protection. The disadvantage to the company is that there is no tax deduction until the benefit is paid. The advantage to the executive is receipt of a greater benefit than otherwise available, at reasonably attractive personal service income rates. However, frequently the executive receives something with lower value than comparable after-tax cash value. Thus, perquisites must be structured very carefully, especially since once implemented there will be continual pressure to extend coverage of existing programs and add new ones for the top executives.

In some instances, perquisites are very significant. Reportedly in addition to a $200,000 annual salary, the President of the United States has an expense account of $50,000 for household expenses and entertainment, as well as $100,000 for travel. Also, there is no rent for using the White House or Camp David, and in addition to a fleet of limousines, Air Force One along with various helicopters are available for use.

Because the main appeal of perquisites is often their restricted use, it is likely they will be employed either (1) to identify a group more exclusive than that covered by the long-term incentive plan or (2) reinforce the distinction between those covered under long-term incentives and the others by defining eligibility as participation in the long-term plan. It appears to be more the former than the latter.

It is important to also realize that perquisites, like benefits, have different tax possibilities. They range from the very attractive "tax deductible to the company and nontaxable to the executive" to the very unattractive "non–tax deductible to the company and taxable to the executive." The appropriate categories and their tax effectiveness (TA) ratios (as discussed in Chapter 1) are shown below.

∞   Nontaxable or taxable but deductible to executive; no expense to company.

1.85   Nontaxable or taxable but deductible to executive; tax deductible to the company.

1.00   Nontaxable or taxable but deductible to executive; not tax deductible to the company.

0.93   Taxable to executive; tax deductible to the company.

0.56   Taxable to executive as ordinary income; tax deductible to the company.

0.50   Taxable to executive; not tax deductible to the company.

0.30   Tax deductible to executive as ordinary income; not tax deductible to the company.

The SEC requires that the value of perquisites be included in column C-2 of the table of remuneration in the annual proxy. Here it is lumped with other employee benefit costs and long-term incentive values. The incremental cost of providing the perquisite is the basis for valuation; however, a *de minimus* rule allows omission if the expense cannot be determined without unreasonable effort. Also if the company cannot determine the specific portion which is personal rather than business and the amount does not exceed $10,000 per individual, it need not be shown. This assumes such omission would not materially misrepresent the remuneration reported.

Footnote disclosure is required when the actual incremental cost is significantly less than the value to the executive. Also, if the value of perquisites exceeded 10 percent of aggregate remuneration, or $25,000, whichever is less, it should be footnoted with a brief description of the perks.

It is important to realize that while the SEC and the IRS have a similar approach, they need not have the same interpretation of what is income, and if income, to what extent. The SEC requirement that an item be disclosed does not constitute an income tax liability; conversely an IRS declaration that an item is taxable income does not automatically mean it must be disclosed in the proxy.

Perquisites will be categorized in the same manner as employee benefits, namely: time off with pay, employee services, nonperformance awards, health care, survivor protection, and retirement.

TIME OFF WITH PAY

Since this form of perquisite is clearly "pay," all forms have a tax effectiveness of 0.93. However, time off with pay often takes rather subtle forms. How many executives who are members of the board of directors of another company take a vacation day to attend the board meeting? Even for those who do, how many use company time to read reports and recommendations preparatory to attending the board meeting? How often are business meetings scheduled at resort facilities with half-day business agendas? Who really watches late arrivals and early departures? Many will argue that most executives put in 60–70-hour workweeks and that such paid time off is a phantom benefit—available but rarely used. This is probably true for hard-driving, results-oriented individuals, but what about those who are no longer reenacting the Charge of the Light Brigade? Perhaps the most accurate conclusion is that use of this benefit is in proportion to the lack of effectiveness of the executive.

Employment Contract

Considered a valuable perquisite by some, the typical employment contract will specify the period of time in which the contract is in effect, what constitutes acceptable performance and what the executive will receive in the way of pay (e.g., salary, short- and long-term incentive amounts, and specific benefit and perquisite coverage). A period of 3 to 5 years is common, along with an automatic renewal clause (probably terminating in case of disability, retirement, or death). A clause may also be included to permit renegotiation upon mutual agreement of the company and the executive. Perhaps executives should employ an agent to negotiate their contracts, as do prominent sports figures. Few can argue that use of agents has not been very successful for these men and women who are being paid whopping amounts of money to continue to play games learned as children.

The employment contract is most prevalent in smaller organizations, although larger companies have used them to obtain a key executive or retain the person (after a successful acquisition or merger). There is no tax effectiveness rating for the contract per se, and its component parts are taxed in the manner they would normally be taxed. The value to the executive is continued employment for a prescribed period of time and a very clear understanding of the compensation to be received; the value to the company is that it has increased its probability of retaining a key executive (especially if the contract includes a noncompete clause in case the executive leaves).

Liberalized Vacation

As indicated in Chapter 5, Employee Benefits, it is not unusual for companies to provide liberalized vacations for certain executives, identified by organizational level and/or title. This may be a flat 4- or 5-week minimum regardless of service (important to the executive recently hired who is in mid-career) or it may be in the form of a supplement (e.g., 2 weeks), so that the executive will always have more vacation than other employees with the same service. In addition, part or all of the executive's vacation expenses may be paid by the company, or the vacation may be combined with a business trip. Another perquisite may be to allow the executives to accumulate the unused portion for 1 or

143

more years—thus providing the opportunity to take a mini-sabbatical, to phase in to retirement, or to soften the blow of termination.

Work at Home

During a liberal portion of the work year, the executive may be allowed to work away from the office. In exchange for allowing the individual to avoid a commute and work in robe and slippers, the company expects to receive a project completed either sooner or better. This is on the assumption there are a number of distractions and interruptions in the office which could easily wait a couple of days.

Disability

One of several legitimate perquisites is sick pay. It is not uncommon to supplement the short- and long-term disability payments by: (1) increasing or completely removing the dollar maximum on benefits and/or (2) increasing the time period of benefits (both for partial and full pay).

Sabbatical

Executives may periodically take a super vacation, or sabbatical. Typically, this might be a 6-month period fully paid (or fully supplemented) during which the individual undertakes a civic responsibility, pursues an advanced degree, or simply "gets away from it all" in order to return to work with fully recharged batteries. Conceptually, sabbaticals are logical and meet an apparent need, but unfortunately, many executives are afraid to take advantage of the benefit. Some are concerned about whether or not the same old job is going to be there when they get back, especially if the sabbatical is for a year or more.

Severance Pay

For those executives who do not meet the minimum performance expectations, the company separation policy of 2 to 4 weeks invariably proves to be inadequate. The termination may be very abrupt: "Here's 6 months' pay, get out today!" Alternatively, "you are hereby relieved of your responsibilities; however, we will provide another office and a secretary for 6 months as you seek other work." In one instance the individual is removed from the site and therefore cannot cause tension by expressing discontent to fellow employees. In the other instance the person is isolated from fellow associates and given a facade for the outside world.

Formulas for determining separation pay usually take into consideration years of service and age. An example of this is the formula below. Note that age is squared and divided by 1600; this simply provides a geometric increase for individuals above age 40 (apparently on the belief that, the Age Discrimination in Employment Act notwithstanding, life may begin at 40 but employment opportunities are more difficult to find). Note also that the minimum allowance in this case is 2 weeks. Fearing such possible minimum stipends, some executives request employment contracts before accepting a new job (thus being assured of, for example, 3 years of pay beginning with the day of employment. Obviously, the individual who is fired immediately has 3 years of pay coming, but the one who is terminated after 3 years of employment might simply receive a handshake.

$$\text{Weeks of pay} = 2 + \left(\text{years of service} \times \frac{\text{age}^2}{1600} \right)$$

Another variation to this formula would be to add a factor for organizational importance by use of job grade. If it was believed inappropriate to give lower-level individuals more than a minimum of 2 weeks, the salary midpoint of a grade (e.g., 15) would be identified as the denominator and divided into the salary midpoint of the terminated executive's grade.

$$\text{Weeks of pay} = 2 + \left(\text{years of service} \times \frac{\text{age}^2}{1600} \times \frac{\text{assigned grade midpoint}}{\text{midpoint grade 15}} \right)$$

To illustrate assume that a grade 24 (midpoint of $59,500) plant manager is being terminated. She is 47 years old, has been with the company 16 years, and is currently earning $62,400 (or $1200 a week). As shown below, she would be eligible for 45.2 weeks of pay or $54,240.

$$\text{Weeks of pay} = 2 + \left(16 \times \frac{47^2}{1600} \times \frac{59,500}{30,400} \right)$$

Another approach is to divide the current pay by a fixed dollar amount (e.g., $2000) and pay the resulting number in weeks of pay. Thus, the person earning $64,200 would be eligible for 32.1 weeks severance at $1200 a week (or a maximum of $38,520). This formula could be modified by the earlier factor of $\text{age}^2/1600$ to recognize the impact of age. The basic formula rationalizes that it will take 1 week of search for every $2000 of earnings; if this does not seem logical, the formula should be adjusted, or perhaps a range should be used to reflect increasing difficulty. Using the formula below, the $64,200 executive described above would receive 23.2 weeks (or a maximum of $27,840).

To $10,000: one week per $5000
$10,000–22,000: one week per 4000
22,000–34,000: one week per 3000
34,000 and up: one week per 2000

In addition to the individual's age and level of compensation, another factor is the general marketability of the departing executive. Other things being constant, a person with experience in several industries probably has an advantage over a person who has spent all his or her life in one industry. Similarly, a person who has management experience in several functional disciplines is probably more marketable than a person who has specialized in one area. While these factors might not be as easily reduced to a formula as age, years of service, and level of compensation, they are probably as important.

Furthermore, notwithstanding the basic formula, companies are likely to be more generous with an individual who has given all the outward appearances of trying, still makes consistently loyal statements about the organization, has made a significant contribution earlier in his or her career, and/or knows the location of a few skeletons. A cynic would argue these are all forms of conscience money; the pragmatist would indicate that any severance pay formula merely quantifies the agreed-to values for determining the amount of pay. The reason for a formula is consistency in application.

Since severance pay is somewhat analogous to alimony, it is logical for the company to make regular payments (not a lump sum which could be rapidly squandered and could also serve as a disincentive for the individual to seek other job opportunities) but only until the individual obtains new work. Some will argue that payments should not cease when a new job is found, for such an approach only encourages the employee to "cheat on the company," and that it is better to consider the remainder a bonus for getting the new job faster than anticipated. However, it may be advantageous to the individual whose employment is terminated late in the year to have a significant portion of the payment deferred to the subsequent year for tax purposes. Such arrangements must be carefully orchestrated to avoid constructive receipt issues.

In addition to severance payments it is logical to continue employee benefit plan participation; perquisites are more logically viewed on an item-by-item basis to determine whether or not the former executive is still eligible. Probably one of the most important perquisites that can be given is no-cost use of an effective outplacement service. Such an organization's services range from assistance in preparing a résumé and preparing for the job interview to psychological counseling to cope with the fact of failure itself.

The Department of Labor ruled in 1979 that retroactive to January 1, 1975, payment of severance benefits must (1) not exceed 2 years of pay and (2) be completed within 2 years of the termination date of employment service (or after normal retirement date if early retirement benefits were elected). In determining the amount of severance benefits, all compensation including employee benefits should be included.

However, the Multiemployer Pension Plan Amendments Act of 1980 amended this restriction and permits the Secretary of Labor to establish rules by which separation plans will be treated as welfare rather than pension plans under ERISA. This change should permit much greater flexibility in design and funding.

Outplacement Assistance

Many terminated executives are also provided this special service by their former employer. Here the executive is counseled either by company consultants or outside specialists on assessment of personal strengths and weaknesses, developing a plan of action for getting a new job, preparation of a résumé, and conducting an effective job interview. All this advice is directed toward assisting the terminated executive get a new job quickly. It also is directed at reducing the anger, frustration, fear, and stress of being fired, or dehired, to use a euphemism. Since the company pays the costs associated with such a plan and it can probably be structured to result in no income to the executive, it has a tax effectiveness rating of 1.85. However, this is really an employee service, a group of perquisites which will be covered in the next section.

EMPLOYEE SERVICES

In addition to the benefits discussed under employee benefits, which are available to all employees, there are a number of perquisites which are employee service in nature.

Company Product Samples

The samples that may be given to the executive for personal use range from large-ticket items such as a car or videotape machine to small disposable items such as magazines or newspapers. In many such situations the company takes the posture that it is really requiring the executive to put the product through extensive product testing and then report back any findings. To the extent such gifts are viewed as income, they have a tax effectiveness of 0.93, but if they qualify as nonincome, the tax effectiveness is 1.85.

Automobile

Use of a car is a rather common benefit for executives—at least a company car for business travel (either specifically assigned or on a first-come, first-served basis). Many go further and allow personal use, with the company reimbursed on either a fixed monthly charge or a mileage basis. These cars are replaced after a specified number of years and/or miles driven. The type of car (and its cost) logically lends itself to the organization level of the individual—the limousine or super-luxury car at the CEO level and a standard model at the entry level of eligibility. In many instances the executive is provided a company-paid chauffeur for business trips.

If the executive is to avoid an imputed income, the company must assess a charge for personal use of the automobile. One approach is to charge the individual a flat amount (e.g., $100 a month); the other approach is to have the executive pay a rate per mile of personal use (e.g., 20 cents). The flat amount is more advantageous when personal use is high, but the per-mile approach is more attractive to the executive when personal use is low. In either situation, the company may have to defend its policy to the IRS and perhaps increase the assessment to avoid an imputed income charge.

Where normal commuting is the issue (and the executive therefore has a tax liability), the company will impute an income either monthly or on the basis of cents per mile (perhaps factoring in an alternative form such as commuter rail cost). In such instances, the perquisites may be perceived as more valuable than the 0.93 effectiveness ratio.

Chauffeured Limousines

Increasingly, companies are providing chauffeured limousines under the guise of protection for the executive. In such cases the view is that the executive's well-being is threatened and the chauffeur is also a bodyguard. To reinforce this view the driver is either a former law enforcement officer or someone who is familiar with bodyguard requirements (possibly licensed to carry firearms) and has gone to driver education schools which teach defensive driving to escape ambushes. While commuting costs are not a business expense, providing for the safety of the executive could be considered a legitimate expense. These situations would probably have to be evaluated on a case-by-case basis.

Security Systems

If personal safety is a factor, the company probably also pays for the installation of an electronic security system in the executive's home. The tax effectiveness ranges from 0.93 to 1.85 depending on whether or not income is attributed to the executive.

Parking

Parking facilities range from a designated space in the company parking lot (or inside a garage), normally very close to the office (tax effectiveness of 1.85), to public parking off the premises at company expense (tax effectiveness of 0.93). The first is more typical of a suburban site, the latter more representative of a metropolitan facility.

Airplanes

Personal use of corporate aircraft has been a very popular perquisite for both business and personal use. As a business form of transportation it affords the flexibility of scheduling not possible under commercial flights. In addition, some locations are not serviced by direct commercial flights, and so use of corporate aircraft allows more efficient use of executive time.

Most company aircraft are nearly as comfortable as first-class commercial service. However, since corporate aircraft usually lack a galley (other than a refrigerator), the food and beverage service is definitely more restricted.

In determining the cost basis the company must select between company cost and fair market value. Using company cost there is no additional expense for allowing an executive to use an empty seat on a corporate jet for personal use when the aircraft is delivering one or more executives to the same city for business purposes; the tax effectiveness is infinity. Conversely if the executive is the only passenger, the full corporate cost could be multiples of commercial flight charges and thereby far exceed 0.93 tax effectiveness. Alternatively, using fair market value would suggest charging the executive the equivalent of first-class commercial fare for a 0.93 tax effectiveness.

Adopting the company cost approach would seem logical for a company that allowed personal use only in conjunction with business flights. Adopting the fair market value would seem more feasible for a company that allowed personal-use-only flights as well as hitchhiking a seat on a business flight. The company cost approach might only include operational expenses such as fuel and landing fees, on the presumption that the crew is paid on a salaried basis and the plane amortization schedule is not affected.

Initially many companies proudly displayed their company name and/or logo on the aircraft, but too many questions from shareholders spotting the planes at resort communities or prominent sporting events (such as the Super Bowl) resulted. In addition, the energy crunch has called for a low profile (and absence of logo), especially when gasoline lines lengthened at the neighborhood station.

Yacht

The complement of the corporate airplane is the company yacht. By necessity this is more restricted in use than airplane if for no other reason than the requirement of proximity to water. Determination of basis, if any, for income is the same as for corporate aircraft. Unfortunately, the 1978 Revenue Act bars company deductions for maintaining a yacht. Presumably, business entertainment on the craft (e.g., catering) would be deductible.

Executive Dining Room

It is not uncommon to have an executive dining room on the company premises. Such facilities range from a separate room serving the same fare as the cafeteria to luxuriously appointed rooms where uniformed waiters serve dry martinis and excellent meals. In fact, the cuisine may be without equal in the city due to the impressive gourmet credentials of the chef. While such facilities are primarily used for luncheons, occasionally they are the site for dinners. The luncheons wane in comparison to the elegant dinners which feature delicate hors d'oeuvres, vintage wine, and fine cigars, all served by tuxedoed waiters.

The dining room or rooms are also physically placed to ensure a marvelous view, probably only matched by that of the president and chairman of the board. Where there is more than one room, they may be of comparable quality in appointments or they may be structured in such a way as to indicate eligibility (e.g., corporate officers use the A room, division presidents and other key executives the B room, and the remaining eligibles the C room). In the latter case, one will usually find differences in room size, elegance of furnishings, type of crystal and china, level of cuisine, and choice of beverages.

Another variation permitting discrimination is reserving certain tables or seats for a handful of the senior officers. This may vary from a table in the executive dining room to simply a table in the cafeteria. This assures the executive of a seating without having to wait in line.

In addition to their convenience, such facilities are often justified in terms of their privacy when executives meet among themselves or with important outside contacts, including customers. Executives are usually charged for a portion of the cost (either a fixed monthly charge regardless of use or on a per-use basis).

Since informal discussion of company business over lunch among company executives has a difficult time meeting IRS requirements for escaping imputed income (and the resulting 0.93 tax effectiveness), some companies have taken the position of scheduling regular luncheon meetings. In some instances the company has been able to successfully argue that the participants are not otherwise available for the meeting. Since the meal has been scheduled for the convenience of the company, there is no imputed income for the individual and, therefore, the tax effectiveness rises to 1.85.

Physical Fitness Programs

These are viewed by some as logical extensions of the medical care program, believing that in the long run they promote good health and lower medical costs. Some argue that stress brought about during work can be relieved through physical activity. Thus, the fitness program is not simply to promote better physical being, but also to assist in shedding the tensions and pressures of work. Since unrelieved stress may lead to depression, this could truly be a perquisite intended to promote happier executives.

Some companies choose to develop their own facilities, but others avoid the construction and related investment costs and join a medically oriented facility near the company site. Exercise equipment ranges from the basic treadmill, rowing machines, stationary bicycle, medicine ball, and weights to more elaborate setups with jogging tracks and courts for basketball, tennis, and volleyball.

Often under the control of the company medical department with staff members trained in exercise physiology, executives are given perhaps three hourly sessions a week to work through a concentrated schedule of activity (usually during normal business hours). These sessions probably lower the risk of coronary artery disease, and in addition, many participants say they feel better and more able to cope with work-related pressures and crises. Increased strength and endurance coupled with concern for proper nutrition and weight management often result in more restful sleep, higher work energy levels, and a more attractive physical image—all very important items to the executive. To date, physical fitness programs have enjoyed a 1.85 tax effectiveness.

Apartments or Hotel Rooms

These are often provided in the city where company offices are located. Such facilities are available for out-of-town company officials as well as key employees working at the location who after attending a late business function stay over rather than face a long commute and little sleep. Due to the business nature, the tax effectiveness is 1.85.

Where the use is strictly business the company has a deductible expense and the executive avoids an imputed income charge. Some companies provide such facilities for key executives to use routinely during the week (almost as a second home); in such instances the individual would probably be subject to imputed income for those non-business-required layovers. Certainly where an apartment, hotel, or house was provided as either a vacation place or a principal place of residence, the individual would have income (and the company a tax deduction), and the result would be 0.93 tax effectiveness.

Legal Services

While it has not been uncommon for executives to draw upon inside counsel for routine matters (e.g., drafting a will or giving an opinion on a personal transaction or possible liability), more and more companies are moving away from this approach, especially in cases of defense against a nonbusiness civil lawsuit or defending against criminal prosecution. It is probably typical that the company does not have a qualified legal services plan for its employees, and even if such a plan existed, it would be short of the services executives might wish. Thus the company involvement ranges from providing a list of attorneys in outside firms indicating type of specialty (with the executive being billed directly) to covering a specified dollar amount and/or list of scheduled services from counselors selected by either the company or the executive. While the company may take a business tax deduction, the executive will have an imputed income for tax purposes, and the tax effectiveness is 0.93.

Tax Assistance

In addition to regularly preparing federal and other income tax returns, it is not uncommon for company legal sources to give executives opinions on significant investment opportunities (e.g., tax shelters). Traditionally, such assistance has been provided by the company tax attorneys; however, a number of executives feel uncomfortable about others in the company knowing their full financial status. Therefore, it is not uncommon for such services to be provided by an outside firm with the company and/or the executive paying the cost. Any portion paid by the company is a deductible expense, and the executive receives a like imputed income charge. However, since all expenses related to taxes are deductible expenses for the executive, this results in little if any income and a tax effectiveness of 1.85, where fully deductible.

Financial Counseling

Financial counseling is the result of extending the coverage of tax planning to include maximizing investment opportunities and adding an analysis of insurance needs. Operating on the belief that executives did not have sufficient time to focus on the long-term financial affairs of the family due to business activities and that such items would not be taxable to the individual, many companies implemented such programs in the past. Typically, the company selected several firms and allowed the executive to choose one or, in some instances, allowed the individual to identify a company outside of those selected. In the latter instance, the company would establish a maximum amount that it was willing to reimburse (e.g., $5000 the first year and $3000 thereafter). At lower management levels, the executives would simply be invited (perhaps with spouses) to attend a seminar. In such instances it may be possible for the expenses to be charged off as management development and no imputed income assigned. Traditionally, computer-produced benefit statements by the company of its benefit programs would be the basis for examining the company coverage.

Today financial counseling programs are in disarray for several reasons. First, while the service was usually quite effective in matters of estate preservation (i.e., minimizing income and estate tax dollars) it was less than perfect in matters of estate building (i.e., increasing the value of the estate through tax shelters and various investments). Second, the IRS stated in Rev. Rul. 73-13 that the full value of financial counseling (while a business deduction to the company) was compensation for services to the executive under Section 61 of the Internal Revenue Code. This aspect however is of minimal importance to those executives who used the service primarily for minimizing taxes since all tax-related expenses can be deducted on the federal income tax returns, thereby giving it a 1.85 tax effectiveness rating. Those portions of the service dealing with the preparation of wills and other matters would probably have a rating of 0.93. As a parenthetical note it is important to distinguish between *tax avoidance* (the legal means by which the individual pays no more tax than is required by taking full advantage of tax law and how different items are taxed) versus *tax evasion* (the illegal means by which the individual pays less tax than is required by understating income and/or overstating deductible expenses).

The importance of tax avoidance is dramatized in Table 6-1 where the pretax yield of an investment subject to ordinary income tax is equated to investment which is not subject to federal income tax. Note that due to the ascending tax rate, it is more impor-

TABLE 6-1 Taxable Yields at Various Tax Brackets of Tax-Free Investments

Executive's taxable earnings	Tax-free yields				
	6 percent	7 percent	8 percent	9 percent	10 percent
$250,000	20.0%	23.3%	26.7%	30.0%	33.3%
200,000	18.8	21.9	25.0	28.1	31.3
150,000	16.7	19.4	22.2	25.0	27.8
100,000	14.6	17.1	19.5	22.0	24.4
50,000	11.8	13.7	15.7	17.6	19.6

tant to avoid taxes as income increases. Therefore, it is possible to take a smaller tax-free return and still be ahead. For example, an executive with $50,000 taxable income would effectively receive a 19.6 percent pretax return with a 10 percent nontaxable form of income. However, an individual in the $150,000 bracket would essentially have the same pretax return (i.e., 19.4 percent) with a 7 percent income not subject to federal taxes.

Tax avoidance is the main attraction of *tax shelters* for many highly compensated executives. The typical shelter consists of a group of investors who have formed a partnership, thus enabling them to claim personal deductions (not available to an association or corporation) proportionate to their personal investment in the partnership.

Tax shelters were created (and are periodically massaged) by Congress to encourage investment in ventures where the risk/reward ratio is otherwise not sufficiently attractive. Contrary to popular belief, they were not designed with the sole purpose of allowing millionaires to avoid taxes. In exchange for the right to currently reduce taxable income and/or receive future income as capital gain (rather than ordinary income), the individual accepts a higher risk of protecting the investment than otherwise might be the case. In real estate, it is speculation that land and property will appreciate favorably in terms of inflation. With gas and oil drillings, it is the probability of a successful strike. With equipment leasing, it is the belief that the supply of equipment will not be greater than the demand for the period of investment. Therefore, it is important that the executive identify and prioritize personal objectives regarding deferral of income, capital gains versus ordinary income, security of investment, and degree of desired liquidity.

While many shelters allow only a pro rata deduction (i.e., the later in the year the investment, the smaller the allowable deduction), others involve property that is eligible for the 10 percent investment tax credit, and thus the tax write-off may approximate the cash investment. However, the provisions of tax law generally limit the deductions under tax shelters to the amount of money "at risk" (i.e., the amount invested and/or liable to pay). Some shelters inflate the amount of deduction by adding a "nonrecourse loan" (i.e., a loan for which the partners have no legal liability) to launch the venture. Thus if five investors each put up $10,000 and a nonrecourse loan of $250,000 was obtained, each would theoretically have a deduction of $60,000. Such situations must be examined very carefully because the IRS has ruled against such deductions in a number of instances.

The problem, therefore, is not finding a tax shelter but, rather, finding one which meets the investment caliber of the executive and provides an opportunity for economic value as well as tax write-offs. One of the major problems facing some executives, who have benefited from significant depreciation write-offs, is how to dispose of heavily depreciated property without massive tax liabilities. Furthermore, many tax shelter opportunities that meet the economic requirements are not timed in an effective manner for a particular executive. Unfortunately, too often executives give more consideration to purchasing a particular $20,000 car than to investing $100,000 in a specific tax shelter.

Today companies have varying degrees of participation in financial counseling programs based on organizational rank. For example, one approach is to include corporate officers and other executives of comparable rank in a personalized program which can cost a minimum of several thousand dollars. The next layer down would be included in a personalized estate preservation analysis, and the last covered group would be eligible to attend a 1- or 2-day seminar (perhaps with spouse) to study the general nature of estate preservation techniques. Under the latter program the individual or family might receive a workbook in which to work out (in conjunction with their attorney and CPA) their own program (e.g., identifying location of all important papers, ensuring wills exist and are current, determining the amount of life insurance needed, and minimizing estate tax liability). Regardless of the type of program, some companies consider it appropriate for the executive to sign a release (allowing the company to provide the financial planner with specific information about the executive's pay and benefit) and a waiver (holding the company harmless for any adverse consequences based on information received).

A key objective in estate planning is not simply to minimize taxes when the executive dies, but to provide an orderly plan whereby the executive's assets are delivered to the proper individuals in the most tax effective manner, which includes minimizing the tax impact on the estate of the executive's spouse.

Certainly the most basic provision is a properly executed will. A person who dies without a will is said to have died *intestate* and the appropriate state law(s) will be applicable. Normally this will specify a certain percentage of the estate to the children and the remainder to the spouse.

Holographic wills (i.e., those completely handwritten by the testator) and *nuncupative wills* (i.e., unwritten wills) may not conform to the appropriate state laws and therefore will not be considered "wills."

Another key requirement of estate planning is to ensure sufficient liquidity exists, not simply to meet estate taxes but also to provide for seizing favorable investment opportunities (e.g., exercising the executive's stock options). Lump sum payments from profit sharing and savings plans, although subject to estate taxes, will provide a form of liquidity in addition to life insurance proceeds.

The 1976 Tax Reform Act had a pronounced effect on estate planning. Among other things it established a unified estate and gift tax table. With the exception of the annual $3000 per person exclusion ($6000 if the spouse consents), all other gifts during the executive's lifetime will be added back into the estate for purpose of determining estate tax liability. Beginning in 1981, there is a lifetime $47,000 exemption for gifts (beyond the annual exclusion); this replaced a $60,000 exemption from estate taxes and a $30,000 lifetime exemption from gift taxes, in effect prior to the 1976 tax law. The $47,000 tax credit is equivalent to a $175,625 deduction from the unified tax schedule shown (before credit for state death taxes) in Table 6-2. This is not a deduction in the normal sense (i.e., off the top) but rather an elimination of tax on the first $175,625. Thus, if the net estate were $675,625, the federal estate tax would be $173,781, not $155,800.

The impact of inflation upon asset values drives home the importance of proper

TABLE 6-2   Unified Estate and Gift Tax Schedule

Amount subject to tax		Tax is		
From	To	This	Plus	Over
$ 0	$ 10,000	$ 0	18 %	$ 10,000
10,000	20,000	1,800	20	20,000
20,000	40,000	3,800	22	20,000
40,000	60,000	8,200	24	40,000
60,000	80,000	13,200	26	60,000
80,000	100,000	18,200	28	80,000
100,000	150,000	23,800	30	100,000
150,000	250,000	38,700	32	150,000
250,000	500,000	70,800	34	250,000
500,000	750,000	155,800	37	500,000
750,000	1,000,000	248,300	39	750,000
1,000,000	1,250,000	345,800	41	1,000,000
1,250,000	1,500,000	448,300	43	1,250,000
1,500,000	2,000,000	555,800	45	1,500,000
2,000,000	2,500,000	780,800	49	2,000,000
2,500,000	3,000,000	1,025,800	53	2,500,000
3,000,000	3,500,000	1,290,800	57	3,000,000
3,500,000	4,000,000	1,575,800	61	3,500,000
4,000,000	4,500,000	1,880,800	65	4,000,000
4,500,000	5,000,000	2,205,800	69	4,500,000
5,000,000	—	2,550,800	70	5,000,000

estate planning. If one assumes a 10 percent increase, the estate will double approximately every 7 years; due to the progressive nature of the tax table, the tax liability will increase even faster. In addition, it should be remembered that nonqualified deferred payments to beneficiaries will probably have their present value included in the estate— a significant drain on the estate values without sufficient life insurance to meet the tax liability.

Some individuals have the mistaken belief that joint ownership will avoid taxation; it does not. It does, however, avoid going to court to transfer title. Thus, joint ownership is convenient since it makes the property immediately available to the spouse at the time of the executive's death. However, leaving half the estate, or $250,000, whichever is greater, to the spouse and the other half to a trust, minimizes the tax consequences. The first half is tax-free as the marital deduction; the second half provides income to the spouse but is held for the children until the spouse dies.

A *trust* is created when an individual takes title to property and administers it for the benefit of the person creating the trust, other identified individuals, and/or the trustee.

There are two types of trusts: inter vivos and testamentary. An *inter vivos trust* is created by the executive while alive; a *testamentary trust* is created by the executive's will. Inter vivos trusts may be either revocable or irrevocable; testamentary trusts are irrevocable. Property transferred through an *irrevocable trust* cannot be withdrawn by the granter. The assets are distributed in accordance with the terms of the trust to beneficiaries designating the occurrence of a specified event or attainment of a point in time. Such trusts can be designed to be either short- or long-term in duration depending on the objective in establishing the trust. For example, an educational trust might be established for 15 years on the child's third birthday to coincide with the completion of high school and beginning of college. The objective of such a trust is to shift income from the highly taxed executive to the low tax bracket applicable to the child. Since capital gains under such trusts invariably are taxable to the person who transferred the property to the trust, not the beneficiary, the optimum approach is to place high-yield rather than high-growth assets in the trust. While the typical investment may be stocks or bonds, real estate could be transferred if it were income-producing through rent. The amounts contributed must be carefully reviewed. Some will conclude it is better to make several annual contributions rather than one large award at the time of establishing the trust in order to take advantage of the annual gift-tax exclusions ($3000 for the individual but $6000 if made jointly with spouse). The executive should be careful not to retain any rights in structuring the trust. For example, if the executive retains the right to replace the trustee (other than by resignation or action of the court), the income in the trust might be considered by the IRS to be part of the estate, since not all rights were relinquished.

Others have concluded that interest-free loans to their children have been almost equally helpful in minimizing taxes. In exchange for the money, the child signs a demand note (a fixed payment date may be ruled subject to gift tax on the theory that a specific value can be calculated) and deposits the money in a high-yield investment. In addition to avoiding the expense of setting up the trust, the filing of federal and state income tax returns is eliminated. While the IRS has consistently attacked such arrangements, the tax courts have been equally consistent in ruling they do not trigger income tax or gift tax liabilities to the lender.

A *revocable* or living trust is a legal entity to which the executive transfers all or part of his or her assets. No longer in the executive's name, the assets still remain under the executive's complete control since the power to add or withdraw assets and amend the conditions of the trust is retained. The advantage of this type of trust is that the beneficiaries will have immediate access to the assets in accordance with the terms of the trust. However the living trust does not reduce estate or income tax liabilities. While the executive is alive, the IRS considers the trust nonexistent, for the income-producing assets are still owned by the executive.

A *generation-skipping trust* is established when the assets provided the executive's children are in trust for the life of the children with the remainder going to their children. Prior to the 1976 tax law this was a very popular device for reducing estate taxes in the future; now the maximum that can be placed in such a trust is $250,000 for each child (not each grandchild).

Some executives have found it appropriate to transfer the ownership of their insurance to an insurance trust and also name the trust as the pension plan beneficiary. Under such an arrangement the surviving spouse could receive the income in much the same way as from an ordinary trust, and while there may be little estate tax saving at time of the executive's death, the amount saved at the time of the surviving spouse's death (for distribution to the children) might be significant. However, there are a number of problems to work out in such a situation (e.g., a gift tax is levied on the cash surrender value of the insurance, and either annual gifts may be made to the trust to pay the premium or income-producing assets may be added to the trust which can be used to pay the premium).

Another common recommendation of estate planners is to purchase "flower bonds" (allegedly named for the floral gifts associated with funerals). These bonds are United States government obligations that sell well below their face value due to their low interest payment; however, they are accepted at full face value for paying estate taxes if owned by the decedent prior to death. Purchase of these bonds has the effect of significantly lowering the estate tax, since while the excess of face value over market value is subject to estate tax, it may not be subject to capital gains or other income taxes.

NONPERFORMANCE AWARDS

There is a fine line between employee services and nonperformance awards. The executive is often afforded the opportunity to receive a number of nonperformance awards beyond those described under employee benefits.

Job Title

The job title is a very visible perquisite which is all intrinsic compensation. Titles are often related to minimal salary and/or organizational levels. In many instances, they have modifiers to denote corporate versus group or divisional level. While corporate officer titles require board of director approval, the approval of group or divisional titles is most likely at the discretion of the company CEO. Central approval is essential to minimize interunit inequities.

In many instances, pay goes with the title, but there are many situations where companies use title instead of increased pay. For many organizations, especially those in the mature phase, the growth in number of vice presidents is faster than the growth in sales! The after-tax value of a job title is infinite, since there is no pay to the executive and no expense to the organization. The new hefty title may not put more groceries on the table, but for most who receive it, the basic necessities of life are already being met. The title of vice president is intended to officially recognize the importance of the individual. Unfortunately, as additional vice presidents are created, the value of the title begins to diminish. First to suffer are the true vice presidents. Their status is denoted by such prefixes as corporate, group, and divisional or executive, administrative, and senior. While these distinctions are helpful, much of the glitter originally part of being a vice president is gone.

Office

The office is another very visible nonperformance award or perquisite. Given the number of variables, it is rather easy to develop a hierarchy to reflect organizational status. In addition to the location of the office, its size (including number of windows), the type of furniture (including armchairs and sofas), the quality of carpets and drapes, and the number and type of paintings and sculptures are visible means to project the degree of the executive's importance. While there have been some questions regarding extremely expensive artwork originals, such items are normally business expense to the company and escape tax liability to the executive, thereby resulting in a tax effectiveness of 1.85.

Executive Washroom

The executive washroom can range from a simple basin and toilet to a facility resembling a Roman bath in style, size, and opulence. Variables include tub, shower, sauna, and dressing table. The location ranges from centrally located communal facilities under special lock to individual rooms located adjacent to the executive offices (usually with private entrances from within the offices). Like the office furnishings, executive washrooms are tax deductible expenses for the corporation without incurring liabilities for the executive, and the tax effectiveness rating is 1.85.

Expense Account

In addition to the normal travel and entertainment policy of the company, certain individuals may be given broader discretion through liberalized expense accounts. Expensive five-star French restaurants normally off limits to other employees may be identified as permissible establishments for conducting business meetings. As long as the situation qualifies for a business expense, it enjoys a 1.85 tax effectiveness. If the use is further liberalized to cover nonbusiness expenses, it is the same as pay and has a 0.93 tax effectiveness.

A variation of this is where the executive is given an expense account of a stated amount (e.g., $25,000) which is not subject to company review. The company considers the total amount compensation expense and the executive uses as much as possible for business-related expenses. Since the company does not reimburse the executive for expenses, the individual will itemize these nonreimbursed items on the tax form. Thus, if executive incurred $20,000 of business expense, he or she would net $5,000 pretax.

Club Membership

Club memberships take different forms, ranging from simple *dining* memberships (sometimes restricted to luncheons) at facilities usually close to the office to the full-range *athletic* or *country* clubs (where indoor and/or outdoor sports as well as dining and dancing are available). The selection of club memberships which will be subsidized or fully paid by the company may be made by the executive, or by the company, or may be mutually decided. In addition, depending perhaps on organizational level, a determination may be made as to how many clubs will be allowed, what portion of costs will be covered (e.g., initiation fee, annual membership, or usage charges), and/or what annual dollar limit if any will apply. For example, the CEO may be allowed three memberships of own choice with a maximum annual subsidy of $10,000. The president may be allowed two memberships with an annual subsidy of $7500, etc.

While the norm is paying all or part of the dues to an exclusive club, some companies go one step further: they own the club. Such situations range from the simple golf club to an exclusive hunting and fishing resort available for private use as well as business entertaining. However, the Revenue Act of 1978 disallows deductions for expenses incurred in connection with the operation of such entertainment facilities. Thus, they have become a very expensive perquisite with a tax effectiveness rating of 0.50.

Where the corporation is able to take a tax deduction, the individual will have imputed income to the extent such charges (i.e., initiation fees, annual membership, and monthly charges) are not directly identifiable as business expenses—namely entertainment. Under Section 274 of the Internal Revenue Code only that portion of dues related to business is deductible and only if that portion exceeds nonbusiness purposes. In other words a 51-49 business/nonbusiness split would qualify for a 51 percent deduction, but a 49-51 split would result in zero deductions. This would suggest that sufficient business luncheons and dinners be scheduled during the year to meet the required usage for deductibility.

Season Tickets

Whether for sporting events or the arts (e.g., opera, ballet, or theatre), season tickets are deductible under the earlier described rules of business entertainment. Therefore, in addition to providing choice locations, often for hard-to-get events, this perk has a very high 1.85 tax effectiveness rating.

Credit Cards

A number of companies provide their executives with credit cards. The company not only pays the annual charge but may in fact pay the full interest on delayed payments (without attempting to separate business from personal usage). In addition, where the company is billed directly it may be slow in requiring reimbursement from the executive for personal charges. These amounts are in effect interest-free loans. Presumably, the situation is therefore the same as described under low-cost loans and club memberships.

Home Entertainment

A variation or in some cases an extension of club memberships is reimbursement for home entertainment expenses associated with business purposes. Activities can range from lawn parties to indoor formal dining with extensive catering, probably the norm rather than the exception. Such a policy may be either a simple reimbursement or a stated annual allowance. In any event, the company receives a deduction for its expenses and to the extent the individual is able to document business expenses avoids an income liability. The tax effectiveness is 1.85.

Domestic Staff

Company provision of personal domestic staff for the executive at either no cost or reduced expense is an extension of the home entertainment expenses. The newspapers and trade journals periodically identify an executive who had company workers build an extension on the house or undertake significant renovation. Thus, such assistance may either be short-term or an ongoing service. Similarly, it may either be provided by company employees or on a contractual basis. Typically, such services would have a tax effectiveness of 0.93, although the perceived value may be greater due to the quality of service received.

Conventions and Conferences

Oftentimes meetings are structured to allow ample time to enjoy golf, tennis, and other recreational facilities nearby. Since the individual's expenses are reimbursed by the company (for which the latter takes a business deduction) without any income liabilities, the executive is in effect receiving no-cost minivacations. Foreign conventions are eligible for the same consideration if it is as reasonable to hold them offshore as in the United States. For some this is added incentive to ensure multinational membership.

First-Class Travel

A well-received nonperformance award is first-class travel on commercial business trips. Certainly it is logical to provide such accommodations for those individuals who are entitled to use the corporate aircraft (since it approaches first-class commercial accommodations). Some companies, however, restrict usage to a certain number of air miles or time in flight before permitting such coverage. For those who do not include coverage to Europe, many unhappy executives are sandwiched in among vacationers and small children—not the most conducive environment for either doing some business work or resting prior to a meeting shortly after arrival. Since this is a business expense, it has a tax effectiveness of 1.85.

Personal Escort

In addition to providing first-class travel, some companies ensure that their top executives are met at the airport and have a personal escort to their hotel. Usually the executive will be checked in and out by the "host," thus saving tedious minutes in lobby lines. It is the host's responsibility also to ensure that the hotel accommodations are fully satisfactory including catering to individual whims (e.g., putting the proper brand of Scotch in the room). The tax effectiveness rating is 1.85.

Spouse Travel

Because of the IRS requirement that a clear business need must exist for the spouse to accompany the executive on a business trip in order for the spouse's travel expenses not to be considered income, it appears that use of this perquisite is limited to this narrow definition. Thus this type of perquisite is determined case by case on the individual circumstances. Due to the business nature, it is possible for this perquisite to extend down rather far in the management ranks depending on the circumstances. In many instances, some level of senior management must specifically approve the individual request and company policy may limit the number of annual trips. However, even when spouse travel expenses are considered income, they may not be considered wages; therefore, while reportable, withholding may not be required. Therefore, the tax effectiveness is either 0.93 or 1.85, depending on whether or not the business expense test is met.

Business Liability Insurance

As some have commented recently, we are becoming increasingly a litigious society. Suing for damages is a fact of life. The executive has both a business and a personal risk. Thus business liability insurance is rather common for corporate officers and members of the board of directors. Also those who have a fiduciary responsibility, as defined by the previously mentioned ERISA, are often covered for their business actions. Whether or not such protection can be purchased by the company is often a function of the state in which the company is incorporated. However, where possible, it is common for the company to purchase the protection, and since it is a business expense the company has a business deduction without creating an income liability for the executive. The tax effectiveness rating is 1.85.

Personal Liability Insurance

Because of the earning level of the executive, many find that the liability maximums on their auto and homeowners' policies are inadequate to cover bodily injury or property damage. Increasingly they are turning to personal umbrella liability insurance. This type of policy provides a stated maximum dollar liability (assuming careful planning) beginning where the auto and homeowners' policies end. Policies up to $5 million are not uncommon at a fraction of the cost of the basic auto and homeowners' protection. If the executive pays the premium, the company is normally able to get a lower rate by arranging for the insurance; if the company pays, it will have a tax deduction but the individual will have an imputed income, for a tax effectiveness rating of 0.93.

Children's Education

This is a perquisite which initially looked very good for apparent tax reasons but has lost a significant part of its appeal. The initial program called for the company to make a payment to an EBT (Educational Benefit Trust) and the trust in turn to bestow scholarships upon children of eligible executives. The thought was that the company could get a tax deduction and the executive and the child would escape tax consequences since scholarships are not taxable, thus resulting in a tax effectiveness rating of 1.85. Or at worst, the monies would be taxable to the child and thereby at much lower rates than to the executive. However, the IRS in Revenue Ruling 75-448 indicated that tuition fees paid on behalf of key employees are considered income (for purposes of FICA, FUTA, and income tax) under a nonqualified deferred compensation plan. Namely, the company could not take a tax deduction until the executive had received the "scholarship" or the restrictions had lapsed and the amount was included in the executive's gross income. Thus, while some companies make educational grants to children of their executives (with possible annual dollar limits) to cover tuition, registration fees, books, and/or room and board, for private secondary education and/or college, they are limited in application due to the delay in taking the deduction. Also the 0.93 tax effectiveness rating is no better than most other perquisites. When benefits are based on need or merit and all employees are eligible, the tax effectiveness rises to 1.85; however, such scholarships are by definition an employee benefit, not a perk.

Loan

A perk that continues to be very attractive is the interest-free or low-interest loan to executives. The beginnings essentially date back to J. Simpson Dean, 35 T.C. 1053 (1961), when the tax court took the position that there was no taxable income to the borrower under an interest-free loan. However, some have pointed out that this position was largely due to the facts of that case, namely that should such a benefit be taxable it would be offset by a corresponding interest deduction. Tax effectiveness, therefore, ranges from infinite (i.e., no company expense and no executive income) to 1.85. Either way, many will argue that there is a greater expense to the corporation. It is equal to the difference between what is received in interest versus what it must pay in borrowings or, even more dramatic, what it earns in capital.

The IRS has challenged such arrangements on a rather consistent basis, attempting to either make the lender pay gift taxes or the borrower pay income tax on the value of the interest discount. Thus far, the courts have sided more with the lender and borrower than with the IRS, though this could change.

Despite the tax effectiveness, sizable loans to executives at low or no interest often attract considerable shareholder heat. Indeed some states require shareholder approval of a loan to a director. Usually these loans are granted to assist the executive in purchasing company stock or financing a stock option, often after the stock price has dropped and the bank is pressuring the executive by calling unsecured demand loans—on the assumption that his or her financial position has deteriorated—or through margin calls on loans for which the stock or other securities have been pledged as collateral.

Few executives have escaped the perils of *margin calls* since buying on margin (i.e., paying only a portion of the stock's cost and borrowing the rest from the broker) is an attractive leveraging technique. By complying with Regulation T of the Federal Reserve, an executive need pay only 50 percent of the stock's cost at time of purchase. Thus, if the executive purchased $100,000 of stock, the broker would send a Regulation T call for $50,000 within 5 business days. However, if the executive already had $150,000 in the account, the Regulation T would simply be entered in the internal account at the brokerage firm (since the $150,000 was greater than the $125,000 needed to cover the combined investments).

With Regulation T satisfied, the next requirement facing the executive is Rule 431 of the New York Stock Exchange, which requires the invester to maintain at least a 25 percent equity position (most investment firms require more). The equity position is determined by subtracting the amount owed the broker from the fair market value of the stock and dividing the balance by the FMV. In the above example, this is $150,000 (i.e., $250,000 less $100,000) divided by $250,000, or a 60 percent equity position. In this example, when the $100,000 owed equals 75 percent of FMV, the minimum equity position of 25 percent has been reached at $133,333 (i.e., $100,000 = 0.75 FMV). Thus, when the stock value drops to $125,000, a margin call will go to the executive to deposit at least $6250 in the account. Thus, the loan will drop to $93,750, resulting in an equity position of $31,250, or 25 percent of the $125,000. A further drop in market value to $120,000 will result in another margin call for $3750.

If the initial $100,000 went to purchase stock A while the $150,000 was invested in stock B, the executive would not receive a margin call on A even if it went to zero, as long as the value of B was at least $133,333.

Many executives also use margin calls to shelter the payment of taxes on their dividends by offsetting them with interest charges. For example, if the stock were paying a dividend equal to a 4 percent yield (i.e., $10,000 or $0.40 a share) and the margin account were charging 10 percent interest (i.e., $10,000 on the $100,000 outstanding), then the interest deduction would offset the dividend income!

It may be argued that the company should not be in the banking business, especially when it is paying twice as much (or more) itself for short-term borrowings. On the other hand, one could argue there is some corporate obligation if it has pressured the executive not to sell any of the company stock holdings. While some companies charge as much as prime rate for any loans, it seems more logical to simply remove any pressures for holding the stock.

Other circumstances warranting a company loan range from company initiated relocation (either a "bridge" loan to cover the equity needs until current residence is sold or an outright loan that otherwise would be covered by a mortgage) to personal expenses of either a routine (e.g., buy a car or finance children's education) or an emergency nature (e.g., extraordinary medical expenses).

Other issues the company must address include: Who will approve the loan (e.g., the board of directors)? What is the allowable term? How is the loan paid if the employee terminates or dies (e.g., balance forgiven, payment schedule unchanged, or payable immediately)? Is there a maximum amount available for loans totally? For any one individual? Will conditions and terms vary by individual?

If the company charges what IRS considers to be a reasonable interest rate, there is no tax liability to the executive, although the company does have a liability on the interest received. If the rate is less than acceptable to the IRS, it may impute an income to the executive. However, the Tax Court has rather consistently struck down this action by the IRS on the basis that there is no taxable income for the difference between the amount of interest charged (if any) and prevailing interest rates because a corresponding interest deduction would be available and thus constitute a wash. Thus while the IRS would consider it an economic benefit given in return for either past or future work contribution, the Tax Court does not consider it income. In either event, it is attractive to the executive since its after-tax value is $1.00. There is no company cost, only lost income opportunity; therefore, the tax effectiveness rating is infinite.

Some companies seeking to avoid publicity associated with executive loans and possible difficulty with IRS simply increase the executive's salary or bonus by the amount of interest it will charge, thereby effectively offsetting the amounts. Namely, if the executive is to be charged $10,000 interest for the year, the executive pays it out of a $10,000 increase in pay—the deduction offsetting the income at time of tax determination. Similarly, the company realizes $10,000 of income but has a compensation expense of $10,000.

HEALTH CARE

Since the coverage described under employee benefits is so extensive, there are essentially only two perquisites that exist under this category: executive physical examinations and full-reimbursement medical plans.

Medical Examinations

Medical exams are very important to the executive as they are intended to identify correctible problems before they have advanced into major concerns. The exam could be given by the executive's own doctor (perhaps up to a prescribed dollar maximum), a clinic (specializing in exams), and/or the company doctor. In some instances the results of the exam are made available to the company (as a tempering effect on manpower planning); invariably the results are given to the executive's own doctor(s).

Some examinations are at the employee's place of work or in his or her own community; others are coincidently located near resort communities. If the latter, the executive is able to conduct his or her own form of cardiovascular risk analysis on the tennis court or golf course.

Eligibility is usually a function of job grade, but the frequency and extent of examination is in some instances related to age. The value of a complete medical exam for a 35-year-old and a 55-year-old are not the same in many eyes.

Medical exams are very cost effective, as the executive has no imputed income whereas the company has a tax deduction, or a tax effectiveness of 1.85.

Supplemental Health Care Coverage

This begins where the basic health care coverage stops. After the executive has been reimbursed to the extent of the plan covering all employees, the balance is quietly reimbursed under the supplemental plan—leaving the executive with no health care expenses. If the executive were not reimbursed, the individual would be able to take a deduction on personal taxes to the extent such expenses exceeded 3 percent of income. However, for the executive earning $100,000 this would mean the first $3000 would not be deductible; furthermore, due to the tax bracket it would also mean the individual would have had to earn $6000 in order to pay these bills.

Under Section 105(h) of the Internal Revenue Code the cost of this supplemental plan is deductible by the company as a business expense but not considered income to the recipient if it is provided under insurance, resulting in a tax effectiveness of 1.85. Payments received under a self-insured (by the company) plan will have such payments considered as income for tax purposes for a tax effectiveness of 0.93 (unless the plan is nondiscriminatory—by definition an employee benefit, not a perquisite).

Some have tried to argue that Administrative Services Only (ASO), where the insurance company simply checks the claim for validity and then writes the check against the company bank account, and 501(c)(9) Trusts, where the company establishes a trust for purpose of making the payments, represent insured plans. However, most pay no state insurance tax on such plans, and therefore, in the eyes of the state insurance commission do not represent insured plans. The company must make a decision about whether the plans are or are not insured. All administrative aspects should then be consistent.

While properly structured supplemental health care coverage is a very cost effective perquisite, it has not received wide acceptance for a simple reason: executives find it difficult to explain to shareholders and lower-paid employees that total health care expenses are being reimbursed only for the top-paid executives. With SEC disclosure requirements intending to surface such plans, it is unlikely that many companies will adopt or retain such a program.

To satisfy IRS requirements it is necessary that supplemental coverage be a formal plan and that it be written; however, due to its simplicity it can be covered in one or two sentences, or it can prescribe what types of expenses either will or will not be reimbursed. However, there is reason to believe that it will only be a matter of time before insured supplemental healthcare will require the same nondiscriminatory coverage as noninsured plans.

In addition to full reimbursement of expenses covered under the basic health care program, the supplemental coverage could include items not covered by the basic plan. For example, massage therapy might be covered under the belief that a relaxed executive is not only a better-functioning executive, but also a better-looking one.

SURVIVOR PROTECTION

In addition to the basic and supplemental life insurance programs described earlier, there are several forms extended on a very limited basis: business travel accident, assignment protection, key employee, kidnap and ransom, Section 79 term/permanent, split dollar, and retired lives reserve.

Business Travel Protection

Some companies liberalize the business travel accident insurance for executives. One approach is to include the executive's spouse (e.g., at half the executive's benefit level) when authorized to travel with the executive on company business. Another approach is to lift an exclusion, such as piloting private aircraft, for executives who use their own planes to fly on company business.

Assignment Protection

As discussed earlier many executives will choose to assign their life insurance policies in order to avoid their inclusion in the estate and, therefore, escape estate taxes. Since the IRS views any assignment made within 3 years of death null and void, there is a 3-year period during which the benefits are at risk. One way in which a company could assist is to take out a separate 3-year term assignment protection policy on the executive equal in amount to the estate taxes on the assigned policy (not the face value) plus the new policy, making the estate the beneficiary. Since the company has no rights of ownership, it could take a tax deduction; the executive probably will have a tax liability in accord with Section 79(c) Uniform Premium Table requirements (see page 101). The tax effectiveness is 0.93.

Key Employee Life Insurance

Key employee life insurance takes one of three approaches; the proceeds are paid to the company (1) as recompense for the value of the deceased executive or (2) to provide monies for a deferred compensation agreement with the executive or (3) to provide the money needed to buy out the deceased executive's ownership in the company. The third approach is more prevalent with smaller companies and partnerships.

Under such insurance the company has ownership rights to the policy; however, it has no tax deduction on the premiums paid [Internal Revenue Code Section 264(a)(1)]. However, the beneficiary does not have an income tax liability on the death benefit proceeds [Section 101(a)(1) of the Code].

Provisions can be made for the executive to buy out the policy at the time of retirement: the assumption is that, by that point, the company has developed a suitable replacement and, therefore, no longer needs insurance to cover the loss. The value to the executive is that permanent insurance protection is obtained to replace the group term insurance in effect during employment. If the key employee insurance is transferred for whatever reason, it is probably best to transfer directly to the insured (perhaps for an amount equal to the cash value). Then the policy can be transferred by the executive to the spouse if desired. If transferred directly from the company to the spouse, the proceeds in excess of the death proceeds may be subject to income tax.

Also, the company should structure the policy so that it can transfer the coverage from executive A to another should the first leave the company. An adjustment on the premium will be required because of differences in the executives' ages and in the length of time the initial policy was in effect.

A variation on the typical key employee policy is keeping the policy in force until the executive's death (even after retirement). Such a policy may be used to provide special pension payments to surviving retired executives. In structuring such a policy, the company must attempt to ensure that the proceeds are sufficient to finance the executive benefit. A key variable is life expectancy when the payments are for life rather than a prescribed period of time. Since the direct linkage of the insurance proceeds to the pensions would subject the executives to unfavorable tax treatment (as prefunded benefits), the life insurance and pensions must not be directly related. Nonetheless, the insurance proceeds provide the financing for the corporation to pay the pension supplements. Under such an arrangement the company typically has heavier cash flow requirements in the early years (i.e., insurance premiums and pension supplements) than without such a plan. As with traditional key employee insurance while the death benefit proceeds are not taxable to the company (since it is the beneficiary), neither are the premium payments tax deductible! However, interest charges are deductible (if 4 of the first 7 years' premiums are paid in cash). By thus borrowing against the policy's increase in cash value, the company is able to lower its cash flow requirements and deduct the interest charges. Since the policy cash values and dividends normally will exceed the after-tax cost of the interest charges, the net result is a positive increase in the value of the initial company investment. This simple fact encourages the company to borrow the premium cost (after paying at least four of the first seven annual premiums) by giving it maximum leverage on use of corporate funds.

Kidnap and Ransom Insurance

This is especially attractive for executives in politically volatile situations overseas. Such policies might have a face amount of $5 or $10 million with a deductible ranging from 1 to 10 percent of policy value. Since this is typically directed at minimizing company loss, it is similar to key employee life insurance; the value to the executive is essentially intrinsic (i.e., knowledge of being sufficiently important to warrant such a policy). Needless to say, companies are reluctant to talk of such insurance policies for fear that knowledge might prompt someone to test the payout provisions.

Combination Term and Permanent Life Insurance

Combination insurance (often called *Section 79* plans) became quite popular during the mid-1960s and the early 1970s. These plans were designed to take advantage of the annual $50,000 benefit exclusion and Uniform Premium Table rates provided under the 1964 addition of Section 79 to the Internal Revenue Code. A popular approach was to place a Section 79 plan on top of an existing group term plan and limit participation to the top executives.

A typical Section 79 plan would call for scheduled amounts of life insurance, a portion being decreasing term and the other part being offsetting increases in permanent protection. The employer would pay the premium on the term portion (deductible under Section 162 of the Code), thus creating imputed income to the executive in accord with the Uniform Premium Table for coverage in excess of $50,000. The executive would pay the premium on the permanent life portion; however, the company would assist in this matter by increasing the salary or bonus by a comparable (or grossed-up) amount. Furthermore, as cash value started to build on the permanent insurance, offsetting the decreases in term coverage, the accumulated cash value often exceeded the actual taxes paid for imputed income. The employer received a tax deduction for group insurance premiums and compensation expense; the executive had income imputed at favorable rates on the term portion and compensation income on the other portion. This structure neatly avoided the issue of non–tax deductibility of permanent life insurance premiums, as well as reduced the amount of term coverage in later years when the Uniform Premium Table rates reflected significant increases which would otherwise result in large imputed income amounts.

The need to separate fairly the two insurance portions in order to receive the benefits of Section 79 was reinforced with Revenue Ruling 71-360. In 1979 the requirements for such plans to qualify under Section 79 were further tightened. Namely these combination plans had to specify in writing the amount of term coverage, allow the executive to decline (or subsequently drop) the permanent insurance without any effect on the group term amount, and provide a group term benefit not less than the total death benefit less the amount of paid-up insurance.

The new rules also provided that the unused portion (if any) allowable under the Uniform Premium Table for the term portion could not be used to reduce the imputed income for the permanent coverage. The effect of this requirement is to increase the imputed income and reduce the attractiveness of such policies. Furthermore, the new rules placed a high value on the cost of permanent insurance due to the conservative interest rate assumption of 4 percent and the 1958 CSO Mortality Table, specified for use by the IRS. This makes it possible, especially for a senior executive after a number of years of coverage, to have the imputed income plus dividends exceed the actual premium cost! Needless to say, these changes by the IRS have significantly cooled the interest in Section 79 plans.

Split Dollar Insurance

In split dollar insurance the beneficiary and the employer split the face value of the policy at the time of the insured's death. Typically, the employer and the executive also split the premium; the company pays that portion of the premium equal to the increase in the cash value during the year. Dividends (under participating plans) may be used to reduce the company contribution, lower the executive premium, and/or purchase additional insurance. Since employer cost is tied to increase in cash value of the contract, the policy must by definition be permanent not term in nature, since the latter has no cash value, providing protection only for a specified period of time. A variation of this standard approach is a level premium payment by the executive over all or a portion of the contract. This has the advantage to the executive of lower payments during the early years when cash flow may be a problem due to family and other financial obligations. Needless to say, it is not as advantageous to the company since it is placing money above the increase in cash value at risk during the early years of the contract.

The company payment is not tax deductible, but the death benefits are not subject to income tax either. However, surrender of the policy will most probably result in a tax liability since the amount by which cash value exceeds payments will be considered income.

These policies may be highly discriminatory in nature when determining eligibility and amounts of insurance. Where the number of executives covered is less than 100, they are exempt from reporting and disclosure regulations of ERISA, other than for a summary plan description. Since split dollar insurance is a welfare, not a pension, plan, it is also exempt from participating, funding, vesting, and plan termination requirements of this same law.

Probably the most typical arrangement is the endorsement method where the company is the owner of the policy. As such, it is responsible for payment of the premiums; however, it makes a separate agreement with the executive stipulating the amount and manner in which the insured will split the premium with the company. In addition, the company allows the insured to name the beneficiary for the amount in excess of the payment to the company to recover its costs.

Another approach is where the employee is the owner of the policy. Here the company agrees to lend the executive annually the amount by which the cash value increases. These loans are either no-cost or low-cost and, as such, may present difficulties in states which restrict such loans to corporate officers and directors. Under this type of plan the insured assigns the policy to the company as collateral for the loans. The company in turn agrees to forward to a beneficiary designated by the insured any proceeds in excess of the loan balance at the time of the insured's death. A variation of this approach is where the intended beneficiary takes initial ownership to the policy. This approach probably will remove the death payment from the estate and, where the beneficiary also makes the partial premium payments, may avoid gift tax requirements. Death payments are, of course, not subject to income tax.

If the beneficiary is not the owner of the policy, it is imperative that the insured has relinquished all rights of ownership to avoid the death payment being included in the estate. Being able to name or even veto the naming of a beneficiary may result in the proceeds being considered part of the estate. When all rights of the policy are assigned to a spouse or trust, the proceeds will not be considered part of the estate if such assignment occurs more than 3 years before the date of the insured's death. However, the economic value of the premiums will be considered as gifts and therefore summed to determine the appropriate estate or gift tax.

The value of the gift each year is the greater of: (1) the amount by which the annual premium exceeds the yearly increase in cash value and (2) the annual P.S. 58 cost. Even if assigned, the insured will have an economic benefit calculation as will be described below.

Initially the IRS ruled, in Revenue Ruling 55-713, that premium payments by the employer did not trigger taxable income to the employee. However, it later amended this view with Revenue Ruling 64-328 which requires a determination of economic benefit in accord with the amount of one-year term insurance rates. This is identified as the P.S. 58 table and is shown in Table 6-3.

The value of the split dollar insurance provided to the executive must be determined annually in accord with Table 6-3 or the insurance company's own individual 1-year term insurance policy rates, whichever is lower. It is also important to realize that dividends paid will also be considered as income to the individual unless the dividends are pocketed by the company or used to reduce its portion of the premium. Any situation where the individual receives an economic benefit from the dividend (e.g., cash, or the purchase of additional term or paid-up insurance) will be viewed as income by the IRS. However, when additional insurance is being purchased with the dividend, that portion of the dividend being used to purchase insurance (to which the company is entitled) is not considered income to the individual. This is in accord with Revenue Ruling 66-110.

Let's assume the company takes out a $500,000 whole life policy for an executive, age 45. The annual premium for this policy is $13,355. As shown in Table 6-4, the executive pays a $12,355 premium since there is a $1000 cash value at the end of the first year. Multiplying the 500 times $6.30 from the P.S. table results in a value of $3150. Since the premium actually paid by the executive (i.e., $12,355) exceeds this amount, there is no economic benefit and no taxable income to the executive.

However, 5 years later the cash value of the policy has started to build, increasing $10,000 over the fourth year (i.e., from $22,000 to $32,000). Furthermore, assume this

TABLE 6-3 P.S. 58 Table: Annual Premium per $1000 Insurance

Age	Premium	Age	Premium
18	$1.52	50	$ 9.22
19	1.56	51	9.97
20	1.61	52	10.79
21	1.67	53	11.69
22	1.73	54	12.67
23	1.79	55	13.74
24	1.86	56	14.91
25	1.93	57	16.18
26	2.02	58	17.56
27	2.11	59	19.08
28	2.20	60	20.73
29	2.31	61	22.53
30	2.43	62	24.50
31	2.57	63	26.63
32	2.70	64	28.98
33	2.86	65	31.51
34	3.02	66	34.28
35	3.21	67	37.31
36	3.41	68	40.59
37	3.63	69	44.17
38	3.87	70	48.06
39	4.14	71	52.29
40	4.42	72	56.89
41	4.73	73	61.89
42	5.07	74	67.33
43	5.44	75	73.23
44	5.85	76	79.63
45	6.30	77	86.57
46	6.78	78	94.09
47	7.32	79	102.23
48	7.89	80	111.04
49	8.53		

TABLE 6-4 Split Dollar Insurance

Policy year	Payments		End of year		Premium 1-year term
	Employer	Employee	Cash value	Dividend	
1	$ 1,000	$12,355	$ 1,000	$ 0	$ 0.00
2	500	12,835	1,500	0	0.00
3	10,000	3,355	11,500	1,165	68.88
4	10,500	2,855	22,000	1,565	144.09
5	10,000	3,355	32,000	1,835	229.11
6	11,000	2,355	43,000	2,250	337.10
7	10,500	2,855	53,500	2,670	459.03
8	11,000	2,355	64,500	3,055	605.01
9	11,000	2,355	75,500	3,380	773.88
10	11,000	2,355	86,500	3,745	968.75
11	11,000	2,355	97,500	4,145	1,193.39
12	11,500	1,855	109,000	4,585	1,458.39
13	11,000	2,355	120,000	5,000	1,756.70
14	11,500	1,855	131,500	5,415	2,105.35
15	11,500	1,855	143,000	5,845	2,503.94
16	11,500	1,855	154,500	6,295	2,958.64
17	11,500	1,855	166,000	7,400	3,475.71
18	11,500	1,855	177,500	7,855	4,060.86
19	11,000	2,355	188,500	8,305	4,713.68
20	11,500	1,855	200,000	8,780	5,467.47

is a participating policy and the dividend at the end of the fifth year is $1835. To ensure the executive's estate has the benefit of the full face value of the policy, a portion of the dividend is used each year to purchase 1-year term insurance equal to the full cash surrender value (which is also the amount the company will reclaim from the settlement). This is what is commonly identified as the *fifth dividend option* (the other four being: payment in cash, payment used to reduce premiums, payment left with insurance company to accrue interest, and payment used to purchase additional paid-up insurance). After 5 years the cash value is shown as $32,000. Subtracting the $229.11 needed for 1-year term from the $1835 dividend leaves $1605.89. This amount is then subtracted from the $13,355 premium, leaving $11,749.11, an amount which is further reduced by the $10,000 increase in cash surrender value (since it is the amount paid by the company). This leaves $1749.11 to be paid by the executive. An alternative would be for the policy to be structured so that the dividend remaining after paying for the 1-year term would be used to buy additional paid-up insurance rather than reduce the split dollar premium.

Let's determine the tax impact. The basic death benefit after 5 years is $468,000 (i.e.,

$500,000 less the $32,000 cash value payable to the company). Multiplying this net amount by the P.S. 58 table value of $8.53 per thousand for an individual age 49 results in a value of $3992.04. To this amount is added the $1835 dividend, resulting in a total of $5827.04. This amount is reduced by the individual's portion of the premium (i.e., $3355); the remainder of $2472.04 is the executive's imputed income.

Since the dividend should be more than sufficient to purchase the needed dollar amount of 1-year term insurance (i.e., equal to cash value), the excess could either be taken as income by the executive or used to purchase either additional term or paid-up insurance. Another variation is when only the first four of seven annual premiums are paid, with the remaining three financed by borrowing against the policy value (the IRS requires that not more than 3 of the first 7 years may be paid by borrowing in order to deduct the interest charges). Similarly, subsequent premiums are paid through a combination of cash payments and borrowings from the policy cash value. The four-of-seven rule has the advantage of minimizing cash flow.

Another approach worth exploring is an increasing contribution by the employee over the life of the contract. Since amounts by which the individual's payment exceeds the P.S. 58 table cannot be carried forward as a credit to offset amounts in subsequent years when the rising cash values result in lower executive premiums, an increasing premium payout by the insured related to the rise in the P.S. 58 table may be an appropriate consideration. Since this requires company premium payments in the earlier years in excess of the cash value increase, the premium structure may also employ the above described four-of-seven rule to more closely approximate the P.S. 58 rates.

If the executive retires, the company is normally reimbursed for its premium payments by the executive. This buy-out can be accomplished normally by a loan against the policy value. More stringent forfeiture provisions can be incorporated into the policy for voluntary separation, especially if the policy is owned by the company, thus structuring golden handcuffs to encourage retention.

However, as stated earlier, if the policy is surrendered, the amount received (i.e., the cash surrender value) less the net premiums paid will be considered ordinary income to the company. If payment is due to death of the insured, then there are no income consequences to the recipients.

In addition to being a definite status symbol, a split dollar insurance program can be of real value where there is a very large estate liability (e.g., a significant amount of deferred stock). Although the insurance settlement is not subject to income tax, it will be subject to estate taxes (unless it has been successfully removed from the estate through assignment). Thus, insurance proceeds can be very helpful in paying the estate taxes on other aspects of the estate (preventing or at least minimizing the degree of their dissolution to pay tax requirements). One should be careful in including shareholder-employees under split dollar plans, for the IRS may rule that the value of the insurance (i.e., the P.S. 58 cost) in excess of that paid by the individual will be considered a dividend.

Probably one of the greatest illustrations of need is when the company has deferred a portion of the executive's pay until after retirement and such payment is made on a scheduled basis (e.g., over 15 years). Although the beneficiary of the deferrals may be subject to the same earn-out schedule, it is most probable that the present value of all future payments will become part of the executive's estate for tax purposes. It is difficult enough to liquidate assets to pay taxes; needless to say, it is much harder to pay taxes when the assets are not available for liquidation.

On the other hand there is not much justification for such a program for a bachelor executive with no family financial obligations. The insurance might simply reduce the stipend otherwise left to some educational or charitable institution.

While there is no impact to the corporate earnings statement, it must be recognized that the company is loaning corporate cash with the benefit of neither tax deduction nor investment opportunity. Covering 30 to 40 executives might well mean an outlay of a million dollars or more a year, depending on the amount of insurance and the premium split. Some policies have attempted to address this shortcoming by paying an interest on the cash value; for most companies, however, this amount is only a small fraction of their normal return on investment. This is of course further compounded by inflation while the contract is in force. Thus, company-paid premiums are significantly deflated in real value when finally returned.

And finally some will argue that similar objectives can be accomplished through the use of less expensive term insurance. This can be done either through individual or group term policies. One such approach is the retired lives reserve (RLR) concept.

Retired Lives Reserve

The RLR concept has the company prefund the executive's postretirement life insurance by making tax deductible contributions to a reserve fund (which in turn pays for the cost of insurance protection after retirement), purchasing a deferred life insurance policy, or continuing premium payments after retirement.

Normally this approach would have a trustee own the policy and be the beneficiary of a post-65 life insurance policy on the executive. If the executive died after retirement, the trust would receive the proceeds and pay them to the beneficiary designated by the executive. If the executive died before age 65, the beneficiary would receive the life insurance proceeds directly from the carrier under the pre-65 policy. An executive who died before 65 would have no rights under the post-65 plan, and the proceeds paid to the trust from the RLR would be used to reduce the company's premium obligations on other covered executives. Proceeds paid directly to the company would be considered taxable income.

Revenue Ruling 69-382 allows deductions by the company of prefunded retirement life insurance if: (1) the reserve is solely for providing life insurance benefits to those covered, (2) the amounts in reserve may not be returned to the company as long as any covered employees or retirees are alive, and (3) annual additions to the reserve are not greater than needed to meet the insurance obligations. This type of deduction was further protected by Revenue Ruling 73-599, which ruled that retired lives reserve plans are not deferred compensation plans. If they were, the company could not take deductions when paid but rather when received by the beneficiary.

The executive has no tax liability under the RLR before 65, although the person is of course subject to imputed income for amounts of insurance in excess of $50,000. Furthermore it appears that as long as the RLR is deemed to be group life insurance after retirement, the retired executive has no new tax liability at that point either. Assuming the individual has successfully assigned the policy it may also be possible to avoid estate taxes, although under Revenue Ruling 76-490 the executive is considered to have made a gift each year of the value of the assigned group life insurance benefit.

Some argue that RLR is a more cost effective approach than split dollar insurance to meet similar objectives. At least the company is obtaining a tax deduction on the RLR cost, and it appears that the executive's tax liability may be more favorable than under split dollar insurance.

However, the IRS may be concerned with the selectivity of RLR policies for executives in mega amounts and whether such insurance is really permanent (not term) insurance. Both strike at the application of Section 79 definitions. If RLR is not Section 79, then the protection while retired may not be free of income tax consequences and the cost may not be deductible to the company until the benefits are paid.

Due to the complexities of insurance plan variations, it is critical that the executive examine the available alternatives very carefully. Due to individual needs and circumstances, one form will be more appropriate than another. Thus, the assistance of an attorney and accountant along with an insurance expert in designing the optimal plan is critical.

RETIREMENT

There are really three types of employees: those who really want to work, those who might want to work, and those who are going to retire at age 65 or sooner. The company's position is either it wants the employee to stay or it is happy to see the individual leave. These combinations are shown in Table 6-5.

TABLE 6-5 Company and Executive Positions on the Retirement Matrix

	The company's position	
The individual's position	Individual should stay	Individual should leave
Wants to stay	A	B
May want to stay	C	D
Wants to leave	E	F

Situations A and F are simple because there is an agreement of opinion. Situation B is where the company must ensure that performance appraisals have been carefully documented in order that the individual may have a graceful exit at, if not before, age 65. The performance records are to ward off age discrimination suits where ADEA executive exemptions are not in effect. If severance of employment is appropriate before age 65, it will be necessary to ensure there is an adequate severance package, such as discussed earlier.

In situation C the company is trying to convince the individual it is appropriate to stay. Here it is important that the intrinsic as well as extrinsic rewards to the individual are carefully laid out and described. Conversely, in situation D the company needs to ensure that a carefully thought-out package for the executive is ready and is supplemented with extensive preretirement counseling, thus providing the basis for the executive to voluntarily retire.

A tough situation is E because the executive wants to leave but the company wants the person to stay, probably a reflection of poor management development and succession planning. Probably the best that can be hoped for is a very short extension of the delay in leaving (e.g., 1 year). By definition the package has to be more attractive than in situation C simply because the executive is more inclined to leave.

There are three approaches to executive supplemental pensions: (1) restoring that amount payable under the formula but limited by ERISA, (2) increasing the formula for all conditions of service and (3) increasing the formula for short-service executives who have had insufficient time with the company to accrue meaningful benefits. These shall be reviewed in terms of the above company/employee position matrix. Furthermore, while noncompete restrictions cannot be added to the qualified defined benefit or contribution plan, since they are in conflict with the vesting requirements of ERISA, such a provision could be added to any supplemental benefits applicable only to executives and not subject to the provisions of ERISA.

ERISA Limit

Restoring the ERISA limited amount is the most common action of the three as it appears that a majority of companies affected have adopted a resolution to pay the difference (if any) between that allowed by ERISA and that payable by terms of their pension plan out of corporate assets. A few have adopted alternative maximums (such as two times ERISA), although one could question whether these maximums have any meaning. The majority take the view that (1) there is a maximum of plan benefits simply through the application of the plan formula, (2) there is no reason for executives to receive less benefit in terms of the formula than anyone else, and (3) establishing a maximum within the plan requires a logic for that value. Furthermore if the maximum is expressed in absolute dollars, the shareholders must periodically be requested to increase the amount—an action that consumes time, effort, and expense.

Benefit Formula Increase

Increasing the formula for all conditions of service is less prevalent than improving the benefits for short-service executives simply because the continuity and smoothness of the annuity as a percentage of pay curve (page 121) is disrupted. Although ERISA permits unfunded pensions for executives, it permits them for only a limited number of people, and thus those falling below this cutoff (which could include a number of very key management people) would probably have the lowest percentage of pay replacement of all employees! Thus, rather than tinker with the pension plan the same objective can be accomplished through deferral features of the long-term incentive plans. Another qualified plan feature that results in low pensions for executives is the exclusion of bonus payments in the definition of earnings. Applying the principle of parsimony would suggest modifying the basic formula definition rather than developing a supplemental plan.

Short-Service Plans

Where short-service supplemental plans exist, they normally are part of an umbrella formula which will include all payments the executive is eligible to receive, including (1) pension benefits from the basic plan, (2) pension benefits from other employers, (3) annuity values from savings or profit sharing plans, (4) social security benefits, and (5) deferred compensation payments from the long-term incentive plan or salary.

How Much to Supplement

In developing supplemental pension plans it is necessary to determine the target amount (normally expressed as a percentage of current salary or total direct pay of salary and short-term incentive in relation to age and years of service). For example, one might conclude that this total should be approximately equal to that for lower-paid employees (i.e., 75 to 80 percent) at age 65 with 30 years of service.

Next the minimum benefit target is determined; assume that this is set at 45 percent (a probable plan benefit for a 65-year-old executive with 30 years of service) for meeting minimum early retirement eligibility of age 55 with 10 years of service. Based on these two targets it is possible to set up a formula for interpolation. For example the 75 percent is based on an age and service combination of 95 whereas the minimum benefit of 45 percent equals a 65 combination. Thus by crediting one point for every year of service and year of age over 65 and adding it to 45, the target percentage can be calculated (e.g., age 63 with 18 years equals 81; $81 - 65 = 16$; $16 + 45 = 61$ percent).

Another way to develop the formula is by setting up a matrix with target percentages of final pay for specific combinations of years of service and age at retirement. The simplified matrix shown in Table 6-6 suggests that 15 years of service with retirement at age 65 should be comparable in benefit to 30 years, retiring at age 50. Some may

TABLE 6-6 Years of Service and
Retirement Age Matrix

Retirement age	Years of service	
	15	30
65	50%	75%
55	25	50

agree, others disagree; the point is simply that a matrix presentation permits examining various combinations easily and quickly, one versus the other.

There are other approaches: (1) increasing the years of service credit (e.g., 30 at 65 or actual, whichever is greater), (2) crediting short service at a higher formula (e.g., first 10 years at 2.0 percent, next 10 years at 1.75 percent, and anything beyond at 1.5 percent), (3) increasing the plan benefit by a stated amount (e.g., 50 percent), and (4) lowering the discount for early retirement (e.g., nonreduced at age 60 instead of 65 with discount beginning at age 60 at 4 percent per year). All these are ways to generate a special executive pension. It should be remembered that, while these approaches relate to the basic plan, they cannot be incorporated into the basic plan without having them apply to all participants.

In addition to such supplements being attractive to the executive they can also be very important to the company to: (1) attract a highly qualified mid-career executive from another company, (2) establish a consistent approach for top people and thereby avoid a number of individual special plans, and (3) terminate an executive no longer meeting performance expectations.

In return for these special supplements some companies require a "no compete" agreement with the executive to ensure that he or she does not hire on with a competitor and work against the company. Similarly such benefits would not apply to a person who, although eligible, resigned to accept other employment (even if outside industry).

Legal Requirements

The federal Age Discrimination in Employment Act (ADEA) prohibits involuntary retirement by the company prior to age 70 except for those individuals meeting certain tests for bona fide executives (e.g., the head of a major local or regional operation and the head of a major department or division) *and* having a combined company pension (e.g., defined benefit and defined contribution), excluding social security and payments from other employers, of at least $27,000. Several states have similar laws. Such individuals, assuming they were bona fide executives at least 2 years immediately preceding retirement, may be retired by the company beginning at age 65 without concern for violating the terms of the act. For many, it is currently far easier to meet the definition of "executive" under the law than to attain the minimum pension; however, since the latter amount is not indexed it means that with pay (and therefore accrued pension benefits) increasing each year, more and more individuals will be come eligible for automatic retirement between the ages of 65 and 70. Although there are exceptions, most companies want their executives to retire not later than age 65 (in order to open promotional opportunities), and therefore offering financial incentives through supplementary pension arrangements is a logical approach—especially if they were structured to only apply before attainment of a certain age. For example, only executives retiring before age 62 would receive the supplemental pension benefits. Even the loss of 3 years of pay (and its impact on the pension benefit) would probably not make up for the loss of the supplement and would result in a lot of retirements at or before age 62. For those who stayed on, the automatic retirement under the $27,000 ADEA requirement would probably catch them at 65.

For some, the ability to voluntarily *defer compensation* is a perquisite; this topic is discussed at length in Chapter 9. The tax effectiveness rating is 0.93, and as the name implies, the tax is deferred until time of payment.

Lump Sum Distribution

Executives may find a lump sum distribution very attractive if they either: (a) need income to start up a new venture or (b) can afford to put it aside in an IRA and live on other income. Another alternative to the IRA is an annuity purchased from an insurance company. This becomes attractive when the lump sum is greater than the amount needed to buy an annuity equal to that available under the company plan. The degree of interest is even greater if the executive's good health lengthens the odds of reaching or exceeding normal life expectancy.

SUMMARY AND CONCLUSIONS

Most companies are troubled with balancing off (1) wanting to do something special for their top executives with (2) not wanting to open the door for broader coverage after others learn of the program. There is no easy answer to the concern: it is a matter of determining the extent to which the company has an egalitarian philosophy versus wishing to single out several individuals as being more equal than others.

The grid in Table 6-7 summarizes the tax effectiveness ratios believed to be in effect. As indicated earlier, since this is a rapidly changing area and much depends on the specifics of the situation, it is important to check the situation with counsel.

In addition to being tax effective, the perquisite must be logical given the SEC rule of disclosure. It was only a few years ago that some companies sought out items which did not have to be identified in the proxy statement. Full-reimbursement medical plans, company cars, and other perquisites became very popular. Since the SEC has lifted the

TABLE 6-7 Perquisite Tax Treatment Summary

	Unattractive	Attractive	Very attractive
Time off with pay			
Employment contract		0.93	
Liberalized vacation		0.93	
Work at home		0.93	
Disability		0.93	1.85
Sabbatical		0.93	
Severance pay		0.93	
Outplacement assistance			1.85
Employee services			
Company product samples		0.93	1.85*
Automobile		0.93	1.85*
Chauffeured limousine		0.93	1.85*
Security system		0.93	1.85*
Parking—company premises			1.85
Parking—other		0.93	
Aircraft		0.93	1.85*
Yacht	0.50		1.85*
Dining room		0.93	1.85*
Physical fitness			1.85
Apartment/hotel		0.93	1.85*
Legal service		0.93	
Tax assistance			1.85
Financial counseling		0.93	1.85
Nonperformance awards			
Title			∞
Office			1.85
Washroom			1.85*
Liberalized expense account		0.93	1.85*
Club membership	0.50	0.93	1.85*
Season tickets		0.93	1.85*
Credit cards		0.93	1.85*
Home entertainment		0.93	1.85*
Domestic staff		0.93	1.85*
Conventions			1.85*
First-class travel			1.85*
Personal escort			1.85*
Spouse travel expenses		0.93	1.85*
Business liability insurance			1.85
Personal liability insurance		0.93	
Education for children		0.93	
Loan			1.85 ∞

TABLE 6-7 Perquisite Tax Treatment Summary

	Unattractive	Attractive	Very attractive
Health care			
Medical examinations			1.85
Supplemental health care		0.93	1.85
Survivor protection			
Business travel			1.85
Assignment protection		0.93	
Key employee insurance			∞
Kidnap and ransom			1.85
Term/permanent		0.93	
Split dollar			∞
Retired lives reserve		0.93	1.85
Retirement			
ERISA supplement		0.93	
Full supplement		0.93	
Short-service supplement		0.93	
Deferral of pay		0.93	

*That portion identified as business expense.

corporate skirts slightly with its perquisite disclosure requirements, some shy executives are blushing from the exposure. Current rules provide that if perks exceed $10,000 for any individual they must be detailed in the proxy (see Table 6-8).

An additional factor is that it is not improbable that the IRS will compare such data with that reported by the individuals in their tax returns. Thus it is critical that the executive have detailed records differentiating personal benefit from business use. In some instances it appears that the cost of establishing procedures and maintaining records will exceed the cost of the perquisite, especially when the IRS and the SEC view the same event differently. For example, hitching a nonbusiness seat on the corporate jet making a business flight may not be considered income by the IRS but is likely to be reportable as remuneration by the SEC.

When executives find they must pay full taxes on some perquisites, the perks lose a significant amount of their appeal. For example if personal use of a company car results in a $2500 tax liability, the executive must earn an additional $5000 to pay for it (one half going to pay for the tax on the salary, the other half for the tax on the perquisites). It is not surprising that some executives and companies substitute pay increases for perquisites—although the company cost to deliver the same economic benefit to the executive is twice as much.

One approach that has some appeal is to give individual executives a perquisite allowance of a specified annual dollar amount. This could be a common percentage of pay (e.g., 5 percent). Thus a $100,000 executive might have a $5000 allowance, while the

TABLE 6-8   Perquisites Proxy Treatment*

Time off with pay
    Employment contract   Column C_1 or D and textual disclosure
    Liberalized vacation   Part of compensation C_1
    Work at home   Part of compensation C_1
    Disability   Part of compensation C_1
    Sabbatical   Part of compensation C_1
    Severance pay   Part of compensation C_1
    Outplacement assistance   May require textual disclosure

Employee Services
    Company product samples C_2 unless all employees eligible
    Automobile C_2 for personal portion not paid by executive
    Chauffeured limousine C_2 for personal portion not paid by executive
    Security system   Probably nothing
    Parking—company premises   Probably nothing
    Parking—other C_2
    Aircraft C_2 for personal portion not paid by executive
    Yacht C_2 for personal portion not paid by executive
    Dining room   Probably nothing
    Physical fitness   Probably nothing
    Apartment/hotel C_2 for personal portion not paid by executive
    Legal service C_2 for personal portion not paid by executive
    Tax assistance C_2 for personal portion not paid by executive
    Financial counseling C_2 for personal portion not paid by executive

Nonperformance awards
    Title   Column B
    Office   Nothing
    Washroom   Nothing
    Liberalized expense account C_1 for nonbusiness items
    Club membership C_2 for personal portion not paid by executive
    Season tickets C_2 for personal use
    Credit cards   Probably nothing
    Home entertainment C_2 for personal portion not paid by executive
    Domestic staff C_2 for personal portion not paid by executive
    Conventions   Probably nothing
    First-class travel   Probably nothing
    Personal escort   Probably nothing
    Spouse travel expenses C_2 for personal portion not paid by executive
    Business liability insurance   Nothing
    Personal liability insurance C_2
    Education for children C_2
    Loan   Possibly C_2 plus textual disclosure

TABLE 6-8   Perquisites Proxy Treatment*

Health care	
Medical examinations	Nothing
Supplemental health care	C_2 plus textual disclosure
Survivor protection	
Business travel	Probably nothing
Assignment protection	May require textual disclosure
Key employee insurance	May require textual disclosure
Kidnap and ransom	May require textual disclosure
Term/permanent	D and textual disclosure
Split dollar	D and textual disclosure
Retired lives reserve	D and textual disclosure
Retirement	
ERISA supplement	Textual disclosure
Full supplement	Textual disclosure
Short-service supplement	Textual disclosure
Deferral of pay	C_2 or D plus textual disclosure

*Executive benefits are to be reported in their incremental cost to the company. Additional footnote disclosure is appropriate if the value to the executive exceeds this cost.

$250,000 person would receive $12,500. There are two ways the program could be constructed; business only and personal only. While the two could be combined, it would create a hybrid tax situation to the executive, who would have a tax liability on the personal items but not the business portion, and therefore the combination approach may not be attractive. The value of this type of program is that it recognizes individuals have different needs and perceived values. Therefore, rather than identifying specific programs and making participation automatic, the programs are available for use based on the individual executive's own interests. The problem with such an approach deals with the administrative design, costing, and record-keeping aspects.

Short-Term Incentives

Since salaries are rarely reduced, they cannot be used effectively to adequately reward outstanding performance for short-term results (i.e., a year) since there is no assurance that the level of performance will be maintained. Short-term incentives therefore are implemented to introduce greater fluctuation in pay in recognition of performance or lack thereof. While there may be hesitancy about granting a $100,000 executive a 40 percent salary increase, there is much less reticence about granting a $40,000 bonus (on the assumption that all or a large part will not be granted the following year if performance drops).

Short-term incentive plans range from highly individualistic rewards for individual accomplishment to sophisticated profit-sharing plans due to the emphasis on corporate, group, and/or division performance with little variance for individual recognition. The main drawback of the latter is that it will overpay the marginal performer in good years and underpay the outstanding performer in the poor years.

Furthermore, a low-salary–high-bonus mix will mean overpaying mediocre performers in good years and losing top-quality executives in poor years. Conversely, a high-salary–low-bonus combination will reinforce mediocre performance in poor years by overpaying the marginal performers.

Thus the incentives are the visible result of a reward (for successful performance) and punishment (for less than outstanding accomplishment) system. Unfortunately as we will see, many companies are more interested in the form than the substance, since too few are prepared to measure performance and pay for the degree of accomplishment. This seems especially true with discretionary plans, which probably have the least degree of fluctuations. Many executives find it easier to hide behind a formula.

While there is no federal law requiring shareholder approval of the incentive plan, some states have requirements for those companies incorporated under their laws. Similarly the stock exchange on which the company stock is listed may have such a requirement (e.g., New York Stock Exchange). Also the SEC requires textual disclosure of how the plan operates for officers and directors.

The basic decisions regarding short term incentives are: (1) eligibility, (2) fund determination, and (3) individual awards.

ELIGIBILITY

Eligibility is normally determined by one of three methods: key position, salary, or salary grade.

Using the *key position* approach means examining each job for appropriateness; this is done when there is a desire to include only those positions with "bottom-line" responsibility. Administratively this has two drawbacks. First, it is possible that two jobs in the same salary grade will be treated differently—one eligible for bonus, the other not. Normally this would require discounting the salary structure for the bonus-eligible by at least a portion of the bonus—usually the normal or minimum award. Second, it will be necessary to review the list of eligibles on almost an annual basis for appropriate

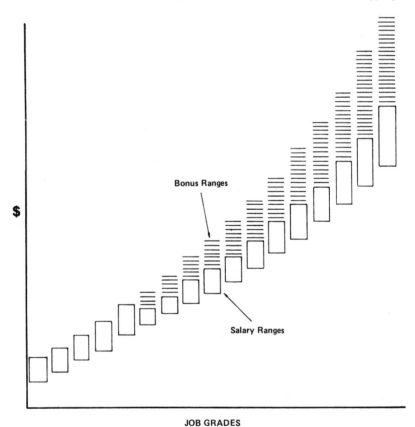

JOB GRADES

FIGURE 7-1   Salary and bonus ranges.

additions and deletions. This approach is generally more prevalent among small than among large organizations. When used it normally results in few if any staff jobs being eligible for bonuses, thus making it more difficult to move individuals internally.

Using *salary* to identify eligibility is much simpler, once the appropriate salary level is identified; however, it also has several drawbacks. First, it gives a false degree of finiteness to eligibility—$50,000 and up "yes" versus $49,999 and below "no." Second, considerable pressure will be exerted by division presidents to move people above the magic cutoff. Third, the cutoff must be adjusted annually in relation to compensation adjustments, for otherwise the size of eligibles will be continually increasing.

The use of *salary grade* to determine short-term incentive eligibility is probably the most common approach among larger corporations. The rationale is simple: the value of the jobs to the organization has already been determined when each job was placed in a salary grade (and given a minimum and maximum range). The approach is superior to use of salary in that it relates to the job, not to the person's earnings. However, it does place the same type of pressure on the compensation program; division presidents will continue to press for upgrading positions into the eligible group. It can also cause some administrative problems since discounting the salary for the bonus will mean the maximum salary for the first bonus-eligible grade may be less than the one immediately below it, as shown in Figure 7-1.

There are no inviolate rules about how far down in the organization short-term incentive plans should go. However they should not go further than where performance can have a significant impact on the organizational unit. For many, bonus eligibility begins somewhere around $40,000 to $50,000. Conversely, if senior executives are included (and it is logical to reward them for short-term success), it is important that the target amounts be carefully examined in terms of potential payouts under long-term incentives. If short-term incentives are financially more attractive, it will be difficult for executives to focus on long-term issues.

In highly profitable, heavily capitalized, high-technology decentralized companies in the maturity phase, 3 percent or more of the total employee population may be affected; in low-profitability, labor-intensive, low-technology, strongly centralized operations in the threshold stage, less than 1 percent may be affected. The specific combination of these factors, as shown in Table 7-1, has a strong impact on the percentage of eligible employees in a specific company.

TABLE 7-1   Percentage of Employee Population Eligible for Short-Term Incentives

Low percent	High percent
Low profitability	High profitability
Labor-intensive	Capital-intensive
Low technology	High technology
Centralized management	Decentralized management
Threshold stage	Maturity stage

Regardless of the basis, it should be recognized that requests for expanding the eligibles will begin within a very short time. Therefore it is necessary not simply to have a rational basis at the time the plan is introduced but also to consider how the eligibles will be expanded and over what period of time. An alternative is to have a firm basis for indicating the demarcation. Unfortunately situations where there is clearly a difference between eligibles and ineligibles are rare. There is almost invariably a gray area. Yet it is a simple "go" or "no-go" situation as viewed by the individuals, who see themselves as either bonus-eligible or not.

Simply the status of being on the bonus plan is sufficient reason for the ineligibles to lobby for expansion. The problem is compounded if there is a significant compensation difference between the lowest and the highest eligibles.

We will return later to the subject of eligibility when we discuss the awards, but first it is necessary to discuss the second element, the fund.

THE FUND

Some organizations do not have a stated formula for developing the bonus fund, or if they do, it varies yearly depending on how much management wishes to pay (e.g. an amount equal to 10 percent of salaries). However, most corporations provide for a mathematical formula that will be applied to corporate financial results to determine how many dollars will be allocated for payment. While formulas vary greatly, as can be seen in Table 7-2, they often begin with a percentage of profits (either pretax or after-tax) and proceed to make some consideration for shareholders' equity or provide for a dividend of a minimum amount. The formula should articulate the basic objectives of the company. Is there a minimum rate to be provided for shareholder return? Is there a minimum increase (dollar or percentage) in earnings before any bonus can be paid? Should executives be rewarded on top-line (pretax) or bottom-line (after-tax) results? The latter increases the identification with the shareholder but does so at the risk of allowing tax policy to have a significant impact on the bonus fund. Will the impact of extraordinary items be removed from the formula values? If so, within the Financial Accounting Standards Board (FASB) requirements, who will make the decision?

It is important to be cognizant of the impact of accounting requirements. For example the issuance in October 1975 of FASB Statement No. 8 has had a significant impact on the P&L of many companies. This opinion, "Accounting for the Translation of Foreign Currency Transactions and Foreign Currency Financial Statements," has in the opinion of some gone counter to generally accepted accounting procedures (GAAP), namely that while potential losses are recognized when they are ascertainable, potential profits should be recognized only when they are actually realized. The requirement of costing inventory at historical rather than current rates of exchange, coupled with the report of unrealized exchange gains, has caused the quarterly earnings statements of a number of companies to resemble gigantic roller coasters. Needless to say this also has a significant impact on the short-term incentive plan if not taken into consideration.

Perhaps payment on definitions that prevailed before issuance of FASB Statement No. 8 is appropriate, but that means a double accounting standard which may be difficult to explain to inquiring shareholders. Another approach would be to develop a basis for averaging the data, such as a moving average linear analysis.

It is important that the formal plan (including the fund formula) be as broad as possible to allow the executive compensation committee to make specific determinations within the plan parameters.

TABLE 7-2   Short-Term Incentive Fund Formulas

1. 12½ percent of consolidated net income less 6 percent of the average common stock equity less the amount of current dividends for the year

2. 10 percent of net income after deducting 5 percent of average capital in business

3. 6 percent of profits after taxes that are in excess of 6 percent of capital

4. 8 percent of the first $5 million net income plus 10 percent of the next $5 million plus 1 percent of the remainder after net income has been reduced by the larger of: (a) 6 percent of average net capital, (b) dividends on preferred stock plus $2.50 per share of common stock

5. 6 percent of net earnings before taxes and percentage compensation or 8 percent of earnings after taxes and percentage compensation

6. 6 percent of net earnings before taxes, after deducting 10 percent of capital employed

7. 10 percent of the excess after dividend requirements of preferred stock plus 5½ percent of the total stated value of common stock plus 5½ percent of the surplus

8. 12½ percent of the amount by which net income exceeds 6 percent of stockholders' equity

9. 15 percent of net income (plus minority interest in net income less variable compensation and interest on long-term debt) less 7 percent of invested capital

10. 20 percent of bonus net income (net income less 6 percent of capital stock and surplus for current and preceding years plus provision for B bonus fund)

11. The amount by which net earnings before taxes plus 10 percent of invested capital exceed $10 million

12. 12 percent of net earnings after deducting 6 percent of net capital

13. 3 percent of the amount by which net income exceeds 6 percent of capital investment

14. 2⅛ percent of the total combined salaries of plan participants multiplied by the percentage points that consolidated income exceeds 35 percent of capital employed—to a maximum of 35 percent of total combined salaries of plan participants

15. 3 percent of the first $15 million net income plus 5 percent of net income exceeding $15 million

16. 6 percent of net income, maximum equal to 25 percent of aggregate paid dividends on common stock

17. 6 percent of the amount by which consolidated pretax earnings exceed 10 percent of shareholder's equity

Once the basic objectives have been identified, the formula values can be set by determining the number of bonus participants and the approximate amount of bonus dollars needed in a good year after viewing the overall profitability, requirements for capital expenditures, and the stability of profits. Certainly, (1) the higher the profits, (2) the lower the capital requirements, and/or (3) the more stable the profits, the lower the formula figures. To the extent any of these three are affected to the contrary, the formula percentages rise to allow for an adequate fund.

To quickly estimate the needed amount, multiply the percent eligible times the percent of their pay to be paid in incentives to determine the percent of payroll. The latter multiplied by the payroll indicates approximate dollars. For example if 20 percent of the monthly paid employees are to be eligible and the awards are to average 10 percent of their salary, then a fund of approximately $2 million is required for a $100 million payroll. It should be remembered this is an approximation that will consistently err on the *low* side because the eligibles are paid more than the average for the total group. This can be easily adjusted if one knows the average salary for the eligibles versus the total payroll. Thus if the eligibles average approximately $50,000 in salary versus $25,000 for all monthly paid, then the fund is $4 million (i.e., $2 million $\times$ 2).

To build the formula, determine how much bonus should be generated under moderate, successful, and very successful financial conditions. By summing the desirable bonus amount for each eligible under the three conditions, it is possible to determine how much total bonus is needed. Normally this is adjusted upward by another 10 to 20 percent (rather err on the high than the low side). Once the amount needed has been calculated, trial and error with various formulas will find the one that best meets the requirements.

One of the main problems in constructing the formula, therefore, is generating an adequate amount. It is here that the very common *deductible* or threshold approach (e.g., X percent of net income minus Y percent of common stock equity) results in a very steep trend line. After a few years, the formula often is generating an embarrassingly high amount because of corporate financial growth (factors in the formula often move faster than the number and base earnings of the eligibles). When the formula generates more than is allocated, a decision must be made (assuming the plan permits) whether to return to net income or carry over a portion to the next year. The rationale for the latter approach is to offset extraordinary circumstances (a real concern if the formula is especially "tight"); the danger is that such an approach may result in paying out almost as much in mediocre years as in outstanding periods—giving confusing signals to both executives and shareholders.

Conversely such deductible formulas cause problems if the company has a loss year. The issue is not with the bonus that year, for obviously there is no bonus (assuming no carryover from previous periods). However, since a loss reduces the company's net worth, it thereby lowers the deductible the following year. Thus the company pays out a greater than planned portion of earnings during profitable years following loss years. To illustrate, assume the formula is 10 percent of the amount by which net income exceeds 6 percent of shareholder equity. At the end of the first year shareholder equity is $100 million, net income is $7 million, and the bonus fund equals $100,000. The second year the company experiences a $1 million loss, thereby reducing shareholder equity to $99 million, and the bonus fund is, of course, zero. The third year the company returns to its profitable ways with an $8.5 million net earnings figure. Assuming no dividends paid during the periods (simply to uncomplicate the example), net worth is now $107.5 million and the bonus fund equals $205,000 (i.e., 10 percent of the amount $8.5 million exceeds 6 percent of $107.5 million). This is $6000 more than if the previous year had been a no-earnings–no-loss year. Even more dramatically, if the company had earnings of $7.7 million the second year (thereby showing a 10 percent increase in both the second and third year), the bonus that year would have been about $124,000, but the bonus the third year (because net worth would be $116.2 million not $107.5) would be $153,000—over $50,000 less.

Some will argue that it is more difficult to show such a turnaround after a loss year; be that true or not, recognize that this type of formula encourages a cyclical earnings pattern rather than steady growth. It is certainly to management's advantage to ensure that all costs that can be taken are taken in a year where it is clear that earnings will not exceed 10 percent of shareholder equity.

For this reason the *limitation* or tandem type formula seems more appropriate (e.g., *A* percent of net income or *X* percent of net income minus *Y* percent of common stock equity, whichever is lower). As shown in Figure 7-2, it gives protection against payout at low net income levels and tempers against runaway conditions for high net income attainment. Since companies in the mature stage are less likely to generate fluctuations of the magnitude of a threshold or growth company, developing a bonus fund is less risky.

Selecting the most appropriate formula is very important. For example, using a deductible formula in regard to return on capital can encourage management to avoid making full use of its borrowing capacity. For example, if the bonus fund is generated by a formula taking 8 percent of net income in excess of 10 percent on capital, any investment return of less than 10 percent (after taxes) would lower executive bonuses.

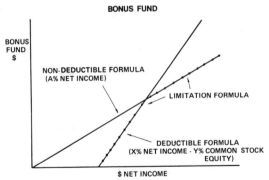

FIGURE 7-2 Bonus fund formulas (deductible—nondeductible—limitation).

Thus it might be attractive from a shareholder viewpoint to borrow at 9 percent pretax (4.5 percent after tax) and get an 18 percent pretax (9 percent after-tax) return but since this action would reduce the bonus fund, it is financially unattractive to management.

Another variation on net worth is use of earnings per share. However, this may place undue emphasis on meeting financing needs by withholding dividends and increasing debt financing, when equity financing might be the most appropriate.

Where two factors (e.g., growth in EPS and return on capital) are prime objectives, a matrix can be built to determine payment level at any combination of performance, as shown in Figure 7-3. For example, if the compound growth in EPS were 11.5 percent and the average rate of return on capital for the same period were 14.5 percent, the normal award would be increased by 25 percent. In constructing such a matrix it is important to test all combinations to ensure the payout level is logical given the other possibilities. In addition, the matrix can be expanded if a third factor is considered essential. For example, to better relate to shareholder objectives, perhaps the compound annual change in the stock price should also be used. Thus if the stock decreased an average of 4.6 percent over the period, then, in our example the normal award would be 119.25 percent of normal award (i.e., 125 percent times 95.4 percent).

Also, formulas which do not take into consideration growth relative to the industry can be either too generous or too conservative. Consider the situation of a company with a consistent 10 percent growth in net earnings over 5 years while its industry has shown 5, 7.5, 10, 12.5, and 15 percent. One could argue that the executives were underrewarded during the first years and overcompensated during the later years on a plan that had a constant percent of net earnings set aside for a bonus fund.

This type of scenario causes many companies to attempt to adjust the bonus fund on performance relative to others in the industry. For example, the EPS of the company could be compared to a select group of companies, and to the extent it was above or below the average of this group the fund would be adjusted, as shown in Table 7-3.

Unfortunately this approach is cleaner in concept than in fact simply because of weight of product mix even among companies that are supposedly comparable. The companies to be included and the basis for weighting are sufficiently open to debate in most cases that, to the extent the analysis does not generate the amount management thinks appropriate, there will be pressure to modify the basis of comparison.

In any event, fund formulas need to be reviewed on a regular basis to ensure they

Compound Growth in EPS Over Period	% of Normal Award Payable				
15% and up	100%	125%	150%	175%	200%
13.0% – 14.9%	75	100	125	150	175
11.0% – 12.9%	50	75	100	125	150
9.0% – 10.9%	25	50	75	100	125
Below 9%	0	25	50	75	100
Average Return on Capital	Below 10%	10.0% – 11.9%	12.0% – 13.9%	14.0% – 15.9%	16% & up

FIGURE 7-3   Award table based on EPS and return on capital.

TABLE 7-3   Bonus Fund versus
Industry Average EPS

EPS as percent of industry average	Adjustment to bonus fund
150%	200%
140	180
130	160
120	140
110	120
100	100
90	80
80	60
70	40
60	20
50	0

are consistent under current company conditions. One reason many plans developed 10 or more years ago are generating excessive amounts today is that the corporate growth has outdated them. This is especially true for deductible plans.

Divisional Funds

From one main corporate fund, divisional funds may be generated by either quantitative formula or qualitative judgment. Unless, in fact, the division is a wholly integrated operation, it is unlikely that the same type of formula used for the corporate fund can be applied at the division level. Even if it could, the number of participating executives (and their level of pay) often does not relate in a consistent fashion to the profit level, thus making a common formula ineffective. More commonly, reference is made to the degree of success in attaining division goals.

Self-standing division formulas are much more likely to be present in nonrelated multi-industry companies when the corporation's role is essentially one of providing capital. Under such a situation it is not unrealistic to have separate bonus plans for each unit based on percentage of profits above a stated return on investment. As the investment in the unit increases, so does the income needed in order to generate a bonus fund.

The basis for judging divisional performance under a corporate fund can range from use of a single factor (such as return on investment for a profit-making unit) to a number of financial and nonfinancial factors. In addition, bookkeeping calculations can be made to adjust financial performance. For example, divisional profits may be reduced by a corporate charge for use of capital. This could be a simple charge on all capital or a higher charge beyond a certain amount. In the first instance if the company is charging 7.5 percent, a division with $100 million of assets would have profits reduced by $7.5

million; in the second approach the same division would be assessed $7.3 million if the charge were 7 percent on the first $90 million and 10 percent on anything above. Both require determining a minimum percentage to ensure divisions recognize the cost of capital and don't simply rush to increase profit without regard to needed capital. The second formula requires determining the desirable capital base (to ensure the division is not undercapitalized, the formula can be changed to charge only above a specified amount, e.g., $90 million). This must be done on a division-by-division basis. For those who find this too cumbersome, an interim step such as a charge on excess inventories can have a similar effect although more narrowly defined (in this case keep inventories down).

While use of one factor is certainly simpler it means no performance reinforcement for other factors. Regardless of the number of factors, ideally the performance should be quantifiable in accord with a previously agreed-to measuring basis and the various scores identified with specific levels of performance. Also the unit being rated should have access to the data during the year, not simply at year end.

Any payment in relation to profit budget places an emphasis on accurate forecasts. To the extent it is imposed by top management, it is outside the unit's control; to the extent the unit develops it, it encourages conservative estimates. It is also important to recognize that a unit may take actions to increase its own profitability (and bonus fund) by taking actions not in the best interest of the company (or even the unit in the long run).

It can be argued that forecasts and performance can always be adjusted for factors outside the unit's control. Conceptually this is logical; unfortunately it is often difficult to quantify, much less identify, noncontrollable factors.

Not to take into account extraordinary circumstances (i.e., to say "Let the chips fall where they may") is to either overreward mediocre performance or underreward outstanding accomplishments. Some try to rationalize having it both ways (i.e., cutting back when outside events would generate too much bonus, but identifying with shareholders when results are negated by outside events). In such situations the only thing that can be said is that the decision makers are consistent in their inconsistency (i.e., they keep bonus amounts down). For many a more rational approach is, within FASB rules, to consider the impact of extraordinary items in determining the bonus fund. Clearly to the extent management is unprepared or unwilling to make adjustments, it places an unrealistic burden on the efficacy of the bonus formula. Conversely it must resist pressure to make adjustments when bonuses are legitimately low due to less than optimal performance without outside factors.

An approach that can be followed in establishing a quantitative reference begins first with identifying the division's goals—both quantitative and qualitative. Quantitative goals are most directly applicable to marketing and production operations, whereas qualitative goals are more compatible with the staff functions of legal, finance, and personnel. Actually, however, there is crossover, and the quantitative and qualitative goals are present in all functions although admittedly to different degrees. The quantitative goals are measured by "how much," the qualitative goals by "how well."

Each division's goals are listed under the two categories, quantitative and qualitative. Before proceeding any further there must be an understanding between division manager and company president concerning the value of attaining those goals. This step is bypassed by many corporations and it is here that they can get into real trouble. One division manager may be the optimistic type, setting very difficult objectives within an almost-impossible-to-meet timetable; another may know how to play the game, setting goals that, although impressively stated and possibly many in number, are rather easy to attain. The president has two alternatives: either readjust all goals to a reasonable level or, following the concept of mutual agreement, leave the goals unchanged but readjust the normal fund for each division up or down in relation to the difficulty of its objectives.

One of the more difficult tasks is to allocate divisional funds under a short-term incentive plan. In spite of all the formulas developed (including performance relative to others in the industry), a subjective judgment must be made about the degree of difficulty which tempered that performance outcome. However hard it may be to make that assessment, the likelihood of inequity in the treatment of two divisions is much less than if no tempering judgment is applied.

Furthermore it is important that divisions understand that divisional targets have equal stretch and degree of difficulty even though the targets are different. Otherwise very profitable divisions, even though falling below that target, will expect a large payout because their absolute level of achievement exceeds other divisions.

Divisional Goals

Having weighted the sum total of the division's goals and objectives against a normal fund, next it is necessary to relate the value of each of the objectives. The simplest technique is to begin by assigning each objective an equal value and then adjusting plus or minus. To make this work quantitatively, assume a total value of 100. If the division has five goals, each begins with an arbitrary value of 20. This value is adjusted by reference of one to another, after the ranking of the five in order of importance. There is nothing magical. It is merely a trial-and-error method of structuring the basis for determining the subsequent size of the divisional fund at the end of the year.

Having weighted each goal, one to another, next it is necessary to determine how to quantitatively measure the attainment of the objective. Two philosophies emerge. The first states bonus should only be paid for outstanding performance (described as attainment of the specified objective; less means no bonus). This binary approach of either "hit" or "miss" makes a bonus program simple to administrate but makes it very difficult for top management to call a very near miss a zero. Also, while such a program adequately differentiates in pay between outstanding and less than outstanding performers, one must question whether or not it adequately differentiates between poor and adequate performers.

The second approach is one that states that there are degrees of success and failure, and bonuses should be structured accordingly. This second view requires the outlining

TABLE 7-4 Point Schedule versus
EPS Attainment

Percent	Points
21.0 and up	45
20.0	40
19.0	35
18.0	30
17.0	25
16.0	20
15.0 and lower	15

and subsequent weighting of each defined goal. Assume that one of five goals for a division is to increase net earnings from 15 to 18 percent. This goal was given a weighting of 30, instead of an unweighted 20 (i.e., a total of 100 divided by 5 goals); plus and minus values were then constructed as shown in Table 7-4. Note that it is even possible to relate attainment in fractions of a point, if such were desirable (e.g., attainment of net earnings in the amount of 18.5 percent would translate to 32.5 points).

The main point is that although numbers may be used to determine the size of the division fund by the measurement of goals and objectives, it is imperative to realize that this is not a magic numbers show. The construction of the weighting scale, especially in the measurement of qualitative goals, is only as good as the judgment of the person doing the rating.

Other Ways of Allocating Funds

Another basic approach to allocating funds is shown in Table 7-5. In addition to the handful of top executives (whose fund is determined only by corporate success) there are three types of divisions: support staff (e.g., finance, legal, personnel), cost centers (e.g., production) and profit centers (e.g., sales/marketing). Two-thirds of the normal fund for support staff is based on corporate success and one-third on the attainment of their objectives; for cost centers the split is 50-50 between corporate success and divisional success; profit centers have two-thirds of their normal fund determined by their own success or failure and one-third by corporate success.

TABLE 7-5 Corporate versus Unit Performance Allocations

	Performance basis, percent	
	Corporate	Own unit
CEO/president and staff VPs	100	—
Support staff	67	33
Cost centers	50	50
Profit centers	33	67

The rationale for the above is, of course, that the top executives are defined as those people who cross divisional lines in their responsibilities and strive for optimization of corporate success, not that of any one division. Support staff has objectives which cross divisional lines, and their success or failure has a definite effect on corporate success (almost always in minimization of expenses or the optimization of output for the same level of expenses). Cost centers can be quantitatively judged on their failure or success in attaining assigned budgets. Profit centers can most assuredly be judged against sales and profit attainment, but to relate them back as a member of the corporate team, a portion of their normal bonus is predicated on corporate success. Paying division heads strictly on the basis of their own accomplishments (such as ROI, sales, and/or profits) is consistent when the divisions are completely autonomous and transfer of top managers between divisions is not a factor.

A variation of this same theme would move the support staff in with the top executives, making both completely reliant on corporate profits, and keep the profit centers unchanged (2 parts division and 1 part corporate), relating the cost centers on a prorated basis to the profit centers they serve. An example of the latter would be the case where a production division's total output was split: 50 percent chemical business, 35 percent pharmaceutical business, and 15 percent agricultural business. These same percentages would make up the total of its normal award (excluding the corporate one-third). Thus if its normal award was $150,000 with $100,000 being for division attainment, $50,000 would depend on the chemical business meeting its profit objectives, $35,000 on the pharmaceutical, and $15,000 on the agricultural. Obviously, these figures could be adjusted upward or downward, depending on the degree of success or failure of each of the businesses in meeting its profit objectives.

Another variation on this approach is to separate the organization in terms of level of unit (e.g., corporate, group, division, and individual) and determine the effect that each will have on a particular job. As in Table 7-6 the CEO/president and staff vice presidents would have their entire bonuses generated by corporate performance. A group president, on the other hand, might have half the bonus contingent on the group's performance and the other half on the corporate (to ensure corporate visibility). A division president within the group might have half the bonus at risk with division performance and the remainder split between corporate and group achievment. Finally a division vice president could have half the bonus based on divisional performance and the remainder on his or her own achievements.

TABLE 7-6 Allocation of Bonuses: Corporate, Group, Division, and Individual, Percent

	Corporate	Group	Division	Individual
CEO/president and staff VP	100	—	—	—
Operating group VPs	50	50	—	—
Division president	25	25	50	—
Division VP	—	—	50	50

The manner in which divisional and corporate portions are structured will reinforce a particular behavior. For example, placing the entire payout on divisional performance (ignoring group and corporate) will have the division manager taking actions which are self-benefiting regardless of long- or short-term impact on the rest of the organization. In this illustration, the division head realizes that half of the bonus will come from outside the division. Thus the person must be responsive to actions beneficial to the group and corporation as well as the executive's own division.

The Brucell Corporation Example

Regardless of the specific nature of the deviation from the basic approach of two or more funds providing the total award, it is probably important to spend a minute to describe how this interaction is done statistically. An example has to be constructed for this purpose. The Brucell Corporation has 40 salary grades and all persons in grade 20 and up are eligible. It has devised a grid to adjust plus or minus the normal bonus for a division based on profit success. This grid, shown in Table 7-7, is used for corporate profit goals as well as, where appropriate, division goals. As can be seen, this is an abbreviated schedule showing only every fifth grade. However, the reader could easily interpolate to determine the factors for any missing salary grade.

Division A attains 105 percent of its profit goal while the corporation only meets 98 percent of its profit objectives. Query: What is the total fund available for division A? Since in this plan three parts of the fund are based on division success and one part on corporate success, it is necessary to first determine the weighted average guideline percentage. This is done for each job incumbent in each salary grade. An example is a person in grade 30 in division A. The bonus target percent of 25 is adjusted by 5 points (i.e., 5 × 1.00), since the division did 105 percent of target, and is given a weight of 3 for a total of 90 (i.e., 30 × 3); the bonus target percent of 25 is reduced by 5 (i.e., 2 × 2.50), since the corporation only did 98 percent of its objective, and is given a weight of 1 for a total of 20 (i.e., 20 × 1). The two are totaled and the sum of 110 is divided by 4 to equal 27.5 percent.

In a similar fashion, the guideline percentage was weighted out for every person in division A, as shown in Table 7-8. The bonus percentage was then multiplied by the

TABLE 7-7   Bonus Percentages by Salary Grade

Salary grade	Midpoint	Minus per 1 percent	Bonus target percent	Plus per 1 percent	Maximum bonus percent
40	$325,000	3.75	37.5	1.50	52.5
35	175,000	3.13	31.3	1.25	43.8
30	100,000	2.50	25.0	1.00	35.0
25	64,000	1.88	18.8	0.75	26.3
20	42,000	1.25	12.5	0.50	17.5

TABLE 7-8 Guideline Bonus Example—One Division

Salary grade	Employees	Average salary	Guide percent	Guide bonus
30	1	$95,000	27.50	$26,125
26	1	73,000	22.00	16,060
25	1	67,000	20.75	13,903
22	2	53,000	16.50	17,490
20	3	44,000	13.75	18,150
Total				$91,728

total salaries in that salary grade and totaled, resulting in a sum of $91,728 available to that division for bonus distribution.

In many instances this type of divisional calculation is a preliminary rather than final step. If there is a corporate formula which generates a total fund from which corporate and divisional awards are to be made, then preliminary divisional calculations have to be summed and related to the available pool on a proportionate basis, as shown in Table 7-9. In this example, division A's available pool has been reduced from $91,728 to $89,213 because the total available for divisional awards is only $265,911 versus $273,384 (sum of the preliminary awards). If the total available were higher than the aggregate preliminary awards, then each divisional final bonus would be proportionately higher.

A variation on this method of determining divisional awards is to express the performance evaluation in terms of an interim score and later convert this score to a bonus percentage. This can be illustrated with a multigoal requirement.

Multigoal Example

Assume that the corporate goal is to increase net earnings by 10 percent, the group goal is to improve net income before allocation by 12 percent, and the divisional goal is to increase income before corporate allocation by 15 percent. Rating scales such as the ones in Table 7-10 might be developed.

TABLE 7-9 Guideline Bonus Example—Four Divisions

Division	Preliminary bonus Amount	Preliminary bonus Percent total	Total available	Final bonus
A	$ 91,728	33.55	$265,911	$ 89,213
B	62,196	22.75	265,911	60,495
C	45,923	16.80	265,911	44,673
D	73,537	26.90	265,911	71,530
Total	$273,384			$265,911

TABLE 7-10 Evaluation Schedule for Corporation, Group, and Division

Evaluation	Corporation increase in net increase	Group A increase in income before allocation	Division A increase in income before allocation	Evaluation
6	13.0% and up	16.5% and up	21.0% and up	6
5	12.0	15.0	19.0	5
4	11.0	13.5	17.0	4
3	10.0	12.0	15.0	3
2	9.0	10.5	13.0	2
1	8.0	9.0	11.0	1
0	Below	Below	Below	0

Note that in these evaluation grids there is equal reward or penalty for a percentage point; the earlier grid penalized below-goal achievement more severely than it rewarded overachievement. The former is more consistent with a company that has discounted its salary line by some portion of bonus and therefore has to be more tolerant of below-expected performance in allowing some bonus; the latter approach is appropriate for a company that has a competitive salary (without discount) and is therefore prepared to cut back sharply on below-target performance.

Note also that the progression on the division performance table is more dramatic than the corporate (even though both are arithmetic constants).

It appears that division A is in an earlier stage of development than the corporation, although new products and/or significant price increases might be accounting for the difference.

A totally different situation is shown in Table 7-11. Here's a division that is obviously in trouble since its objective is to just break even. Note that the objective is expressed in absolute rather than relative terms (i.e., dollar amount of profit or loss rather than percent change).

Let's assume that division A has several other objectives: sales, return on capital, and

TABLE 7-11 Additional Example of a Divisional Performance Schedule

Income before allocation, millions	Evaluation
$1.5	6
1.0	5
0.5	4
0.0	3
−.5	2
−1.0	1
More	0

TABLE 7-12   Multiple Performance Criteria for One Division

Performance	Increase in net sales	Return on capital	Percentage point increase in parity goal
6	21 % and up	19.0% and up	9.0 and up
5	19.0	18.0	8.0
4	17.0	17.0	7.0
3	15.0	16.0	6.0
2	13.0	15.0	5.0
1	11.0	14.0	4.0
0	Below	Below	Below

affirmative action achievement. The first two are financial, the latter a nonfinancial EEO goal. Shown in Table 7-12 are possibilities for each.

In this instance it could be argued that the three financial objectives are interrelated (i.e., it will be difficult to do poorly on one and well on the other two). This may be true, but identifying and defining performance on each makes the division president more aware of the three.

In this instance the goals have been weighted in the following manner:

Income before allocation	40%
Increase in net sales	30
Return on capital	10
Increase in parity goal	20

The attractiveness of the above-described goals is their quantitative nature. Sometimes the nonfinancial goals are more qualitative in nature, possibly including manpower planning and development, efficacy of long-range planning, and organizational effectiveness. In most instances these and other worthy goals are not included simply because it becomes so difficult to agree on the levels of performance *and* how to measure them.

But back to our example. After the conclusion of the year, the results are tallied and reveal:

Corporate earnings increase	11.5%
Group A income increase	12.0
Division A	
Increase in income before allocation	17.4
Increase in net sales	16.3
Return on capital	17.0
Percentage point increase in parity goal	8.8

The next step is to identify the performance for each goal. Notice that most require interpolation between values. Thus a 17.4 percent increase in income before allocation for division A is a 4.25 rating.

$$19 - 17 = 2 \qquad 17.4 - 17 = 0.4 \qquad 0.4 \div 2 = 0.25$$

In a similar manner the performance ratings for each of the other objectives may be calculated, resulting in the following:

Corporate earnings increase	4.5 %
Group A income increase	3.0
Division A	
Increase in income before allocation	4.25
Increase in net sales	3.65
Return on capital	4.0
Percentage point increase in parity goal	5.8

Determining the overall divisional performance is a matter of adjusting these scores by their respective weights and dividing by 100.

$$\frac{4.25(40) + 3.65(30) + 4.0(10) + 5.8(20)}{100} = 4.4$$

By weighting the corporate, group, and division performance ratings in a similar manner, the combined rating is calculated.

$$\frac{4.5(25) + 3.0(25) + 4.4(50)}{100} = 4.1$$

To use this rating to determine the bonus fund, it is necessary to have established a bonus table similar to the one in Table 7-13 (which relates to the salary schedule on page 45). As can be seen, bonus percentages are established by grade for each level of performance. The amount of reward should be proportionate to the degree of risk; therefore, bonus percentages increase as one moves upward through the salary structure. By many standards, this would be considered a relatively modest level of payout at the upper end of the structure. Certainly this would be true in the absence of long-term incentives. In this particular example, bonus eligibility begins with grade 20, which has a salary midpoint of $43,400 (see Table 4-3).

Since the combined weighted performance rating in our example is 4.1, it is necessary to interpolate 10 percent of the difference between columns 4 and 5. The appropriate percentage for each grade is then multiplied by the average salary and the number of employees as shown in Table 7-14 to generate a guideline bonus total.

It can be argued that bonus, like salary, should vary not only with performance but also with position in range, for otherwise the company runs the risk of losing an out-

TABLE 7-13   Bonus Guidelines Grades 20 to 40

	Bonus guidelines						
	Performance levels						
Salary grade	0	1	2	3	4	5	6
40	0%	10.0%	20.0%	30.0%	40.0%	50.0%	60.0%
39	0	9.7	19.3	29.0	38.7	48.3	58.0
38	0	9.3	18.7	28.0	37.3	46.7	56.0
37	0	9.0	18.0	27.0	36.0	45.0	54.0
36	0	8.7	17.3	26.0	34.7	43.3	52.0
35	0	8.3	16.7	25.0	33.3	41.7	50.0
34	0	8.0	16.0	24.0	32.0	40.0	48.0
33	0	7.7	15.3	23.0	30.7	38.3	46.0
32	0	7.3	14.7	22.0	29.3	36.7	44.0
31	0	7.0	14.0	21.0	28.0	35.0	42.0
30	0	6.7	13.3	20.0	26.7	33.3	40.0
29	0	6.3	12.7	19.0	25.3	31.7	38.0
28	0	6.0	12.0	18.0	24.0	30.0	36.0
27	0	5.7	11.3	17.0	22.7	28.3	34.0
26	0	5.3	10.7	16.0	21.3	26.7	32.0
25	0	5.0	10.0	15.0	20.0	25.0	30.0
24	0	4.7	9.3	14.0	18.7	23.3	28.0
23	0	4.3	8.7	13.0	17.3	21.7	26.0
22	0	4.0	8.0	12.0	16.0	20.0	24.0
21	0	3.7	7.3	11.0	14.7	18.3	22.0
20	0	3.3	6.7	10.0	13.3	16.7	20.0

TABLE 7-14   Evaluated Performance and Bonus Example — One Division

Salary grade	Number of employees	Average salary	Guide percent	Guide bonus
30	1	$95,000	27.4	$26,030
26	1	73,000	21.8	15,914
25	1	67,000	20.5	13,735
22	2	53,000	16.4	17,384
20	3	44,000	13.7	18,084
Total				$91,147

TABLE 7-15   Bonus Guidelines for Grade 30 by Position in Range

Performance	Position in salary range grade 30				
	Below minimum	Lower one-third	Middle one-third	Upper one-third	Above maximum
6	60.0%	50.0%	40.0%	30.0%	20.0%
5	50.0	41.7	33.3	25.0	16.7
4	40.0	33.4	26.7	20.0	13.3
3	30.0	25.0	20.0	15.0	10.0
2	20.0	16.6	13.3	10.0	6.6
1	10.0	8.3	6.7	5.4	3.5
0	0.0	0.0	0.0	0.0	0.0

standing individual who is low in range, while proportionately overpaying a person high in range. Addressing this objective requires adding the dimension of position in range to the bonus guidelines in a manner similar to the rework of grade 30 shown in Table 7-15.

Following the same method of interpolation as in the previous example would result in the values shown in Table 7-16 for a 4.1 rating, depending on the position of the individual within the salary range. Thus, if the individual were in the lower one-third, a guideline percentage of 34.2 percent would be applied to the individual's salary. Using the salary schedule on page 45, this would mean a salary somewhere between $78,100 and $92,700, or a bonus value ranging from $26,710 to $31,703 for an individual in grade 30. It can be seen that such an approach can mean not only higher bonus percentages for those low in range, but also higher bonus dollars (e.g., compare $26,710 and $31,703 in this example with $26,030 in Table 7-14).

While such an approach is more logical, it is also more cumbersome and for this reason many would not see it as administratively practical.

Impact of Minimum Performance on Divisional Funds

However the guideline bonus fund is to be generated, it is important to ensure that the plus and minus variations from the desired payout are in the desired relationship. To illustrate: Employing the concept advanced in the earlier discussion on fund formulas

TABLE 7-16   Interpolated Bonus Guidelines Using Position in Range

Below minimum	Lower one-third	Middle one-third	Upper one-third	Above maximum
41.0%	34.2%	27.4%	20.5%	13.7%

TABLE 7-17   Performance versus Target for Four Divisions

Division	Dollars, millions		Relationship
	Minimum	Actual	
A	$10	$9	0.90
B	— 2	2	∞
C	16	20	1.25
D	15	16	1.07

(page 200), assume it is desirable to have a minimum growth below which nothing is paid. Thus we could express actual growth (e.g., income before corporate allocation) in terms of expected minimum to determine a divisional bonus relationship, as in Table 7-17. Note the problem with a projected loss situation.

However, by introducing targeted growth we can express the relationship of actual to targeted versus minimum in a manner which will cancel out the problems of negative values. Note that the formulas will always generate a positive number as long as target is greater than minimum (a logical requirement) and actual is greater than minimum (when it is less there is no bonus pool).

$$\text{Relative performance} = \frac{\text{actual} - \text{minimum}}{\text{target} - \text{minimum}}$$

Continuing our example, we will use "income before corporate allocation"; however, this approach can be employed for any quantifiable measurement (e.g., pretax dollar profit, pretax profit percentage, return on investment, net dollar profit, or net dollar percentage). As shown in Table 7-18, actual performance for both division B and division C exceeded their respective minimums by $4 million. However, division B had the higher performance using the above formula because its relative growth was higher.

The importance of accurate minimum and target values is demonstrated by the following example. Shown in Table 7-19 are three divisions with a common minimum but varying targets. Given three different actual performance levels, note the differences,

TABLE 7-18   Relative Performance versus Target for Four Divisions

Division	Minimum	Target	Actual	Performance
A	$10	$12	$ 9	0.00
B	— 2	0	2	2.00
C	16	20	20	1.00
D	15	18	16	.33

recognizing that if all three *should* have had the same target (e.g., $20 million), then division A is being overrated and division C underrated. Note further that the impact of erring on the low side is more dramatic than erring on the high side (e.g., at $21 million the A division receives 34 percent more than it should, whereas C is reduced by only 20 percent). Compare also the average rating with the division B rating.

The same types of problems occur with misjudging the "minimum." Thus this approach requires a high degree of confidence in being able to equitably set "minimum" and "target" for each division. Furthermore the rating relationship generated must adequately reflect the bonus position. In the example in Table 7-20, assume that the minimums and targets are accurately reflected as shown; further assume that all divisions have a guideline normal bonus of $100,000. Given the results, does Table 7-20 appear to be appropriate for the performance generated?

To the extent that Table 7-20 is not considered to be an equitable balance, an additional factor(s) must be introduced to adjust the funds. Either that or an alternative formula(s) must be developed.

Some plans require that whatever has been generated, and allocated, must be distributed. However it is believed that a much more logical approach is to simply have the fund serve as the maximum limit. Furthermore, as indicated earlier, in a number of instances the plan formula provides that the unused amount may be carried over—in many cases, indefinitely. Some form of carryover is needed to provide for the contingency of an insufficient amount provided by the company formula to compensate divisions with outstanding years.

When a carryover of unused funds is not permitted, there will be greater pressure to adjust targets during or after the year based on factors which divisions consider to be beyond their control (e.g., late release of new product). While there may be sufficient justification for such actions, management must be careful to avoid charges of simply changing the targets to ensure an adequate payout. Some might logically ask why the payout targets for the professional manager should be lowered when the owner-manager does not have the same opportunity.

TABLE 7-19 Performance Rating by Sales Attainment for Three Divisions

Division	Dollars, millions		Performance rating by sales attainment, millions		
	Minimum	Target	$19	$20	$21
A	$16	$19	1.0	1.33	1.67
B	16	20	0.75	1.00	1.25
C	16	21	0.60	0.80	1.00
Averages			0.78	1.04	1.31

TABLE 7-20 Bonus Pool by Sales Attainment for Three Divisions

Division	Dollars, millions		Bonus pool by attainment, millions		
	Minimum	Target	$19	$20	$21
A	$16	$19	$100,000	$133,000	$167,000
B	16	20	75,000	100,000	125,000
C	16	21	60,000	80,000	100,000

THE AWARD

The award, the third and last bonus element, consists of three subelements: the amount, the form, the timing.

The Amount

In determining the size of the award, one again must consider the degree of selectivity in determining the recipients. Is it only for very good and outstanding performance or will in fact a lesser amount also be paid for acceptable performance? The decision, of course, must be consistent with the earlier decision of how the salary schedule was to relate to the going rate in the labor market. Companies that have discounted the average total compensation paid in the labor market, to determine their own salary structure, must be certain to add back the amount of the discount—this being the normal bonus award.

If, in the previous example (see Table 7-13), the 3 level of award reflected the discount in the salary midpoint to market, it would mean anyone not receiving at least a 3 level bonus would be under a competitive pay level.

In many instances the division president receives a fund to be allocated which has already been reduced by the president's own award (normally the guideline amount). Typically, he or she does not have carte blanche on the distribution but must submit a list of proposals for review and approval by either the CEO or the compensation committee of the board.

To illustrate, using the example in Table 7-14, the division president who is a grade 30 would receive $26,030 (or $26,000 if the company prefers rounding). The remaining $65,117 is available for distribution among the remaining employees. If the seven bonus eligibles all performed at exactly the same level of proficiency in relation to their assigned targets, then each would get the bonus percentage used in generating the fund (e.g., the grade 26 would receive an amount equal to 21.8 percent of salary). Since this is highly unlikely, the amounts should be plus or minus from the guideline percentage depending on the level of performance attained. Some would be inclined to reserve half

TABLE 7-21 Bonus by Individual Based on Own and Division Performance

Grade	Employee	Salary	Performance	Individual Bonus Unadjusted	Individual Bonus Adjusted	Division bonus	Total Unadjusted	Total Adjusted
26	AB	$73,000	4	$ 7,775	$ 7,667	$ 7,957	$15,624	$15,600
25	BC	67,000	5	8,375	8,259	6,868	15,127	15,100
22	CD	56,000	2	2,240	2,209	4,346	6,555	6,500
22	DE	50,000	5	5,000	4,931	4,346	9,277	9,300
20	EF	46,000	6	4,600	4,536	3,014	7,550	7,500
20	FG	44,000	4	2,926	2,885	3,014	5,899	6,000
20	GH	42,000	3	2,100	2,071	3,014	5,085	5,000
Total				$33,016	$32,558	$32,559	$65,117	$65,000
Variance				458	0	0	0	(117)

TABLE 7-22 Bonus by Individual Based Only on Individual Performance

Grade	Employee	Salary	Performance	Bonus percent	Bonus Unadjusted	Bonus Adjusted	Bonus Adjusted
26	AB	$73,000	4.2	22.4	$16,352	$15,274	$15,300
25	BC	67,000	5.3	26.5	17,755	16,584	16,600
22	CD	56,000	2.5	10.0	5,600	5,231	5,200
22	DE	50,000	5.1	20.4	10,200	9,528	9,500
20	EF	46,000	6.0	20.0	9,200	8,594	8,600
20	FG	44,000	4.1	13.6	5,984	5,590	5,600
20	GH	42,000	3.3	11.0	4,620	4,316	4,300
Total					$69,711	$65,117	$65,100
Variance					$ 4,594	0	$ (17)

of the guideline amount for each individual as payment for sharing in division perfor-mance. The remaining $30,000 plus would be allocated based on individual achieve-ment. For several this might mean no bonus, for others a significant amount. Table 7-21 shows how this 50 percent division and 50 percent employee performance approach might be utilized. Note that the performance rating is used to look up the appropriate bonus percentage for that grade (see Table 7-13) but only half is used (since one half has already been set aside for division performance). The sum of these bonuses is $33,016 or $458 more than allowable [i.e., $65,117 − $32,559 (for division set aside) = $32,558]. Therefore the awards are proportionately reduced, using the ratio that $32,558 is to $33,016, or 0.9862. Adding the individual adjusted amount to the division bonus produces an unadjusted total for each person. This amount is then rounded if deemed appropriate to finalize the calculation. Note that the division is $117 under its allocation.

If the decision is to determine the executive's bonus totally on his or her own per-formance, the calculations are similar to those in Table 7-22. Note also that performance in this instance is expressed to the nearest tenth of a percent. Using the individual's grade and performance rating the appropriate interpolation is made within the figures on Table 7-13. This amount multiplied by the salary generates an unadjusted bonus. The sum of the latter is $4594 over the allowable divisional total so each award is proportionately reduced by the ratio that $65,117 is to $69,711, or 0.934. These figures are reported in the adjusted column, and if desired they may be rounded as shown in the last column.

The essential difference between the combination division-individual and the individ-ual-performance-only approach is that the first smoothes out bonus variations (at the expense of holding back on the outstanding performer and being somewhat generous with the marginal performer). The attractiveness of the combination approach is that it rewards group achievement (the one-for-all philosophy). This is critical if teamwork is needed and the individual is expected to not advance individual performance gains at the expense of the unit.

A variation on both of these examples is to use the bonus percentage against the midpoint of the range rather than the individual's actual salary. The latter emphasizes the importance of structure and will result in a greater award for an individual below midpoint and less for a person above midpoint than using actual salary. Tying bonuses to the midpoint emphasizes competitive levels of pay; basing the bonus on actual salary emphasizes the importance of current salary. The latter is an advantage to those better performers who have been in the grade longer and are therefore above the midpoint, but it is a disadvantage to better performers who are low in range because of brevity of service.

Another variation on determining the individual award, particularly at the corporate end, is to do it strictly by a formula set for that year. Assume there are seven top corporate officers and that the normal compensation relationship among the seven (based on compensation midpoints) is as shown in Table 7-23.

Based on targeted net income of $100 million (an increase of $10 million over the

TABLE 7-23 Incentive Compensation versus Midpoints for Seven Officers

| | Compensation midpoint ratio | Incentive bonus basis | |
		Corporate	Group
CEO	100	100%	—
President	75	100	—
VP—group A	60	50	50%
VP—group B	50	50	50
VP finance	40	100	—
VP legal	35	100	—
VP personnel	30	100	—

previous year), a formula is set for the CEO which is expected to generate a $60,000 bonus.

Bonus = 0.0002 (net income)

$\qquad$ + 0.004 (net income minus previous year net income)

The president's award would be set equal to 75 percent of the CEO's (unless there was a specific reason to make it different). The staff vice presidents would also have percentages comparable to the pay relationship as shown above unless a specific need for a different relationship were important. If so that would be reflected in an adjusted percentage.

The bonuses for the group vice presidents would be determined half by corporate and half by their own group performance. Thus, the group A VP would not have 60 percent of the CEO's bonus for corporate, but rather 30 percent (i.e., 60 percent × 50 percent). Furthermore, since budgeted income for group A is $70 million (an increase of $5 million over previous year), the following formula might seem appropriate:

Group bonus 0.00015 (group net income) + 0.0015 (increase in group net income)

Assuming the corporate and group targets were met, the bonus would be:

CEO bonus = $60,000
Group A VP bonus:
$\qquad$ Corporate portion = 0.30 ($60,000) = $18,000
$\qquad$ Group portion = 0.00015 ($70,000,000) + 0.0015 ($5,000,000) = $18,000
$\qquad$ Total bonus = $36,000, or 60 percent of CEO bonus

Note that in the above example the group VP would have received a greater or smaller group portion depending on group performance. To the extent group performance was better than budgeted, the VP would have a bonus higher than 60 percent of the CEO's; to the extent group A's performance was less than budgeted, the VP's bonus would have been less than 60 percent of the CEO's incentive payment.

A comparable calculation can be made for the other group VP; note that the bonus percentages will have to be different from the other group VP in order to attain the desired relationship to CEO pay since group B's targeted income is $30 million (an increase of $5 million). Perhaps 0.00025 of sales while retaining the 0.0015 of increased net income would be justifiable. This would be a targeted bonus of $15,000 which, when added to the $15,000 for corporate (i.e., $60,000 × 0.5 × 0.5), would yield a total of $30,000 or 50 percent of the CEO's bonus.

If "income before allocation" is deemed more appropriate for determining group performance incentive, comparable values can be determined in a similar manner through a series of trial-and-error calculations until acceptable formulas are developed.

It is imperative that such formulas be reexamined each year to ensure that the values are still appropriate. In most cases it will be found necessary to make at least minor adjustments in the formula values. Such minor annual adjustments preclude major problems in future years.

There is a reluctance on the part of a few companies to give large bonuses for fear of poor shareholder relations. These companies are misdirecting their apprehension; the focus of concern should not be the size of the bonus but rather the level of the total compensation package! As a matter of fact it is to the shareholder's best interest that a large segment of top management's total compensation be in bonus incentives structured to reward success and penalize failures. How often would a corporation reduce the salary of one of its managers if the division did not meet its objectives?

To illustrate that raising or lowering performance can have an impact on total compensation, let's continue our example for the executive in grade 25. We showed earlier that the executive received a $16,600 bonus for a 5.3 rating; assuming the same rating was used for salary purposes, the $67,000 salary (which was in the middle one-third) was probably increased 11 percent, or $7400, using the earlier described performance matrix (Table 4-17). Thus, the individual received $91,200. Now let's examine the dollar impact of varying levels of performance the following year on current compensation using Tables 4-17 and 7-13. Table 7-24 shows the salary increases and bonus amounts for different levels of performance. Salary increases are for the middle one-third (on the assumption the structure increased sufficiently for the individual to retain the position; if not and the executive is now in the upper one-third, the salary increases should be reduced $200 to $300).

Note that because the individual had such a high rating (and resulting high bonus) last year, anything less than a 4 will result in a decrease in total compensation (even though there will be a salary increase). Conversely, if last year's performance rating (and bonus) had been lower, there would have still been a possibility for less compensation (for significantly lower performance rating) but the upside potential would have been proportionately greater. This specific example can be broadened to a full test of the "stretch" by examining all performance possibilities (current versus previous year) for the highest grade (e.g., 40) and the lowest (e.g., 20). Shown in Table 7-25 are the results of such a test. Note that there are 49 (last year versus current year performance) combinations, although pragmatics would challenge the likelihood of dramatic changes (e.g., 6 last year and 0 this year). However, even an examination limited to plus or minus one

TABLE 7-24 Individual Bonus Examples Based on Different Performance Ratings

Current salary	Last bonus	Performance	Salary increase	Bonus	Total	Variance Amount	Variance Percent
$74,400	$16,800	6	$9,700	$22,300	$106,400	$15,200	16.7
		5	8,200	18,600	101,200	10,000	11.0
		4	6,700	14,800	95,900	4,700	5.2
		3	5,200	11,200	91,100	(100)	(0.1)
		2	3,700	7,400	85,500	(5,700)	(6.2)
		1	2,200	3,700	80,300	(10,900)	(12.0)
		0	0	0	74,400	(16,800)	(18.4)

TABLE 7-25 Compensation Comparison Using Current Year and Last Year Performance

Change in total compensation—grade 40

Last year's performance	This year's performance						
	0	1	2	3	4	5	6
6	(34.6)	(26.1)	(18.3)	(10.4)	(2.6)	5.2	13.1
5	(31.0)	(22.1)	(13.8)	(5.5)	2.7	11.0	19.3
4	(26.8)	(17.3)	(8.6)	0.2	9.0	17.8	26.6
3	(21.9)	(11.7)	(2.4)	7.0	16.4	25.7	35.1
2	(16.0)	(5.1)	5.0	15.1	25.2	35.2	45.3
1	(8.8)	3.0	13.9	24.9	35.8	46.8	57.7
0	0.0	10.0	25.0	37.0	49.0	61.0	73.0

Change in total compensation—grade 20

Last year's performance	This year's performance						
	0	1	2	3	4	5	6
6	(14.4	(9.0)	(4.4)	0.0	4.7	9.3	13.8
5	(13.1)	(7.6)	(2.9)	1.7	6.3	11.0	15.6
4	(10.9)	(5.3)	(.4)	4.3	9.0	13.8	18.5
3	(8.5)	(2.8)	2.2	7.0	11.8	16.8	21.6
2	(6.0)	(0.7)	5.0	10.0	15.0	20.0	25.0
1	(3.1)	3.0	8.2	13.4	17.2	23.7	28.9
0	0.0	6.3	11.7	17.0	22.3	27.8	33.3

level of performance (e.g., 4 last year could be 3, 4, or 5 this year), as shown in the banded area, results in appreciable change in rate of movement. For example in grade 20 a person with a 3 rating last year would receive 2.2, 7.0, or 11.8 percent, depending on whether this year's rating was 2, 3, or 4.

In comparing the results from the two grids, it is also apparent that there is considerably more upside and downside risk in compensation at grade 40 than at grade 20, although repeating the same performance would generate about the same increase. For example while a 3 last year would receive 7 percent if a 3 again this year in both schedules, the impact of being a 6 this year would be a 21.6 percent increase in grade 20 versus a 35.1 percent adjustment in grade 40. Stated another way, there is a greater proportional reward for improving performance in the upper grades as well as a more dramatic drop in pay for not retaining previous performance levels.

The amount of impact a lower performance rating has on total compensation is a function of the salary and bonus guidelines. The more spread in both for differences in performance, the greater the downside risk for reduced compensation if performance drops off.

TABLE 7-26   Form versus Timing of
Short-Term Incentives

Timing	Forms		
	Cash	Stock	Combination
Current	1	4	7
Deferred	2	5	8
Combination	3	6	9

Form and Timing

It is difficult to discuss the last two subelements separately. The *form* of the bonus is cash and/or stock and the *timing* is current and/or deferred.

The matrix in Table 7-26 shows the nine possible combinations of form and timing ranging from an immediate lump-sum cash settlement to a combination of cash and stock, part paid immediately and the remainder in deferred installments.

Certainly the current *cash* payment has the greatest impact on the lower-level executive. Even though a third or more of the award may be lost in taxes, the balance can still represent a significant increase in the recipient's income. Due to family obligations (e.g., mortgages and college tuition) this time-form combination is probably most popular with persons in their thirties or forties.

If the award is all in *stock*, the recipient usually has difficulty in paying the taxes without selling some of the stock, thereby partially defeating the initial objective of giving the executive an investment in the future growth of the organization. For this reason a combination form of stock and a sufficient amount of cash to pay taxes on the total award is a logical approach. For many, this would argue for half the value in stock and the other half in cash (to meet tax liabilities). Where city and state taxes exist, a split such as 40 percent stock and 60 percent cash may be more appropriate.

Also, use of company stock should not be restricted to corporate staff. Using it for divisional awards reinforces (at least on a future basis to the extent the executive holds the stock) identification with corporate success, not simply divisional performance.

Companies that pay a large amount of the award in company stock must realize that they are placing heavy liquidity pressures on the individual unless the person is free to sell a portion of the amount. For companies that give the total award in stock, this is very significant because of the tax requirements. Even those that give half in cash and half in stock must realize that if the individuals are discouraged from selling any stock, they in essence have a salary reduction plan with a heavy shift to deferred income.

Paying all or a portion of the award in stock also can cause a problem to a corporate officer due to the requirements of Section 16(b) of the Securities Exchange Act. It stipulates that any profit made by an officer or director of a company by purchasing shares of the company within 6 months of selling similar shares must be returned to the company.

In general, payment of stock under an incentive program is not considered a purchase by the Securities and Exchange Commission (SEC). However, subsequent sale by the executive is considered a sale under the definitions of the act. This becomes important where the company also has a stock option or other long-term incentive plan using company stock.

Whether the individual receives the award in cash or something other than cash (e.g., company stock), the tax treatment is the same: personal service income tax on the value of the award on the date when received (deferred income is discussed in Chapter 9).

It is important that the individual award relate to the person's performance—especially for the better performer. When the recipient believes the award is less than appropriate given performance, the plan is in trouble. When a plan gives essentially the same award to both the marginal and the outstanding performer, two things happen. The marginal performer is not going to be very attentive to requests to improve performance; the outstanding performer is going to either lower future performance to meet the award level (by increasing off-the-job activities for either intrinsic or extrinsic compensation) or be receptive to job offers from other companies. Most companies would not find these two results desirable.

SPECIAL AWARDS

Besides short-term incentives a number of companies also have a special award program with the avowed aim of recognizing any singularly notable accomplishment that contributes to the successful conduct of the business. The emphasis on accomplishment separates such programs from suggestion system programs where a recommendation on a product or process improvement is submitted and a payment given in relation to some formula related to cost savings (e.g., 15 percent of the first year's net labor and material savings).

Typically, the special award program has a number of levels. It may range from a token recognition award often paid in nonmonetary awards such as dinners, theater tickets, and merchandise (perhaps with a maximum of $200) to the chairman's award for a major research discovery or outstanding financial contribution to the corporation (with perhaps a minimum value of $25,000). In between are various levels of departmental and divisional awards, all with different levels of accomplishment and payouts.

A problem with such programs is being able to define the level of contribution which will qualify the person for an award. In addition, financial controls and feedback procedures have to be established to ensure interunit equity.

Companies with such programs must be careful to ensure that they are not being utilized to overcompensate for poorly performing short-term incentive programs. Normally such misuse occurs only with the programs which can be approved within the division. A review of number and size of awards by organizational level, coupled with special attention for individuals repeating as recipients, should be able to indicate degree of misuse.

SUMMARY AND CONCLUSIONS

Tax treatment of short-term incentives typically results in an 0.93 effectiveness rating, tax deductible to the company and reportable as personal service income to the executive. Proxy treatment is equally simple: column C when paid (or if vested) and column D for nonvested contingent awards. Apparently the bonus should be reported in column C_1 if paid in cash and C_2 if paid in stock. The SEC also requires textual disclosure of how the plan operates for officers and directors, including formulas and schedules determining payment.

Although all companies provide salary and benefits (and possibly some perquisites), it is not axiomatic that they need provide short-term incentive opportunities. By definition, results have to be measurable within a short period (e.g., 1 year). It is not sufficient to assume that simply because the company produces an annual earnings statement it needs a variable compensation plan tied to its results. The annual model cycle in an industry (e.g., automobiles) is a classic situation arguing for an annual incentive plan. However, to the extent eligibility goes beyond those making the decisions impacting on results, the plan has shifted to a profit sharing plan.

To be cost effective, performance must be commensurate with incentive. By definition, overpaying those whose performance has slipped narrows the pay difference between barely acceptable and outstanding performance. Unfortunately some managers expect the bonus system to automatically preclude this from happening. They have confused the ends with the means. The incentive plan is merely a pay delivery system; it has no native intelligence. Certainly, it is unrealistic to assume that in developing an incentive plan, all possible conditions can be examined and factored into the formula.

To the extent the incentive plan correlates positively with performance, it will be possible to retain aggressive, results-oriented individuals—as well as attract new ones to the company. These are people who are more concerned with self-actualization and ego reinforcement than security. The mere existence of an incentive plan will not assure their presence; it is, however, the payoff which will determine their interest in remaining with the company.

Some companies rely strongly on the noncommittal or "golden gut" approach; "Just do a good job and we'll take care of you." Unfortunately, it is very difficult for the executive to identify strongly with this tpe of organization inasmuch as specific objective results related to bonus payment are nonexistent.

Companies with divisional allocations should be careful not to overpay profitable divisions and underpay unprofitable ones. Is it logical to pay a highly profitable division more than an unprofitable one if the former is losing market share while the latter is achieving a miraculous turnaround? In many instances relative performance is more important than absolute. Also how much of the credit for success or failure should go to the present management team? Were they the decision makers or were they simply in the chairs at the time the results were measured? Consider the executive who never held an assignment for more than 3 years and in each instance the unit showed marvelous results (only to sink to lower depths after the individual's departure). Was the executive the solution or part of the problem?

Low bonus potential in problem divisions may also be a significant retardant in getting highly qualified executives to accept a transfer from a profitable division.

Consider the division president who agrees to an unrealistic increase in wages to settle a union contract and avoid a loss in sales. This action may place undue pressure on the other units of the company regarding the size of their settlements or increases to nonorganized employees. Also one must question how long it is possible to pass these increased costs along in the way of price increases.

Conversely it is not very logical to adopt a short-term incentive plan where key decisions are few, results cannot be judged for years, only a handful of executives make the decisions (except perhaps for an active committee system), and a comfortable environment exists in which inadequate performance is seldom penalized.

More so than any other compensation element, because it can go up and down within a year's time, short-term incentive programs provide the vehicle for reinforcing desirable performance and penalizing undesirable results. Unfortunately, because of design flaws and management reticence in administration, the degree of success in meeting this objective is more apparent than real.

Many plans fail because of poor performance appraisals and inadequate financial controls. However, the surest way to ensure plan failure is to have those responsible for administration not prepared to penalize failure (rewarding success is a problem only relative to rewarding mediocrity). The CEO and compensation committee must firmly believe in the incentive principle and be prepared to make it work. Lacking this conviction and resolve, the best plan is doomed to failure.

Because of the complexities of corporate responsibilities today, the authoritarian CEO is an anachronism; most decisions are reached by consensus among management committees. Given this climate, it is unrealistic to assume the CEOs will make unpopular decisions regarding subordinate pay increases. Need for objectivity seems to increase with the distance from the rater and ratee! Most executives find it difficult to be objective with their own subordinates but fully expect them in turn to pay their subordinates in relation to attainment of objectives. Many a well-designed incentive plan has failed simply because it has not recognized this basic truth.

Companies with bonus plans generally are reported to be paying 20 percent or more for comparable positions than non-bonus-paying companies. For some companies these additions to the executive payroll are cost effective; for others they are additional expenses which have little to do with pay for performance. The hypothesis that companies with incentives outperform those without has been challenged by many. It is possible to construct a study to prove that nonbonus companies outperform bonus companies. Nonetheless, others will argue that companies should not abandon pay for performance because of problems in performance measurement, but rather should work to improve the performance criteria.

217

Long-Term Incentives

The essential difference between long- and short-term incentives is the length of the performance period; while short-term are typically 1 year, long-term are multiyear in nature. Some will argue that there is a mid-term (e.g., 3 to 5 years such as restricted stock and performance unit plans) as well as a long-term plan (e.g., more than 5 years such as stock options and SARs). This chapter will combine these two categories under "long-term incentives."

The earlier issues of determining eligibility are similar, except it is assumed only those executives whose performance period exceeds a year (because it takes longer to determine the impact of the decisions) are included in long-term incentives.

This is not to say that a portion of the executive's total compensation cannot consist partly of short-term incentives, but rather that a significant portion should be based on the longer time span for adequate assessment.

The forms of long-term incentives, similar to short-term, are expressed in terms of those dependent upon stock price and those independent of stock price (this section will deal with non-market-related plans). However, due to their longer-term nature, there are considerably more variations within each that can be employed.

STOCK OPTIONS

A stock option is the right to purchase a stated number of shares of company stock at a stated price during a stated period of time. Executives must be careful they do not trigger a *wash sale* transaction. This would occur if the individual acquired stock through an exercise of an option within 30 days before or after selling any stock of the same company at a loss. The IRS would deny recognition of the loss but will include the amount of the loss in determining the FMV of the stock acquired under exercise.

The receipt of a stock option grant has no tax or SEC consequences; however, the exercise or purchase of stock under an option carries tax consequences (as will be discussed later) and is considered a purchase under Rule 16(b) for purpose of the 6-month test on "insiders." An *insider* is defined by the Securities and Exchange Act as any person who owns 10 percent or more of any class of stock in a publicly held company or is an officer or director of the company.

Stock options are either qualified or nonqualified. The former was the successor to the restricted stock options of the fifties and widely used until recently. The 1969 Tax Reform struck a mortal blow at the after-tax effectiveness of the qualified option to those above approximately $50,000; the 1976 Tax Reform Act legislated it out of existence after May 20, 1981. Any qualified stock options that were not exercised by that date will be taxed as nonqualified options.

Qualified Stock Option

Qualified stock options are defined in Section 422 of the Internal Revenue Code and include those which meet certain requirements, namely: the option price must be not less than 100 percent of fair market value at time of grant, the period of option must be not more than 5 years, and retention of stock received by exercising the option must exceed 3 years. The spread between option price and fair market value at time of exercise is not taxed until sold (although it is considered tax preference income in the year of exercise for purpose of determining minimum tax). However, it changes dollar-for-dollar income otherwise eligible for the 50 percent maximum tax to "other income" with the 70 percent maximum.

If the stock is not held for more than 3 years, the executive is considered to have made a *disqualifying disposition* and the spread at exercise is taxable at personal service income rates in the year of sale. At that point, the company takes a like amount of deduction for tax purposes. A qualified option may not be exercised while a previously granted option at a higher price is outstanding.

Nonqualified Stock Option

By definition the nonqualified option is an option that fails to meet all requirements of a qualified option. The most common form is a nondiscounted 10-year grant, probably due to a carryover of the former SEC rules that an option for insiders could neither be discounted nor exceed 10 years in duration in order to be an exempt transaction at time of grant (i.e., neither a purchase nor a sale).

While the recipient does have a tax liability at time of exercise (equal to the spread between fair market value and option price), it is considered personal service income under Section 1348 of the Internal Revenue Code (and according to Revenue Ruling 78-359) and the company has a comparable tax deduction. Furthermore Revenue Ruling 67-257 requires the company to withhold on this spread. Failure to do so will result in loss of the company tax deduction as a result of a 1978 amendment by the Treasury of Section 83 of the Code. To receive capital gains treatment (on the spread between fair market value at time of exercise and time of sale) the recipient must hold the stock for more than 1 year after exercise.

Exercising a nonqualified option may not be a simple low-risk situation—even when sale is at option price. Since the Revenue Act of 1978 establishes a maximum annual capital loss write-off of $3000, it would take 10 years to write off a $30,000 loss. Such could occur if an executive exercised an option at $30 when the stock was selling at $40. Later when selling the 1000 shares at $30, the individual learns it is not a simple canceling of the gain (even during the year of exercise)!

With the lifting of the SEC no-discount rules, some nonqualified options were discounted. The discount is determined either at time of *grant* (e.g., 85 percent of fair market value) or at time of *exercise*. The latter is determined by formula (e.g., for every $1 the fair market value exceeds the price at date of grant the option price is reduced by a like amount) normally with a minimum price (e.g., one-half of fair market value at date of grant). Thus an option granted with the stock selling at $100 would be reduced to $50 if the optionee exercised it at a time when the fair market value was $150. The corporation could take a tax deduction for $100 since the executive would have personal service income in the same amount. Unfortunately APB Opinion No. 25, "Accounting for Stock Issued to Employees," issued in 1972 by the Accounting Principles Board, would require the amortization of this value while the option was outstanding by flowing the amount through the earnings statement.

Another variation would be to set the future price in relation to prescribed percentages of fair market value (e.g., 95 percent after 1 year, 90 percent after 2 years, etc.). It is believed such a plan would meet the 16(b) requirements of the Securities and Exchange Act that the plan must set the stock price. In this instance it establishes the price by formula rather than in absolute terms.

Why Stock Options?

For years, stock options have been one of the more acceptable forms of incentive compensation to shareholders because (1) the executive must put up some of his or her own money, (2) the value, like the shareholder's, is at risk with the price of the company stock, and (3) assuming no discount, there is no charge to corporate earnings. Options are a form of profit sharing which link the professional manager's financial success to that of the shareholder.

While such programs have been widely used in many companies, there are organizations where they are not available as a compensation device. For example, federally chartered savings and loan institutions could not use them because there is no stock for use.

Since a company does not pay federal income tax on any profits it may realize in selling its own stock, stock options are expensive to the company in direct proportion to the realized value the executive receives in appreciation. Heavy use of stock options in such situations results in a significant loss of income to the company. For example, assume an individual receives an option of 10,000 shares at $50 a share. The individual exercises the option when it is selling at $60 a share. The executive has a tax liability on $100,000 (i.e., 10,000 shares × $10). Similarly the company has a tax deduction of $100,000 or a reduction in taxes of $46,000 (assuming the 46 percent rate is in effect). If par value of the stock is $1, par value of $10,000 is added for the additional 10,000 shares now outstanding, and $490,000 (i.e., $500,000 — $10,000) is added to the capital surplus account as is the $46,000 resulting from the savings in taxes for a total of $536,000. However, had the company sold the stock at $60, capital surplus would have been increased by $590,000 (i.e., $600,000 — $10,000). Thus the option has "cost" the company $54,000 (the difference between $590,000 and $536,000) or the portion of the $100,000 gain not reimbursed (e.g., $100,000 less a $46,000 reduction in taxes).

Treasury Method

Another way to evaluate the cost of stock options is to determine the extent of dilution to equity. A popular method for calculating this is the *treasury method*. This assumes that the proceeds from the stock option plus the tax benefit received are used to purchase shares of the company stock on the open market. Dilution is therefore a function of spread of market value over option price. For example, using the same 10,000 shares described above at an option price of $50, the company received $500,000 from the executive plus $46,000 (assuming a 46 percent tax rate) in tax benefits from the $60 market price. This $546,000 can be used to purchase 9100 shares at $60 a share. Thus, the dilution of equity is 900 shares. The Financial Accounting Standards Board (which replaced the Accounting Principles Board in 1973) allegedly was considering excluding the tax benefit (since there is no charge to earnings under stock options) in a clarification to APB Opinion No. 15 (which deals with earnings-per-share calculations). However, FASB Interpretation No. 31, "Treatment of Stock Compensation Plans in EPS Computations," reaffirmed the use of the tax benefit in calculating fully diluted EPS.

Questions and Considerations

While there is no governmental requirement that shareholders approve the stock option plan, it may be a requirement of the exchange on which the stock is listed. Furthermore, the grant of stock options under a plan not approved by the shareholders will not be considered an exempt transaction by SEC, and therefore shareholder approval of stock option plans is the rule, rather than the exception.

An additional question is whether or not to register the stock. In those companies which do not undertake the expense of registration, the executive must make an investment representation before exercising the option. The negative aspect of such a representation is that the executive cannot sell the stock for 2 years without incurring a high penalty discount on the value. Not too many executives find this restriction an attractive motivational compensation technique.

If a company is acquired by another, it is appropriate to restate the option price for purchase of the acquiring company in relation to their respective prices. For example, if company B's stock was selling at $50 with an option in effect at $30 when it was acquired by company A whose stock was then at $75, the option for B stock at $30 could be restated to $45 for A stock without changing any other terms of the option on a share-for-share basis. Since 30/50 equals 60 percent, then 60 percent of $75, or $45, would be the new option price. Alternatively, it might be set at $55, reflecting the same dollar difference (i.e., $50 − $30 = $20; $75 − $20 = $55).

Many companies do not grant options to those close to normal retirement age, although some would argue this may be counter to the age discrimination laws. Better to make the grant but limit the exercise period after retirement. On the other hand a few plans will permit the optionee to exercise after retirement to the full term of the grant, thereby removing another barrier to retirement. Those who argue that the option is in part a reward for past efforts (especially a factor in determining number of shares) are even questioning the 10-year limit on the option. Why not 15, 20, or more years?

Should the individual terminate employment, many plans provide a very limited exercise window (e.g., 90 days). In cases where the individual is quitting or being terminated for cause, it is not illogical to have the option cease on date of termination. Periods of 6 months to 1 year, on the other hand, are not uncommon after termination due to disability or death. On the other hand, many plans simply use the IRS rules for qualified plans, namely 90 days from date of termination except for death where it is 1 year, for nonqualified plans as well. A few companies take a more liberal view for reasons such as retirement and allow the option to run to its normal expiration; however, a more common approach is to allow the option to expire 2 or 3 years after retirement.

Most plans have a minimum *waiting period* (e.g., 1 year) before the option can be exercised. After that time the grant may or may not have additional restrictions. While some plans permit exercise on any or all of the grant after that period, many have an installment feature (e.g., 25 percent of the shares after 1 year, 50 percent after 2 years, etc.). This approach is designed to encourage exercise and hold by spreading the buying over the period of the option, but more importantly it is designed to penalize executives who leave, since they will have to forfeit the remaining portion of the grant.

The *stock-for-stock exchange* allows the company to help the executive avoid financing problems: namely it permits the optionee to use stock already owned to meet a portion of the exercise cost. For example, assume the executive owns 10,000 shares of company stock and decides to exercise an option for 5000 shares at $41 a share. The cost to exercise is therefore $205,000. Assume, further, the fair market value (FMV) is $50 a share at time of exercise. By transferring to the company 4000 shares already owned (purchased at $30 per share) the executive need only write a check for $5000.

The executive would receive two certificates, one for 4000 (replacing the one transferred to the company) and another for 1000. Since the first was a tax-free exchange, the 1000-share certification is considered compensation in the amount of $45,000 (1000 shares × $50 FMV, minus the $5000 check). This amount is the same as if the executive simply exercised the option with a check in the amount of $205,000. Namely, the difference between option price and FMV of $9 multiplied by 5000 shares equals

$45,000. The cost basis for the 4000 shares remains $30 a share; the cost basis for the 1000 shares is $50 per share.

Had the individual sold the 4000 shares in order to obtain funds to exercise the option, and had the sale qualified for long-term capital gains, the tax could have been as high as $22,400 (i.e., 28 percent on $80,000). Therefore, the additional cash needed to exercise the option would have been $27,400 since the net proceeds from stock sale were only $177,600. If the optionee were a 16(b) executive, this action would be precluded unless at least 6 months had lapsed between sale and exercise.

The IRS stated in Rev. Rul. 80-244 that an employee could deliver stock owned as payment for exercising a nonqualified stock option without incurring a taxable event on the unrealized appreciation on the shares delivered. At about the same time, the SEC amended Rule 16b-3, enabling insiders to engage in such transactions, and also stated that shareholder approval of such a feature was not necessary. As a result, a number of companies not only incorporated this method of exercising stock options in their subsequent grants but also amended outstanding options to permit payment with company stock. However, companies must be careful to ensure that such stock received is not "tainted" in the eyes of SEC as this would preclude "pooling-of-interests" accounting.

Another device used is one that provides the executive with cash equal to some percentage of the spread between option price and fair market value. If the objective is to ensure that the executive does not have to sell any stock to meet tax liability, it would be logical to give an amount comparable to the spread (on the assumption the individual is in the 50 percent marginal tax bracket). Needless to say, this can be rather expensive to a company with extensive use of options, especially when the spread becomes appreciable.

A variation of the cash supplement described above is a *buy-back* program in which the company buys back a portion of the exercised option, lessening the executive's financing requirements and the dilution of equity to the company. Thus, an executive who exercised an option to buy 5000 shares at $40 a share when the market value was $50 would have to dig up $200,000 to exercise the option plus an additional $25,000 (assuming the 50 percent tax rate) to meet the tax bill.

If the buy-back were designed to simply provide sufficient cash to meet the tax liability, the company would buy back 500 shares at $50 a share. Such plans have to be examined very carefully for 16b-3 executives.

For companies that have both stock options and stock purchase plans, it is not illogical to preclude the executive from participating in the first while holding options in the latter. After the individual exercises all the options, they expire, or the executive voluntarily surrenders the grants, the person is again eligible for the stock purchase plan. Such an action is plausible if the stock has been underwater for a time; conversely it would not seem as logical if the company stock were experiencing strong growth, as the spread under the option would probably exceed the 15 percent discount under the stock purchase plan.

Options are non-goal-oriented plans (i.e., the company does not have to prescribe certain goals which must be achieved in order to receive payment). This is, however, a two-edged sword, for while the above may be an advantage, market swings (probably more dependent upon investor view of equities in general than this stock in particular) may make the option very lucrative or literally worthless. For example, a rise in interest rates usually means falling stock prices as investors shift from the stock to the bond market.

Some have said that all options do is motivate the recipients to increase the price of the stock, rather than improve company performance, which in turn would, it is hoped, result in a higher price. The cynics argue that the latter is about as successful as pushing on a string. Similarly, it is much easier to pull that string (and pull the stock price down) by announcing glum news, since the stock price is essentially future earnings discounted to a present value. With the Stock Exchange, SEC, IRS, and FASB monitoring activities, stock price manipulation is virtually impossible without some form of legal action falling on the company.

Many believe the market to be a good indicator of coming recession or recovery, namely that the market will drop prior to a recession. As the recession continues, the stock prices increase in anticipation of a recovery. Once the recovery has been assured, the stock is vulnerable to dropping off. This lag between economic performance and stock prices is important to understand if using company stock. Unfortunately, it is easier to understand than to utilize due to the uncertainty of predicting economic conditions—except on a historical basis at which time it is too late.

History of Stock Options

The first stock option form receiving favorable tax treatment was the "restricted" option as defined in Section 424 of the Internal Revenue Code. It came into being with the *Revenue Act of 1950* and lasted to the Revenue Act of 1964, when it was replaced by the "qualified" option. The "qualified" option lasted until the Tax Reform Act of 1976 legislated it out of existence (the burial was on May 21, 1981). However, it was subjected to heavy attack by changes in the 1969 Tax Reform Act as well. However, like Lazarus, restricted or qualified stock options may return to the world of the living, as several attempts have been made in Congress to restore them to life.

The essential features of the restricted option included (1) an option price as low as 85 percent of market value at time of grant, (2) capital gains treatment on the difference between market value at time of sale and option price for stock held more than 6 *months*, (3) a period as long as *10 years* during which the grant could be exercised, and (4) *no restriction* as to which sequence options need be exercised.

The *Revenue Act of 1964* introduced a new form of statutory option (i.e., "qualified") while terminating the restricted form. Like the restricted option, the qualified imposed no tax liability on the holder at either time of grant or time of exercise; however, (1) the grant could not be for less than *100 percent* of market value at time of grant, (2) capital gains treatment was available only if the stock was held for more than *3 years*, (3) the option period could not exceed *5 years*, and (4) an option could not be exercised while the holder had outstanding an earlier granted qualified option at a higher price.

Thus while the qualified option was not as attractive as its predecessor, the restricted, it still was more palatable than anything else, given (1) a rather favorable growth in stock prices during the period, and (2) marginal tax rates as high as 70 percent (91 percent before the 1964 Revenue Act).

The *1969 Tax Reform Act* took three further swings at the attractiveness of the qualified option. First, it lowered the maximum marginal tax rate from 70 to 50 percent on earned income (namely payment arising out of employment).

Second, the long-term capital gains tax maximum of 25 percent was increased to one-half the ordinary income tax rate (maximum 70 percent) except for the first $50,000, which was still subject to a 25 percent rate. Thus the tax spread between salary and bonus versus stock option was reduced from a difference of 70 percent versus 25 percent to a difference of 50 percent versus 35 percent.

Third, it introduced a new form of tax—a minimum which would be applied to certain items (i.e., preference income). This tax preference income (TPI) would be taxed at the rate of 10 percent above a $30,000 exclusion. However this exclusion was further increased by the amount of tax liability for the current and up to 7 prior years. The spread between market value and option price on the date a qualified option was exercised met the definition of tax preference income (unless sold within the same tax year) as did one-half of the long-term capital gains at time of sale.

Assume the executive exercised the option and the "spread" equaled $50,000. Further assume that the individual paid $22,000 in federal taxes. Since the $30,000 exclusion plus the tax liability exceeded the TPI, there was no tax liability. However, any TPI over the $30,000 exclusion reduced dollar-for-dollar the earned income subject to the 50 percent maximum tax, thus making it subject to a possible 20-point increase in taxes.

In spite of prophecies that the qualified option was dead, it continued to be a viable part of the compensation program—especially for those under the 50 percent maximum tax bracket—primarily because the stock market continued to produce profits.

The downturn in the stock market was coupled with the *1976 Tax Reform Act* which legislated the qualified stock option out of existence on May 20, 1981. Furthermore it made use of such options less attractive during their remaining life by (1) eliminating the $30,000 annual exemption, (2) increasing the minimum tax to 15 percent, and (3) lowering the overall exemption to the greater of $10,000 or one-half of the regular income tax for the current year (the carryover of unused previous years' credit was eliminated).

The Conference Report accompanying the 1976 Tax Reform Act requested the IRS to develop and promulgate rules which would govern an individual's election to have the option valued at time of grant rather than exercise and sale. In addition to the option price and length of the option, some estimation of future earnings of the company was to be considered. To date the IRS has been reluctant to take this action, perhaps since the future aspects of the company success make it unlikely that the value will be "readily ascertainable" as required in Section 83(3).

The *1978 Revenue Act* reduced the portion of long-term gains subject to taxes from half to 40 percent, thus effectively lowering the maximum capital gains tax from 35 percent (i.e., 50 percent of income $\times$ 70 percent of tax rate) to 28 percent. In addition, the untaxed portion of capital gains income was no longer subject to the 15 percent preference tax. Also, the reclassification of $1 of personal service income as ordinary income for every $1 of untaxed capital gain income was eliminated. However, these two tax features still applied to the difference between fair market value and option price at time of exercise.

Each of these legislated changes made nonqualified stock options comparatively more attractive. In the eyes of many, the official death of the qualified in 1981 was more a "mercy killing" than a vicious act. Assuming the 50 percent marginal tax income bracket is not indexed or at least periodically increased, few middle managers would be unaffected by these taxes, assuming compensation growth for the last several years basically continues.

The stripping away of the tax advantages of the statutory options coupled with a lackluster stock market has sent many pay planners back to the drawing boards to create something as attractive.

Are Stock Options Still Viable?

For those who feel comfortable with long-term stock market performance, nonqualified options are still attractive. Like the statutory option, there is no tax liability at time of grant; however, at time of exercise the spread between market value and option price is taxed (at the earned income, or as now defined "personal service income," 50 percent maximum). Since it is taxed as income the TPI does not apply at time of exercise although 60 percent of the gain at time of sale (assuming long-term capital gains treatment) will be subject to the alternative minimum tax without adverse maximum tax consequences. The holding period to achieve long-term capital gains is the same as for other holdings (i.e., more than 1 year).

The company finds the nonstatutory option more tax effective since it has a deduction at time of the optionee's exercise. The only way the company received a similar deduction under the qualified option was if the optionee sold the stock short of the "more than 3-year" holding requirement. This premature sale was called a disqualifying disposition and allowed the company to take a tax deduction equal to the spread between market value at date of exercise and option price.

Some companies granted both qualified and nonqualified stock options to executives. If each option was self-standing (i.e., not affected by the other) it was a *parallel* grant. If the exercise of one reduced the number of shares exercisable under the other, it was a *tandem* grant.

To illustrate, the executive might receive 5000 shares of a nonqualified option for 10 years and 5000 shares of a qualified grant for 5 years—each at the same price. This would be a parallel grant. If, however, the individual received a grant of 10,000 of each but the exercise of one would proportionately reduce the other, this would be a tandem

227

grant. Thus exercising 2000 shares as a qualified grant would lower the maximum available under each grant to 8000 shares.

Just as companies were warming to this approach, Revenue Ruling 73-26 rendered it useless. It stated that whenever the action on a nonstatutory option affects the exercise rights of a qualified grant, that qualified grant becomes a nonqualified option for all purposes (except remaining in effect for exercise sequence issues). Pay planners giveth and the IRS taketh away!

Who Is Eligible for Stock Options?

As with the short-term incentive plans, eligibles may be determined by base salary, job grade (or job evaluation points), a banding of comparable level positions, or on a job-by-job selection basis. The degree of penetration from the CEO down is normally not as deep as with short-term incentives, although the extent of coverage is a function of corporate objective. Very limited participation is connected with a view that only a limited few can have sufficient impact on corporate earnings (which, it is assumed, will result in a higher stock price, assuming no revaluation of the stock earnings multiple).

Rather broad coverage is consistent with a desire to place a large number of executives and managers "at risk" with stock price and thus more closely associated with other shareholders. Admittedly individuals further down in the organization may not have the same impact on corporate performance, but many will argue that they will be more interested in effecting economies and improving performance if they are part owners. The price for broader coverage is greater dilution to shareholder equity since more shares must be placed under option.

How Big a Stock Option?

Determining the number of shares to give under option to each executive is very important since it defines the absolute amount of opportunity for appreciation for that executive and the amount relative to other executives. As expected the most shares are given to the CEO, and executives at lower levels of management get successively smaller numbers of shares. Classically the CEO receives not only more shares than the next job down but also a greater award *relative to compensation*. Thus a CEO earning $500,000 might receive 50,000 shares (a 10:1 ratio) whereas the president earning $375,000 might receive 30,000 shares (an 8:1 ratio).

The most frequently employed technique in structuring options is the multiple. As shown below, the number of shares to be granted under the option is determined by multiplying the individual's salary (or salary plus bonus) times a value (the assigned multiple) and dividing the product by the fair market value of a share of stock.

$$O = \frac{P \times M}{S}$$

O = number of optioned shares of stock
P = individual's pay
M = assigned multiple
S = FMV of one share of stock

Periodically studies are made of the multiples being used by companies in making their option grants. Usually such studies calculate the multiples based on the actions taken, rather than reporting the actual multiple formulas used in setting the awards. Logically one might expect the reported multiples to be subject to pressure to decrease during periods of falling stock prices and to increase during periods of rising prices. Furthermore one should expect higher multiples in mature companies than in their growth counterparts (i.e., the less the believed potential for increase, the higher the multiple).

In addition, it is important to attempt to separate companies relying solely on stock options from those who combine stock options with other forms of long-term incentive compensation. Presumably, the multiples for the first would be higher than the second. If the two are combined in a survey, a company using only stock options is likely to grant fewer shares than competitively appropriate. Conversely, the company using other plans as well is likely to grant more options than competitively suggested.

The data is typically reported in a manner similar to that shown in Figure 8-1. As

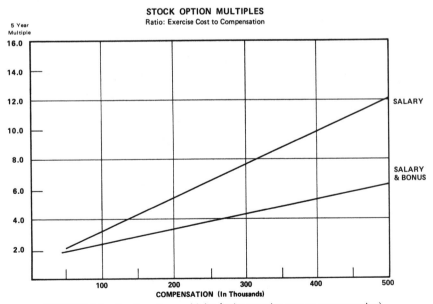

FIGURE 8-1 Stock option multiples (ratio: exercise cost to compensation).

TABLE 8-1   Multiples by Salary and Total Compensation Brackets

Multiple	Salary	Salary plus bonus
12.0	$477,500 and up	$972,500 and up
11.0	432,500–$477,499	877,500–$972,499
10.0	387,500– 432,499	787,500– 877,499
9.0	342,500– 387,499	687,500– 787,499
8.0	297,500– 342,499	592,500– 687,499
7.0	252,500– 297,499	497,500– 592,499
6.0	207,500– 252,499	402,500– 497,499
5.0	162,500– 207,499	307,500– 402,499
4.0	117,500– 162,499	222,500– 307,499
3.0	72,500– 117,499	117,500– 222,499
2.0	37,500– 72,499	52,500– 117,499
1.0	Up to $ 37,500	Up to $ 52,500

one would expect, the multiple for salary is higher than that for salary plus bonus (proportionate to the ratio of salary alone to salary plus bonus). When using such data, it is useful to know whether the average represented is the mean or the median; the former is often easier to calculate, but it is subject to influence by a limited number of very high or low values.

Note that one can establish compensation brackets by selecting various points on the line and extending a plus and minus value parallel to the X compensation axis. In this fashion a table such as the one in Table 8-1 can be constructed (values above 6.0 multiples for salary and bonus were projected from the curve).

Note that the Y axis in the multiple chart indicates "5-year," and thus the values are appropriate when granting options every 5 years. If options are granted more frequently, a proportionately lower multiple is appropriate (e.g., every 3 years would be 60 percent of a 5-year multiple; conversely every 5 years would be 167 percent of a 3-year multiple). A graphic illustration is shown in Figure 8-2, contrasting 5-year and 3-year multiples.

It should be noted that these stock multiple exhibits are intended to be illustrative, rather than indicative of prevailing practices. There are, however, a number of studies on the size of multiples published each year by various management consulting firms and management associations. The classic multiple could be modified with additional input (e.g., promotability). For example, executives considered immediately promotable would have their multiple adjusted by 1.25 (giving a 25 percent premium). Conversely, executives considered either at their peak or no more than long-term promotionable candidates would be adjusted by a 0.75 factor (a 25 percent reduction).

Perhaps a simpler way is to develop a minimum, normal, and maximum award (expressed in shares of stock) for each eligible as shown in Table 8-2. Using a sum of the normal awards to construct a division total, the unit head could then work out the appropriate awards using the range (except when a zero award was appropriate). Such

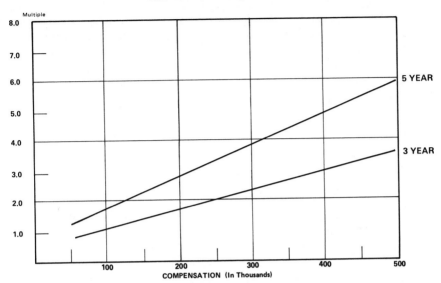

STOCK OPTION MULTIPLES
Ratio: Exercise Cost to Salary Plus Bonus

FIGURE 8-2   Stock option multiples: 3-year versus 5-year.

an approach permits the management compensation committee to adjust the control totals up or down for divisions to reflect unit performance.

This approach functions much in the same way as a salary range; therefore, the width is a function of the degree of deviation management wishes to make at a given salary level. Recognize that the greater the spread, the greater the overlap in ranges above and below the one being examined. Thus it is more likely for a department head to get an

TABLE 8-2   Award Range by Individual Example, Shares of Stock

| Employee | Grade | Award range | | | Proposed |
		Minimum	Normal	Maximum	
AB	26	0	2,000	4,000	2,000
BC	25	0	1,800	3,600	2,000
CD	22	0	1,100	2,200	800
DE	22	0	1,100	2,200	1,200
EF	20	0	900	1,800	1,200
FG	20	0	900	1,800	1,000
GH	20	0	900	1,800	500
Total			8,700		8,700
Variance to control total					0

award equal to or greater than the supervisor with a ± 100 percent spread than a ± 25 percent range.

One should be cautious about using multiples without ensuring they are reasonably current since the curve will drift up and down in response to market value of the stock. To illustrate: a CEO earning $500,000 in salary plus bonus might receive $1,750,000 worth of stock under an option if the stock were selling at $100 (i.e., 17,500 shares), but it is unlikely the successor would receive 35,000 shares if the stock dropped to $50! It is this very movement of stock prices that causes the most problems with the multiple approach.

Prospective Valuation of the Stock Option   Another issue is how to value the stock option (a critical issue when comparing it with alternative forms of compensation). Some argue that an option given at 100 percent of FMV by definition has no value. On the surface this may seem valid, but it is simply not logical. Since the option is a contract to purchase in the future a stated number of shares of stock at today's price, its present value is a function of future stock price. It is without value only if the future market price is equal to or less than the current price.

Thus if an option for 10,000 shares at $25 were extended to an executive, it would have a present value of $96,522 (assuming a 5 percent compound growth in stock price over 10 years) or $153,674 (assuming a 10 percent increase over 10 years). This is shown in Table 8-3. The market value was determined by compounding the present stock price by 5 percent and 10 percent for 10 years. After subtracting the purchase price from the market value, the gain or spread was then discounted by a value equal to the growth percentage (i.e., 5 percent or 10 percent) to calculate present value.

In this type of valuation there are three factors involved: rate of growth in stock price, number of years of growth, and discount value to determine present value. *Rate of growth* is really a combination of estimated growth in earnings and price-earnings multiple. If earnings per share is estimated to increase at 10 percent per annum and the price earnings multiple remains constant, the rate of growth is a simple compound 10 percent. More sophisticated models can be developed with varying annual rates of growth and annual variances in price-earnings multiple if desired, although the sophistication probably greatly exceeds the validity of the assumptions.

The *number of years of growth* can be anywhere up to but not beyond the length of the option. Some will argue that use of 5 years is better than 10 on the belief that

TABLE 8-3   Present Value Example for Stock Options

	Compound growth rate	
	5 percent	10 percent
Purchase price ($25 × 10,000)	$250,000	$250,000
Market value 10 years later	407,224	648,436
Gain	157,224	398,436
Present value of gain	96,522	153,674

TABLE 8-4   Another Present Value Example for Stock Options

Period of measurement, years	Compound growth rate	
	5 percent	10 percent
5	$48,111	$106,314
10	76,284	193,319

executives do not wait until the very end of the option period to exercise but rather are exercising throughout the period. In the above example, if the period had been halved to 5 years, the present value would have been $54,118 and $94,770, respectively.

While it may be logical to assume the same *rate of discount* as used for market growth, some will argue that an alternative use of money is more appropriate, such as interest on tax-free municipal bonds. For sake of illustration assume that the rate is 7.5 percent. The impact of this discount rate on the 10- and 5-year periods is shown in Table 8-4.

As one would expect, in comparison with Table 8-3 this results in a lesser value compared with the 5 percent discount and a greater value in relation to the 10 percent discount. Furthermore, it should be remembered that these are average compound rates; the year-to-year rates could vary significantly. Nonetheless, one must pick average rates which seem attainable. Even sophisticated adjustments based on historical trend analysis often suggest future values that are significantly off the mark. Thus rather than either completely ignoring the present value or attempting to be too precise, it is probably more appropriate to give a range to the present value by using two growth numbers that bracket most probable growth. Perhaps it could be agreed that a 5 to 10 percent growth rate in stock price is most probable; in the above situation this would mean giving an option with present value of approximately $100,000 to $150,000.

Historical Valuation of the Stock Option   Easier than predicting what an option might be worth is examining on a retrospective basis what previous options have been worth—especially important in studies of competitive total compensation packages. Unfortunately even here there is considerable debate as to the correct approach. The possibilities include: (1) total gain between selling price and option price, (2) spread between option price and fair market value on date of exercise, and (3) hypothetical gain.

The most troublesome of these three approaches is the one utilizing total gain between selling price and option price. The complications of tracking options over varying time intervals and attempting to relate their gain to a specified time frame are awesome, but more important, doing it is believed to be inappropriate. Once the executive has received the stock, when to sell is the individual's decision (except for the 6-month limitation imposed on insiders); thus the person is like any other stockholder in the company. In retrospect the decision to sell may run the gamut from propitious to disas-

TABLE 8-5 Illustration of Hypothetical Gain on Stock Option

Option price	Valuation price	Difference	No. of shares	Total value
$25	$40	$15	5,000	$25,000
33	40	17	3,000	21,000
37	40	3	7,000	21,000
42	40	−2	8,000	0
36	40	4	9,000	36,000
Total			32,000	$153,000
Average (5 years)				$ 30,600

trous. Nonetheless, the selling decision is not a function of the executive compensation program.

Admittedly, using the spread between fair market value and option price on date of exercise as the basis for measurement has the logic that this approach is consistent with the tax rules. Unfortunately the problem with using total gain is also a factor here. Since the date of exercise (within certain limitations of the grant) is at the discretion of the executive, it too is a market investment decision (similar to selling). In retrospect the amount of the gain may either be overstated or minuscule in relation to the total gain (if any) realized at time of sale. The argument for using this approach is threefold: (1) the appreciation is real, (2) it is directly a function of the form of compensation, and (3) presumably the executive is exercising at the point in time believed to be most advantageous.

The third possible approach, hypothetical gain, is designed to ignore individual investor decisions on exercise and sale. It simply calculates the spread between any options granted and the fair market value at the end of a prescribed period. Since many companies grant options on less than an annual basis, it is important to use a sufficiently long period; 3 years might be adequate, but 5 is probably better. As shown in Table 8-5, the spread between option price and market price at a prescribed date (or the average over 10 days to minimize market swings) is calculated and averaged over the period of time examined. Its advantage is also its disadvantage: it bears little or no relationship to what the executive actually realized as gain.

Frequency of Grants It used to be common practice to grant options every 3 to 5 years, yet the trend appears to be in the direction of the more logical approach of granting them annually—appropriately adjusting the multiple. Fewer shares on a more frequent basis minimizes the impact of rising compensation and swings in the price of the stock, as well as the visibility of large options to insiders. If options are not granted on an annual basis, it is also necessary to make interim (off-year) grants to new hires and recently promoted.

In an interim or catch-up grant, it is necessary to adjust the regular stock option grant guidelines by: the estimated future market value, the previous grant (number of shares and option price), the extent of lapsed time since the regular grant, and the current option price. These requirements are expressed in the formula shown in Equation 8-1.

EQUATION 8-1 Formula for Interim or Catch-up Stock Option

$$RT[NS_g(FMV - OP_M)] - [NS_M(FMV - OP_M)] = NS_c(FMV - OP_c)$$

RT = percentage of time remaining before next major grant
NS_g = number shares granted this grade in last major grant
NS_1 = number shares granted this person in major grant
NS_c = number shares to be granted this person in catch-up
FMV = fair market value of stock at time of next major grant
OP_M = option price of last major grant
OP_c = option price of catch-up grant

Assume 1 year later one individual has been promoted and another hired into grade 21 (which last year during the major grant called for a normal award of 1000 shares with the stock price at $50). The stock is currently at $55, and the growth rate is still anticipated to be 10 percent a year (or $66.50 a share 2 years hence at the time of the next major grant). The known values are shown in Table 8-6. Rounding the results would suggest granting 1000 shares to the new hire and an additional 200 shares to the recently promoted individual.

It is recognized that the formulas in Table 8-6 erroneously equate a straight-line relationship of time with an increasing value effected by compound growth; however, this is not believed serious given the fact that the solved unknown is most likely to be rounded and otherwise adjusted by management judgment. In addition formulas can be developed to use present value if that is deemed appropriate. Regardless of the approach the basic logic is give options to recent hires and promotions which will equate them

TABLE 8-6 Example of Stock Option Catch-up Grant

	New hire	Promoted
RT	0.67	0.67
NS_g	1,000	1,000
NS_1	0	800
NS_c	?	?
FMV	66.50	66.50
OP_m	50	50
OP_c	55	55

Promotion
$$0.67 [1,000 (66.50 - 50)] - [800 (66.50 - 50)] = NS_c (66.50 - 55)$$
$$NS_c = 192.3$$

New Hire
$$0.67 [1,000 (66.50 - 50)] - [0 (66.50 - 50)] = NS_c (66.50 - 55)$$
$$NS_c = 961.3$$

with the major grant optionees *only for the remaining time until the next grant.* Using the above approach (or for that matter any time-adjusted formula), the catch-up grant will be too generous vis-à-vis the previous major if the stock price is greater than assumed; conversely it will be too low if the growth in the stock price is less than assumed. In our example, plus or minus the assumed $66.50 a share is the issue.

If the stock price not only does not rise appreciably, but drops to a level where it is believed it will probably not rise to the option price before the grant expires, it is not illogical to recycle the option by replacing the old ones with new grants at the current lower price. This cancel-and-reissue or "swap" program can get a company into trouble if it has not received approval from the shareholders for such an action. Whether the same number of shares, or more, or less, should be extended in this recycling should be based on an assessment of probable growth.

The more liberal approach would argue for a higher number of shares (even assuming the same dollar per share increase over the coming 10 years) than was projected when the earlier option was extended. The increase would be based on the recouping of the lost time. For example if an option was extended at $50 a share 5 years ago and the market price is currently $25, it might be decided to give twice as many shares.

Conversely others argue that the swap should be for fewer shares since a lower option price has been established. Such a philosophy is based on the assumption that the value (i.e., spread between option price and market value at some designated point in future time) will be greater under the swap than what was assumed for purpose of the original grant. For example, if the option price for the original grant was $50 and it was assumed it would be worth $100 after 7 years, a swap at $25 should be made for fewer shares if it is assumed the market value will exceed $75 within the prescribed time frame.

The other decision to be made when swapping options is what to use for an expiration date. Should it be the date of the old option or should it run for a full cycle (e.g., 10 years)? The answer is a function of whether the swap is simply a rescue operation or is being combined with a regular option review. The former would suggest use of the original grant's expiration date, and the latter would indicate a full time frame would be more appropriate.

These problems of catch-up grants and swaps are essentially eliminated with the use of annual grants. In addition to responding to organizational changes they allow fine tuning with regard to the stock price—a form of dollar value averaging. They also permit a form of deferred compensation similar to the cash award that has to be earned out over 5 years. By establishing a 1-year waiting period and then a maximum exercise of 25 percent of the total option in each of the succeeding 4 years, the recipient has a layered series of parts of five different options after 5 years. Furthermore, the executive will *never* be able to exercise all the outstanding options if terminating employment, except as permitted under the plan for retirement, disability, and death.

The consideration of downside risk is also important in stock option plans. The executive is placed in a precarious position when having to borrow to exercise the stock option if the intent is to hold it for some time. Consider this illustration: the individual borrows $250,000 at 10 percent interest to exercise a 5000-share option at $50. Since the market price is currently $75 there is a paper profit (and either tax preference or personal service income depending on whether there is a qualified or a nonqualified option of $125,000). Furthermore, unless the dividend is at least two-thirds of the interest rate (i.e., $250,000 loan versus $375,000 market value of acquired stock), the dividends will not cover the interest, much less any repayment of principal. Nonetheless things aren't too bad—and then the stock starts to slide. With each drop the bank becomes more vocal about additional collateral. Obviously if the price drops below $50, the executive has a paper loss. To the extent this necessitates sale of the stock, the executive may have lost money at a point above $50 a share (based on the manner in which the gain at exercise was taxed versus the loss realized).

Proxy Statement Disclosures   Until the 1979 proxy season, most companies simply included a table reflecting the number of shares: under option, exercised, and granted during the year by individual and/or officers and directors. The individuals were the same as those identified in the remuneration table; the price was often the average of all grants outstanding, granted and/or exercised, rather than price by grant. For 1979 and 1980, companies were required to report the gain between fair market value and option price for options exercised during the period as part of the number in the C_2 column, in addition to the option table information.

With the 1981 proxies, companies are required to again provide only separate information on stock options for the same individuals identified in the remuneration table along with aggregate totals for all directors and officers as a group. This information can be shown in a table indicating the number of shares granted during the last fiscal year (and their average option price), the number of shares exercised, the net gains resulting during the period, and the number of shares unexercised (and their potential or unrealized value as of year end). No option data is to be reported in the remuneration table.

These changes apparently were initiated by the SEC in reaction to criticisms of the inclusion of option data in the proxy statement and in an attempt to give shareholders a better picture of the stock option program. These changes also recognize that simply including option gains in the remuneration table was combining value received for services during the reported fiscal year and (in the case of options) value realized from awards of earlier periods. In addition, the negative values being generated by SARs also caused the SAR disclosure requirements to be changed.

STOCK APPRECIATION RIGHTS

Another feature employed by many in conjunction with a nonqualified option is the *stock appreciation right*, or SAR (attaching it to a qualified option would automatically make it a nonqualified option). The SAR permits the optionee to receive the appreciation of FMV over option price in stock and/or cash without providing funds for the option price. The SAR is an alternative right to the stock option itself; self-standing SARs are really phantom awards, since there is no accompanying stock option. Such a plan must be designed carefully to avoid an IRS ruling of constructive receipt due to lack of alternative right. An important point to remember in structuring a plan to avoid constructive receipt is the basic principle that if income is available only if the individual forfeits a valuable right, then income is subject to a substantial limitation and not constructively received. In Rev. Rul. 80-300 the IRS, applying this logic, indicated that since the exercise of the SAR would mean the loss of a valuable right (namely the chance for further appreciation in the market price) the gain should not be recognized as income until the rights are exercised.

Normally the number of SARs is equal to the number of shares under option; however, one variation would be to attach SARs to only half the stock options and require that a stock option be exercised with every SAR. Plans may allow for issuance only at time of option grant or, as is more logical, anytime during the life of an outstanding option, since this more carefully limits the charge to earnings problem. The SAR may be eligible for the full market gain over the option price or artificially limited (e.g., no more than a 25 percent increase); this will minimize the exercise of SARs when larger gains are attainable by exercising the accompanying option. The settlement in some plans permits only stock whereas others allow a combination of stock and/or cash settlements. Some plans provide for a supplementary cash payment to cover the estimated tax liability; such provisions are more logical when settlement is in stock as the executive will not be forced to sell stock in order to meet tax obligations. This could be accomplished by giving an SAR payable in cash in addition to stock received in exercising the option.

Here's how the typical SAR works. Assume the executive was granted an option of 10,000 shares at $50 a share with SARs attached to all shares. Several years later the stock is selling at $70, and the executive, rather than seek financing, wishes to exercise 5000 shares through appreciation rights. The 5000 shares have an aggregate option price of $250,000 and a fair market value of $350,000. This $100,000 difference divided by the market price of $70 a share would mean the executive would receive 1428 shares of stock worth $99,960 plus $40 in cash (if cash settlement were allowed by the plan) or any combination of stock and cash totaling $100,000 (if permitted by the plan and in conformance with SEC requirements). The corporation would have a deduction for $100,000 and the executive a tax liability for a comparable amount of personal services income. The executive would still have 5000 shares remaining under option, and if the plan permitted, (1) 1428 shares would have been charged against any plan maximum in effect per participant, not 5000, and (2) 3572 shares, the difference between 5000 and 1428, would have been returned to the plan for future grants!

The grant of an SAR is not considered a purchase under SEC rules; at the time of exercise, stock received is considered to be a purchase and the 6-month rule is invoked. Until recently, the SEC viewed the receipt of cash in lieu of stock as a simultaneous purchase and sale and therefore a prohibited transaction with all gains forfeitable to the company. After further reflection the SEC agreed to permit the payment in cash provided certain rules were met. These include:

1. The SAR must be administered by a disinterested board of directors or by a committee of three or more disinterested persons.

2. The SAR cannot be exercisable for the first 6 months.

3. The SAR can be exercisable only between the third and twelfth business days following the release of quarterly company earnings data.

The third requirement can be bypassed if the allowable date of exercise is outside the control of the individual and specified in advance in the plan.

Not too surprisingly stock appreciation rights are very popular. Unfortunately most are premature in the assignment (as well as too liberal in the eligibility). Rather than automatically attaching them at the time of grant, it is more rational to monitor the performance of outstanding options before making a decision. For example, after 5 years (on a 10-year option) it is logical to ascertain whether there is sufficient spread to obviate the need for SARs (i.e., whether fair market value is significantly above option price) except perhaps for insiders with financing difficulties. If not, perhaps 25 percent of the option should have an SAR attached (at a price equal to the original grant). The following year the review is made again and if the stock market is still sluggish another 25 percent of the grant could be covered by the SAR.

The advantage of waiting is that the impact upon the earnings statement is more closely monitored (APB 25 again) and statements are issued only on a need basis. Accounting regulations require quarterly determination and accrual of compensation expense liability based on change in the market price of the stock. Therefore, sharp rises or drops in company stock price can have a significant effect on earnings if SARs are used extensively within a company.

FASB Interpretation No. 31 requires that when stock or cash is available under payout, it will be assumed to be stock unless there is a reasonable basis for assuming otherwise. A resolution by the compensation committee to make SAR settlements in cash would presumably meet this reasonable basis. However, if the executive had the choice it would probably be necessary to assume a stock settlement. However, if the executive decided to exercise the stock option rather than take the SAR, the accruals established as a charge to earnings logically would be eliminated since the SAR liability has been removed. The advantage of paying the 16(b)3 executive in cash rather than stock is that the individual has no downside risk during the 6-month period following exercise. However, cash settlements of SARs are not as attractive to the company since they result in negative cash flow (versus the positive cash flow resulting from the tax benefit if stock is issued).

In the earlier example, assuming the stock price dropped from $70 to $60 during the 6 months following exercise, the market value of the stock received under the SAR feature would be $85,680 (i.e., $60 × 1428 shares). If the 5000 shares had been exercised as an option, the market value would be $300,000; however, the executive's gain would be only $50,000—since the individual had to invest $250,000 to acquire the stock. In the latter case, this would about equal the individual's tax liability, whereas in the former situation the executive would still have a reasonably good profit without having to worry about financing and carrying charges.

While it would be nice to extend SARs to all with options (and thereby minimize the amount of new stock issued), the existence of APB 25 and the required charge to the earnings statement makes it prohibitively expensive. Therefore the individual can achieve the same net gain by purchasing and quickly selling the portion needed to cover financing and perhaps income taxes, but the other shareholders experience the resulting decrease in earnings per share through increased dilution.

Some plans put limitations on this tandem option-SAR arrangement by requiring a minimum percentage of the option which must be exercised for the full stock—thereby putting a portion of the executive's potential growth at risk with this investment (exercise price). This approach would be very unattractive to 16b-3 executives due to the financing problems and the risks associated with the 6-month rule.

Other plans allow recipients to exercise the SAR only within prescribed time periods (i.e., windows) each year. Such periods may be limited, such as the 10 days following quarterly earnings statements, and may apply to 16(b)3 executives and others, for stock as well as cash settlements. It would not be surprising if a few companies decided to handle the exercise of the stock option in the same manner.

In addition, companies need to decide whether or not to keep the SAR open after death or other termination. If so, they may want to limit the number of shares (i.e., the spread) available on date of termination (rather than allow continued recognition of market growth) or value at time of exercise, whichever is less.

SARs are attractive in times of high interest rates and low stock price appreciation. Due to purchase and sale restrictions on insiders and the charge to the earnings statements, such alternative rights should logically therefore be restricted to those with 16(b) problems.

The popularity of SARs, however, may wane with the spread of stock-for-stock exercise of stock options, since the executive ends up with the same number of shares that would have been received through exercise of the SARs. To illustrate, assume the executive has an option for 10,000 shares at $40 a share along with a comparable number of accompanying SARs. If the executive exercises the SARs when the market price is $50, he or she will receive 2000 shares of stock (i.e., $100,000 divided by $50). Assume the executive also owns 10,000 shares of company stock acquired before this transaction with a cost basis of $30 a share. The individual now owns 12,000 shares of company stock, 10,000 at $30 and 2000 at $50 for subsequent sale purposes. Conversely, if the executive exercised the entire option using stock, he or she would turn over 8000 shares (i.e., $400,000 value based on $50 a share) to the company and receive two certificates in return—one for the 8000 shares tendered and another for the 2000-share appreciation. The executive now owns 12,000 shares (i.e., the 2000 retained, the 8000 exchanged, and the 2000 in appreciation). Of this total, 10,000 would still have a $30 value basis and the 2000 would be valued at $50 for purpose of subsequent sale.

While either transaction brings a tax deduction to the company, the SAR results in a charge to corporate earnings whereas the stock-for-stock exchange does not. Since there is no difference in result to the executive, one could conclude that a number of companies will switch from SARs to stock-for-stock exchange as a manner of exercising the stock option.

However, for the stock-for-stock exchange to be attractive the executive must possess sufficient stock to be able to use it for exercising the option. In the above example, the executive needed 8000 shares to be able to exercise the grant. How can the individual accomplish this if he or she only owns 2000 shares? The answer: Pyramid the exchange. Namely, give the company the 2000 shares, receiving 2500 in return, turn back the 2500 and receive 3125 back, etc. Using this process a total of 4 times, the individual is able to exercise the full grant.

	Shares			
Transaction	Turn in	Retain	Receive	Remaining under option
1	2,000	—	2,500	7,500
2	2,500	—	3,125	4,375
3	3,125	—	3,906	469
4	375	3,531	469	—
	—	469		
Total		4,000		

It is important to remember that SEC has ruled that stock-for-stock exchanges do not constitute a sale. Thus, for 16b purposes, even though there may be more than one purchase within 6 months, there is no prohibited transaction since no sale is involved. However, at time of printing it was unclear as to the SEC view of this type of pyramiding transaction. Also important, was the fact that IRS had not commented on this type of multiple transaction.

Proxy Statement Disclosure

Also for the 1979–80 proxy period, companies were required to report the accruals for SARs in tandem with stock options and free-standing in column D of the remuneration table; any gain of exercised SARs not previously accrued was to be reported in column C_2. Furthermore, decreases in stock price would result in credits to SAR accruals which in turn could produce a negative amount in column D.

Beginning with 1981, the SEC requires that SARs in tandem with stock options be excluded from the remuneration table and instead be reported separately and preferably in the stock option table. Free-standing SARs require separate disclosure, again preferably in a separate table. This table should show the number of SARs granted during the period, exercised during the period, and outstanding at the end of the period. Furthermore, the amounts received as a result of the exercise of such rights should be reported along with the value of unrealized gains from rights outstanding at the end of the reporting period.

STOCK PURCHASES

While stock options promote ownership among key employees, excessive use will dilute shareholder equity. An alternative form of promoting ownership is the executive stock purchase plan. The key difference between the option and the purchase plan is that the latter has a much more limited period in which the executive decides whether or not to buy the stock. While the stock option may allow up to 10 years, the purchase plan typically allows a month or two.

The executive stock purchase plan should not be confused with the purchase plans described in Chapter 5, Employee Benefits. Those plans require nearly all employees to participate and allow up to 27 months for the individual to purchase stock as low as 85 percent of market value (determined either at time of offer or time of purchase depending on the structure of the plan). Such plans are developed in accord with Section 423 of the Internal Revenue Code and must be nondiscriminatory in participation. Executive stock purchase plans are much more flexible in design and limited in participation. Executive plans can be described in terms of the basis for determining cost of the shares and the basis for payment. Since each can be either fixed or variable in nature, the result is four possible combination plans.

Fixed Cost and Fixed Basis for Payment

Typically the cost is market price of the stock at the time the offer is made; the basis for payment is a specified yearly schedule which will pay for the stock over a stated period of years. Such arrangements are attractive because typically the company gives the executive a low-interest or no-interest loan to purchase the stock (see Chapter 6, Perquisites). Ideally the executive's annual bonus is sufficient to meet the loan repayment amount. However, since the bonus is of course taxable, this would suggest that a $20,000 bonus is necessary to retire $10,000 of the loan in a given year. In addition it may be appropriate to structure the loan so that after a period of years the executive can cancel the loan balance by returning to the company the number of shares whose market value equals the loan balance. Should the executive leave the company, typically such loans are required to be paid in full immediately (although a forgiveness clause might be structured in the event of the executive's death).

Since the executive will have personal service income at time of purchase, equal to the difference between purchase price and fair market value, it is desirable from the executive's point of view to immediately purchase all the shares (when this difference is little or nothing) through a loan arrangement. However, the company must be careful to ensure that the Federal Reserve margin requirements are followed when shares are used as collateral.

If the purchase price is discounted, the stock is typically given to the executive with a number of restrictions regarding disposition. The discount may be a stated percentage (e.g., 50 percent) or a stated value (e.g., par or book value). Discounted stock purchase plans are designed to ease the financing (by lowering the cost) and minimize the negative impact of a drop in the market price (by setting the purchase price significantly below market value). The restrictions are placed on the executive to minimize temptations to sell the stock prematurely for a quick profit. The restrictions also affect the tax treatment since the company deduction and executive's personal service income are both deferred until the restrictions lapse. Such restrictions can be of the installment nature (e.g., 10 percent a year for 10 years) or all or nothing (e.g., 100 percent after 5 years but zero vesting before then). While the restrictions are in effect, the shares of stock affected generate dividends which are subject to the personal service income maximum. The discount value must be recognized by the company as a charge to the earnings statement.

Fixed Cost and Variable Basis for Payment

Given an amortization schedule to retire the loan, it may be possible to establish a formula indicating the portion of that annual payment which may be canceled by corporate performance. These "earnouts" are charged to company earnings, reported as personal service income to the executive, and taken as a company tax deduction.

As an example, the schedule may call for an annual $10,000 payment toward retiring the loan. However, this amount can be reduced by $1000 for every 1 percent increase in EPS beyond 10 percent. Thus, a 15 percent increase in EPS one year would only require a payment of $5000 with the other $5000 being "forgiven." In addition, or in lieu of the performance variable, a time-in-job factor could be designed. For example, $1000 might be forgiven each year for each year of service since receiving the stock. Thus, $9000 would be required after the first year, $8000 after the second, and so on. This accelerated "earnout" makes staying with the company very attractive to the executive.

Variable Cost and Fixed Basis for Payment

Rather than set the purchase price for all shares at the time of agreement to buy, it is possible to annually determine the cost of the shares to be purchased that year. The amount of annual discount is taken as a charge to the company earnings, reported as personal service income to the executive, and identified as a company tax deduction.

For example, the formula might prescribe 50 percent of market value each year for 5 years. If 10,000 shares of stock were involved, this would mean that the value of 2000 shares would be determined each year in relation to the then current market value. Or on the assumption that price should really be a function of earnings, some multiple assigned to EPS could be used. For example, if a multiple of four were used, the cost for year 1 would be $12.00 for each share, or $24,000 if the EPS were $3.00, whereas it would be $13.20 per share in year 2, or $26,400 if the EPS were $3.30.

Variable Cost and Variable Basis for Payment

This is simply a combination of two variable formulas, one which determines the cost and the other which determines the extent of forgiveness. By definition, it is not only the most complicated combination, but it is also the one most subject to dramatic swings in the amount of value delivered to the executive.

STOCK AWARDS

Essentially a stock award is a stock purchase with a 100 percent discount. It too can either be given immediately or restricted with ownership deferred to a future date(s) with much the same treatment as outlined above for stock purchases.

A restricted stock plan is structured around a conditional transfer of the company stock to the executive. While the individual is prevented from assigning, transferring, or selling the stock without a taxable liability, the executive has the right to vote the stock, receive dividends, and even possess the stock certificate (although it is noted on its face as being restricted in sale).

Let's examine how a restricted stock award might operate. Eligible executives are given stock awards every 3 years in accord with the schedule in Table 8-7. Using our earlier identified salary schedule, let's assume the chairman and CEO is in grade 40 with a current salary of $300,000. Using the table value of 1.5 would require a restricted

TABLE 8-7 Stock Award Multiple by Grade Example

Grade	Award multiple
40	1.5
39	1.4
38	1.3
37	1.2
36	1.1
35	1.0
34	0.9
33	0.8
32	0.7
31	0.6
30	0.5

TABLE 8-8 Restricted Stock Award Based on EPS

Compound growth in EPS over period, percent	Percent of restricted award released
12 or higher	100
10.0–11.9	75
8.0–9.9	50
6.0–7.9	25
Below 6	0

stock award worth $450,000. If the stock were currently selling at $50 a share, the CEO would receive 9000 shares.

If the restrictions are lifted simply in accord with continued employment, it may be logical to assume the charge to earnings is based on the value at time of grant. If, however, the amount of award is also related in any manner to company success, it would be appropriate to also accrue for the subsequent appreciation in determining the earnings charge. This would be consistent with the treatment of performance shares (which will be discussed later in this chapter). In any event, the company takes a tax deduction for the FMV of stock in the year restrictions lapse—including appreciation plus initial stock value. The deduction is thus equal to the amount the executive realizes as compensation, which is treated as personal service income subject to the 50 percent maximum tax. When the stock is sold, the difference between value at time taxed and selling price is eligible for long-term capital gains if more than 12 months have lapsed.

The restrictions on the award can be set in a variety of ways, the simplest being continued employment. For example our CEO is placed on a 33⅓ percent per year earnout. Thus, after 1 year the individual would own outright 3000 shares, after 2 years 6000, and concluding the third year, all 9000 shares. Usually such plans would allow earnout also in case of disability, retirement, or death, but not other breaks in employment. Restrictions can also be related to company performance, as shown in Table 8-8, but such plans are commonly identified as performance share plans and will be covered later in this chapter.

Recognizing that the recipient has personal service income on the full fair market value of the stock for which restrictions lapse, it may be necessary for the executive to dispose of some of the stock in order to meet the tax liability. One way to solve this liquidity problem is to grant a contingent cash bonus tied to company performance. Table 8-9 indicates the amount of cash to be paid under prescribed company performance.

Thus if the EPS increase over the first year was 12.0 percent, the CEO would receive not only 3000 shares of stock but also a cash value equivalent to its market value. Let's assume the stock price had increased from $50 to $55. Thus the cash bonus would be $165,000—hypothetically a sufficient amount to pay the tax liability on both the stock and the cash without having to sell any stock! Note that if the cash bonus is set in terms of FMV at time of award it will not be sufficient to meet tax liabilities at the time

TABLE 8-9 Contingent Cash Bonus Based on Company Performance

Compound growth in EPS over period, percent	Percent of FMV of stock paid in cash
12 or higher	100.0
11.0–11.9	87.5
10.0–10.9	75.0
9.0–9.9	62.5
8.0–8.9	50.0
Below 8.0	0

restrictions come off to the extent the FMV has increased! Conversely it could be greater than required to the extent FMV has decreased.

In the second year, the EPS increase is 9 percent, but when combined with the first-year increase of 12 percent the annualized compound average equals 10.4. This would result in an award of 2250 shares (i.e., 3000 × .75) and a cash award equal to 75 percent of the FMV of the stock. If the stock is now selling for $60 a share, the CEO will receive a cash award of $101,250 (i.e., 2250 × $60 × .75). Assuming no other liquidity, the executive would sell 282 shares (12.5 percent of the 2250 awarded, leaving 1968 plus 3000 from the previous year) to generate $16,920, which when added to the $101,250 would total $118,170—just over one-half the combined value of 2250 shares at $60 a share plus a cash bonus of $101,250.

Alternatively, the plan could be described to pay simply for that year's performance rather than the annualized compound average. In this instance half the shares (i.e., 1500) would be released and $56,250 (i.e., 62.5 percent of the stock's FMV) would be paid in cash.

After a similar calculation was made for the third year, a new table would be devised for another 3-year period. At such time the list of eligibles would again be reviewed. Some companies freeze the eligibles for each 3-year period, thus precluding any additions. Others make additions (usually as a result of replacing a terminated executive) but are careful to stay within a control total number of shares.

In our example we have used a 3-year award period with annual earnouts. A similar result can be effected with annual awards and 3-year earnouts (after a phase-in over the first 2 years). Thus there is greater design flexibility in structuring the award and earnout periods.

In structuring the restricted award, it is necessary to determine how much (and if appropriate under what company performance) will be given on an annual basis. This can then be factored down in component parts (e.g., restricted stock and contingent cash bonus). In our illustration it was considered appropriate to give the CEO a payout equal to salary if EPS were 12 percent or higher with proportion reductions to half-pay for at least an 8.0 percent EPS growth but no payout if company performance falls below a 6.0 percent EPS growth.

It should be noted that the executive could receive capital gains treatment under current tax rules for appreciation from time of award until the date restrictions lapsed. However, the conditions are sufficiently onerous that very few executives will take the needed action. To be eligible for capital gains tax the executive makes a Section 83 election to voluntarily pay tax on the value of the stock on the date it's awarded, recognizing that unless the terms of restriction are fulfilled it will not be possible to ever take ownership! Furthermore if the executive does not receive the stock, there is no credit for the tax paid. Needless to say the executive has to be *very* confident to pay the tax at the time of award rather than waiting until the restrictions lapse.

In addition, restricted stock plans currently have a unique tax characteristic; the dividends paid while the stock is under restriction are a deductible expense to the corporation and considered as personal service income to the executive! In other words dividends paid during the restricted period are treated as compensation, not as dividends! How long this remains in effect is debatable. While this is an attractive advantage for restricted stock plans, it is certainly not sufficient to preclude adopting a different form of plan—especially a more appropriate one, given industry characteristics and company needs.

A variation on the restricted award where the executive automatically vests (attains an unforfeitable right) a portion each year is where the executive is to repay the company a portion of the value of the stock each year. However, this amount will vary depending on company performance. Example: an individual receives $500,000 worth of stock today and is to pay the corporation $100,000 a year over the next 5 years. However, if the corporation attains a 10 percent growth in EPS, that year's $100,000 payment is forgiven, 9 percent reduces it to a $20,000 payment, 8 percent to a $40,000 amount, etc.

Restricted stock awards may be especially attractive in a number of situations. Included among these are:

- A front-end bonus to hire a top executive without distorting the compensation program
- A privately held company interest in tying payment to book value, thus avoiding the market swings of FMV or publicly traded stock
- A company in the mature phase with reduced opportunities for growth in market value of company stock
- A form of golden handcuffs to a retiring executive to ensure the individual does not join the competition

Immediate vesting power, stock in hand, opportunity for long-term capital gains, and no financing problems make these programs very attractive to many individuals. Some shareholders, however, are less than enthusiastic about giving stock away to executives when the stockholders themselves have to buy it.

PERFORMANCE SHARE PLANS

A major variant on the stock award is the performance share plan. The original form (which will be called the classic plan) indicated the number of shares which would be awarded at varying levels of prescribed company performance (individual performance is rarely considered in these plans). To illustrate this type of incentive plan let's go back to our restricted stock example. First let's convert the award multiple to number of shares of stock in relation to either actual salary or midpoint of range and based on current selling price of $50 a share as shown in Table 8-10.

Further let's assume that after an analysis of competitive pay and desired position, the decision makers (e.g., the compensation committee) believe the above is appropriate *after* tax assuming the company attains a compound average increase in EPS of 10 percent over the coming 3-year period. Let's also assume that the company is prepared to proportionately increase the payout for performance above 10 percent up to a maximum of double for 15 percent or more. Conversely for growth less than 10 percent the payout should be reduced proportionately with no payment for less than a 6 percent compound growth.

To achieve the net tax position we can either simply double the number of shares of stock or leave the shares as stated but indicate an equal cash bonus will be paid. The former is appropriate if the executives have sufficient means to pay the tax liability without selling the stock (e.g., large short-term incentive payments); the latter is more logical in the absence of such liquidity as it precludes short-swing trade problems with the insiders, who might be forced to sell stock to meet their tax obligations.

For our example let's assume strictly a stock payout. Thus instead of 9000 shares for

TABLE 8-10 Example of Performance Share by Grade

Grade	Award multiple	Shares of stock
40	1.5	9,000
39	1.4	7,700
38	1.3	6,400
37	1.2	5,200
36	1.1	4,300
35	1.0	3,500
34	0.9	2,800
33	0.8	2,300
32	0.7	1,800
31	0.6	1,400
30	0.5	1,000

TABLE 8-11 Example of Performance
Share Corporate Formula

Compound average percent increase in EPS over 3 years	Percent of stock to be paid
15 or more	200
14.0	180
13.0	160
12.0	140
11.0	120
10.0	100
9.0	80
8.0	60
7.0	40
6.0	20
Under 6.0	0

grade 40 it is 18,000. But remember the decision was to increase or decrease the number proportionate to growth in EPS. Based on the desired relationship, Table 8-11 is constructed.

Thus, if the company compound growth rate in EPS over the next 3 years is 15 percent or more, the CEO (grade 40) will receive 36,000 shares of stock (i.e., 200 percent of 18,000 shares). Such a table could also allow for interpolation (e.g., 14.5 percent = 190 percent, or 34,200 shares for the CEO).

It is important to remember that this is an annualized compound growth rate over the 3-year period, not one that has to be attained in each and every year. Thus increases of 15, 10, and 9 percent for the 3-year period would be an average compound growth rate of 11.3 percent, or in this case an award of 126 percent of normal, or in the case of our grade 40 CEO, 22,680 shares.

In establishing the multiple-year target, one must be careful not to fall into a mathematical logic trap if a multiple-year base is used. For example, a 15 percent annual compound growth in EPS is equivalent to a 23 percent increase over a 2-year base and a 31 percent increase over a 3-year base (assuming annual 15 percent increases). As shown below, the average of the first 2 years is $107.50. Although the third year amount of $132.25 is 15 percent larger than the previous year's $115.00, it is 23 percent greater than $107.50. A similar calculation can be performed using a 3-year average for base.

Year	First-year average	Second-year average	Third-year average
1	$100.00	—	—
2	115.00	$107.50	—
3	132.25	123.51	$115.75

TABLE 8-12 Performance Share
Payout versus Industry Performance

Percent of industry average	Percent of stock to be paid
150	200
140	180
130	160
120	140
110	120
100	100
90	80
80	60
70	40
60	20
Under 60	0

An alternative to company EPS targets would be to set company growth (measured in terms of EPS or return on capital) in relation to other key companies within the same industry as shown in Table 8-12. Or the award could be split so that half was dependent upon company performance, and the other half on this performance relative to the identified key companies.

Initially companies established the payout only after the third year with no payments after the first and second. Needless to say this caused significant blips in earnings for top people. The first refinement was to make prorated payments after the first and second years. Normally this meant a simple one-third of the payment after the first year, but in the second year it was necessary to first calculate two-thirds of the earned award and then subtract the actual first-year payout. A similar calculation was then made in the third year by calculating the 3-year award and netting out the amounts paid after the first and second.

To illustrate, assume the company increase in EPS after the first year was 10 percent: the CEO would receive one-third of the 18,000 shares (i.e., 6000). After the second year the company EPS experienced an 8 percent increase or a compound average of 9 percent. The calculation for the second-year award for the CEO would be two-thirds of 18,000 times 80 percent less 6000 shares, a calculation which would result in an award of 3600 shares. After the third year the EPS increase was 13 percent, or a compound average for the 3-year period of 10.3 percent. Thus the third-year award for the CEO would be 18,000 shares times 106 percent less 9600 (i.e., 6000 + 3600) = 9480 shares.

The above prorating approach resulted in a payout very similar to a short-term annual incentive and, without additional controls, could result in a greater than desired payout (e.g., significantly better EPS growth in the first year than subsequent years). Therefore few companies have retained such a feature, especially since business journals find it easy to make the calculations and add it to salary and short-term incentives whereas other long-term plans are ignored because of difficulty in calculations and multiple years earnings basis.

What a number of companies have done is establish annual awards with payouts after 3 years. Initially this required making three contingent awards: a 1-year, a 2-year and a 3-year. After the first year each award is for the future 3-year period. Unless there is a need for a significant increase in compensation, this approach also allows a gradual buildup in the compensation as well; one-third of the increase the first year, two-thirds after the second, and only after the third year is the full increase in effect. For companies that are fully competitive and are merely changing emphasis within the elements, this allows a 3-year wind-down of the other elements.

Additional advantages of such an approach include: (1) annual adjustments for eligibles rather than several years of waiting, (2) increased retention factor since portions of two awards (i.e., a one-third and a two-thirds) are always outstanding, (3) a smoothing of payout from one year to the next, and (4) the unlikelihood of the annual payments being added to short-term incentive payments by business journals (since they are attributable to 3 years' performance). The impact of the annual payout of multiyear performance versus the single-year payout is demonstrated in the chart in Figure 8-3. After 6 years both plans have paid out the same amount, but the impact on total pay during each of the last 6 years is quite different.

Unfortunately this type of stock award plan results in a double whammy to the earnings statement under APB 25 as shown in Figure 8-4. First, the probable number of shares of stock (at initial market value) that will have to be paid must be amortized. Second, the increase or decrease in stock price has to also be included in the estimated cost of the plan. Thus if the stock price doubles during the period, the impact on the earnings statement will be twice as large as was intended when the award period began.

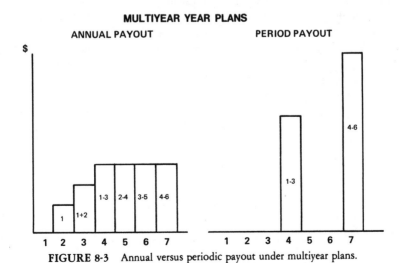

FIGURE 8-3 Annual versus periodic payout under multiyear plans.

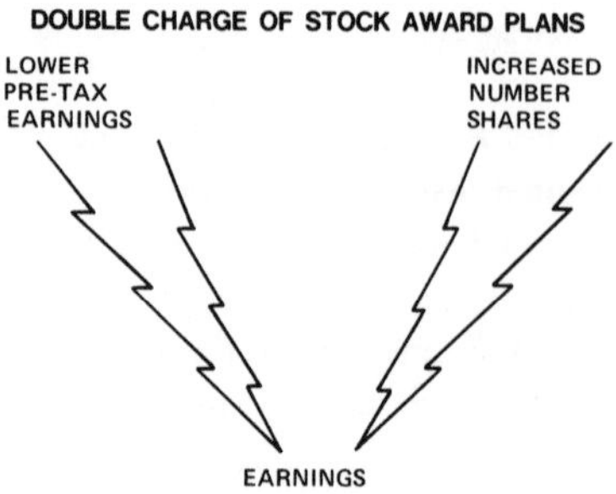

DOUBLE CHARGE OF STOCK AWARD PLANS

LOWER
PRE-TAX
EARNINGS

INCREASED
NUMBER
SHARES

EARNINGS

FIGURE 8-4 Double charge to earnings under performance share plans.

In addition to the above described accounting problems this approach requires a fair degree of ability to quantify objectives with varying degrees of plus and minus performance over the next several years. Not too surprisingly, most plans provide for some form of adjustment in objectives as the plan is operating. While this is necessary to offset changes in accounting and tax treatment unknown when the plan was established, it will be tempting to also adjust for business conditions—and thereby in part defeat the purpose of the plan. This has prompted some cynics to state that a good incentive plan is invariably adjusted after a bad financial year. The inference is that because performance was below bonus levels and people didn't get paid, it needed adjustment.

While it is logical to adjust targets when conditions outside the executive's control dictate, it is important to resist changing simply because of the manifestation of normal business risks. The rationale for midcourse change is that if such factors had been known at the beginning of the period, the goal would have been appropriately modified. Thus midcourse corrections require separating impacting factors from actual performance— a measurement more conceptually understandable than practically administered in many situations. Furthermore, it is important to remember that the true entrepreneur has no one changing his or her goals and profit targets—that individual is stuck with making the best of a bad situation. Some argue that it should not be any different for the professional manager.

For those concerned about altering goals during the period, it is logical to keep the plan cycle as short as possible. By definition the further out in time the plan, the more suspect the conclusions. Therefore, a 3-year plan is less likely to need change than a 5-year program. Even so, setting targets as short as 3 years may be very hazardous in cyclical industries.

PERFORMANCE UNIT PLANS

The uncertainty of the stock price 3 years in the future means the company could be delivering more or less than considered appropriate for a stated level of corporate performance under a classic performance share plan. Both of these deviations could be corrected by converting the performance share to a performance unit plan; the APB requirement of accruing for increases in the value of company stock is then no longer a factor.

Rather than making a contingent award of company stock the current value of the stock is used to develop a dollar allocation. In Table 8-13 the performance shares in the earlier example have been converted using a $50 share (i.e., FMV).

This dollar allocation is adjusted by company performance in relation to Table 8-11. Thus if the corporate 3-year EPS average were 15 percent, instead of 18,000 shares the payment would be $900,000 worth of company stock. If the stock were still selling for $50 a share the payout would be 18,000 shares. However, at $60 a share the executive would receive 15,000 shares. Since the plan is insulated from market factors, it will exactly equal the dollar value believed appropriate at a prescribed level of performance. While the expected dollar allocation must be amortized in accord with APB 25 there is no adjustment for movement in company stock since its market value has no impact on the dollar value of the award.

Needless to say the executive likes the downside risk protection under the performance unit plan but is not very happy if the stock is appreciating (since the individual would have benefited from this in the performance share plan). This is easily negated by attaching a nonqualified stock option for the same 3-year period (or longer depending upon the largesse of the compensation decision makers) for the same number of shares used in developing the dollar allocation. Therefore our grade 40 executive has a $450,000 allocation (subject to upward and downward adjustment in relation to EPS attainment) plus a 9000 share option at $50 a share, good for 3 years.

Going back to the situation with company stock selling at $60 a share and a 15 percent EPS attainment, the executive would receive 15,000 shares but the stock option would be increased to 18,000 shares, thereby allowing $180,000 gain (since the number of shares under option is determined by the same EPS schedule). This combined value of $1,080,000 (i.e., $900,000 plus $180,000) is the same as if the contingent award had

TABLE 8-13 Example of Performance Unit by Grade

Grade	Shares of stock	Dollar allocation
40	9,000	$450,000
39	7,700	385,000
38	6,400	320,000
37	5,200	260,000
36	4,300	215,000
35	3,500	175,000
34	2,800	140,000
33	2,300	115,000
32	1,800	90,000
31	1,400	70,000
30	1,000	50,000

been for 18,000 shares of stock under a performance share plan (i.e., 18,000 × $60 = $1,080,000). However, since gain to the executive of a stock option plan is not charged to earnings, the company has charged $900,000 under the performance unit plan whereas it would have charged $1,080,000 under a performance share plan. Note that it would be of no value to add appreciation rights to the stock option plan as the appreciation would have to be charged to the earnings statement—thus having the same full effect as a performance share plan.

VALUE COMPARISON

It is possible to compare and contrast the degree of downside risk with upside growth potential for each type of plan. Shown in Figure 8-5 is a comparison of 1000 shares under a stock option at $50 a share, a performance share plan of 500 shares at $50 a share, and a performance unit plan of $50,000. Note that all three will generate $50,000 if the stock prices rise to $100 a share—not an unrealistic assumption about 7 years out, assuming no change in price-earnings multiple and a constant increase in earnings per share of 10 percent. However, everyone is familiar with the problems in assuming such a constant relationship. As seen, the stock option is the most highly leveraged form—worthless below $50 a share and worth $100,000 at $150 a share. Conversely the performance unit has no leverage; only the number of shares awarded is adjusted inversely in relation to market direction. The performance share plan is right between the two.

By combining plans it is possible to essentially eliminate the negative aspects. For example, by targeting the performance fund at $50,000 for 100 percent attainment of

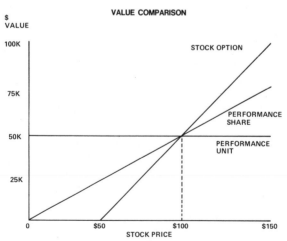

FIGURE 8-5 Value comparison of stock option, performance share, and performance unit.

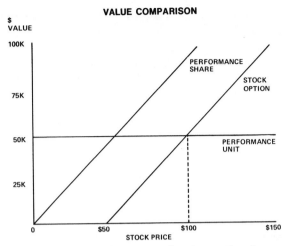

FIGURE 8-6 Value comparisons of options and performance unit versus performance share.

objectives and giving the individual an option for 1000 shares at $50, we have: (1) avoided the accrual for increases beyond $50 a share, and (2) given the executive the opportunity to participate in growth of company stock price. Following this approach the chart values would be additive (e.g., assuming 100 percent attainment of target and stock price at $100 the performance unit would generate $50,000, or 500 shares, and the stock option would be worth $50,000, or 500 shares, through the exercise of a stock appreciation right). As shown in Figure 8-6 this is the equivalent of having given the executive 1000 performance shares; however, in this case the change to earnings is one-half that required by the performance share plan.

PHANTOM STOCK PLANS

Phantom stock plans are a form of incentive pay that uses company stock as the basis for measurement but not necessarily for form of payment. There are three forms: dividend equivalents, appreciation, and total market price.

Dividend Equivalents

The recipient is awarded an equivalent for a stated number of shares of company stock. The executive does not receive the stock but will each year receive an amount (cash or stock) equal to the dividend paid. Thus an executive who received 1000 shares with dividends equaling $1.00 a share would receive $1000. The following year if the executive received an additional 1000 units and the dividend was increased to $1.10, payment would total $2200. Such grants are often in effect for long periods of time, e.g., until death or age 85 whichever comes last. The company receives a deduction and the employee receives personal service income; however, APB 25 has caused significant complications as highlighted earlier. In addition the early death of an executive could cause considerable cash liquidity problems for the estate. However, income received while the executive was either employed or retired (in the form of deferral payments) would probably qualify for the 50 percent personal service income maximum tax.

Appreciation

Phantom units at a prescribed price are given to the executive with a specified date of valuation usually stated. Thus at valuation date the difference in fair market value and price at time of grant is given to the executive in stock and/or cash. The company has a deduction at time of payment and the executive has a comparable amount of personal service income, but the company has had to amortize the compensation liability under the rules of APB 25.

A variation on the appreciation from fair market value at time of grant is a discount which can be prescribed at time of grant or by formula and calculated at time of valuation. If the discount were 100 percent, it would be a "total market price" as described below and would be similar to a deferred stock bonus (especially if payment were in the form of company stock).

Total Market Price

The total market price approach is the same as the appreciation approach except that appreciation is from first dollar to fair market value at date of valuation. In other words the price at time of grant is zero rather than current fair market value.

NONMARKET LONG-TERM INCENTIVES

In general, anything that can be done with market value plans can also be done with nonmarket plans. In addition nonmarket value plans have probably the most attractive, certainly the simplest form—cash.

However, their strength is their weakness. Just as they are not likely to go "below water" or remain flat for prolonged periods, so too they are not capable of rising dramatically in times of a bullish stock market. Such characteristics have caused some to look on such plans as a form of guaranteed payout profit sharing. Of course, this view can be thwarted by establishing a minimum rate of growth before payment.

Cash

The formula, instead of being tied to company stock in any way, specifies the amount of cash that will be paid under certain objectives (note that earlier described performance unit plans, paying in cash, not stock, would meet this description). The amount can be paid immediately or deferred over a period of time. The company has a deduction at the time of payment equal to the amount the executive has earned in the way of personal service income. The charge to the earnings statement is clearly prescribed.

Nonmarket Phantom Stock Plans

This form of incentive compensation deals with appreciation in a manner similar to that of phantom stock plans related to company stock except by definition this uses some other measuring devices. Some plans are constructed around book value (i.e., assets minus liabilities divided by number shares of stock outstanding)—the thought being that, unlike those related to company stock which can bounce up and down, reflecting market assessment of macroeconomic issues rather than company success, book value usually has a nice steady progress. Another variation deals with earnings per share; such plans are likely to use a moving multiyear average (or total) to remove small annual swings. Still another variation for those in mining or drilling might relate to established reserves; certainly this would place a significant emphasis on adding new discoveries.

Book value plans have been used primarily by privately held companies, although publicly held companies have recently expressed interest, due to the lackluster performance of the stock market in recent years. Simply stated, such plans offer executives an opportunity to receive company stock at its book rather than its market value. This may be accomplished either by allowing the executive to purchase stock at its current book value (e.g., repaying the loan with dividends received) or by giving the stock to the executive. Using the example shown in Table 8-14, assume an executive received 10,000 book value units valued at $25.00 a share. If the plan specified that payment could be

TABLE 8-14 Example of Book Value Stock Purchase

	EPS	Allocation of EPS		Book value
		Dividend	Retained	
Base		—	—	$25.00
1	$ 4.00	$ 1.50	$ 2.50	27.50
2	4.40	1.65	2.75	30.25
3	4.84	1.81	3.03	33.28
4	5.32	2.00	3.32	36.60
5	5.86	2.20	3.66	40.26
6	6.44	2.41	4.03	44.29
7	7.09	2.66	4.43	48.72
8	7.79	2.92	4.87	53.59
9	8.57	3.21	5.36	58.95
10	9.43	3.54	5.89	64.84
Total	$63.74	$23.90	$39.84	
Appreciation				$39.84

made from dividends, in this example the executive would have received almost enough (i.e., $23.90 a share) in dividends after 10 years to pay off the price of the stock. The stock would be worth $648,400 (i.e., 10,000 shares at $64.84 a share).

If the executive were simply given appreciation units, there would be no investment required and the executive would have $398,400 worth of investment, plus $239,000 worth of dividends received during the 10 years if dividend equivalents were also a feature. Properly structured, the dividends would be ordinary income but subject to the personal service income maximum. The appreciation would be subject to long-term capital gains when the units were sold back to the company.

Typically, the executive must sell the stock back to the company when employment is terminated. Assuming favorable conditions (e.g., death, disability, or retirement) such stock may be bought back at current book value. However with voluntary terminations some form of penalty may exist (e.g., buy-back at original book or forfeiture of all gains for the previous 5 years). It may be possible to defer the long-term capital gains tax by effecting a tax-free transfer into company market value stock, and then the tax would be effective when such shares were sold.

Stock Options

Rather than give an option to buy common stock, the option to purchase is given on book value (or some other internally valued stock). A variation would be book value plus dividends paid. The advantage of this approach is that a change in the level of earnings retained has no impact on the valuation. Remember book value is by definition equal to book value at beginning of period plus earnings per share less dividends paid.

Following the same example discussed in the previous section and repeated in Table 8-15, the option at $25.00 would be given to the executive. If the executive exercised the option 5 years later, the gain would either be $15.26 (i.e., $40.26 − $25.00) or $24.42 (i.e., $49.42 − $25.00) per share depending on which definition of book value was used for purposes of the option.

At the time of exercise the executive would have personal service income in the amount of $152,600 or $244,200 (again depending on the definition) assuming 10,000 shares of option were exercised. Assume the individual retires 5 years later when the book values are $64.84 and $88.74, or $648,400 and $887,400 respectively, for 10,000 shares. The difference of $495,800 and $643,200 respectively would be eligible for long-term capital gains taxation.

The company would have a tax deduction and charge to earnings equal to the amount the executive received as personal service income, and the tax effectiveness rating would be 0.93. Furthermore, the company would accrue the liability for future expense in accord with APB 25. The increases represented at retirement, either $495,800 or $643,200, would have been charged to earnings, but since there would be no compensation expense (simply a long-term capital gain) the company would have no tax deduction! The result: a tax effectiveness rating of 0.72.

TABLE 8-15   Example of Book Value Stock Option

		Allocation of EPS		Book	Book value
	EPS	Dividend	Retained	value	plus dividend
Base	—	—	—	$25.00	$25.00
1	$ 4.00	$ 1.50	$ 2.50	27.50	29.00
2	4.40	1.65	2.75	30.25	33.40
3	4.84	1.81	3.03	33.28	38.24
4	5.32	2.00	3.32	36.60	43.56
5	5.86	2.20	3.66	40.26	49.42
6	6.44	2.41	4.03	44.29	55.86
7	7.09	2.66	4.43	48.72	62.95
8	7.79	2.92	4.87	53.59	70.74
9	8.57	3.21	5.36	58.95	79.31
10	9.43	3.54	5.89	64.84	88.74
Total	$63.74	$23.90	$39.84		
Appreciation				$39.84	$63.74

Except for acquisitions, spinoffs, changes in accounting procedure, or other unusual events which could affect book value (all of which can be netted out), the appreciation of this type of value is a direct function of corporate financial success not subject to external factors in determining value. Thus, the executive is not concerned with the stock market's assessment of corporate performance, for as long as shareholder equity is increasing on a per-share basis, the potential value of the incentive is also increasing. It is not surprising, therefore, that the executive's degree of interest in book value options is almost directly inversely related to the direction of movement in the common stock. Great interest in times of bear markets, little interest during bull markets.

COMBINATION PLANS

Stock options for years were essentially the only form of long-term incentive compensation for many companies. However, they found that when price-earnings multiples increased, the levels of compensation were significant—creating more than one millionaire. Conversely, when the multiples dropped, increases in EPS were meaningless in terms of stock prices as many options went underwater. This volatility caused many companies to cut back on the use of options and introduce an additional form of compensation such as the performance unit plan (which is not affected by the market price of the stock).

Many company plans provide for two or more forms of long-term incentives, but that does not mean they are all being employed. Even where they are being utilized, they may be used separately at different levels (e.g., performance unit plan for the top

20 executives and stock option for the next 100 key people). However, the more classic situation calls for either parallel (additive) or tandem (payment from the more beneficial plan) coverage.

It is very logical to develop combination plans since in doing so it is possible to neutralize some of the individual disadvantages. A good example of this is how the unknown stock price impact of the classic performance share plan was neutralized by developing a performance unit plan and attaching a stock option. A stock award coupled with sufficient cash to cover tax liabilities makes sense, especially to those with short-swing profit problems. Also, putting the executive at risk with company stock value can be coupled with a nonmarket value plan to provide some protection.

Here's an illustration of how a combination market and nonmarket stock option can be structured. Let's go back to our previous book market plan example. The company's current book value is $25.00 a share, and it is assumed earnings will increase at a compound growth rate of 10 percent a year for the next 10 years. Further assume that the company plans on maintaining a dividend policy equaling 37.5 percent of earnings per share. The estimates of EPS, dividends, retained earnings, and book value for the time period are reported in Table 8-16. Note that the common share stock price has also been increased on the same progression (retaining its ten times price-earnings multiple).

Assume that it is decided that the executive should receive an option whose estimated appreciation 10 years hence should be worth $500,000. If a nonqualified market value option were to be given, it would probably be for about 22,400 shares (i.e., $500,000 ÷ $58.30 − $36.00). However, the same value could be extended by giving a nonmarket value option for about 33,700 shares of book value (i.e., $500,000 ÷ $39.84 − $25.00) or 12,900 shares of book value plus dividends (i.e., $500,000 ÷ $63.74 − $25.00). The advantage of using the latter over the former book value defi-

TABLE 8-16   Ten-Year Projection of Book Value and Stock Price

		Allocation of EPS		Book value	Book value plus dividend	Common stock price
	EPS	Dividend	Retained			
Base	—	—	—	$25.00	$25.00	$36.00
1	$ 4.00	$ 1.50	$ 2.50	27.50	29.00	40.00
2	4.40	1.65	2.75	30.25	33.40	44.00
3	4.84	1.81	3.03	33.28	38.24	48.40
4	5.32	2.00	3.32	36.60	43.56	53.20
5	5.86	2.20	3.66	40.26	49.42	58.60
6	6.44	2.41	4.03	44.29	55.86	64.40
7	7.09	2.66	4.43	48.72	62.95	70.90
8	7.79	2.92	4.87	53.59	70.74	77.90
9	8.57	3.21	5.36	58.95	79.31	85.70
10	9.43	3.54	5.89	64.84	88.74	94.30
Total	$63.74	$23.90	$39.84			
Appreciation				$39.84	$63.74	$58.30

TABLE 8-17   Book Value versus Market Value Stock
Option Comparison

| | Number of shares under option | | |
| | Market value | Nonmarket value | |
		Book value	Book value plus dividends
Independent	22,400	33,700	12,900
Combination Parallel			
A	11,200	16,850	
B	11,200		6,450
Tandem			
A	22,400	33,700	
B	22,400		12,900

nition is, it may be recalled, that any change in the dividend policy has no impact on the calculation. Under the straight book value approach an increase in dividend payout has an adverse effect on the increase in book value.

Rather than give an option under any one of the three, a combination plan can be set using either a tandem or parallel approach as shown in Table 8-17. Under the *parallel* approach each option is self-standing and unaffected by any exercise actions on the other option. Although any desired relationship can be set, a logical choice might be that half of the estimated $500,000 value should be attained from each option. Thus the number of shares available as an independent or separate option are reduced by half as shown on the grid. Thus under the A plan the executive would receive 11,200 option shares for common stock at $36 a share and 16,850 shares of a book value option at $25.00. Under the B plan the person would receive 6450 option shares of book value (defined to include dividends) plus a 11,200 share nonqualified market value option.

Under the *tandem* approach the same number of shares is given under both market and nonmarket value options that would have been given if it were the only plan. However, as the individual exercises shares under one plan a comparable number are forfeited under the other plan. For example in plan A the executive would receive 22,400 shares of common stock at $36 a share and 33,700 shares of book value at $25 a share. Assume that the executive exercised 3400 shares of the market value stock 2 years later. Not only would that reduce the maximum remaining number of shares under the market value option to 19,000, it would also reduce the number of shares under the book value option by 5116 (leaving 28,584). This was determined in the following manner: Since 3400 is 15.18 percent of 22,400 then 15.18 percent of 33,700 results in 5116. Namely, for every share of common stock exercised the book value option will be reduced by almost a share-and-a-half. Conversely, for every 3 shares of book value exercised the common stock option will be reduced by approximately 2 shares.

TABLE 8-18 Book Value versus Market Value Restricted Stock Award Comparison

| | Number restricted shares awarded | | |
| | | Nonmarket value | |
	Market	Book value	Book value plus dividends
Independent	8,500	12,500	7,800
Combination			
Parallel			
A	4,250	6,250	
B	4,250		3,700
Tandem			
A	8,500	12,500	
B	8,500		7,800

Plan B under the tandem approach functions the same way. The only difference is that a different definition has been constructed for value (i.e., book value plus dividends).

Thus it can be seen that the tandem approach is a hybrid independent and parallel plan, in that it allows the recipient to choose how to exercise the option. Note that if all the options under the market value plan are exercised, it is the same as if the executive received only a market value option; the same is true for completely exercising the nonmarket value option. Exercising half of each has the same effect as the parallel option.

A similar approach can be employed with stock awards. Using a phantom common stock restricted award coupled with the book value plan, the executive could receive the same number of shares in the above example, either tandem or parallel, assuming payout was only on *appreciation*. Assuming the same anticipated stock values 10 years hence, the number of restricted shares to be awarded if payout was on total value (not simply appreciation) are as shown in Table 8-18.

SUMMARY AND CONCLUSIONS

Long-term incentive plans are designed to reward executives for long-term results. However, their nature is by definition a large part of their problem—predicting performance expectations for several years in the future. The difficulty of setting such targets is a function of the degree of cyclical fluctuation within the particular industry. In some, such as chemicals and paper, production capacity within the industry is a very significant factor in defining probable success.

As illustrated in Table 8-19, there is little difference in tax treatment of the basic forms of long-term incentives. Essentially they are deductible to the company and subject to tax to the executive as personal service income. All the plans which are paid in company stock have the subsequent opportunity to receive long-term capital gains (beginning from the income level previously recognized for tax purposes) and the 0.72 rating. All dividends paid on company stock are nondeductible to the company and subject to ordinary income tax to the executive (0.30 rating), except for dividends under restricted stock which are treated as compensation and receive a 0.93 rating.

Stock acquired by the executive's exercise of an option, warrant or right will be construed to be a purchase under Rule 16b-3. However, when acquisition is not subject to the executive's control and discretion, it will probably be an exempt transaction for purpose of short-swing profit situations.

The proxy disclosure treatment of long-term incentive compensation is shown in Table 8-20. Essentially, these payments in cash are reported in column C_1 (except for SARs), payments (including deferred but vested) in stock (excluding gains on exercising stock options) are included in column C_2 and deferred, and nonvested or contingent compensation is reserved for column D.

Incentive plans cannot be developed and turned over to the accountants on the assumption that they will be self-monitoring. Adjustments are often required during the incentive period, not to mention the time and effort required at the close of the period to determine the extent to which performance was positively or negatively affected by factors outside the executives' control. In some plans such action is needed to adjust individual payments; in all it is a requirement for setting future targets—for even the stock option grant must make some assumptions about the future.

TABLE 8-19   Long-Term Incentive Tax Treatment

	Unattractive	Attractive	Very attractive
Market-related			
Stock options	0.30	0.72	0.93
SARs	0.30	0.72	0.93
Stock purchases	0.30	0.72	0.93
Stock awards	0.30	0.72	0.93
Performance share	0.30	0.72	0.93
Performance unit	0.30	0.72	0.93
Phantom			
Dividend equivalents			0.93
Appreciation			0.93
Total market price			0.93
Nonmarket-related			
Cash			0.93
Nonmarket stock			0.93
Nonmarket options			0.93

TABLE 8-20   Long-Term Incentive Proxy Treatment*

Market-related	
Stock options	Grants and exercises in separate table
SARs	Grants and exercises in separate table
Stock purchases†	D for contingent accrual
	C_2 for exercised gain not previously reported in D
Stock awards†	D for contingent accrual
	C_2 for value received not previously reported in D
Performance share†	D for contingent accrual
	C_2 for value received not previously reported in D
Performance unit	D for contingent accrual
	C_2 for value received not previously reported in D
Phantom	
Dividend equivalents	D for contingent accrual
	C_2 for value received or credited not previously reported in D
Appreciation‡	Grants and exercises in separate table
Total market price‡	Grants and exercises in separate table
Nonmarket-related	
Cash	D for contingent accrual
	C_1 for value received not previously reported in D
Nonmarket stock	D for contingent accrual
	C_1 for value received not previously reported in D§
Nonmarket options	C_1 for value received not previously reported in D§

*It is believed there is still room for misinterpretation of the SEC proxy disclosure requirements until further clarification is received. Therefore, this whole subject should be reviewed very carefully with legal counsel.
†Depending whether the accruals, if any, relate to market price, stock purchases, stock awards, and performance shares these also could be reported outside the remuneration table.
‡May require disclosure in the remuneration table.
§Assumes cash payment, however, disclosure in column C_2 may be required.

In smaller organizations the contact between the CEO and key executives is on a daily basis; in larger organizations the contact may be almost as frequent, but the additional layers of management with their own needs and perceptions cannot be given the same degree of personal involvement. Thus it is necessary that a more formal basis of identifying objectives and evaluating performance be adopted. For some this is the long-term incentive plan. By specifying the basis for payment, all executives are inclined to determine how such performance (and payment) can be maximized. However, this means that individuals may be encouraged to take actions which are not in the best interests of the company. For example, a plan based on return on assets might have an enterprising executive selling some assets (and leasing them back) to improve performance.

However, if real growth rather than current dollars were the basis for payment, it would be difficult for some companies to show positive growth rate. These are companies far into the maturity stage, if not already in the decline phase, which are essentially liquidating themselves by paying out dividends which should be reinvested in the business. Performance share and unit plans would bring additional attention to paying executives for apparently riding the corporation to its final internment. Performance unit and share plans work better in noncyclical industries than in those with periodic ups and downs, since the latter require continually adjusting targets which in retrospect are either too liberal or too restrictive. Companies in such industries would probably be better off either using market value stock options or book value plans.

Some will argue that long-term incentive plans do not provide incentive to executives to work harder or smarter. Assuming this is true, it still seems logical to pay them in relation to key measurements of corporate success. Simply paying a salary or a short-term incentive based on current earnings is insufficient for a CEO, because a longer-term pay delivery system is needed for a significant part of such an executive's earnings. How else can shareholders be assured that the CEO is focusing on strategies to optimally position the company in the next 5 to 10 years?

Some companies discourage executives from selling stock they have acquired through exercising options, SARs, or receiving stock awards. The normal message is that such plans were approved by shareholders to promote a common interest in the company's growth. A measurement of confidence in this growth is expressed through holding rather than selling stock.

In determining which type of long-term incentive plan is to be used, it is necessary to sort through the company's priorities. Stock options and stock appreciation rights are structured to maximize compensation in terms of rising stock market prices. Performance share and fund plans are designed to relate individual performance to attainment of corporate objectives. Nonmarket plans are designed to provide steady if unspectacular compensation insulated from the vagaries of the marketplace. Essentially they are all group rather than individually oriented. The extent of participation is a function of organization level rather than individual performance.

Deferred Compensation

Deferred compensation is an agreement between a company and an individual employee that all or a portion of compensation will be paid over a stipulated period of time, beginning at present, or a stated period of years from now, or upon retirement. Thus, deferrals can be either short- or long-term in nature. Payment which is deferred is similar in result to restricted compensation plans where the executive has to earn out the full rights to ownership unless the benefits are nonforfeitable. Many would indicate that the latter is usually done for the executive's benefit whereas the former is a form of golden handcuffs benefiting the company.

The objective of deferrals is to shift income from current to future years in order to maximize meeting personal income needs. One should clearly understand that deferring or not deferring is an investment decision, but only after it is determined that money is not needed currently for personal or family obligations (e.g., education and health care). Included in the decision to defer are assumptions about current and future events (e.g., taxes, inflation, risk of forfeiture, investment opportunities, and need for liquidity). Some take the simplistic view that it will always be beneficial to defer dollars (which will be highly taxed now) to a point in the future when income (and tax rates) will be lower. While this may have been true 20 years ago when marginal taxes were as high as 91 percent, it is not true when marginal maximums are 50 percent, since the opportunity for significant difference is reduced. Furthermore, while the 50 percent maximum tax can now be applied to deferred personal service income, there is less of an executive need to defer due to improved pension plans and more favorable estate tax situations in many instances.

Deferred compensation is either voluntary or mandatory in nature, and can be applicable to each of the five compensation elements (i.e., salary, short-term incentives, long-term incentives, employee benefits, and perquisites). Under a mandatory plan the company unilaterally defers a portion of compensation in accord with a schedule (e.g., equal installments from the short-term incentive award over 3 years beginning now or equal installments from a long-term incentive plan over 10 years beginning at retirement). Under voluntary plans the individual enters into an agreement with the employer to defer a portion of compensation (e.g., salary, short- or long-term incentive payment) for a stated number of years. Such plans range from qualified retirement plans (where deferral is an inherent characteristic of the defined benefit or defined contribution plan) to personalized employment contracts. Thus, the spectrum runs from arrangements open to all to individually negotiated agreements, the latter often in conjunction with employment negotiations.

TYPES OF DEFERRED COMPENSATION

Plans are either funded or nonfunded, qualified or nonqualifed, and forfeitable or non-forfeitable. As shown in the Table 9-1 matrix, this results in eight possible combinations.

A *funded* plan is one where the benefits promised by the employer are secured by rights to property (e.g., stock, insurance, or some other negotiable item). Distinction may be drawn between informal or indirect funding and formally funded plans. In the former the company sets up a reserve or possibly even takes out an insurance contract for the amount of the liability but retains sole control over its application. Thus, in case of financial failure of the company, the employee stands in line as a general unsecured creditor seeking settlement of a claim. In a formally funded plan the funding of the liability is direct and the payment will be made from the property set aside. A nonfunded plan is one backed simply by a promise of the employer to pay.

If the company wishes to fund the payments through a life insurance contract on the executive's life, it will probably use a paid-up policy at 65 with a cash value. However, the company could also choose an ordinary life contract, expecting to pay the designated beneficiaries in case ot the executive's death before retirement, from the face value of the contract. Conversely, if the executive outlived payment of the deferrals, the company might decide to cash in the policy and use the cash surrender value to finance all or a portion of the deferred payments. To the extent cash surrender value exceeded premium paid, the company would have ordinary income. Such plans may either be participating (i.e., they may pay dividends which can be used to build up cash value, reduce premiums, or buy additional insurance) or nonparticipating. Where there is a

TABLE 9-1   Type of Deferred Compensation Matrix

	Forfeitable	Nonforfeitable
Funded		
Qualified	1	3
Nonqualified	2	4
Nonfunded		
Qualified	5	7
Nonqualified	6	8

desire to provide a preretirement death benefit, a term insurance program will probably be used. Other ways in which the employer can fund the payments include mutual funds, company stocks (own or others), and/or bonds (governmental or corporate).

A *qualified* plan must meet a number of tests dealing with such items as: permanency, nondiscriminatory coverage and nondiscriminatory benefits (these cannot favor higher-paid employees), and nonrecoverability of employer contributions. The advantage of such plans, covered by Section 401 of the Internal Revenue Code and the Employee Retirement Income Security Act of 1974, is that while the employer receives a tax deduction in the amount of the contribution to the plan, the employee's tax liability is deferred until benefits are actually received. A nonqualified plan is one not meeting the requirements of Section 401 of the Code; therefore, there is no tax deduction until the employee receives taxable income.

A *forfeitable* benefit is one in which the employee must earn out the benefit. Typical arrangements would call for a time period—either a stated number of years (e.g., 5) or upon retirement. In addition some plans will require that the employee not engage in any activity which can be viewed by the company as being in competition with its lines of business. A *nonforfeitable* benefit is one in which the executive is completely and immediately 100 percent vested.

Now, let's examine the essential characteristics of each of the eight combinations to determine their degree of plausibility and attractiveness to employer and to employee.

1. *Funded, qualified, forfeitable plan* This type of plan, due to its qualified nature, has very definite limitations on the degree of forfeitability. By definition it cannot be any more severe than that allowed by ERISA (see the section on Retirement in Chapter 5, Employee Benefits, for a description). These plans are probably not very attractive to the executive because their qualified nature limits the extent of benefits the company is prepared to give—since they must essentially apply to all employees. Other than for the basic retirement benefit, this is not an attractive alternative to either employer (due to cost) or executive (due to limitation on amount of benefit).

2. *Funded, nonqualified, forfeitable plan* This plan is identical to the one just described except that the employer can tailor the plan to a small group of employees or even one individual. Payments are secured by nonqualified trust, insurance contract, or reserve account. Since the payments are subject to a substantial degree of forfeiture, the employee has no income tax liability until such restrictions are removed. However, the employer is similarly barred from taking a tax deduction until the restrictions are removed. Thus, while this plan is quite attractive to the employee, it is not very attractive to the employer (which must set aside nondeductible dollars to fund the benefit).

3. *Funded, qualified, nonforfeitable plan* This is the same as the first plan described except that employees have 100 percent immediate vesting. Thus, it is even less attractive to employers than the first alternative, for in addition to all the limitations of a qualified plan, the cost of this type of plan is even greater since there are no

forfeitures which can be used to offset funding the nonforfeited benefits. Since employers will be forced to lower benefits in designing such a plan, it is not very attractive to executives because, of the eight alternatives, it will probably provide the lowest benefit for the highly paid.

4. *Funded, nonqualified, nonforfeitable plan* While at first glance this plan should be the most attractive to the executive (since risk is eliminated and the nonqualified nature permits a generous benefit design), it is rarely used. The reason: because it is funded and nonforfeitable, the IRS will consider payments made by the employer to the "fund" to be currently taxable income to the employee. Thus, the employee will have a tax liability without the benefit of having received the payments!

5. *Nonfunded, qualified, forfeitable plan* By terms of ERISA, it is not possible to have a qualified, nonfunded plan. To be qualified it must be properly funded. Thus, this alternative does not exist.

6. *Nonfunded, nonqualified, forfeitable plan* Until recent years, this probably was the most typical form of executive deferral. Because this plan is nonqualified, it enables the employer to design a very attractive personal package. Because it is nonfunded and forfeitable, the executive accepts the unsecured tenuous nature of future payment in exchange for no current tax liability. The company has no tax deduction until payments are made, but since it also has no funding requirement there is no immediate cash flow problem.

7. *Nonfunded, qualified, nonforfeitable plan* By terms of ERISA, it is not possible to have a nonfunded, qualified plan.

8. *Nonfunded, nonqualified, nonforfeitable plan* This is even more attractive to the executive than number 6, since the benefit is 100 percent vested. Although this situation was covered in Revenue Ruling 60-31, for years companies included some degree of forfeiture to minimize any possible claim by IRS of constructive receipt. The Revenue Act of 1978 reaffirmed that this type of plan, properly designed and administered, will not place the executive in the position of constructive receipt. From the employer's point of view, it is a little less attractive than number 6 since ability to retain the executive is lost with the full vesting. As with other nonqualified plans, the company has no tax deduction until the executive receives payment.

CONSTRUCTIVE RECEIPT

A number of the bonus plans in existence call for payments in several annual installments, usually not more than five. The rationale for such an approach on timing is (1) it cushions the effect of one low-bonus year, (2) it helps to retain executives, since the payment of deferred awards is often contingent upon continued employment with the company, and (3) it spreads the tax bite. Concerning this last point, it is imperative that any deferred payments be viewed in light of the IRS doctrine of constructive receipt in order to avoid taxation to the recipient in the year in which granted. This was defined in Revenue Ruling 60-31, which said, "Under the doctrine of constructive receipt, a taxpayer may not deliberately turn his back upon income and thereby select the year for which he will report it."

The *doctrine of constructive receipt* is defined in Section 1.451-2(a) of the Treasury Regulations. It states: "Income, although not actually reduced to a taxpayer's possession is constructively received by him in the taxable year during which it is credited to his account, set apart for him, or otherwise made available so that he may draw upon it at any time, or so that he could have drawn upon it during the taxable year if notice of intention to withdraw had been given. However, income is not constructively received if the taxpayer's control of its receipt is subject to substantial limitations or restrictions." In other words, if the executive could reach out and take the money (regardless of whether or not he or she did), it will be considered taxable income.

The chances of such an interpretation being made is minimized if the individual makes a determination before the amount is earned: some interpret this as before January 1 of the year on which the bonus is calculated, not simply a couple of months before the calculation is made. They cite Revenue Ruling 69-650 which indicated that a decision by December 31 was required in connection with compensation to be earned during the following year. Although this applied to deferral of a portion of salary (not bonus), it is presumably a sound position that the more time between the decision and the event, the less likely there is to be a problem with the Internal Revenue Service. Revenue Procedure 71-19 sets forth the conditions under which IRS will issue advance rulings in this matter.

In addition, if the executive indicates a preference but final decision is in the hands of a compensation committee, the likelihood of a problem with constructive receipt is also minimized. Thus, in adopting a deferred compensation approach the issues of "who makes the determination" and "at what point in time" are critical coniderations.

ECONOMIC BENEFIT

Another tax principle closely allied with the doctrine of constructive receipt is the theory of economic benefit. Here the IRS interprets an action by the employer as resulting in something of value being bestowed upon the employee. For example, the mere promise by the company to pay in the future (rather than currently) has no economic value; however, if the payment is funded through a "split-dollar" insurance contract providing a death benefit, then an economic value can be calculated on a yearly basis by comparing the employee's cost with the imputed value of the premium.

Similarly, if the employer sets up a trust to which the employee has nonforfeitable rights, then the amount of annual contribution will be construed to be an economic benefit and the employee will be taxed that year on the value of that contribution. Note

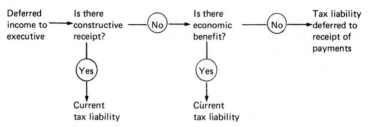

FIGURE 9-1 Constructive receipt and economic benefit matrix.

that this is not an issue of constructive receipt because the trust specifies when in the future the executive will receive payments. However, if there were a substantial risk of forfeiture associated with these payments, then the economic benefit theory would not apply. One should recognize, however, that the IRS may look to an individual's age to determine whether continued employment is really a substantial risk of forfeiture. A 60-year-old executive with 30 years of company service (and a handsome pension accruing) is not as likely to depart as, say, a 40-year-old individual with only 5 years of service. The impact of constructive receipt and economic benefit is shown in the flow chart in Figure 9-1.

ACCOUNTING IMPACT OF CASH VERSUS STOCK

While the amount deferred under a cash bonus plan is charged against pretax earnings in the year earned, it is not tax deductible until paid. However, the company is able to lower its provision for federal income taxes by the amount taxes would be reduced if the amount were paid in the year in which earned. Thus, a bonus of $50,000 deferred over 4 future years would reduce pretax earnings by $50,000. The $10,000 paid immediately would reduce current taxes by $4600 (assuming a 46 percent tax rate) and earnings by $10,000. The remaining $40,000 deferral would reduce the deferred provision for federal income taxes by $18,400 (i.e., $4600 × 4 years). The latter is a liability on the balance sheet which is reduced annually over the 4 years by $4600 as each portion of the deferred compensation is paid. These payments have no future effect on earnings (only cash flow).

The treatment for deferred stock is more complicated but, excluding appreciation, has the same results. Assume the $50,000 is converted to 1000 shares of stock (based on current market price of $50) and spread over 4 additional years. Instead of assuming an additional 1000 shares will be issued, assume the company takes the $50,000 and buys 1000 shares on the open market and deposits these in the treasurer's vault—thereby not increasing the number of shares outstanding. This approach results in a negative cash flow since the outlay for stock is only partially offset (i.e., 46 cents on the dollar) by the deduction to pretax earnings. Conversely, issuing new stock would increase cash and shareholder equity by like amount. After-tax earnings in either situation have been reduced by $27,000 (i.e., $50,000 less a $23,000 provision for federal taxes, assuming a 46 percent tax rate).

The following year an additional 200 shares are given to the executive except now the stock is selling at $55 and therefore the value is $11,000, not $10,000. The provision for federal income tax is reduced by $4600 (reflecting the $10,000 portion), and stockholder equity is increased by $460 (the reduction in federal taxes for the $1000 portion). Since the $10,000 portion increased shareholder equity by a like amount in the year earned, shareholder equity has now been increased by $10,460. Cash flow has been increased by $5060 as a result of the tax benefit. This amount can be used to purchase 190 shares (i.e., $10,460 ÷ $55) or used for capital investment needs. If used to buy treasury stock, total shares outstanding have only been increased by 10 shares; if used for other needs, the number outstanding is increased by 200. Significant uses of deferred stock can therefore have a definite impact on EPS—by increasing the denominator as well as decreasing the numerator.

PRE-1969

Prior to the 1969 Tax Reform Act a number of deferred compensation plans used restricted property. A typical example would be to give the individual shares of stock in the company indicating that the restrictions would lapse according to a schedule. For example an executive might be given 1000 shares of company stock (then selling at $100 a share) and told that restrictions would lapse at the rate of 100 shares a year for the next 10 years. Not only was there no tax liability at time of grant, but when the restrictions were removed the value would be subject to ordinary income tax on the lesser of fair market value at time of award or when restrictions lapsed. Thus, if the value of the stock rose, there was a capital gains opportunity; if it dropped, the tax would be based on the fair market value at time of receipt.

The Tax Reform Act of 1969 added a new section to the Code—Section 83, which deals with the taxation of property. It states that the fair market value of the property will be that when the restrictions lapse, at which time it will be considered ordinary income. To delay recognition of income the restrictions must include substantial risk of forfeiture. IRC Section 83 (c)(1) states: "The rights of a person in property are subject to a substantial risk of forfeiture if such person's rights to full enjoyment of such property are conditioned upon the future performance of substantial services by any individual."

Thus, if the property is actually transferred to the employee, the substantial risk of forfeiture is a requirement. However, if the company retains these rights, the property does not fall under the definition of restricted property and therefore the risk of forfeiture is not a requirement. Needless to say, the 1969 Tax Reform Act dampened the use of restricted property plans.

THE EARLY 1970s—SALARY REDUCTION PLANS

During this period, the "salary reduction" plan became popular. It effectively allowed the employee to have a portion of salary deferred by placing it in a money-purchase-type investment plan.

It worked like this. An executive would be hired at $100,000 but would agree that $10,000 of this would be invested in a Section 403(b) tax-sheltered annuity program. The executive would have $90,000 (not $100,000) of reportable income; however, the company could claim a $100,000 compensation deduction ($90,000 for salary and $10,000 for contribution to the money purchase plan). Effectively it allowed the company to take a deduction before the executive had a taxable event!

During the mid-1970s these plans were allowed to continue by the IRS, but new plans lost the attractive tax feature. More specifically such contributions were considered to be made by the *employee;* thus the person had $100,000 salary with a $10,000 contribution made from after-tax income. The company had a $100,000 deduction for salary.

Beginning in 1979, the same favorable tax treatment has been returned. Now qualified profit sharing plans may include a provision which allows the covered employee to elect either to take the employer's contribution in cash or have it contributed to the trust. Tax treatment will be based on the action *taken*. Thus, if elected to be received as cash, it will be taxed when received; if deferred, the normal rules for payment from a qualified trust apply.

Going back to our earlier example, this would mean hiring the executive at $90,000 salary and indicating that the $10,000 generated by the profit sharing plan could be received as cash or contributed to the trust. If deferred, the executive has $90,000 of reportable income, the company a $100,000 tax deduction. If received as cash, the employee has $100,000 of reportable income, while the company still has a $100,000 deduction.

TODAY

The Tax Reform Act of 1976 made deferred compensation generally attractive. It amended the definition of "personal service income" (which it substituted for "earned income") to include amounts received as annuities, pensions, or other deferred compensation. Thus, properly designed deferred compensation plans are subject to the same 50 percent maximum tax in effect when the monies are earned. Prior to this act it might be subject to a 50 percent tax when earned, but if deferred, it could be subject to the full 70 percent tax bite, if received later than the year following the year in which it was earned. The 1-year grace period then in effect was helpful only in exempting short-term incentive awards usually paid in the first part of the year subsequent to the year in which earned. The 1976 Tax Reform Act allows both qualified and nonqualified deferred compensation to be subject to the 50 percent personal service income maximum tax.

DEFERRAL ADVANTAGES

There currently are a number of advantages to deferring compensation. These include:

1. Unlike many IRS rules requiring no discrimination in favor of higher employees, nonqualified deferred agreements can be set up on a highly discriminating "pick-and-choose" basis.

2. If the amount earned is paid interest or otherwise invested, the individual does not experience a loss in value due to inflation. And (if geared to appreciation in interest ratios, the value of stock or other property which reflects the inflation factor); the amount is allowed to grow at a tax-free compound rate until time of payment, when all dollars are subject to the personal service income maximum.

   This is especially advantageous for long-term deferrals. For example, if a $20,000 payment is deferred for 5 years at 7 percent of pretax interest and then paid out, the $28,051 is worth $14,026 after taxes (assuming the entire amount is subject to 50 percent personal service income maximum). This is $2013, or 16.8 percent more than the after-tax value of $20,000 paid out immediately and then invested at 7 percent (because the amount available for investment was $10,000, not $20,000, since it was immediately subject to taxes). As shown in Table 9-2, the posttax values increase to $19,672 and $14,836, respectively, for a $4836 or 32.6 percent variance. This increase in absolute and relative differences is also shown for 15 and 20 years.

3. In accord with Revenue Rulings 68-99 and 72-25 it would appear that the employer can fund the deferred compensation obligation without triggering an income liability to the employee *if* the company owns all policy rights, including designation of beneficiary.

4. If the individual has significant preference income and/or ordinary income currently, the marginal tax rate may be less at a subsequent date. (However, the possibility of higher marginal rates in the future through new tax legislation is a high offsetting risk).

5. An unfunded plan is not subject to ERISA funding requirements (but is probably covered by the reporting requirements) as long as such benefits are in excess of

TABLE 9-2   Pre- and Post-Tax Comparisons with Current and Deferred Income

Years	$10,000		$20,000		Posttax variance	
	Pretax	Posttax	Pretax	Posttax	Amount	Percent
5	$14,026	$12,013	$28,051	$14,026	$ 2,013	16.8
10	19,672	14,836	39,343	19,672	4,836	32.6
15	27,590	18,795	55,181	27,590	2,795	46.8
20	38,697	24,349	77,394	38,697	14,348	58.9

defined benefit or contribution plan limits and/or deferral arrangements are limited to more highly compensated individuals.

6. Generally, social security benefits are not affected by the amount of deferred payments received. However, care should be taken in developing such arrangements because payment (which permits the company to use the individual as a consultant) may be regarded as wages for purpose of reducing social security payments. This may be only a short-term issue, however, since after 1981 individuals age 70 and over are permitted unlimited earnings without reducing social security benefits.

7. If amounts deferred are under risk of forfeiture for executives who leave the company for reasons other than death, disability, or retirement, the individual's inclination to join another company may be retarded.

8. A large portion of the deferred income can be passed on to the beneficiaries through properly designed trusts and supplemental insurance coverage (e.g., split dollar) provided by the employer.

9. Short-term deferrals significantly reduce sharp year-to-year fluctuations to incentive payments and smooth out the taxable earnings of the executive. This is important when high marginal tax rates are in effect.

10. Nonfunded deferred compensation plans enable the company to preserve capital by withholding a portion of compensation to a future date. This may be especially important to a threshold or emerging company. However, APB Opinion No. 12, "Deferred Compensation Contracts," should be examined carefully to ensure the expensing of future benefits is properly reflected.

11. The company benefits to the extent it recaptures forfeited payments since these would have been lost if paid when earned. In addition, it will benefit to the extent it credits the deferral with a value less than the cost of borrowed capital.

DEFERRAL DISADVANTAGES

Conversely there are a number of disadvantages to deferring compensation. These include:

1. Unless the amount deferred is protected against inflation, it will have significantly less value when received than when earned, even under the most favorable tax circumstances. Or even if it is vested and has less value when received than the executive believes could have been obtained, the executive will not be very happy. The $40,000 deferred over 4 future years in the earlier discussion would amount to a total of $52,432 if credited at 7 percent interest. Assuming the 50 percent marginal tax is in effect, this amount is reduced to $26,216. Contrast this with the $40,000 paid immediately and half of it paid out for taxes. If the remaining $20,000 were invested in 5.5 percent tax-free bonds it would net $24,776 after 4 years—

$1440, or 5.5 percent, less than deferred net payment. Thus, while the deferral is better, it may not be considered sizable enough to be worthwhile. This is especially true if the recipient believes the $20,000, if invested in stocks, real estate, art, or the like, would have a much greater net appreciation (after deducting capital gains taxes at the time of sale).

Application of a rate of interest to preserve purchasing power is, therefore, very logical, especially during periods of inflation. Approaches include: a specific percentage (e.g., 7 percent), a noncompany index (e.g., prime, passbook savings, or 90-day treasury notes) or a company index (e.g., return on assets, investments, borrowed capital, or shareholder equity). The latter two approaches may make an additional adjustment (e.g., prime rate less 1 percent or one-half the rate of return on shareholder equity). In addition, two or more of these can be placed in a combination (e.g., prime or one-half return on equity, whichever is lower).

In using rates it is important to identify when the measurement will be taken and how long it will be in effect. For example, using 90-day treasury notes, one could agree that the averages for the last weeks in March, June, September, and December would be the applicable rates for the respective quarters. For reference to company data it logically would be calculated after the close of the year.

2. The buildup in deferred compensation resulting from an interest rate or other inflation factor is currently considered compensation (subject to the personal service maximum) when received. However, the rules could change, resulting in this being subject to the ordinary income tax rate, or even worse, from the company's perspective, the increase might be ruled unreasonable compensation and therefore not deductible by the corporation. It would seem the risk of this occurring is greatest when the value increases at a rate significantly greater than the rise in inflation over the same period.

3. Deferred compensation in closely held corporations has the additional problem that a tax deduction for a deferred payment to a controlling shareholder must be permanently forfeited unless the compensation is paid (and the deduction taken) within 2½ months after the close of the taxable year. This is in accord with Section 267 of the Code.

4. The tax situation must be thoroughly reviewed on a state as well as federal basis to ensure it results in lower taxes. For example, some states may apply an exit tax on any deferred compensation earned in that state but not taxed at time of relocation. This certainly makes less attractive a move from a high-tax to a low-tax state at time of retirement. Furthermore the federal tax rates may be higher when received than when earned.

5. An unfunded plan makes the executive a general creditor of the company. While every company expects to exist in perpetuity, there are enough bankruptcies each year to require an assessment of the probability of this occurring to the company in question. Establishing a trust without forfeiture requirements will probably mean the executive will be taxed when money is deposited in the trust; including a for-

feiture clause will probably defer income tax liability to the executive; however, the company may not be able to take a tax deduction until monies are paid from the trust (thereby resulting in negative cash flow).

While bookkeeping reserves may be established, no funds can be set aside to meet the obligation. Furthermore, no annuity contracts or life insurance policies can be purchased for the employee; however, it is possible that such might be accomplished by the employer as long as the latter retained full ownership and the proceeds were not directed toward fulfillment of the deferral obligation.

6. The deferred compensation plan, especially if funded, may come under the definition of security as defined by the Securities Act of 1933 and the Securities Exchange Act of 1934. If it is deemed a security and a sale is involved, it will mean registration with the SEC, proper disclosure to those covered, and concern that no fraud charge can be directed to the "securities" management.

7. Deferred amounts are subject to the social security tax when paid in accord with Social Security Administration SSR 73-30 (SSR 75-2 gives state employees the choice of considering the amounts as income in the year in which earned or in which paid). For many this is an extra tax that would have been avoided had the amount been paid during the period in which earned since the executive's other salary and bonus payments exceeded the taxable earnings base. Since it is deferred, the amount is not only taxable to both employer and employee at time of payment but, considering the continually escalating tax rate, is probably at a higher rate as well.

The Internal Revenue Code specifies that for payment to be excluded from FICA and FUTA, it is necessary that payment occur due to termination of the employment relationship because of death, retirement for disability, or retirement after attaining an age specified in the agreement or the pension plan. Furthermore, such payments must be in accord with a plan clearly describing a class of employees. These requirements were further highlighted in Revenue Rulings 77-25, 78-263, and 79-328. If payments begin prior to meeting such requirements then they will continue to be subject to FICA and FUTA even after one of the three acceptable termination points is attained.

However, it may be possible to avoid such taxes after retirement if a consulting agreement is the basis for such payments *and* it contains a very restrictive noncompete clause. The rationale for no tax is (*a*) the person is no longer an employee and (*b*) the individual is not engaged in a consulting trade or business because the terms of the contract bar such service other than to the former employer.

8. Since the amount deferred proportionately reduces current total compensation, the executive may be more vulnerable to offers at slightly more than the current total package but with no deferral requirements. This is true during the early years of a short-term deferral program (see the example below, a 5-year deferral plan) and during all active years under payments deferred until retirement.

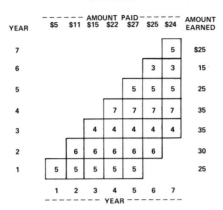

FIGURE 9-2 Amount earned versus paid under multiple-year plans.

9. Conversely, executives may demand more current compensation. To the extent the corporation acquiesces, it will pay more under a deferred compensation plan than if all compensation were paid currently.

10. Due to the partial payment of a number of years of service, it is difficult for the executive to see the impact of performance on the bonus. For example, in year 5, as shown in Figure 9-2, the executive received payments totaling $27,000 that year. The following year the bonus earned dropped $10,000 (from $25,000 to $15,000) but the amount received fell only $2000 (from $27,000 to $25,000). Conversely, the next year the amount earned rose $10,000 (from $15,000 to $25,000), but the amount paid slipped from $25,000 to $24,000. Given such a correlation in amounts earned versus paid, one must question the extent to which the individual truly receives reinforcement for the level of performance attained under deferred compensation plans.

11. Compensation deferred cannot be considered pay during the period of deferral for purposes of determining benefits under qualified pension and profit sharing plans (care should be taken to ensure that life insurance and disability protection is not similarly reduced). Thus, while this has little effect on the short-term deferrals (except for installments payable after retirement), it has considerable impact on long-term deferrals not payable until after retirement. The result can be a very significant reduction in the company pension plan payments—the magnitude being a factor of the percentage of earnings deferred. Such a position was described by the IRS in Revenue Ruling 68-454 when it disallowed compensation deferred by certain officer-employees. However, in accord with Revenue Ruling 69-145 it would appear that such compensation could be recognized *if* all employees were eligible to defer compensation. Revenue Ruling 80-359 added that if the proportion of

lower-paid employees who made deferrals was equal to or greater than the higher-paid, the basis for calculating benefits would not be viewed as discriminatory in favor of the prohibited group.

12. Payment beginning at the time of retirement from the company can create another problem, namely when the individual is "retiring" from company A to join company B. The earnings from the new employer will significantly reduce if not totally eliminate any tax advantage the executive hoped to receive on the deferred payment. However, careful planning and specific language in the deferral contract can essentially eliminate this problem. Namely the contract with company A should indicate that payments begin when the employee ceases full-time employment (not simply employment with company A). In addition, it may be advantageous to indicate that payment should begin the year *after* the year in which full-time employment ceases. In case of a person retiring late in the year, sufficient earnings may have been accumulated to eliminate favorable tax treatment of any deferral payments that year.

13. Some committees only allow the executive to state preferences (current versus deferred) in percentages (e.g., 25 percent immediate and 75 percent deferred). This approach does not recognize that the individual's current needs are absolute, not relative. Thus, using the above percentage example, everything would be fine if the total award were $20,000 and the individual's current needs were $5000. But what if the committee decided the executive should only receive a total of $10,000? In this case the immediate amount would be one-half of the needed $5000.

This problem can be overcome simply by allowing the executive (at the beginning of the agreement, so as to obviate constructive receipt problems) to indicate the dollar amount desired currently or deferred, with the balance going to the other. Thus, the executive could indicate a preference for the first $5000 in cash with the rest deferred or conversely the first $10,000 deferred with the rest payable currently. An additional refinement would be to combine the absolute and the relative (e.g., the first $5000 or 25 percent, whichever is greater, payable immediately with the balance deferred).

14. If the deferred payments are designed to continue after the death of the employee, such payments will probably be included in the decedent's estate in accord with Section 2039 of the Code. In addition, if the payment would have been considered taxable income to the decedent, it may also be considered income to the beneficiary. This double taxation (estate tax and income tax) can cause significant liquidity problems without sufficient life insurance to cover the tax liabilities.

15. While deferred compensation plans are often described as golden handcuffs locking the executive to the corporation, many have learned that only the marginal performers are the ones really shackled to the company. Top-quality performers invariably find someone with the key (namely comparable compensation to that forfeited). The result is that not only do deferrals not retain the top performer in many

situations, but equally bad, they make it difficult for a less effective executive to seek alternative career opportunities.

SUMMARY AND CONCLUSIONS

As the list of advantages and disadvantages would suggest, deferred compensation is not for everyone. From the individual's point of view, it is a needs-investment decision. What are my current cash needs? What is the after-tax value of the award today? What is it likely to be at the time the deferral ends? What is the compound rate of return on the investment? What is the projected inflation and value of the dollar at the end of the deferral? The executive must attempt to place future, as well as present, values on the chart in Figure 9-3 before determining the extent to which deferred compensation is appropriate. The before- and after-tax positions will vary by individual based on the person's assumptions.

Let's review several of the key issues which impact on the appropriateness of deferring compensation.

First, it must be remembered that, although the amount is being deferred for tax purposes, it is also being deferred for investment purposes! It is logical to defer if the investment growth is judged to be the same for both current and deferred payments. However, the situation must be carefully examined if the growth rate on deferred payments is less than that available under other opportunities if received immediately. In this case, the deferral may actually cost the recipient more than is saved in taxes, even if some form of interest is added to the deferred amount.

Second, the younger executive is usually at an income level that is too low to provide

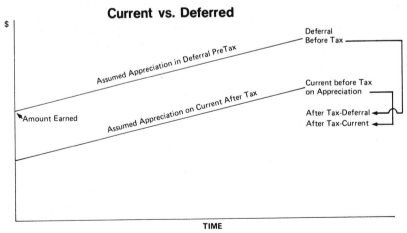

FIGURE 9-3 Current versus deferred compensation after-tax comparison.

any real tax advantage. Even if this is not the case, he or she by definition has more years in which to build up a postretirement income. Obviously, the more the deferred income increases through pension annuities, savings, and other forms of deferrals, the higher the income tax and the less the tax saving over current rates.

Third, the recipient may need the money now to meet mortgage and college tuition costs even though the net may be less than in later years. The countering argument is that financial needs will be correspondingly less in postretirement years.

Fourth, since the main justification for deferring income is to optimize the individual's net income it is imperative that the act of transferring income from years of employment to years of retirement be carefully examined. Pension and long-term profit sharing plans should be examined in relation to the amount deferred until retirement, through salary and incentive plans, to determine the total package available at postretirement as replacement income. Forgotten considerations include looking at the loss of income in determining retirement annuities—especially those that call for a percentage of last 5 or 10 years of earnings. Often overlooked is what the recipient's total postretirement income will be. Some companies have found that, taken individually, each plan provided a tax savings, but when combined with other plans the tax savings was either greatly reduced or eliminated. Examples can be found of executives who retired at higher incomes than earned in their last year of employment.

Fifth, not only are deferred bonus arrangements difficult to construct from a value to the recipient's point of view, but they are also complicated from the viewpoint of applicable taxes. To determine when they should begin and how long they should last, a number of assumptions and calculations must be made. Specifically, an estimate must be made of the recipient's income (from all sources) for the years in question and the applicable tax rates at those times (a very tenuous assumption when dealing 5, 10, or even 20 years in the future). Due to this high degree of uncertainty in both income and tax rates, deferred compensation payments are logical only if a considerable safety margin exists.

Sixth, the current tax rate is always a given, but the tax structure even several years from now is an unknown. What is known is that we get a new tax law about every other year. Who's to say that the 50 percent maximum tax on personal service income will not be increased? Recall the 91 percent marginal rate in effect in the early 1960s and the 70 percent rate in the late 1960s? Perhaps an additional tax on deferred compensation, either during the period of deferral or upon receipt, will become law.

Seventh, the longer the period of deferral, the greater the risk that one or more of the assumptions will incur significant deviation (e.g., need for current cash, tax structure, and alternative investment opportunities).

Probably the greatest drawback to deferred compensation lies in its motivational appeal, or more properly stated, its lack of motivational appeal. Since the reward is separated in time from the performance of the act, it is often difficult to relate the two. This is especially true when the deferral is until retirement.

However, just as important is that as deferrals build up there is a natural reluctance

282

to do anything which will jeopardize the receipt of such payments. For the truly outstanding performer this is no problem because he or she will either succeed with the current employer or find another who is willing to "buy off" the deferrals. However, for the maturing executive whose performance has plateaued there is reluctance to accept risk ventures outside the current employer, causing the forfeiture of unpaid bonus monies. Therefore, it is not too surprising that, given the present tax situation, current rather than deferred payment is very popular.

The Compensation Committee

No longer are compensation levels or programs subject solely to scorn by a professional shareholder at the annual meeting. The audience may include retired employees, union representatives, legislative aides, institutional investors, and government officials. In most instances management still has sufficient control of proxies to ensure the outcome on key issues (e.g., new compensation plan), however it must be prepared to hear dissenting views from other shareholders. The earlier reticence of the shareholder to express concern is fading.

Increasingly prevalent is the establishment of a committee of the board of directors responsible for the pay of the corporate officers and employee directors. In addition to approving the design and mix of the compensation programs, it is also responsible for the administration of such plans. Thus, it is accountable not simply for the form in which the corporate officers are paid but also the level of such payment. This committee, consisting solely of outside directors (similar to the audit and nominating committees), may also address itself to succession and other management development issues for the same group—namely, the review of replacement charts for key officials including the interviewing of candidates before appointment. This could include responsibility for selecting a new CEO subject to board approval.

To ensure comparable treatment, the committee logically would also review (for information purposes) pay increases of other nonofficer executives within the company who are at a comparable level of pay.

COMMITTEE MEMBERSHIP

Depending upon the makeup of the particular board, the committee could consist of former government officials, bankers, lawyers, academicians, or executives of other firms. Some people are critical of companies whose board membership consists of retired members of management and those considered to be suppliers of contractual services (e.g., bankers, outside counsel, and management consultants). The retired executive may have fraternal ties to existing management, having hired and trained them. The presence of suppliers on the board may give a false signal to others that this company is "tied up" with the supplier.

Regardless of type (except for retired executives), committee members usually have one thing in common: very limited capital investment in the company which has engaged them for board work. Not uncommon is a holding of 100 shares. This limited risk factor, combined with knowledge of executive compensation programs essentially limited to salary and a conceptual understanding of short-term incentive plans paying out some form of earnings, can be a significant obstacle in attempting to sort out the pros and cons of alternate plans (e.g., a performance unit plan coupled with nonqualified stock options versus a nonmarket book value and market value tandem stock option). This is one reason having a compensation committee consisting mostly of executives from other companies makes a lot of sense, since they are more likely to be knowledgeable about a wider range of forms of compensation.

Another excellent candidate for the compensation committee is the professional director (i.e., someone whose only employment is serving on a number of boards) who is a retired executive. This may become a very attractive second career for many who wish to take early retirement within their own firms, especially if shrinking inside-board sizes have precluded being elected while working.

However, from the viewpoint of knowledge, the best candidate is an executive compensation consultant or similar individual in the employ of another company. Either of these individuals would be a candidate where eligibility for the committee required simply that candidates be "disinterested parties" and not that they necessarily be also members of the board of directors. Where a company is using several consultants, it may find the industry expert more appealing, not only to bring another dimension but also to avoid potential conflict-of-interest charges.

ROLE RESPONSIBILITY

Some directors feel they are responsible to management rather than the shareholders and the public. This is logical given the proximity of management and the vagueness and distance of shareholders. In addition, some professional directors, seeing their financial dependence upon board membership being contingent on favorable review by senior management, don't do the job. They fail to recognize that if they are really good they will be able to get employment on other boards—for there is no surplus of talented outside directors.

Probably the greatest obstacle facing the committee is simply "getting up to speed" with the forms of compensation and their relationship to specific accounting, tax, and company situations. Unfortunately, too few committee members are well schooled in executive pay programs; some can't tell the difference between a stock option and a stock award. The task is difficult enough given the myriad pay delivery forms, and it is unduly complicated by media messages promising 101 ways to reward executives effectively. Too often these are shallow gimmicks rather than creative new techniques.

Because of their fiduciary role to the shareholder, it is logical to expect the members of the committee to be performance-oriented in direction but cautious in specific plan design. A plan looking very much like one in a number of other companies (especially the same industry) is more likely to be acceptable than an innovative creation.

In large part this conservative approach is believed attributable to a lack of knowledge by which to adequately judge the efficacy of a new approach. It is much easier to rely on the judgments of other boards: "If they have it and apparently it is not causing problems, then it is probably right for us also." This is not to imply that compensation committees are unique in this respect. It is not uncommon for some executives to be more risk-taking in their rhetoric than in their actions.

The compensation committee, in addition to having to absorb a significant amount of compensation design coupled with basic accounting and tax considerations, must be able to see the areas likely to be applicable as well as those which are inappropriate. Having discarded the latter, the committee must focus on determining the appropriate program(s) for this company's elected officers. It must be conscious of relative pay levels on a total compensation mix, for to the extent salaries are high any incentive payment may be superfluous.

Logically the committee should state a desired pay philosophy. A beginning point would be to look at the philosophy of the rest of the organization. It would not seem rational on the face of it to pay at the median of defined industry competition for the nonofficer group but at the 75th percentile for the officers. This is not to say the pay philosophy has to be the same, but certainly there should be a quantifiable reason for degree of difference. The above identified 50th and 75th percentile situation could be rationalized if the nonofficer group, while adequate, was not considered likely to provide officer replacements—almost all of whom therefore would come from outside the company at significant increases in pay above the community median.

USE OF CONSULTANTS

To assist the committee in sorting through these issues, many companies are turning to outside consultants. This is not a slap at the competency of the inside executive pay planners but again a reference to fiduciary trust. It seems a little less than an "arms-length" transaction to have the inside executive pay planner (who is in the reporting chain to the CEO) advise the compensation committee on the appropriate form and level of pay of the CEO. It would seem unlikely that many CEOs would advance the report (or in the long run, retain the pay planner) if it were not favorable. One answer is to have the pay planner report directly to the committee, although the career possibilities of such an individual would be questionable. The other alternative is to utilize an outside consultant.

Rather than immediately sign up a consultant, it would seem appropriate to do a little market research. Some consulting firms have broad-gauge management views: "We can tackle anything." Others are more specialized in nature, ranging from total compensation planning to executive pay design. Each have their advantages and disadvantages. Broad-gauge management consulting firms are more likely to design a program related to the company short- and long-term needs; however, the extent to which such plans reflect a creative approach will be a function of the degree of executive compensation knowledge, or lack thereof, of the compensation consultant assigned. On the other hand, a top-notch pay planner from a more specialized firm will be more likely to custom-tailor a plan. However, the individual may not have sufficient broad-gauge management background to have accurately assessed the corporate needs.

Few committees seem to approach the problem objectively. Rather than identify one firm, several should be selected on the basis of proposals (after of course providing sufficient data to allow them to assess the problem). Each proposal should be analyzed to determine the extent to which the problem has been accurately defined as well as whether the approach suggested is feasible. A cost-benefit analysis of the proposal should be prepared including such items as consultant charges, company time, disruption, and program cost.

In looking at consultants, one should also attempt to identify which have been identified as loud proponents of a specific form of plan. If Ms. X is recognized as a performance share advocate, the company should be more interested in how she will justify that type of plan within the company than surprised that she recommends such a program. She has a solution in search of a problem. Unfortunately, unless the problem meets the definition, the misapplied solution subsequently becomes part of the problem.

It would be logical to engage as a consultant to the compensation committee an executive compensation specialist who is neither an employee nor engaged in consulting assignments with the company, thus avoiding potential conflict-of-interest situations. The individual could be employed to review the quality of recommendations and/or to develop specific recommendations based on committee objectives.

An extension of this would be to appoint the consultant as a permanent member of the committee with the written agreement that the person will not work for management. As indicated earlier, an executive compensation expert in the employ of another company might also be a candidate for membership in the compensation committee. Even combining these two sources, there are many more opportunities than there are knowledgeable individuals.

During the research phase it is also necessary to identify the real reason (not the obvious avowed response to fiduciary trust) for engaging a consultant. Possible reasons include:

- Image—engaging an individual and/or firm well recognized for preeminence in the area of executive compensation design is an overt signal to the outside world that this committee is "doing right"—excellence by inference. With "so-and-so" as the consultant, one must conclude the company has an effective pay delivery system.

- Buffer—employing a consultant prepared to support the position of the committee gives face validity to the program if challenged by a shareholder.

- Magician—belief that the individual engaged will bring forth powers of alchemy. With a wave of the person's wand the laborious design process will be circumvented by the materialization of a simple, easy-to-understand, and easy-to-operate plan which will be perceived as equitable by all parties concerned. Committees with this approach probably still believe in the tooth fairy.

- Resources—limited time frame and/or lack of executive compensation plan design within the company could necessitate going to a consultant who can provide the know-how and sufficient resources to accomplish the job quickly.

On the other hand, some companies look to the auditing firm to comment on the appropriateness of the design of a pay package and its level of payment. The first is a logical extention of what they may later have to comment on anyway; the reasonableness issue is one that will have to be addressed with the IRS if not with shareholders. The auditing firm has an advantage over another consulting firm in that it knows the company rather well.

When the compensation committee engages a consultant, it presents management with an interesting problem: does it hire a different consultant (it would seem a potential conflict of interest to have the same consultant for both management and the compensation committee), or does it ensure that internal staff is experienced enough to take on the consultant? If there are two different consultants, professional courtesy might preclude concise summaries of differences. Thus the companies with top-flight executive compensation pay planners appear to have a distinct advantage. Since the supply is significantly less then the increasing demand, it is predicted that a two-tier market in levels of pay will thus emerge, separating the "pros" from the "adequates." Internal relationships will be reassessed, and many will see that an additional $25,000 or more in pay for such a person is extremely cost effective given the total executive payroll. It is also less than might be incurred in consulting fees.

Once a consultant has been selected and has prepared a proposal, the specific plan alternatives must be reviewed in terms of anticipated performance and level of payment over the prescribed time period. Only by simulating results and examining payment will it be possible for the committee to judge the efficacy of the proposals. It would also be logical to have the consultant attend the annual shareholder meeting, not simply in those years in which a plan change is proposed but in the other years as well.

COMPANY COMPENSATION EXPERT

Even if management consultants are employed, it is critical that a large company have an internal executive compensation expert. That individual could be appointed as secretary to the compensation committee and, in that role, work with the chairperson in establishing the agenda. In addition, the individual would be responsible for preparing the necessary materials for each meeting, briefing members individually on items of concern, recording the minutes of the sessions, and following up on items identified by the committee.

To be successful, the individual must have sufficient rapport with counterparts in other companies to be able to obtain needed data. In addition, the person must be articulate in speech and writing, analytical but practical, and emphatic but independent.

Ideally, the individual should also be sufficiently versed in all forms of executive pay to provide another dimension to material advanced by the external consultants.

COMMITTEE RESPONSIBILITIES

Thus, it is critical for the compensation committee to have sufficient knowledge of company objectives and compensation design to be able to judge the efficacy of a specific proposal. It is as important to ask whether this is the optimum solution as to ask whether the proposed course of action itself needs some modification. In other words, before being certain that the specific plan has no inconsistencies or inaccuracies, be certain that a more desirable plan has not been overlooked or incorrectly discarded! This can only be accomplished by reviewing *all* the forms of executive pay design and indicating why each is appropriate or inappropriate for this company. It is insufficient to test the efficacy of a proposal simply on the basis of whether or not it appears to reflect good staff work. In a number of situations these committees are initiating their own studies and proposals instead of passively awaiting a proposal from management. Many suffer from a plethora of reports and recommendations to digest, and from little staff support to ensure efficacious analysis.

On the one hand, it is important to ensure that the pay package is attractive and competitive; on the other hand, it is necessary to ensure that the compensation package is not considered by shareholders to be a waste of corporate assets—for, if so, a lawsuit may very well follow. Just because several companies in a desperate need to obtain a particular CEO have offered a million-dollar bonus is no rationale for increasing the pay of several vulnerable people by a couple of hundred thousand dollars.

In order to meet its social responsibilities and shareholder obligations, the committee should ensure that its pay delivery system for top managers is consistent with expected short- and long-term results. This is the optimum. The minimum is to ascertain that pay is not inconsistent with company goals. Between these two is the "no-man's-land" into which the majority of pay systems fall. Many a compensation committee has heard the plea to change the plan because "it isn't paying anything." This may be the best indication that it is a good plan. It may not be paying because performance is not adequate. However, few resist the temptation to change the goals or the plan in order to make an adequate payout. Performance becomes in these situations a secondary consideration.

Once the specific plan or combination of plans and the defined level of pay for the officers under specific conditions of company performance have been chosen, it is probably necessary for the plans to be formally drafted by counsel and submitted to the full board for approval. A company may choose one form over another simply because of the low profile it may be given in the proxy statement. Classically, stock options have had much less visibility than stock awards in isolating individual gains. In almost every case the plan would also be submitted to shareholders after the board approval, although awards could be made contingent on shareholder acceptance.

The compensation committee would also determine how much should be paid from the sum of previous carry-forwards and current year performance. It would also typically authorize the amount to be carried forward to the next year. This could simply be the total available less this year's awards; however, to the extent this is in excess of what would be perceived needed to cover warranted bonuses for several lean years, it would be reduced.

Typically, one would expect the committee to make decisions on the CEO, review recommendations on the other top 10 to 20 executives and make a decision, after reviewing the actions on the next 20 to 50 individuals (perhaps decided by a separate committee) for informational purposes. When determining the form in which to distribute the award, the executive's stated preference should be considered. However, it is also important to examine the company needs. If the company is in a cash bind, it should lean toward distribution in the form of company stock; if there is a concern for dilution of equity, then distribution is in cash. To the extent it is both, a combination award will be made to lessen the impact of dilution and cash flow.

After the awards have been made, the committee is responsible for monitoring the activity of the plan performance and acting upon salary recommendations for the officers. Some committees consider it logical not only that they be responsible for the pay of the corporate officers but also that they be fully appraised of succession plans. Thus, the committee has a basis for judging the depth of management talent or lack thereof. It is also helpful in understanding differences in recommended pay increases (one is on the inside track and the other an outside shot, at best). Some request that management succession plans be reduced to writing and reviewed at least annually.

Administration of the actual pay program will focus on all five components of the officers' pay package, including their relative mix. It is therefore assumed the committee will be responsible not only for approving any recommendations on salary increase but also the units of participation under both the short- and long-term incentive plans. Modifications to basic employee benefit plans (such as allowing an unfunded plan to restore benefits curtailed by ERISA maximums) and eligibility for specific perquisites would also be determined by this committee.

Logically, the various actions should be identified, the basis on which a decision is to be made should be stated, and the respective roles of responsibility for proposing and approving various actions should be indicated. Table 10-1 shows how the five compensation elements might be handled for a company having two compensation committees, an executive compensation committee for elected corporate officers consisting solely of nonemployee directors and an employee compensation committee consisting of the CEO, vice president of personnel, and one or more top operating heads.

TABLE 10-1   Relative Roles of Responsibility

Action	Basis	Proposed by	Approved by
		For salary	
Obtain competitive data	Comparable size/ industry	Director, compensation and benefits	Executive compensation committee (corporate officers)
		Division personnel vice president	Director, compensation and benefits (all others)
Approve job gradings	Competitive data Internal equity	CEO (corporate officers)	Executive compensation committee
		Director, compensation and benefits (others above $75,000)	Employee compensation committee
		Division personnel VP (those below $75,000)	Director, compensation and benefits
Approve salary structure and guidelines	Competitive data	CEO	Executive compensation committee (corporate officers)
		Director, compensation and benefits	Employee compensation committee (all others)
Allocate divisional salary budgets	Compa-ratio Unit performance	Director, compensation and benefits	Employee compensation committee
Approve salary changes	Unit and individual performance	Immediate supervisor ↓ Division president	Employee compensation committee (except corporate officers)
		Employee compensation committee	Executive compensation committee (corporate officers)
		For employee benefits	
Obtain competitive data	Comparable size/ industry	Director, compensation and benefits	Employee compensation committee

Action	Basis	Proposed by	Approved by
Amend pension plan	Competitive data Employee attitude surveys	Vice president personnel/finance ↓ Employee compensation committee	Board of directors
Establish/amend other plans	Competitive data Employee attitude surveys	Director, compensation and benefits	Employee compensation committee (over $25,000 per year)
		Director, compensation and benefits	Vice president personnel (all others)
For perquisites			
Obtain competitive data	Comparable size/ industry	Director, compensation and benefits	Executive compensation committee (corporate officers)
		Director, compensation and benefits	Employee compensation committee (all others)
Establish/amend plan	Competitive data Internal equity	CEO ↓ Executive compensation committee	Board of directors
		Director, compensation and benefits	Employee compensation committee
Give to individual	Job grade Salary level Organizational level		Executive compensation committee (for CEO)
		CEO	Executive compensation committee (corporate officers)
		Director, compensation and benefits	Employee compensation committee (all others)
For short-term incentives			
Obtain competitive data	Comparable size/ industry	Director, compensation and benefits	Employee compensation committee

TABLE 10-1 Relative Roles of Responsibility (*Continued*)

Action	Basis	Proposed by	Approved by
Obtain competitive data	Comparable size/ industry	Director, compensation and benefits	Executive compensation committee
Amend plan	Competitive data Company performance	Vice president personnel/finance ↓ Employee compensation committee ↓ Executive compensation committee	
		Board of directors	Shareholders
Establish targets	Competitive data Company short-range forecasts	CEO ↓ Executive compensation committee	Board of directors
Allocate divisional funds	Unit and corporate performance	CEO	Executive compensation committee
Grant individual awards	Individual performance		Executive compensation committee (for CEO)
		CEO	Executive compensation committee (other corporate officers)
		Division president ↓ Director, compensation and benefits	Employee compensation committee (others above $75,000)
		Immediate supervisor	Division president (others)

For long-term incentives

Action	Basis	Proposed by	Approved by
Obtain competitive data	Comparable size/ industry	Director, compensation and benefits	Employee compensation committee
		Director, compensation and benefits	Executive compensation committee

Action	Basis	Proposed by	Approved by
Amend plan	Competitive data Company performance	Vice president personnel/finance ↓ Employee compensation committee ↓ Executive compensation committee ↓ Board of directors	Shareholders
Establish targets	Competitive data Company long-range forecasts	CEO ↓ Executive compensation committee	Board of directors
Determine eligibility	Job grade Salary level Organizational level	Director, compensation and benefits	Employee compensation committee (nonofficers)
Grant individual awards	Corporate performance Unit performance and potential	CEO Division president ↓ Director, compensation and benefits	Executive compensation committee (corporate officers) Employee compensation committee

TABLE 10-2 Timetable for Compensation Actions

	Division president	Director, compensation and benefits	VP personnel	Employee compensation committee	Executive compensation committee	Board of directors	Shareholders
January							
• Allocate divisional salary budgets				X			
• Allocate short-term incentive funds to division					X		
• Allocate long-term incentive funds to division					X		
• Review individual performances	X			X	X		
February							
• Establish short-term incentive targets					X	X	
• Establish long-term incentive targets					X	X	
March							
• Approve salary changes	X			X	X		
• Approve short-term incentive awards				X	X		
• Approve long-term incentive awards				X	X		
• Identify competitors				X	X		
April							
• Amend short-term incentive plan							X
• Amend long-term incentive plan							X
May							
• Obtain competitive data		X					

296

Month / Activity					
June					
• Obtain competitive data	X				
July					
• Analyze competitive data	X				
August					
• Approve job gradings	X				
• Analyze competitive benefit data	X				
September					
• Approve job gradings			X	X	
October					
• Amend short-term incentive plan			X		
• Amend long-term incentive plan			X		
November					
• Amend pension plan			X		
• Amend other benefit plans		X	X		
• Approve perquisite plans			X	X	
• Determine perquisite eligibility			X	X	
• Determine long-term incentive plan eligibility			X		
December					
• Amend pension plan					X
• Amend short-term incentive plan					X
• Amend long-term incentive plan					X
• Approve perquisite plans					X
• Approve salary structure and guidelines			X		

Table 10-2 is a timetable illustrating how the various responsibilities meld together for the year. In this illustration salary actions are affected on a common date (April 1) rather than distributed throughout the year; short- and long-term incentive awards are made at the same time. However, benefit and perquisite actions are affected the first of the year.

The committee's task is not an easy one; it must balance financial expectations of management with degree of difficulty in goal attainment and cost to shareholders. In many instances simply quantifying corporate strategy and goals in a manner that will allow structuring a short- or long-term incentive plan is a challenge by itself. Add to this the need to relate to pay levels of officers of other companies after adjusting for profit performance, and it is easy to see the responsibility is more easily defined than accomplished.

A logical requirement is an annual report reflecting pay levels for a specified list of companies. This could be prepared either by an internal staff or by an outside consultant. Using this data the committee could ascertain what level of adjustment is appropriate for the affected group. This in turn might be reviewed with an outside consultant for reasonableness.

UNREASONABLE COMPENSATION

A major concern of the compensation committee is whether or not the pay of the executives will be viewed as reasonable. Have the executives really earned their pay? To date the courts have been reluctant to substitute their judgment for that of the board of directors or its appropriate committee. Primary attention has been directed toward whether or not there has been an abuse of fiduciary trust, lack of good faith, or outright fraud.

However, when the courts have been required to determine whether or not the compensation is reasonable, they have looked to the specific facts about the company and the executive. Listed in Table 10-3 are situations that tend to either support the compensation as being reasonable or suggest that it is not.

It is difficult to generalize, since each case will be judged on its special merits. However, the likelihood of a favorable ruling is enhanced if more facts fall to the right side than the left in the above listing.

In addition to shareholder suit, the committee has to be aware of potential tax problems. The prime interest by the IRS is to ensure that all the earnings of the company are not paid out as compensation to the owners, thereby avoiding tax on the profits. Furthermore, the shareholder-executives are eligible for the 50 percent maximum tax on pay versus the 70 percent maximum for dividends. If the IRS rules a portion of the compensation to be unreasonable, that portion cannot be claimed as a business expense. Furthermore, it is logical that the portion of compensation ruled as being unreasonable will also not be eligible for the 50 percent maximum tax on personal service income. Thus, the tax effectiveness drops from 0.93 to 0.30 (i.e., 30 cents net income divided

TABLE 10-3 Unreasonable Compensation Checklist

	Level of compensation	
	May be unreasonable	May be reasonable
Company	Privately held	Publicly held
	Family-controlled	Diffuse ownership
	Small company	Large company
	No or low dividends	Attractive dividends
Executive	Little experience	Extensive experience
	Light work schedule	Works long hours
	Either significant increase in pay or no change for years	Increase in pay consistent with growth of company, increase in responsibility, or back pay for lean years
	Pay significantly higher than for other companies or data not available	Pay is basically consistent with comparable-size companies in comparable industries
	Pay set near end of year (when profits can be more exactly measured)	Basis for pay clearly set at beginning of year
	Pay of shareholder-owners higher than comparable nonshareholder employees	Pay of shareholder-owners comparable to or lower than others in firm with similar responsibilities
	Stockholder of significant holdings of company stock	Nonstockholder or one with insignificant percentage of ownership

by $1 net expense). This risk has prompted some companies to establish a repayment provision in the executive's contract requiring that the individual repay the company for that portion of compensation ruled to be unreasonable. This eliminates the company expense and drops the executive's net income from 30 cents on the dollar to zero (but presumably the person would be taken care of in other ways, perhaps at a future date). However, such an agreement is considered by some as giving the IRS additional reason to examine the level of compensation on the presumption that such an agreement wouldn't exist unless there was possible cause for a case of unreasonable compensation.

A concern facing some companies with forms of restricted compensation is that if the property (e.g., company stock) has significantly appreciated in the period between the award and when the restrictions lapse, it may be challenged. It will be remembered that deductions on restricted property can be taken only to the extent restrictions lapse (or the executive voluntarily recognizes it as income when awarded).

If the company is challenged to demonstrate that a reasonable relationship exists between the value of pay versus the value of the service provided by the executive, it may be helpful to point to total compensation, not simply salary and bonus. If employee benefits and perquisites are significantly less liberal than for comparable companies, it would be logical to include these costs in a total compensation review. Otherwise a company with competitive total compensation but almost all its pay in salaries and bonuses may find it difficult to demonstrate a competitive position.

Fortunately the IRS appears to be content with determining reasonableness in terms of what other employers in like businesses of comparable magnitude are paying their executives. Thus all could be overpaying (underpaying would be unlikely), and there apparently is no problem. Apparently this is the same basis the courts are using to determine reasonableness in a tax case; as indicated, they have been chary of looking behind the decision of level of pay in a corporate law case.

NONEMPLOYEE DIRECTOR PAY

A separate issue is who is responsible for pay decisions with respect to outside directors. It is not uncommon for the corporate secretary to draw together data on competitive practice and present it to the CEO, who will analyze it and make a recommendation to the full board. Logically the nonemployee directors would abstain from voting. The role of the company pay planner in this process is a function of his or her creditability.

Recognizing that surveys exist to identify the competitive levels of directors' fees, few examine the level of remuneration in terms of what consultants would receive for a half-day or day of work. This could be accomplished by estimating the hourly rate (i.e., total fees and attendance) and comparing it with the billing rates of senior management consultants, attorneys, or accountants. Perhaps one can adjust this in some relation to value received; however, the degree of responsibility of the individuals is different. Few would argue that advisers should be paid as much as those responsible for the decisions.

Furthermore, it is curious that all directors (assuming same committees and attendance) are paid the same. The same pay is valid only if one accepts that all outside directors are of equal ability when assigned comparable responsibilities (i.e., all committees are equally important) and that they are equally proficient in discharging these responsibilities. That assumes a lot of equality! Why then are they all paid the same? Essentially, because the compensation programs have not caught up with the change in importance of outside directors. Modest remuneration of equal amounts for all was certainly appropriate when board membership was more honorary than risk-oriented. The $20 gold piece at the director's place was probably a reasonable compensation level given the responsibilities. Some might argue that restoring this practice (given the premium prices for mint-condition $20 gold pieces) would be reasonable in today's times as well. However, in today's situation treating all the same is not automatically synonymous with treating everyone equitably.

It is interesting that while most companies review the pay package of their executives, a number do not review the pay program for outside directors. Objectivity notwithstanding, it is difficult for some directors to understand why they should approve annual salary increases or short-term incentive awards to the senior management when their compensation has been the same for several years. Furthermore, in addition to varying the compensation package (depending on the role played and the number of committees involved), it may be necessary to have a front-end, one-time recruiting cash payment or (more appropriately) stock award for troubled companies.

Again the basic issues: form and level. Probably the most prevalent practice is a combination of annual retainer and meeting fee. Other arrangements could be simply one without the other. Companies that have retainer and attendance fees for the full board implicitly state that there is an ongoing responsibility and away-from-the-site work plus a need to attend meetings in order to discharge these responsibilities. Those with only a retainer are reflecting that regardless of attendance the director is responsible for board actions; those with only an attendance fee are requiring the director to appear and make his or her position known. To the extent the practice is not consistent with the philosophy, obviously the practice should be changed. Too many companies are mesmerized by survey data without attempting to relate to the philosophy. For example, a company might conclude that the ongoing responsibility and attendance are of about equal value. Assuming 12 board meetings a year, the attendance fee should logically be $\frac{1}{12}$ of the annual retainer. Typically, the size of such payment is related to size of organization, with the multibillion companies paying significantly more than those a fraction their size.

In addition to the normal director's compensation most companies apparently pay extra for serving on board committees. In some instances they pay the traditional retainer plus a per-meeting fee. However, it appears that simple compensation in terms of meetings attended is more common. There is a difference among companies about whether to pay only one attendance fee per day, regardless of how many meetings are held, or pay for each meeting regardless of the number. The determining factors in setting the policy should be level of desired payment, importance of attendance, and inconvenience of travel. The increased cost for paying for more than one meeting a day could be significantly offset by travel expense savings.

If most of the directors are only an hour or so away from the meeting site, scheduling more than one meeting a day is as much a convenience for them as for the company. Even so, many would state it is unfair to penalize them so drastically as to pay for only the first meeting in the day. Perhaps half the normal fee for the second and all additional meetings during the day would be reasonable. In addition, a number of companies do provide a separate annual retainer for the chairman of each committee in recognition of organizational responsibilities (e.g., developing agendas, meeting with management, coordinating staff work, and reviewing recommendations), in addition to or in lieu of annual retainers for other committee members.

Probably the most prevalent practice is for a company to pay the same fee for attending a committee meeting as a board meeting. This may be appropriate but the company should examine the relationship. For those who conclude that much of the critical work is done in the committee and that the board meetings are more perfunctory, the decision should be to have committee fees higher than board attendance fees. Conversely, if the board is the focal point and the committees are more information-gathering in nature, perhaps board fees should be higher. The important point is that the impact of each should be assessed in setting the fee structure. A related issue is what to pay for visits to company sites.

The problem with flat retainers and meeting fees is that it assumes not only that the relative responsibilities are the same but that each director is performing equally well. The problem in pay for performance is: Who would make the determination? It would either be the chairman of the board or the entire board. In either event, one could argue that it might disrupt the harmony of board activities.

Some directors are interested in deferring part or all of their retainer and/or meeting fees. Such deferrals may be at a specified rate of interest, tied to a specific financial vehicle (e.g., 6-month Treasury bills or the prime interest rate), and/or tied to company stock performance. As explained in Chapter 9, Deferred Compensation, this type of decision is a wager by the individual on the probable tax rate, amount of inflation, and lack of attractiveness of alternative forms of investment. Another alternative is investment in the Keogh plan described in Chapter 5, Employee Benefits.

Few companies provide any direct compensation other than the annual retainer and/or the per-meeting fee. It could be argued, however, that the directors should increase their identification with the shareholder and be given stock awards and/or stock options. These could either be real or phanton plans. Essentially, any plan described earlier for executives could be developed for nonemployee directors. However, a key planning consideration is the limited period many will serve as directors. Thus, a 10-year non-qualified stock option is probably not very attractive. However, a stock purchase plan where director purchases are matched in whole or in part by the corporation may be very attractive. On the surface it seems logical that a director with 10,000 shares of company stock has a different perspective than one with 100 shares.

Like executive pay, the pay for directors is increasing, and more rapidly than in previous years. In the past it was not uncommon to set the directors' fees and not change them for years. Now it is more common to adjust them more frequently, if not annually. The rationale is simple: Why should the outside directors have less frequent adjustment than their employee director counterparts?

Some have argued that responsibility of the board is easily as much as that of the CEO and therefore the pay of the directors should be proportionate to the CEO in terms of amount of time. Thus if the CEO is paid $500,000 an outside director should receive approximately $2000 for every day spent on board work. If it were assumed that each board meeting required at least a day of preparation or follow-up, an annual retainer of $24,000 and meeting fees of $2000 each with 12 meetings per year could be justified.

Very few companies have a fee arrangement anything close to this probably largely due to slowness in recognizing that the role of the director has changed significantly in the last few years. Membership is no longer an honorary function. Board work is much more demanding due to social responsibility and other issues. Directors are liable to lawsuits in instances where it appears that they have not prudently governed the business. Even where director and officer liability insurance would reimburse losses, few like the thought of the annoyance of a legal action and the public embarrassment of being charged with negligence. As indicated earlier, an up-front sign-up bonus similar to that used in professional sports may become necessary, especially for troubled companies, to make the position sufficiently appealing.

For tax purposes these persons are not "employees" of the company but rather self-employed individuals. Thus, including them under company benefit plans is more difficult. For example, they cannot be included under qualified defined benefit or contribution plans since such benefits can only apply to employees. An identical plan paralleling the benefits can be established; however, this could require compliance with ERISA and careful design to ensure the income was not taxed until received. However, Keogh plans enable directors to set aside a portion of their retainer and fees.

Also, it is common to include outside directors in the company travel accident insurance plan, the matching gifts program, and a director and officer liability insurance plan, as well as to reimburse them for business travel expenses. Some outside directors are also entitled to personal use of company aircraft, medical examinations, and personal umbrella liability coverage.

Some companies provide life insurance to their nonemployee directors either at no or reduced cost. The amount may either be a flat amount (e.g., $100,000) or a multiple of earnings (although this means coverage is a function of number of meetings attended where per-meeting fees exist). It is important to remember that the $50,000 life insurance exclusion applies only to employees; also, the less favorable P.S. 58 rates (not the Uniform Premium Rate table) is applicable. It would also be logical to consider including directors in health care coverage (with coordination of benefits under other policies), disability programs, and survivor benefits. Unfortunately, state requirements and ERISA could present obstacles.

Since director compensation is self-employment income it is subject to social security taxes in the year received. In addition, the director who is receiving social security benefits may be subject to an earnings test for level of benefits. However, this may be waived in the first year of retirement if the services rendered are not substantial in time. Less than 15 hours a month may eliminate any earnings test. In any event, after 1981 there is no earnings test for an individual age 70 or older. Thus to the extent there is a problem it is only for 5 years (age 65 to 70). Perhaps this problem could be eliminated by deferring all of the director's compensation to age 70.

While many companies require directors to retire upon attaining age 70, this policy may disappear, possibly before it is legally mandated, as top-quality directors become more difficult to find.

SUMMARY AND CONCLUSIONS

If one accepts that the human resources are the most important assets of the company, then it is imperative that pay programs for the top executives especially be equitable and cost effective. It is simple logic that the likely need of attaining desired financial and social objectives will be maximized if capable people are in the positions of authority and are rewarded in proportion to their success. By definition this also means being punished for degree of failure by the amount of pay withheld. Obviously there is a point at which failure is handled by dismissal, but a successful pay delivery system reinforces desired performance as well.

To date, few compensation committees have taken responsibility for initiating studies of the executive pay delivery systems. Rather they review and approve those prepared by consultants and compensation staff at the request of senior management. However, more and more are taking the responsibility for establishing the executive compensation program, not simply approving or modifying requests from management.

Such committees define their role as taking the corporate objectives established by the board and relating them to a pay delivery system which will reward in proportion to accomplishment. In addition, they attempt to determine the extent to which performance is being measured and the basis for salary increases and bonus awards—not simply for corporate officers but also for other key members of management. Such committees also recognize the need to be competitive; however, they temper the input of firms that offer multimillion dollar packages in a desperate attempt to buy management needed to "turn a company around."

Probably most important of all, committees are realizing that executive pay programs are a means to an end and not an end unto themselves. They are sometimes complicated and too often don't work well, but they are the best technique available for ensuring that shareholder interests are placed in proper focus.

Plan Objectives

Before deciding on the types of short- and long-term incentive plans that are appropriate, it is necessary to determine the plan objectives. The optimum plan for a specific company will be consistent with its basic objectives and delivery of rewards in a cost effective manner. Listed below are some of the major considerations, along with some commentary on their potential impact.

POSSIBLE CONSIDERATIONS

1. *How much of the reason for adopting an incentive plan is to be in vogue and how much to truly pay in relation to performance?*

    One approach will require significant effort to design a meaningful plan, the other is much easier since the plan is more pro forma.

2. *What portion of the executive pay (at varying levels) should be at risk with the stock market (and therefore closely associated with shareholder interest)?*

    Incentive plans dealing with company stock (especially options) were very popular devices for allowing boards to indicate the professional managers were at risk with the market just as the shareholders were. To the extent the market softened, stock options were shored up with appreciation rights and performance share plans. Thus while there was still identification with the shareholder, the degree of risk was significantly lowered.

    To the extent stock options are employed, the company is saying that it wishes its key employees to share in this growth. Conversely few seem to recognize that they are also saying we aren't prepared to give anything if the stock does not appreciate! When this happens and the company has utilized only stock options, not surprisingly it scurries for alternative programs (especially if the lack of stock growth is inconsistent with corporate performance).

    Although use of the company stock (especially options)

has a high degree of identification with the shareholder, a more basic issue is the extent to which the incentive plan is a risk-reward vehicle. Shareholders seem to accept high payouts for very exceptional performance, but they also expect the payout to drop in some relationship with less than outstanding achievement. Thus plans that have little variance in payout for varying levels of financial success, especially marginal levels, may be subject to significant shareholder criticism.

3. *Having identified how much should be paid at varying levels of performane, what percentage of the total should be salary and short- and long-term incentives?*

Given target dollar amounts, the higher the salary, the less available for incentive pay. Many will argue that the more volatile company performance, the more should be put at risk with incentive pay; however this means publicity during big payout periods and unhappy executives during low payout periods. Thus it is not too surprising that many companies increase the salary portion and lower the incentive in volatile earnings situations—thereby smoothing out the earnings swings of executives. Companies with smaller fluctuations put more at risk and allow the executive to participate in company success or lack thereof.

A related question needing answering is: are these relationships based on competitive data or value assessments about what is right with the company?

4. *Is it understood that the incentive plan will have to be reviewed annually in terms of appropriateness to industry, company, management, tax, accounting, and SEC issues?*

Unfortunately the view of almost everyone is that after sweating through the installation of a new pay program they can forget about it at least for several years. The result is that, after such a time span, the plan requires major surgery and continuity is significantly jolted.

Fund formulas should be reviewed periodically. Old and outdated formulas will typically provide greater funds than required because they were established when earnings were smaller. One test of efficacy is ascertaining whether the same amount of discipline is exerted as when the formula was last modified. A related question is whether the budgeted targets have similar stretch to earlier goals.

Conversely, financial performance will be more positive under historical-cost accounting than if those figures are adjusted for inflation and present-day cost of replacing assets. Therefore, formulas based on the former, to generate short- or long-term incentive payouts, should be examined very carefully before being modified.

Parenthetically, it should be noted that while most are able to deal with the results associated with FIFO (first in, first out), LIFO (last in, first out), and NIFO (next in, first out), no one has been able to develop a meaningful incentive plan when FISH is employed (i.e., first in still here).

5. *If corporate staff functions are to be included, what will be the basis for the evaluation?*

Some plans will be restricted to those with bottom-line accountability and thereby cause varying levels of participation. Such an approach is based on a position-by-position analysis to determine eligibility. Those not eligible are under either straight salary or a short-term incentive plan based on degree of accomplishment of annual objectives.

6. *How important is clarity of the eligibility definition?*

   As soon as the level of eligibility is defined (by job level, salary amount, or position-by-position inspection), pressure will develop to include those just below the cutoff. This factor probably more than any other causes a good plan to go bad as those brought in do not have the degree of impact being measured in the plan. Some argue such plans should not be tied to salary levels for this reason because it places additional pressure on upgrading. Admittedly it does, but it also allows the needed review of total pay.

7. *Are the goals of top executives quantifiable in terms of performance and time span needed to measure degree of success? To what extent are they shared with others?*

   The ideal plan would have a payout scale for each objective determined at time of closure. Thus one goal might be adequately assessed after 3 years and constitute a value of zero to $25,000, while another might not be ascertainable for 5 years with a range from zero to $10,000.

   Everyone would agree that while not all objectives have the same time frame or end on the same date, few are prepared to develop a payout scale on this basis.

8. *Is the company prepared to define and evaluate individual or unit performance for incentive plan purposes?*

   It is an anomaly to talk about incentive plans based on performance and then to be very mushy about what constitutes performance.

   Furthermore most of the studies reveal that individual performance plans are more effective in behavior modification than group plans, yet most of the executive incentive plans are based on group performance (e.g., corporation, group, or division)—not individual.

9. *What is the long-range planning period?*

   As one might expect, it is logical to tie the long-range incentive plan to the same cycle used in the management planning and review process. Unless there are mitigating circumstances, one would not expect a 5-year performance-measuring period for incentive plan purposes to exist in a company with 3-year forecasts and appraisals.

10. *Will individual performance be assessed for the purpose of adjusting group unit performance?*

    Most plans that will pay individuals in relation to corporate performance will not attempt to adjust for individual performance. However the next allocation of units (or bonus range) will probably be adjusted in relation to how the individual

307

performed. Unfortunately this means the individual will probably be underrewarded at one time and overcompensated at another or vice versa.

11. *To what extent is it desirable to lock in the executive with golden handcuffs to the firm through restricted pay devices?*

While many consider this a practical solution to retaining executives, it is necessary to understand that golden handcuffs have varying strengths. They are most effective with the least attractive (to other companies), low-mobility (unlikely to change jobs) executive. In other words the forfeited value can always be offset by another company if the executive is that good.

12. *How important are tax avoidance and minimization?*

To the extent this is a basic concern, one must be prepared for a number of major revisions in executive pay on almost a regular basis. It will be a constant effort of altering form and timing to optimize this approach. These major changes (rather than oblique movements) will make any type of continuity highly unlikely.

13. *Given EPS and financing goals, how much stock is the company prepared to offer executives over the short and long term?*

If significant stock is available it allows considerable flexibility in incentive design; however, if the amount is restricted this impacts upon the type of plan (e.g., stock options require more than stock awards since the value of the former is only through appreciation) and number of participants.

14. *Will significant increases in total pay for top executives be desirable in terms of employee relations?*

What pressure at the bargaining table or nonorganized dissatisfaction will occur if top management is receiving pay increases in multiples of others? Is it of concern that the hourly employee may receive an 8 percent adjustment while senior managers get 15 to 20 percent?

15. *To what extent are shareholder relations a concern?*

With many companies the holdings are shifting from the individual investor to the large institution which is capable of greater impact on the stock price (by buying or selling). To the extent this is a concern, there will be a desire to: limit perquisites and other special pay arrangements not related directly to performance, separate salary from incentive pay (especially in cyclical performing companies) and report the bonus in the immediately succeeding year (delaying an additional year might result in big bonuses being reported after a poor financial year), and ensure the short-term incentive fund formula, while adequate, does not generate excessive amounts (especially in poorer-performing years). Some institutional investors have become more critical of executive compensation plans and levels of pay which they believe are unwarranted in terms of corporate performance.

16. *What is the likelihood of wage controls being again imposed?*

    This type of concern would suggest wider salary ranges (in case no structural adjustments would be allowed, although the company might be permitted to operate an existing program within such a program) and documented administrative procedures within a written plan. For many the period 1971–1974 is only a bad dream; to others it is a departure point for the next go-around (whenever it happens).

17. *What will the replacement needs be for senior executives in the next 5 to 10 years?*

    If the company is shifting into the upper portion of a mature stage, it may have little in the way of needs other than for attrition. An emerging company however will be faced with significant growth in manager positions. These two situations face significantly different needs. On the one hand, merit pay will have to be adequate for most of the people, but on the other hand, promotional adjustments will be able to offset modest merit increases. Some have said that about two-thirds of top executives' salary today has come through prior promotional adjustments (taking new jobs) with only one-third for merit (job performance). Fast trackers expect to double their pay every 5 years—a virtual impossibility without significant promotional adjustments, and a high rate of inflation.

    Need for executives must also be examined in terms of availability. The bulge in the population's 25–44 age group will create a large potential supply of managers by the mid-1980s and senior executives by the 1990s.

18. *Is a particular type of executive needed?*

    A high-risk situation within the company will need someone attracted to this setting. It is very unlikely that such a person will be brought in without an opportunity to earn a very high bonus (based on degree of success). The individual willing to accept high risk is also likely to seek high rewards; the company is unlikely to offer suitable rewards in a straight salary, and therefore it needs some type of performance-related payoff.

19. *What is the desired relationship of total pay and the relative emphasis of components to the defined executive labor marked?*

    Inasmuch as it is very difficult to obtain data on long-term incentive plans in a compensation survey, it is possible to be fully competitive on salary and short-term incentives, yet either be significantly overgenerous or undercompetitive on total compensation—depending upon the magnitude of the long-term incentive programs. Undercompetitiveness is likely to show up before overgenerosity: underpaid people are more likely to leave than are those who are overpaid.

20. *To what extent is the company willing to define performance objectives and evaluate the degree of achievement?*

    Most will agree that evaluating performance is rather difficult; however, after-the-fact assessment of performance is still considerably easier than defining in advance proper corporate and individual goals. Yet the need for accuracy in defining an appropriate target and measuring the extent of attainment is basic to all incentive plans, although perhaps to different degrees.

The incentive impact must be tempered to the extent these factors are not definable or measurable and/or are subject to considerable fluctuation by factors outside the incentive recipient's control.

21. *What is an acceptable discount price from market value for company stock before alternative forms of nonequity debt financing become attractive?*

   This question strikes directly at the stock option program. Some delude themselves into thinking that there is no cost for such a program since the company receives capital. However, the cost to the company can be measured in terms of (*a*) dilution and (*b*) the dollar gap between fair market value and option price.

22. *Given the financing and earnings-per-share objectives, how much additional stock is it appropriate to issue?*

   Certainly the greatest diluter of the EPS is the option, and the smallest is the stock bonus, among stock-based awards. However, the option does aid the financing objective (albeit at a lower price than market), whereas the stock award returns no capital (other than in the form of a tax deduction).

23. *To what degree will "performance" relate to objective factors?*

   It is virtually impossible to build an incentive plan (short of straight profit sharing) that is self-administering. Therefore, one must determine the extent to which the performance factors must be measured and the validity of the selected measuring sticks. For example, plans based on EPS will encourage a move to long-term debt (even though this might cause later difficulties in a recession). Conversely plans using ROA are subject to swings in inventories and accounts receivable (usually financed by short-term borrowing). In other instances one will attempt to objectively evaluate subjective factors. Under such conditions it is important to remember that the measurements used should not be more sophisticated than the ability of the rater to measure.

24. *What is the role of the top executive group? Is it actively involved in planning and decision issues, or is it a resource generation and allocation vehicle for its captive companies?*

   The former describes a company where divisional results are strongly influenced by the corporate officers and therefore divisional funds must be strongly influenced by corporate results. The latter describes a situation more conducive to separate divisional or group incentive plans with little if any adjustment for corporate performance.

25. *Is management prepared to estimate the cost of the incentive plan to the company versus the value to the individual?*

   Whereas one is forced to do this with cash awards, many shy away from attempting a similar analysis for other forms—especially stock options. Yet if options are to be used, it seems logical to make such an attempt. Just as performance share values can be estimated based upon a stated compound growth in earnings per share, so too can stock options be estimated after factoring in the assigned price-earnings multiple. Granted the control of this multiple (especially in the two-tier market compounded by the bull and bear cycles) is outside management's hands, nonetheless management must still make an attempt to estimate the future value if the option is to be part of the executive compensation package (otherwise how can it be compared with alternative forms of compensation).

26. *To what extent will individual executive achievement in meeting the corporate objective(s) be recognized?*

Since most agree that pay will not motivate unless there is some identifiable linkage by the recipient between degree of successful performance and extent of reward, structuring the magnitude of the latter requires a direct link with ability to measure performance. This question also leads to other questions: To what extent is it appropriate to identify 5 to 20 people within the corporation to participate in an incentive pay program? Or is it more desirable to have an egalitarian approach with extent of participation defined in terms of a smooth line directly correlating with organizational structure?

27. *Is the CEO prepared to make pay differences among those reporting to him or her?*

A CEO who believes it appropriate to pay two group vice presidents the same salary even though they have significant differences in level of sales and profits may be unlikely to accept an incentive plan that will result in a different payout for each.

28. *Is the CEO prepared to make unpopular decisions regarding objective achievement?*

An incentive plan that requires appraisal of goal achievement in terms of modifiers (extent of difficulty) is completely inconsistent with a CEO that operates within an environment of participative management. Modifying goals or adjusting results in subjective terms requires making unpopular decisions.

29. *Is divestment of unprofitable operations a significant requirement in attempting to shift back to a more attractive position in the marketing life cycle?*

Rather than simply condition an incentive payment on the sales per se, a market-related incentive plan paying for every full point increase in the company stock might be feasible. For example, if the stock were selling at $25, it might be appropriate to pay a bonus of $25,000 for every point above that 5 years hence. A nonmarket plan (e.g., book value) would be troublesome in structure if the sale of assets actually reduced book value per share.

30. *Are two or more divisions essentially in competition for the same sales dollar?*

In such situations it is not uncommon to find these units competing more avidly against each other than the rest of the market. Developing separate divisional funds with little or no group or corporate identification will simply reinforce such behavior.

31. *Is management interested in influencing factors not in the incentive formula (e.g., strategy planning and certain policy issues)?*

To the extent management does have such interests, it logically should adjust the formula-suggested awards by the assessed impact of these other factors. To fail to do so is to diminish the degree of impact on nonincentive factors.

32. *Is the organization still run by its founder or an heir?*

A founder or one who has taken an organization through periods of major growth is not likely to be interested in diffusing ownership (through stock-based plans) or extending liberal incentive plans. For some the organization is an instrument of power and position within the community; having attained it the individual may not be inclined to adopt programs which will diffuse this position.

33. *What is the relation between pay increases for corporate officers and those for outside directors of the board?*

Is it logical that pay of corporate officers increases annually while that of directors is adjusted only every several years and then by a comparatively modest amount? Most organizations state that the pay of their employees is in relation to their responsibilities; does this apply to outside directors as well? If not, why not? Isn't their responsibiity increasing at least at the same rate as that of the senior corporate officers? In recent years there has been increasing emphasis on the role of the director in responsibility for setting corporate policy. Board membership is no longer simply a prestigious honor; failing to discharge properly the fiduciary role to shareholders can result in litigation.

34. *Is the shareholder's return on investment consistent in terms of increases in compensation and benefits of top management?*

Some might wish to set a corporate objective that dividend increases will not be less than pay increases for corporate officers or dividends plus appreciation in stock price. Granted, such an approach has significant problems in application (e.g., is stock price measured at beginning and end of year, or is it averaged per quarter, per month, per day?). Also, how do you calculate a percent increase in dividends if the previous period had a zero payout? With dividends rising 7 percent in each of the last 2 years, how do you ensure that average executive pay which is 50 percent higher than last year but only 10 percent higher than 2 years ago is understood by shareholders?

Perhaps the problems of application make this approach inappropriate, but that does not preclude its consideration.

35. *Is the payoff from short- and long-term incentives in reasonable relationship to each other?*

Too much emphasis on short-term profit results will do little to encourage the executive to look at long-term impact of current decisions. Conversely too much emphasis on long-term results may mean underpaying the individual for current performance and thus increasing market vulnerability (losing the executive to another firm).

36. *Is the company in an industry that is recession-resistant?*

If "yes," earnings are more predictable, and short- and long-range incentive formulas easier to construct. If "no," not only is care needed in developing the incentive formulas due to cyclical swings in profits, but stock options also become even more unpredictable (assuming the price-earnings multiple remains constant). Optionees are likely to relive the pauper to prince, or prince to pauper tale.

Relating the Corporate Objectives to the Pay Program

By identifying the most significant objectives and relating them to the key forms for each of the compensation elements, it is possible to determine the desirable emphasis, not simply the mix of executive pay programs. In identifying the objectives, one will note they fall into one of two camps: those we wish to maximize and those we wish to minimize. Let's assume our three key objectives are maximizing the retention of executives, development of stock ownership, and minimizing the dilution of shareholder equity.

Since each of the basic forms of compensation will be examined in terms of their degree of success in attaining the stated objective, it is necessary to develop brief definitions for each objective—ranging from 0 for no positive impact to 1 for fully meeting the objective. Such definitions might be as follows:

Retention of executives

1	Very considerable holding power
0.5	Some holding power
0	No holding power

Development of stock ownership

1	Keeps all or almost all of stock
0.5	Keeps only a portion of stock
0	Keeps no stock

Dilution of shareholder equity (using Treasury method*)

1	No dilution
0.5	Dilution but amount is tax deductible
0	Dilution and amount is not tax deductible

If desired a more detailed set of definitions can be developed; for example the stock ownership can be described using specific percentages (e.g., 100 percent equals 1, 90 percent equals 0.9, etc.).

In our abbreviated example we will examine how well salary (current versus deferred), retirement benefits, stock options, and DEPS (dividend equivalents on phantom shares)

---

*The Treasury method assumes the money received and/or cash flow created by tax deductions when issuing stock is used to purchase stock. Thus, new stock is issued only to the extent Treasury stock is not obtained under this method.

TABLE 11-1   Compensation Forms versus Objectives

Objectives	Weighted	Salary		Benefits	Incentives	
		Current	Deferred	Retirement	Stock options	DEPS
Maximize						
Retention	2	0	1	1	0.5	1
Stock ownership	1	0	0	0	0.5	1
Minimize						
Dilution	2	1	1	1	0.5	1
Totals						
Unweighted		1	2	2	1.5	3
Weighted		2	4	4	2.5	5

relate to the identified objectives. Many of the determinations are strictly value judgments. For example some will argue that salary deferred until retirement (with forfeiture clauses) will have "very considerable holding power" or a value of 1, others will admit only to "some holding power" and a value of 0.5. Even given these differences in perceived values, it is believed this type of exercise is useful, if for no other reason than to have the rater's values surface. Having each of the members of the compensation committee undertake this type of evaluation provides the basis for a discussion among the group of the differences. Until these are resolved, or at least identified, it will be very difficult to proceed on the analysis of the compensation program.

But back to our example. While it has no impact in this situation, since DEPS is the clear-cut winner, it may be desirable to weigh the various objectives as shown in Table 11-1. In other words, instead of assuming all objectives are of equal importance, perhaps it is appropriate to indicate that the retention and dilution issues are twice as important as the stock ownership factor. The total scores would be determined by multiplying by 2 each of the values on the retention and dilution lines. Thus deferred salary would have a value of 2, not 1, on both those lines.

The specific implications for plan design of the above data would probably have the company liberalize the deferred salary aspect, improve the retirement benefits by emphasizing earnings just prior to retirement (e.g., final pay plan) and adopting a conservative vesting provision (e.g., rule of 45), cutback on stock options, and develop extensive use of DEPS. However, another company examining the same possibilities but adding a fourth item with a weight of 3 ("minimizes the impact on earnings") would find stock options as important as any of the other items simply because it is the only item in the list which has no charge to the earnings statement. The other forms have either a known or an unknown amount incurred either once or over a period of time.

Admittedly, few will undertake such an exercise because of the effort involved in identifying and defining the objectives and then evaluating each of the compensation forms in terms of degree of success in meeting the objective. However, that does not make it any less valid as an appropriate planning device.

Do You Really Want Incentives?

There is a more basic question: are incentives worth the effort involved in constructing and administering them? For those pondering this issue, the following self-examination is offered. Answer either "yes" or "no" to each of the following questions:

1. Do you believe pay is a significant vehicle for reinforcing desired performance?
2. Can the desired levels of performance be sufficiently expressed in quantitative terms?
3. Are you prepared to "level" with your subordinates regarding their performance shortcomings?
4. Is performance completely within the control of the individual (i.e., are there no company decisions or forces outside of the company impacting on level of performance attainment)?
5. If there are factors outside the individual's control, can their impact be quantitatively assessed?
6. Can you develop targets with equal stretch for each of your subordinates?
7. Will performance goals set at the beginning of the period be unlikely to change?
8. If performance goals are changed during the year, can they be reset to ensure the same stretch as at the beginning of the period?
9. Will you be prepared to reduce a subordinate's total pay by giving no bonus in an "off year"?
10. Will you be able to identify the extent of "lowballing" by managers who attempt to negotiate easily attainable goals?

A "yes" to 7 or more of the above questions makes the individual a prime candidate for an incentive plan; conversely 4 or fewer positive responses means, regardless of the efficacy of the plan design, incentives are probably doomed to failure. Scores of 5 and 6 are in the gray area; if the incentive plan is properly structured and the individual is continually aware of its shortcomings, it may still be an effective part of the total compensation program.

SUMMARY AND CONCLUSIONS

The problem in developing an incentive program is not a lack of alternatives but rather how to narrow the possibilities to determine the one which is best. Given financial performance as a criteria for incentives, one can select from: profits before taxes, profits after taxes, return on investment, return on equity, return on capital employed, and earnings per share. These measurements can be expressed in absolutes or as relative amounts of change. They can be based on corporate and in many instances group or divisional results. Too many executive compensation programs are extensions of previous company programs or faddish adaptations of another company's plan. Lacking is a basic examination of how the program should be structured given individual and corporate objectives versus the impact of federal pay policy (e.g., taxation) and perception of the public (including shareholders).

The company must sort through these factors and array them in importance. Different businesses, like different industries which are in different stages in their market cycle, have different needs. For example, the late-threshold–early-growth-stage company has a strong capital need for future growth. Therefore, it is not logical to place much emphasis on current profits because of the need to reinvest profits to promote future growth.

Examining the needs and impacting factors carefully will not guarantee success, but ignoring them completely will almost guarantee failure. Since recognizing failure is easier than quantifying success, it will also mean either continually tinkering with the plan or abandoning it in complete disgust.

Conclusion

This book has identified the basic elements of the executive compensation package, and has defined them and described their key features. The objective was to give the reader a frame of reference for subsequently discussing any element or segment in perspective to the total package. While the emphasis was on concepts and approaches rather than specific solutions, it has been liberally supported with charts and tables for those interested in a more detailed analysis. Where specifics were added, it must be remembered that items such as accounting, legal requirements, and tax treatment are subject to change and that such change may alter significantly the attractiveness of a specific alternative. In any event, although this material reflects the author's understanding, the material should *not* be relied upon without verification by the company's own accounting, tax, and legal experts.

It is important to remember that while the standard cliché is an effective compensation program should attract, retain, and motivate, at the least it should not repel, encourage turnover, or demotivate. Not all plans will have positive results, but they should at the minimum avoid negative responses. In earlier days the executive owned the business, much as he or she does now for threshold companies. But the executives in growth, mature, and declining companies are essentially professional managers. Their individual stock holdings are usually well under 1 percent of the outstanding shares—far short of enabling direct control. Their risks, like their rewards, are different.

The plan for a specific company can only be structured by reviewing the objectives, assessing their priority and degree of importance, and creating a delivery system which facilitates their attainment in a cost effective manner. Too often the right decision is made at the wrong time (e.g., give more stock options because the stock is performing well, or adopt a non-market plan because the stock price is low). In other instances, the priorities are confused (e.g., placing tax effectiveness ahead of individual needs and corporate objectives).

Ideally, the best way to develop the incentive plan is for the CEO and others responsible for pay determinations to identify and weigh the various objectives (as described in Chapter 11). Unfortunately, the temptation is strong to immediately look at several alternative plans. For those who do the latter, it is still

317

imperative to examine these alternative plans in terms of their strengths and weaknesses before moving beyond the conceptual stage. For example, stock options are positive vehicles for raising capital but significantly affect the dilution of shareholder equity.

The compensation program, when properly structured and controlled, is probably the most potent weapon the chief executive officer has in his or her arsenal of reward-and-punishment devices for motivating individual executives to higher levels of performance. Optimum usage of this arsenal, therefore, calls for plus and minus deviations to the individual's package in direct relation to performance.

Companies should reconcile the differences between what they say and what they do with regard to pay for performance. If companies are unwilling or unable to take valid measurements, they would do better to honestly admit that performance is only marginally important than to claim they want to pay for performance but no one has developed the right pay system for them. In many instances, companies need to challenge their manpower planning groups to develop effective training programs to assist in managing preformance appraisal. Invariably the executive gets a very impressive manual explaining in detail how much to give for a certain level of performance. What is lacking is the mechanism to effectively assess level of performance. This is where most companies and compensation plans fail. It is one thing to say the company has a performance management program; it is something quite different to indicate that all managers have been trained in the process and do it!

Some companies are apparently guided by the philosophy "Let's adopt the plan which gives the best payout." In this case "best" is defined as biggest rather than most cost effective given corporate performance. These companies might be typified by frequent very radical departures in plan programs (e.g., stock options one year, performance shares the next, stock appreciations rights the year after, etc.). A study of their compensation for top corporate officers would result in little correlation with performance in return on equity, earnings per share, or other indicators of corporate success. This is especially true when a large portion of total compensation is in salary and benefits, but even multiyear incentive plans which smooth out annual fluctuations and emphasis on stock market–related awards will do little to aid achieving a high correlation.

It is difficult to believe a company is really interested in the incentive aspect of short- and long-range compensation programs when it continually adjusts targets after the fact, apparently in order to ensure adequate payout for the executives. Such situations have made cynics out of many who believe the prime objective of such plans is have a structure that will obfuscate, hide, and serve as the culprit for huge incentive awards. Conversely, those who believe that the perfect executive incentive plan is "just around the corner" are about as optimistic as those who describe a recession as a short interval of below-average economic expansion.

The one manner in which level of executive pay can be justified is in terms of what other companies are paying for comparable responsibilities. Some, however, argue that this approach is a never-ending spiral of pay adjustments as companies chase each others' pay actions. They find it difficult to believe that a corporate executive should be paid more than the President of the United States or amounts as high as 50 times that of the lowest-paid worker in the organization. In part, executives have contributed to the pressure to increase their pay as they have approved the addition of extra layers of management within the organization—obviously resulting in compression of pay. Therefore, there is little sympathy among the public and politicians about executive pay compression problems. Some have suggested that the pay of every executive be viewed as a corporate asset: is the shareholder receiving at least as high a return as on the company net assets? This negative view is frustrating to executives, especially since they are more concerned about the relative (i.e., in relation to pay of other executives) than the absolute level of pay. Furthermore, higher marginal tax brackets notwithstanding, they believe that their predecessors fared better due to favorable stock market gains than can be achieved under current conditions.

While most companies review programs in terms of competitiveness, some are reluctant to adopt any programs that are not consistent with a majority of the companies studied. Adopting such a policy results in a paradox—programs completely justifiable in terms of the business world but probably inappropriate for a specific company because too often the average is simply a measure of a central tendency that describes few if any real situations.

Conversely, resistance to change, that natural enemy of progress, and fear of accepting a plan that may be less than perfect have resulted in many corporations doing less than they should in structuring their executive compensation program. Interestingly enough, this often means staying with an old, outdated, but familiar program rather than developing an improved compensation plan.

The person charged with the responsibility of developing and maintaining the compensation package, especially at the executive level, must be not only a good administrator but also sharp, creative, and able to assess and respond to the needs of the corporation and its individuals. Although a number of statistical techniques are available for use in establishing and monitoring a program, the pay planner must be able to adapt conceptually to a profession which is more art than science. Compensation programs are only as good as the judgment of those involved in their construction and maintenance. Consistency is pertinent only to the extent that deviations are not in fact justifiable. The program must be flexible and responsive to the corporation's need; it should bring order into the system, but not inflexible discipline.

The responsibility of senior management is to assess competitive strengths and weaknesses and then develop and execute a strategy which will best utilize available corporate assets. The compensation program's responsibility is to reward the extent of success achieved.

However, there are a number of obstacles in the path; some are so consistent and so predictable that the author has set them down as ten "laws." They are:

Ellig's Laws

1. Treating everyone the same is inconsistent with treating each individual equitably in relation to contribution.

2. Individuals believe that others in similar positions work less and are paid more.

3. Appearance is at least as important as reality (e.g., pronouncements are often accepted as performance).

4. Performance ratings will always support the recommended pay action.

5. The highest performance ratings will go to the immediate subordinates of the manager.

6. Complete flexibility usually results in less rather than greater use of discretion.

7. An action correcting an inequity results in creating a new inequity.

8. Formal procedures and programs apply to those one level below the executive making the pronouncement.

9. A decision is difficult to modify even though the parameters have changed, because the action is not examined in terms of the changing situation.

10. An arithmetic increase in the number of people involved results in a geometric increase in the time required to reach agreement.

Optimum usage of the compensation package is only made possible when an informed, risk-taking top management team interfaces with a competent tax counsel and a bright, imaginative compensation executive who is soundly oriented to compensation theory but not wedded to the stilted and often archaic text of the past—a person who not only does not use yesterday's solutions to solve today's problems but is also looking to tomorrow and its challenges. The only difference between stepping-stones and stumbling blocks is perception and perspective.

For those who consider the foregoing too time-consuming and are looking for a simple, albeit sophisticated-appearing, manner of setting pay levels for executives, the formula in Figure 12-1 is offered. It reads: Compensation of the executive is a function of job value between the limits of zero and infinity (no need to arbitrarily limit the earning potential) times the hat size of the executive (rough indicator of cerebral capacity) times his or her weight (should be prepared to reward a heavyweight) times size of mouth divided by shoe size (indicating ability to put foot in mouth) times speed in running the 100-meter dash (need for a fast-tracker) is a function of the individual's degree of willingness between the limits of zero (no) and one (yes) to fight a tiger barehanded (degree of risk taking).

$$C_E \longrightarrow \int_0^\infty JV \left[H_E \cdot W_E \right] \cdot \left[\frac{M_E}{S_E} \right] \cdot 100\,MD \int_0^1 FT$$

FIGURE 12-1 Compensation formula.

The importance of a systematic, logical, and orderly review process cannot be emphasized too strongly. Conversely it is critical to keep the analysis phase in perspective. It is easy to become inundated with data or, even worse, subject the data to measurement far more sophisticated than needed or required. This analysis-paralysis can mesmerize one into being ruled by the data, rather than using it as the basis for making decisions on executive pay.

Unfortunately there are only imperfect solutions for an imperfect world. Che sará sará.

Index

Achievement:
  level of, 26–27
  related to pay, 26–28
Achievement/pay combinations, significance of, 27
Adjustment (see Structural adjustments)
Advancement opportunities as retention factor, 23
After-tax cost to company, 4–6
After-tax effectiveness, 4–6
  (see also Tax effectiveness)
After-tax value to executive, 4–6
  related to after-tax effectiveness, 4–6
  by type of income, 4–5
Age Discrimination in Employment Act, 105, 144–145, 176, 178–179
Airplanes:
  determining basis of use of, 148–149
  as perquisite, 148–149
  proxy treatment of, 182
  tax effectiveness of use of, 149, 180
Analytical techniques for salary surveys, 53–63
  company tax deductions for, 151
  as perquisites, 150–151
  proxy treatment of, 182
  tax effectiveness of, 151, 180
Assignment of insurance policies, 107–108
Assignment protection:
  company tax deduction for, 166
  as perquisite, 166
  proxy treatment of, 183
  tax effectiveness of, 166, 181
Attendance bonuses, 92
Attraction of executives:
  factors affecting, 20–21
  related to compensation elements, 19–21
Automobiles:
  approaches to charging for use of, 147–148
  determining cost of use of, 147–148
  as perquisites, 147–148
  proxy treatment of, 182
  tax effectiveness of use of, 148, 180

Bankruptcy, 277
Benefit formula increases, 177
Benefit plans (see Defined benefit plans)
Benefits (see Employee benefits)
Bereavement pay, 88
Bonus fund formulas, 188–193
  deductible, 190–191
  limitation, 191
  need for review of, 192–193
  nondeductible, 191
Bonus funds, 188–193
  allocation of, 195–198
    affecting behavior, 198
    corporate versus unit, 196–197
    in terms of level of unit, 197–198
  determination of award of, illustrated, 198–199
  determination of divisional awards of, multigoal example, 199–204
  estimating needed amount of, 190
  formulas for developing, 188–193
  generated by corporate or divisional performance, 196–199
  impact of accounting requirements on, 188–189
  (See also Divisional funds; Short-term incentives)
Bonus ranges compared with salary ranges, 186
Bonuses (see Short-term incentive awards; specific types of bonuses)
Book value plans as nonmarket long-term incentives, 257–259
Book value of stock:
  related to stock prices, 16
  used for nonmarket phantom stock plans, 257
Book value stock options for nonmarket long-term incentives, 258–259
Burnout, executive, 37
Business liability insurance:
  company tax deductions for, 161
  as perquisite, 161
  proxy treatment of, 182
  tax effectiveness of, 161, 180

Business travel accident insurance, 108, 166
  premiums for, used as company tax deductions, 108
  proxy treatment of, 183
  tax effectiveness of, 181

Capital gains, 127, 133, 136
  long-term, 4–5
  on sale of stock, 220–221
  short-term, 3
  and stock awards, 247
Career advancement, executive need for, 23
Career earnings plans, 111–113
Career service plans, 111
Cash:
  as nonmarket long-term incentive, 256–257
  versus stock, accounting impact of, 272–273
Cash availability at different stages of market cycle, 12–14
Cash-deferred profit sharing, 129–130
Children's education:
  as perquisite, 162
  proxy treatment of, 182
  tax effectiveness of, 162, 180
Class year vesting, 126–127
Classification method of job evaluation, 41
Club membership:
  company tax deductions for, 159
  as perquisite, 159
  proxy treatment of, 182
  tax effectiveness of, 159, 180
Collective bargaining agreements affecting compensation, 2
Combination plans:
  for long-term incentives, 259–262
  parallel approach to, 261–262
  tandem approach to, 261–262
Combination term and permanent life insurance:
  company tax deductions for, 168
  Internal Revenue Service regulations for, 168–169
  as perquisite, 168–169
Communication of pay program:
  extent of information included, 31
  methods of, 31

Communication of pay program *(Cont.)*:
  and motivation of executives, 30–31
  need for, 29–31
Company, market cycle of, compared with industry, 16–17
Company compensation cost:
  after-tax, 4–6
  related to employee value, 4–6
Company pension plan providing annuities, 108–109
Company product samples:
  as perquisites, 147
  proxy treatment of, 182
  tax effectiveness of, 147, 180
Company size used to determine level of competitive pay, 62
Company structure and responsibility, 10
Company success used to determine level of competitive pay, 62
Company tax deductions, 4
  for deferred compensation, 269, 270, 272, 274, 277
  for employee benefits, 95, 97, 101, 108, 110, 126, 129, 132, 137
  for long-term incentives, 245, 247, 256–258
  for nonperformance awards, 92–94
  for perquisites, 151–153, 158–162, 165–168
  for short-term incentives, 216
Compa-ratio, 69–70
Compensation:
  deferred (*see* Deferred compensation)
  divided between salary and incentive pay, 306
  effect of public pressure on, 2
  externally competitive, 1
  extrinsic versus intrinsic, 22–24
  forms of, 3, 9–17
  impact of collective bargaining agreements on, 2
  internally equitable, 1
  intrinsic, 22–24, 157, 168
  merit pay matrix of, 75–76, 81–83
  need to relate differences in, to performance differences, 28–29
  and performance, 10–11
  rate of change in, compared to rate of change in sales, 55–62
  and recognition, 21–22

Compensation *(Cont.)*:
  Securities and Exchange Commission disclosure requirements relating to, 6–7
  unreasonable, 6, 298–300
  (See also Pay; Salary)
Compensation committees, 285–304
  executive compensation consultants as members of, 286
  handling of compensation elements by, 291–295, 298
  industry experts as members of, 286
  membership of, 285–286
  pay philosophy of, 287
  and problems with unreasonable compensation, 298–300
  professional directors as members of, 286
  and reasons for engaging consultants, 288–289
  responsibilities of, 290–298
  role responsibilities of, 286–287
  shareholder obligations of, 290
  timetable for compensation actions of, 296–298
  use of outside consultants by, 287–289
Compensation consultants:
  cost effectiveness of, 289
  hired by compensation committees, 286, 288–289
  hired by management, 289–290
Compensation elements, 3, 9–17
  and attraction of executives, 19–21
  choice of, and stage of market cycle, 15–17
  and company objectives, 313–314
  emphasis on: at different levels, 10–11
    by market level, 14–15
  employee benefits as *(see* Employee benefits)
  handling, by compensation committee, 291–295, 298
  impact of market cycle on, 11–14
  and job value, 10
  long-term incentives as *(see* Long-term incentives)
  and motivation of executives, 19–20, 24–29
  perquisites as *(see* Perquisite)
  relative importance of, 10–11
  and retention of executives, 19–24
  salary as *(see* Salary)
  short-term incentives as *(see* Short-term incentives)

Compensation elements *(Cont.)*:
  tax considerations of, 3–6
  and types of executives attracted, 20
Compensation expenses:
  company options and tax impact, 4–6
  options, 4
Compensation level increased by job changes, 20
Compensation programs:
  as component of the organization, 2
  developing, 317–318
  eligibility for, 306–307
  need for performance for, 318
  objectives of, 26
  and organizational objectives, 2
  salary as a cornerstone of, 39
Competitive pay, determining level of, 62
Competitive pension position, determining, 120–124
Competitive position of company and adjustment of salary structure, 65–66
Compression *(see* Pay compression)
Constructive receipt, 270–271
  avoiding, 238
  doctrine of, 271
  and economic benefit, 272
  taxation of, 6
Consumer price index, 68
Contribution plans *(see* Defined contribution plans)
Conventions and conferences:
  company tax deductions for, 160
  as perquisites, 160
  proxy treatment of, 182
  tax effectiveness of, 180
Conversion privilege for insurance, 105
Converted insurance coverage, 105
Cost of living and pay program, 68
Counseling *(see* Financial counseling)
Court leave as employee benefit, 88
Credit cards:
  as perquisites, 159–160
  proxy treatment of, 182
  tax effectiveness of, 180
Credit unions as employee benefit, 92
Current compensation versus deferred compensation, after-tax comparisons of, 281
Current income versus deferred income, pre-and post-tax comparisons of, 275
Customized benefit packages, 137, 140

Decision making at different stages in market cycle, 11–14
Decline stage of market cycle, 13–14, 16
Deductible formulas for short-term incentive bonus fund, 190–191
Defense Production Act, 87
Deferred compensation, 109, 179, 267–283
  advantages of, 275–276
  affecting benefits under pension and profit sharing plans, 279–280
  after-tax situation of, compared with current compensation, 281
  and company benefits, 277
  conditions for taxing payments of, 278
  disadvantages of, 276–281
  and doctrine of constructive receipt, 270–271
  effect of inflation on, 276–277
  estate tax liability of, 280
  and executive preference for current cash versus delayed payment, 280
  and forfeitable benefits, 269–270
  funded plans for, 268–270
    formally, 268
    nonqualified: forfeitable, 269
      nonforfeitable, 270
    qualified: forfeitable, 269
      nonforfeitable, 269–270
  as golden handcuffs, 267, 280–281
  impact of performance on, 279
  informally funded plan for, 268
  mandatory, 267–268
  methods of financing, 268–269
  as needs-investment decision, 281
  for nonemployee directors, 302
  nonforfeitable benefits of, 269–270
  nonfunded plans for, 268–270
    nonqualified: forfeitable, 270
      nonforfeitable, 270
    qualified: forfeitable, 270
      nonforfeitable, 270
  nonqualified plans for, 269–270
  objective of, 267
  as part of estate, 280
  pre- and post-tax comparisons with current income of, 275
  present tax position of, 274
  prior to 1969 Tax Reform Act, 273
  proportional to current compensation, 278–279

Deferred compensaton (Cont.):
  qualified plans for, 269–270
  reasons for choosing, 267
  reducing pension plan payments, 279–280
  and salary reduction plans, 274
  as security, 278
  and social security benefits, 276
  and social security tax, 278
  stock options as, 236
  tax aspects of, 267
  tax disadvantages of, 276–278
  tax effectiveness of, 179, 181
  and theory of economic benefit, 271–272
  and timing of beginning of payments, 280
  types of, 268–270
  using restricted property, 273
  voluntary, 268
Deferred pay, 274
  retirement benefits as 110, 173–174
Deferred tax liability, 125, 133
Defined benefit plans, 110–114
  career earnings, 111–113
  career service, 111
  and defined contribution combined, 131
  final pay, 19, 111–113, 117
Defined contribution plans, 110, 124–136
  cash-deferred, 129–130
  employee stock ownership, 131–132
  hardship withdrawals from, 127
  investment of contributions to, 125, 130
  mandatory versus voluntary employee contributions to, 129
  maximum amount of employer contributions to, 125–126
  partial withdrawal from, 127
  profit sharing, 129–131, 274
  savings, 124–128
  taxation of withdrawals from, 127–128
  withdrawal options in, 127–128
Dependents life insurance, 109
Deviation, regression analysis, 43–44
Differential between organizational levels, 2–3
  effect of pay compression on, 2–3, 64–65, 77
  reduced by structural adjustments, 64–65
  size of, needed to provide incentive, 65

Dilution of equity, 222
Disability pay:
  as employee benefit, 89
  as perquisite, 144
  proxy disclosure for, 182
  tax effectiveness of, 180
Disability plans, 89
  long-term, 89, 122
Disclosure requirements (*see* Proxy disclosure requirements)
Disqualifying disposition of stock, 220
Diversification, reasons for, 13–14
Dividends, tax effectiveness of, 263
Divisional funds, 193–195
  allocation of, 195–198
  formulas for developing, 193–194
  impact of minimal performance on, 204–207
  qualitative judgment used for developing, 193–194
  (*See also* Bonus funds; Short-term incentives)
Divisional goals, 194–196
  identifying, 194–195
  quantifying to determine bonus eligibility, 195–196
  weighting to determine bonus eligibility, 196, 201–204
Divisional incentive plans, 15
Divisonal pay programs, 15
Divisional performance, basis for judging, 193–195
Doctrine of constructive receipt:
  defined, 271
  (*See also* Constructive receipt)
Dollar return versus market performance, 14
Domestic staff:
  as perquisite, 160
  proxy treatment of, 182
  tax effectiveness of, 160–180
Downside risk with stock options, 236–237

Early retirement, 120–124
  and retirement benefits, 122–124
Economic benefit:
  and constructive receipt, 272
  taxation of, 6
  theory of, 271–272
Education of children, 162, 180, 182

Educational assistance programs, 92–93
Educational Benefit Trust (EBT), 162
Effort:
  importance of, 25–26
  rate of return on, 26
  related to performance, 24–26
    and to pay, 25–26
Ellig's laws, 319–320
Employee benefit(s), 9–11, 87–140
  and attraction of executives, 19–20
  company coverage as, 100–102
  as compensation element, 9–11
  court leave as, 88
  credit unions as, 92
  customized benefit packages as, 137, 140
  definitions of, 87–88
  disability plans as, 89
  educational assistance as, 92–93
  employee services as (*see* Employee services, as employee benefits)
  endowment policies as, 99
  funeral leave as, 88
  handled by compensation committees, 293
  health care programs as, 95–98
  insurance coverage as, 98–109
  legal services as, 91
  life insurance as, 98–100
  loans as, 92
  matching gifts plan as, 93
  and motivation of executives, 19–20
  nonperformance awards as, 92–94, 162
  paid holidays as, 88
  preemployment physical as, 95
  preretirement counseling as, 92
  proxy disclosure requirements for, 139
  relocation expenses as, 93–94
  and retention of executives, 19–20
  retirement as, 109–136
  scholarships as, 93, 162
  service awards as, 92
  severance plans as, 89–90
  survivor benefits as, 100
  survivor protection as, 98–109
  tax effectiveness of, 138
  time off with pay as, 88–90
  travel and entertainment expenses as, 94
  vacation allowance as, 88
Employee Retirement Income Security Act (ERISA):
  executive benefits permitted by, 126
  fiduciary responsibility defined by, 161

Employee Retirement Income Security Act (ERISA) *(Cont.):*
  pension requirements of, 109, 122, 125, 176
  regulations of: for deferred compensation plans, 269, 270
    for reporting and disclosure, 169
    for severance plans, 146
    for vesting, 109, 126–127
Employee services:
  as employee benefits, 91–92
    credit unions, 92
    insurance, 91, 98–109
    legal services, 91
    loan policy, 92
    preretirement counseling, 92
  as perquisites, 147–157
    airplane use, 148–149
    apartments or hotel rooms, 150–151
    automobile use, 147–148
    chauffeured limousine use, 148
    company product samples, 147
    executive dining room, 149–150
    executive washroom, 158
    financial counseling, 151–157
    legal services, 151
    parking facilities, 148
    physical fitness programs, 150
    security services, 148
    tax assistance, 151
    yacht use, 149
Employee stock ownership plans, 131–132
Employee stock ownership trust, 131
Employee value:
  after-tax, 4–6
  related to company cost, 4–6
Employment contracts, 143, 145
  proxy treatment for, 182
  tax effectiveness rating of, 180
Entertainment expenses, 94
  (See also Home entertainment)
Equity theory of motivaton, 24
ERISA *(see* Employee Retirement Income Security Act)
Estate planning, 154–157
  trusts in, 155–157
Estate tax liability, 154–155, 157, 170
  on deferred compensation, 280
  lowered by government bonds, 157
Estate taxes, 107–108, 173
Executive(s):
  after-tax value of, 4–5

Executive(s) *(Cont.):*
  assessing goals and performance of, 307
  attraction of, 19–21
  defined, 7
  fear of failure of, 32
  group, 20
  identifying with superiors, 33–34
  impact of stress on, 35–36
  importance of appearance for, 34
  importance of pay to, 29
  incorporated, 37
  interacting with peers, 34
  marketability of, 145–146
  mid-career crisis of, 36
  motivation of *(see* Motivation of executives)
  need of: to assess priorities, 32, 35
    to be effective subordinates, 33–34
    for career advancement, 23
    to identify management style of superiors, 33
    to organize time, 34–35
    for recognition, 33
      beyond pay, 21–22
    for replacement, 309
    to understand pay program, 29–31
  pay-value combinations for, 22–23
  preferences on pay of, 37, 280
  reasons for termination of, 90
  relationships with subordinates of, 34–35
  relationships with superiors of, 33–34
  retention of, 19–24
  security consideration for, 148
  supplemental pensions for, 176–178
  termination of *(see* Termination of executives)
  types of compensation sought by, 22–23
  as workaholics, 36
Executive burnout, 37
Executive compensation consultants:
  hired by compensation committees, 286, 288–289
  hired by management, 289–290
Executive dining room:
  proxy treatment of, 182
  tax effectiveness of, 150, 180
  used as perquisite, 149–150
Executive income related to company cost, 5–6

Executive pay:
  associated with shareholder interest,
    305–306
  increases in, affecting employee relations,
    308
  portion at risk with stock market, 305–
    306
  related to company performance, 305–
    306
Executive pyramid and upward movement,
  23
Executive qualities, 31–37
  executives' perceptions of, 31–33
Executive search firms used as insurance
  against raiding, 20–21
Executive stock purchase plans, 242–244
Executive washroom:
  company tax deductions for, 158
  as perquisite, 158
  proxy treatment of, 182
  tax effectiveness of, 158, 180
Expectancy theory of motivation, 24–25
Expense accounts:
  as perquisites, 158
  proxy treatment of, 182
  tax effectiveness of, 180
Externally competitve compensation, 1
Extrinsic compensation, 22
  versus intrinsic compensation, 22–24

Federal Reserve Regulation T, 163
Fifth dividend option, 172
Final pay, social security as percentage of,
  114
Final pay pension plans, 111–113, 117
  impact on retention of executives, 19
Financial counseling:
  based on organizational rank, 153–154
  company tax deductions for, 152, 153
  for estate planning, 154–157
  as perquisite, 151–157
  proxy treatment of, 182
  tax aspects of, 152
  tax effectiveness of, 152, 180
First-class travel:
  company tax deductions for, 161
  as perquisite, 160–161
  proxy treatment of, 182
  tax effectiveness of, 161, 180
Forfeiture, substantial risk of, 273, 276

Fringe benefits (see Employee benefits)
Front-end bonus, 21
Funded plans for deferred compensation,
  268–270
Funeral leave as employee benefit, 88

Generation-skipping trust, 156
Geographic differentials in levels of pay,
  68–69
Gift tax exclusions, 154, 156
Gift taxes, 154–156, 170
Golden handcuffs, 267, 280–281, 308
Government bonds affecting estate tax, 157
Group executives, 20
Group insurance, 99
Growth stage of market cycle, 12, 15–16
Guaranteed income contracts (GICs), 125

Health care:
  as employee benefit, 95–98
    methods of providing coverage, 95–96
    preemployment physical, 95
  as perquisite, 164–166
    medical examinations, 164–165
    supplemental coverage, 165–166
Health care maintenance organizations, 95–
  96
Health insurance:
  administrative services only (ASO) as
    form of, 97, 165
  contracts for, 96
  extent of coverage under, 97–98
  premiums for, 96–97
  programs for, 95–97
  self-insured companies, 97
Health Maintenance Act, 95
High grade/high performance syndrome,
  74–75
Home entertainment:
  company tax deductions for, 160
  as perquisite, 160
  proxy treatment of, 182
  tax effectiveness of, 160, 180
Hotel rooms:
  company tax deductions for, 151
  as perquisite, 150–151
  proxy treatment of, 182
  tax effectiveness of, 151, 180
House value in retirement planning, 136

Immediate participation guarantee, 125
Imputed income, 6
  avoidance of, 92, 147, 150, 151
  from club membership, 159
  from insurance coverage, 107–109, 168, 169, 175
  and low interest rates on loans, 164
  reducing, 105
  worksheet for, 101–102
Incentive compensation, drawbacks of, 24
Incentive pay:
  linked to corporate objectives, 311
  phantom stock plans as, 255–256
  and retention of executives, 24
Incentive plans:
  control of, 28
  cost to company versus value to individual, 310–311
  divisional, 15
  objectives for, 305–316
  relating corporate objectives to pay program, 313–314
  and responsibilities of corporate officers and outside directors, 312
Incentives:
  as compensation element, 9–11
  divisional, 15
  long-term (see Long-term incentives)
  short-term (see Short-term incentives)
Income:
  after-tax, 3–4
  imputed (see Imputed income)
  Internal Revenue Service interpretation of, 142
  ordinary, 3, 5
  personal (see Personal service income)
  psychic, 22
  Securities and Exchange Commission interpretation of, 142
  tax preference, 226–227
Income loss, determining for insurance purposes, 102
Income needs approach for calculating insurance requirements, 103–105
Incorporated executive, 37
Individual pay actions, 69–84
  adjusting merit increase guidelines for, 80–83
  adjusting for unit performance, 79
    and position in range, 79
  developing merit budget for, 77–79

Individual pay actions (Cont.):
  and frequency of review varied by performance, 77
  and frequency of salary review, 76–77
  performance appraisal for, 71–75
  and promotion increases, 83–85
  and timing of salary action, 76
Individual Retirement Accounts (IRAs), 123, 128, 133–135, 179
  compared with Keogh plans, 135
  conditions for, 134
  tax penalties for not meeting conditions of, 134
Industry market cycle stage compared with company stage, 16–17
Inheritance tax, 98
Insider, defined by Securities and Exchange Act, 220
Insurance, 91, 98–109
  accidental death coverage by, 100
  and assignment of policies, 107–108
  for assignment protection, 166
  borrowing against cash value of, 98–104
  for business travel protection, 108, 166, 181, 183
  calculating requirements for, 102–105
    income needs approach to, 103–105
    net income approach to, 102–103
  combination term and permanent life, 168–169
  and company coverage, 100–102
  and company response to executive need, 105–108
  conversion privilege of, 105
  and coverage by age, 105–106
    versus need, 104–105
  coverage after retirement, 107
  definition of pay for, 106–107
  as employee benefit, 91, 98–109
  and endowment policies, 99
  forms of settlement of, 108–109
  group term, 99
  health (see Health insurance)
  imputed value of, 107–108
  for key employee life, 167–168
  for kidnap and ransom (see Kidnap and ransom insurance)
  liability, 161–162, 180, 182
  life (see Life insurance)
  for nonemployee directors, 303
  premiums for, as company tax deductions, 101

Insurance *(Cont.):*
versus salary and total compensation, 107
and Section 79 plans, 168–169
split dollar *(see* Split dollar insurance)
supplementary pay-all program, 102
term, 99–100
whole life, 98–100
(See also Survivor protection)
Insurance needs, company response to, 105–108
Insurance premiums, company tax deductions for, 101, 167
Insurance trust, 157
Inter vivos trust, 155–156
Internal equity retained by promotional pay policy, 84
Internally equitable compensation, 1
Intrinsic compensation, 22
versus extrinsic compensation, 22–24
job title as, 157
kidnap and ransom insurance as, 168
Irrevocable trust, 156

Job analysis, 39–40
need for, 40
objective of, 39
Job change:
expectations from, 21
to increase compensation level, 19–20
Job description, 39–40
Job evaluation, 40–49
choice of system used in, 40
classification method for, 41
market pricing method for, 47–49
maturity method for, 46–47
objective of, 40
point factor method for, 41–46
problems with traditional methods of, 47
ranking method for, 40–41
for salary surveys, 52
Job grade inequity, 46
Job grades:
compared with curves, 44, 46
in constructing salary ranges, 43–46
developed from job value, 42–43
need for, 66–67
need for communicating to employees, 67
for point factor method of job evaluation, 42–46
without positions, 68

Job grades *(Cont.):*
and problems with grade structure, 44, 46
problems with lack of, 67
and problems with point cutoffs, 44, 46
for senior executives, 66–67
Job matching:
to ensure comparability of data for job surveys, 50–51
problems with, 50
stratifying data for, 51
techniques for, 51
Job regrading, 62
Job title, 40
as intrinsic compensation, 157
as perquisite, 157–158
proxy treatment of, 182
tax effectiveness of, 180
Job value converted to job grade, 42–43

Keogh plans, 135–136
compared with Individual Retirement Accounts, 135
Key employee life insurance:
as perquisite, 167–168
proxy treatment of, 183
tax effectiveness of, 181
used to provide pension payments, 167
value to executive of, 167
Key position approach to determine eligibility for short-term incentives, 186–187
Kidnap and ransom insurance:
as intrinsic compensation, 168
as perquisite, 168
proxy treatment of, 183
tax effectiveness of, 181

Legal services:
company tax deductions for, 151
as employee benefit, 91
as perquisite, 151
proxy treatment of, 182
tax effectiveness of, 151, 180
tax features of, 91
Length of service bonuses, 92
Leveling technique in job matching, 51
Leveraged employee stock ownership plans, 131
Liability insurance, 161–162, 180, 182

Liberalized vacation:
  as perquisite, 143–144
  proxy treatment of, 182
  tax effectiveness of, 180
Life insurance, 98–109
  for dependents, 109
  group term, 99
  for key employees (*see* Key employee life
    insurance)
  ordinary, 98–100
  payments of premiums for, 100–101
  proxy treatment of, 183
  tax effectiveness of, 181
  term, 99–100
  whole life, 98–100
  (*See also* Insurance; Survivor protection)
Limitation formulas for short-term incentive
    bonus funds, 191
Limousine:
  as perquisite, 148
  proxy treatment of, 182
  tax effectiveness of, 180
Living trust, 156
Loan policy as employee benefit, 92
Loans:
  Internal Revenue Service challenges to,
    162–164
  as perquisites, 162–164
  proxy treatment of, 182
  salary increases to offset interest on, 164
  for stock purchases, 163–164
  tax effectiveness of, 162–164, 180
Long-term capital gains, rate of taxation of,
    4–5
Long-term disability plans, 89, 122
Long-term divisional incentives, 15
Long-term incentives, 9, 219–265
  and attraction of executives, 19–20
  combination plans for, 259–262
  as compensation element, 9–11
  during different stages of market cycle,
    15–16
  handling, by compensation elements, 295
  and motivation of executives, 19–20
  nonmarket, 256–259
  performance share plans as, 248–252
  performance unit share plans as, 252–
    254
  phantom stock plans as, 255–256
  proxy disclosure requirements for, 263–
    264
  and retention of executives, 19–20

Long-term incentives (*Cont.*):
  stock appreciation rights as, 237–242
  stock awards as, 244–248
  stock options as, 219–237
  stock purchase plans as, 242–244
  tax treatment of, 262–263
  valuation techniques as, and stage of mar-
    ket cycle, 16
  value comparison of plans for, 254–255
  (*See also* Incentive plans)
Long-term profit sharing plans, 129
Lump sum distributions, 128–129, 179
Lump sum payouts, 128–129

Management depth and market cycle, 11–
  14
Margin calls, 163
Market cycle:
  cash availability at different stages of, 12–
    14
  decision making at different stages of,
    11–14
  differences in, company versus industry,
    16–17
  emphasis on compensation elements at
    different stages of, 15–17
  impact on compensation elements of, 11–
    14
  management depth at different stages of,
    11–14
  personal relationships at different stages
    of, 12–13
  and product lines, 11–14
  stages of, 11–14, 15–17
    decline, 13–14, 16
    growth, 12, 15–16
    maturity, 12–13, 16
    threshold, 11–12, 15
Market performance versus dollar return,
  14
Market phase, identifying by product, 14–
  15
Market pricing method of job evaluation,
  47–49
  principles for, 48
Market stages (*see* Market cycle, stages of)
Market value of stock and stage of market
  cycle, 16
Marketability of executives, 145–146
Matching gifts plans, 93
Maturity data, 46–47

Maturity method of job evaluation, 46–47
Maturity stage of market cycle, 12–13, 16
Medical examinations:
    company tax deductions for, 165
    as perquisites, 164–165
    proxy treatment of, 183
    tax effectiveness of, 165, 181
Medical expenses, company tax deductions for, 95–97
Merit budget, methods for developing, 77–79
Merit increase guidelines, adjusting, 80–83
Merit pay matrix:
    amount versus timing, 76
    performance versus positon in range, 75, 81–83
Merit pay and rate of inflation, 80
Merit program, ceilings within range, 76–77
Mid-career crisis, 36
Motivation of executives:
    and communication of pay program, 30–31
    equity theory of, 24
    expectancy theory of, 24–25
    relationship of compensation elements to, 19–20, 24–29
Multiemployer Pension Amendments Act, 146
Multiple regression analysis for salary surveys, 52–53, 62–63

Net income approach for calculating insurance requirements, 102–103
Nondeductible formula for short-term incentive bonus funds, 191
Nonemployee director pay, 300–303
    deferred, 302
    form and level of, 301–302
    and Keogh plans, 302, 303
    and pay for performance, 302
    programs for, 300–301
    and social security liability, 303
Nonemployee directors:
    insurance coverage for, 303
    perquisites for, 303
    role and responsibility of, 302–303, 312
Nonfunded plans for deferred compensation, 268–270
Nonlinear pay curve, 43

Nonmarket long-term incentives, 256–259
    cash as, 256–257
    phantom stock plans as, 257–258
    stock options as, 258–259
Nonmarket phantom stock plans, 257–258
Nonmarket stock options, 258–259
Nonperformance awards:
    as employee benefits, 92–94
        educational assistance, 92–93
        matching gifts plan, 93
        relocation expenses, 93–94
        scholarships, 93, 162
        service awards, 92
        travel and entertainment expenses, 94
    as perquisites, 157–164
        business liability insurance, 161
        children's education, 162
        club memberships, 159
        conventions and conferences, 160
        credit cards, 159–160
        domestic staff, 160
        executive dining room, 149–150
        executive washroom, 158
        expense accounts, 158
        first-class travel, 160–161
        home entertainment, 160
        job title, 157–158
        loans, 162–164
        office accommodation, 158
        personal escort, 161
        personal liability insurance, 161–162
        season tickets, 159
        spouse travel, 161
Nonqualified plans for deferred compensation, 269
Nonqualified stock options, 220–221
    discounted, 221

Office accommodation:
    company tax deduction for, 158
    as perquisite, 158
    proxy treatment of, 182
    tax effectiveness of, 158, 180
Offset approach for integrating social security and pension benefits, 117, 120
    advantages and disadvantages of, 117
Open pay systems and pay performance, 29–30
Ordinary income:
    rate of taxation of, 5

Ordinary income *(Cont.):*
  tax liability on, compared with personal
    service income, 3
Ordinary life insurance, 98–100
Organization structure and type of executive needed, 20
Organizational objectives and compensation program, 2
Outplacement assistance:
  as perquisite, 146–147
  proxy treatment of, 182
  tax effectiveness of, 147, 180

Paid holidays as employee benefits, 88
Parking facilities:
  as perquisites, 148
  proxy treatment of, 182
  tax effectiveness of, 148, 180
Pay:
  deferred, 110, 173–174, 274
  defined for insurance, 106–107
  disability, 89, 144, 180, 182
  executive, 305–306, 308
  final, social security as percentage of, 114
  geographic differentials in, 68–69
  importance of, 29
  and individual preferences, 37
  nonemployee director, 300–303
  perception of, by executives, 19–38
  related to achievement, 26–28
  related to performance, 24–25
  and sales, 62
  severence *(see* Severence pay)
  for time not worked *(see* Time off with
    pay)
  (See also Compensation; Salary)
Pay/achievement combinations, significance
  of, 27
Pay action *(see* Individual pay actions)
Pay adjustments, need for objective measurements of, 28
Pay communication system, 29–31
Pay compression, 2–3, 77
  affecting differentials, 2–3
  factors affecting, 2, 64–65, 77
  and starting salaries, 2
Pay delivery systems, 1
Pay elements, quantification of, 62
Pay-for-performance concept:
  and incentive plans, 28–29, 318
  for nonemployee directors, 302

Pay-for-performance concept *(Cont.):*
  and open pay systems, 29–30
  problems with, 28–29
  variation in, used to indicate poor performance, 90
Pay incentive:
  reduced by adjusting salary structure,
    64–65
  (See also Incentive pay)
Pay objective, assessment of, 1
Pay philosophy and type of talent attracted,
  21
Pay policies and sales, 53–54
Pay preferences, 37
Pay premiums and geographic differentials,
  69
Pay program(s):
  and cost of living, 68
  divisional, 15
  need for annual revision of, 306
  need for communication of, 29–31
  need for executive understanding of, 29–
    31
  for nonemployee directors, 300–301
  relating corporate objectives to, 313–314
  shareholder reactions to, 308
  tax considerations of, 308
Pay program designs, need for training in,
  25
Pay relationships, indexing, 63
Pay value combinations, 22
  for executives, 22–23
Peer relationships, importance of, 34
Pension earnings, 112–113
  proxy disclosure requirements for, 123
Pension plans *(see* Retirement plan; Supplemental pensions)
Pension surveys, 118–119
Performance:
  and effort related to pay, 25–26
  versus position in range, 75
    and simulation of movement through
      range, 81–84
  related to effort, 24–26
  related to pay, 24–25
Performance appraisal, 71–75
  distribution of performance ratings in,
    73–75
  goal-oriented, 72
  high grade/high performance syndrome
    in, 74–75
  and merit review, 72–73

Performance appraisal *(Cont.):*
need for, 71
need for interaction between supervisor
and supervisee in, 73
and quality versus timeliness matrix, 70
raising standards in response to, 74–75
related to planning of pay programs,
307–310
timing of, 72–73
types of, 71–72
and types of incentive programs, 310
Performance evaluation programs, 26–27
Performance ratings, 71–75
distribution of, 73–75
and position in salary range, 81–83
used for developing merit budget, 78–79
Performance share plans, 248–252
adjustment of targets, 252
award based on company earnings per
share targets, 248–249
award based on company growth relative
to industry performance, 250
combined with other long-term incentives, 259–262
compared with performance unit and
stock option plans, 254–255
impact on earnings statement, 251–252
prorated payments, 250–251
types of payment plan, 250–251
Performance unit plans, 252–254
accounting requirements for, 253
combined with other long-term incentives, 259–262
compared with performance share and
stock option plans, 254–255
nonqualified stock attached to, 253
Perquisite(s), 9, 141–184
airplane use as, 148–149
apartment use as, 150–151
assignment protection as, 166
and attraction of executives, 19–20
automobile use as, 147–148
business liability insurance as, 161
business travel protection as, 166
chauffeured limousine as, 148
children's education as, 162
club membership as, 159
combination term and permanent life insurance as, 168–169
company product samples as, 147
company tax deductions for, 151–153,
158–162, 165–168

Perquisite(s) *(Cont.):*
as compensation element, 9–11
conventions and conferences as, 160
credit cards as, 159–160
disability pay as, 144
domestic staff as, 160
emphasized during stages of market cycle,
16
employee services as *(see* Employee services, as perquisites)
executive dining room as, 149–150
executive washroom as, 158
expense accounts as, 158
financial counseling as, 151–157
first-class travel as, 160–161
handling, by compensation committees,
293–294
health care as, 164–166
home entertainment as, 160
hotel rooms as, 150–151
job title as, 157–158
key employee life insurance as, 167–168
kidnap and ransom insurance as, 168
legal services as, 151
liberalized vacation as, 143–144
loans as, 162–164
medical examinations as, 164–165
and motivation of executives, 19–20
for nonemployee directors, 303
office accommodation as, 158
outplacement assistance as, 146–147
parking facilities as, 148
personal escort as, 161
personal liability insurance as, 161–162
physical fitness programs as, 150
product samples as, 147
proxy disclosure of, 142, 182–183
and retention of executives, 19–20, 22
retired lives reserve as, 174–175
retirement benefits as, 175–179
sabbatical leave as, 144
season tickets as, 159
Section 79 plans as, 168–169
security systems as, 147
severance pay as, 144–146
split dollar insurance as, 169–174
spouse travel as, 161
supplemental health care coverage as,
165–166
supplementary basic benefit programs as,
141
survivor protection as, 166–175

Perquisite(s) *(Cont.):*
tax assistance as, 151
tax effectiveness of, 142, 180–181
time off with pay as, 142–147
vacation time as, 143–144
work at home as, 144
yacht use at, 149
Personal escorts:
as perquisite, 161
proxy treatment of, 182
tax effectiveness of, 161, 180
Personal liability insurance:
company tax deduction for, 162
as perquisite, 161–162
proxy treatment of, 182
tax effectiveness of, 162, 180
Personal relationships at different stages of
market cycle, 12–13
Personal service income:
deferred, 267
and deferred compensation, 275–277
defined by Tax Reform Act of 1976, 274
from nonmarket long-term incentives,
257–258
from phantom stock plans, 256
related to stock awards, 245, 247
tax liability of, compared with ordinary
income, 3
taxation of, 5–6
Personal service income tax and unreasonable compensation, 298–299
Phantom stock plans, 255–256
appreciation form of, 256
dividend equivalents form of, 255–256
nonmarket, 257–258
total market price form of, 256
Physical fitness programs:
as perquisites, 150
proxy treatment of, 182
tax effectiveness of, 150, 180
Point factor method of job evaluation, 41–
46
developing job grades for, 42–43
developing structure for, 42–44
using job grades for, 42–46
Point factor plans, construction of, 41–42
Position description, 39–40
Preemployment physical as employee benefit, 95
Premium used to attract executives, 20
Preretirement benefit, 122

Preretirement counseling as employee benefit, 92
Product innovations, comparing growth of,
16
Product lines and market cycle, 11–14
Product samples:
as perquisites, 147
proxy treatment of, 182
tax effectiveness of, 147, 180
Professional directors, 286
Profit, ascertaining for divisions, 15
Profit sharing plans, 129–131, 274
combined with pension plans, 131
company tax deductions for, 129
current versus deferred payment, 130
nondiscriminatory rule for deferrals in,
130
Revenue Act of 1978 requirements for,
129–130
Promotion increases, 83–85
Promotional pay policy and retaining internal equity, 84
Proxy disclosure requirements, 6–7
for employee benefits, 139
for long-term incentives, 263–264
for pension payments, 123
for perquisites, 142, 182–183
for salary, 85
for short-term incentives, 216
for stock appreciation rights, 241–242
for stock options, 237
Psychic income, 22
Public pressure affecting compensation, 2

Qualified plans for deferred compensation,
269
Qualified retirement plans *(see* Retirement
plan)
Qualified stock options, 220, 225–226
Qualities of executives, 31–37

Ranges *(see* Salary range)
Ranking method for job evaluation,
40–41
Rate of compensation and rate of increase
in sales, 55–62
Recognition and compensation of execu-
tives, 21–22
Red circles, 75

Regression analysis, 42–44
  multiple, 52–53, 62–63
  and pay policies, 53–54
  use of sales in, 53–54
Regulation T of the Federal Reserve, 163
Relocation expenses:
  assignment policy for, 94
  company tax deductions for, 93–94
  as employee benefits, 93–94
Restricted stock awards, 245
Retention of executives:
  compensation elements related to, 19–24
  factors affecting, 21–24
Retired lives reserve:
  as perquisite, 174–175
  proxy treatment of, 183
  tax effectiveness of, 181
Retirement:
  early, 120–124
  as employee benefit, 109–136
  encouragement of, 175–176
    by supplemental pensions, 179
  insurance coverage after, 107
  legal requirements of, 178–179
  as perquisite, 175–179
  and preretirement counseling, 92
  proxy treatment of, 183
  and stock options, 223
  tax effectiveness of, 181
Retirement benefits:
  basis for, 109–110
  calculating, 112–113
  determining competitiveness of, 120–124
  and early retirement, 122–124
  increasing the formula for, 177
  integrating with social security, 114–117, 120
  as part of deferred pay, 110, 173–174
  related to pay received, 111
  restoring Employment Retirement Income Security Act limit on, 176
  and short-service plans, 177
  and supplemental pensions, 176–178
  tax effectiveness of, 181
  years of service versus remuneration for estimating, 123
Retirement income objective, 117

Retirement matrix, 175
Retirement plan(s):
  company tax deductions for contributions to, 110, 126
  compared, 111–113
  as deferred compensation, 109
  defined benefit (see Defined benefit plans)
  defined contribution (see Defined contribution plans)
  eligibility of employees for, 110
  Individual Retirement Accounts as, (see Individual Retirement Accounts)
  Internal Revenue Service requirements for, 110
  Keogh plans as, 135–136
  need for integrating with social security, 111
  Simplified Employee Pension as, 135–136
  stock purchase, 132–133
  types of, 110–111
  vesting formulas for, 109
  (See also Supplemental pensions)
Retirement planning, value of house in, 136
Revenue Act of 1950 and stock options, 225
Revenue Act of 1964, impact on stock options of, 225
Revenue Act of 1978:
  disallowing deductions for club expenses, 159
  and educational assistance benefits, 92
  and profit sharing plans, 129–130
  and risk of constructive receipt from deferred compensation, 270
  and Simplified Employee Pensions, 135–136
  and stock options, 221
  and taxes on long-term gains, 226–227
Review date:
  performance appraisal, 72–73
  salary, 76–77
Revocable trust, 156

Sabbatical leave:
  as perquisite, 144

Sabbatical leave (Cont.):
  proxy treatment of, 182
  tax effectiveness of, 180
Salary, 9–11, 16, 19–29
  associated with promotion, 19
  and attraction of executives, 19–21
  as compensation element, 9–11
  as cornerstone of compensation program, 39
  emphasized during stages of market cycle, 16
  as function of value of work, 39
  handled by compensation committee, 292
  and motivation of executives, 19–20, 24–29
  proxy disclosure requirements for, 85
  and retention of executives, 19–24
  starting, 2
  tax effectiveness of, 85
  used to determine eligibility for short-term incentives, 187
  (See also Compensation; Pay)
Salary grade, 44–45
  used to determine eligibility for short-term incentives, 186–187
Salary range(s), 43–45, 60–71, 81–84
  compared with bonus ranges, 186
  position in, 69–71
    after merit adjustment at various percentage spreads, 81–84
  rate of progression through, 81–84
  simulation of movement of different level performers through, 81–84
  spread in, 44–45
Salary reduction plan, 274
Salary reviews:
  and advantages and disadvantages of common review date, 76
  frequency of, 76–77
  time intervals between, 2–3, 76–77
  timing of, 76
Salary structures:
  adjusting (see Structural adjustments)
  and geographic differentials, 68–69
  range widths in, 43–45
Salary surveys, 49–64
  analysis of data from, 53–63
  defining appropriate community for, 49
  developing appropriate questions for, 52–53

Salary surveys (Cont.):
  and indexing pay relationships, 63
  and industry analysis for industry sensitive jobs, 49
  across industry lines, 49
  methods of comparing jobs for, 50–55
  need for horizontal representation in, 50
  need to include total salary and incentive pay in, 53
  need for vertical representation in, 50
  projecting and updating survey data, 63–64
  selecting jobs to be surveyed by, 50
  use of average pay increases by, 67
  use of multiple regression analysis by, 52, 62–63
  use of step-progression analyses by, 52
  used to adjust structures, 64–69
Sales:
  and pay, 62
  and pay policies, 53–54
  rate of change in, and rate of change in compensation, 55–62
Savings plans, 124–128
Scholarships:
  as employee benefits, 93, 162
  as perquisite, 162
Season tickets:
  company tax deductions for, 159
  as perquisites, 159
  proxy treatment of, 182
  tax effectiveness of, 159, 180
SEC (see Securities and Exchange Commission)
Section 79 plans as perquisites, 168–169
Securities and Exchange Commission (SEC):
  definition of insider, 220
  disclosure requirements relating to compensation, 6–7
  interpretation of income, 142
  requirements for short-term incentives, 216
  roles for stock appreciation rights, 238–239
Security systems:
  as perquisites, 147
  proxy treatment of, 182
  tax effectiveness of, 147, 180
Senior executives, forms of pay for, 3
Service awards as employee benefits, 92

Severance pay, 89–90
  Department of Labor rulings on, 146
  formulas for determining, 144–146
  as perquisite, 144–146
  proxy treatment of, 182
  tax effectiveness of, 180
Severance plans as employee benefits, 90
Short-service plans, 177
Short-term capital gains, rate of taxation of, 5
Short-term disability plans, 89
Short-term incentive awards, 207–215
  allocated from two or more funds, 196–199
  amount of, 207–213
  bonus guidelines for, 199, 203–204
  and bonus percentages by salary grade, 198
  in cash, 214–215
  in cash and stock combinations, 214
  combinations of form and timing of, 214
  determination of amount of, 207–213
    based on individual and division performance, 208–209
  determination of divisional, 198–204
  determination by formula of, 209–211
  evaluation of performance for, 199–204
  form of, 213–214
  linked to performance ratings, 211–213
  matrix used to determine payment level of, 192
  performance criteria for, 201–202
  and position in range, 202, 204
  related to performance and total compensation, 211–213, 215
  related to salary schedule, 207
  in stock, 214–215
  target values for determining, 205–206
  tax considerations of, 214–215
  timing of, 213–214
Short-term incentives, 9, 185–217
  and attraction of executives, 19–20
  awards based on growth in earnings per share and return on capital as, 192–193
  as compensation element, 9–11
  determination of elegibility for, 186–188
  emphasized during stages of market cycle, 16
  handled by compensation committee, 294–295

Short-term incentives (Cont.):
  key position approach to determining eligibility for, 186–187
  and motivation of executives, 19–20
  percentage of employee population eligible for, 187
  proxy disclosure requirements for, 216
  and retention of executives, 19–20
  salary grade approach to determining eligibility for, 187
  salary used to determine eligibility for, 187
  Securities and Exchange Commission requirements for, 216
  tax effectiveness of, 216
  (See also Bonus funds; Incentive plans)
Short-term profit sharing plans, 129
Simplified Employee Pension (SEP), 135–136
Social security:
  benefits, 111, 113–114
  integrated with employee benefits, 114–117, 120
  as percentage of final pay, 114
  taxes, 115
Special awards, 215
Split dollar insurance:
  approaches to, 169–170
  characteristics of, 169
  drawbacks of, 174
  Internal Revenue Service rulings on, 170, 173
  as perquisite, 169–174
  premium table for, 171
  proxy treatment of, 183
  tax effectiveness of, 181
  tax impact of, 172–173
  value to executive of, 170–173
Spouse travel:
  as perquisite, 161
  proxy treatment of, 182
  tax effectiveness of, 161, 180
Stabilization Act, 87
Starting salaries and pay compression, 2
Step-progression analysis for salary surveys, 52
Step-up approach for integrating social security and pension benefits, 114–116
Stock:
  versus cash, accounting impact of, 272–273

Stock *(Cont.)*:
  disqualifying disposition of, 220
  lag between performance and price of,
    225
  as short-term incentive award, 214–215
Stock appreciation rights, 237–242
  accounting regulations for, 239–240
  compared with stock-for-stock exchanges,
    240–241
  proxy disclosure requirements for, 241–
    242
  Securities and Exchange Commission
    rules for, 238–239
  in tandem with stock options, 240–242
  and termination, 240
  variations of, 238
Stock awards, 244–248
  and capital gains, 247
  in cash to meet tax liability, 245–246
  combined with other long-term incen-
    tives, 259–262
  setting restrictions on, 245
  situations for use of, 247
  tax considerations for when restrictions
    are lifted, 245
Stock-for-stock exchange, 223–224
  compared with stock appreciation rights,
    240–241
Stock option multiples, 228–232
  ratios used in, 229–231
Stock option plans:
  compared with performance share and
    performance unit plans, 254–255
  compared with stock purchase plans, 133,
    242
  cost to company of, 310
Stock options:
  annual grants of, 234, 236
  as deferred compensation, 236
  buy-back program for, 224
  cancel-and-reissue program for, 236
  cash supplement to, 224
  catch-up grant of, 234–236
  combination market and nonmarket,
    260–262
  combined with other long-term incen-
    tives, 259–262
  when a company is acquired by another
    one, 222–223
  cost to company of, 221–222
  defined, 219
  discount on nonqualified, 221

Stock options *(Cont.)*:
  downside risk in, 236–237
  eligibility for, 228
  factors affecting present valuation of,
    232–233
  formula for interim or catch-up option of,
    234–235
  frequency of grants of, 234–237
  gains on, 233–234
  historical valuation of, 233–234
  history of, 225–227
  interim grant of, 234–236
  legislation affecting, 225–227
  as long-term incentives, 219–237
  multiple technique for structuring, 228–
    232
  nonmarket, 258–259
  nonqualified, 220–221
  present viability of, 227–228
  prospective valuation of, 232–233
  proxy disclosure requirements for, 237
  qualified, 220, 225–226
  and registration of stock, 222
  related to performance, 224–225
  and retirement, 223
  revenue acts and, 221, 225
  shareholder approval of plans for, 222,
    224, 236
  size of, 228–237
  stock-for-stock exchanges of, 223–224
  swapping, 236
  in tandem with stock appreciation rights,
    240–242
  tax consequences of purchase of stock us-
    ing, 219–220, 222, 224
  tax considerations of, 220–222, 226
  and termination, 223, 236
  treasury method for evaluating cost to
    company of, 222
  valuation of, 232–234
  waiting period for, 223
  wash sale transaction in, 219
Stock plans, phantom (*see* Phantom stock
    plans)
Stock prices:
  rates of growth in, 232
  related to book value, 16
Stock purchase plans:
  company loans for, 242, 243
  compared with stock option plans, 133,
    242
  discounted, 243

Stock purchase plans *(Cont.):*
  as employee benefits, 132–133
  fixed cost and fixed basis payment in,
    242–243
  fixed cost and variable basis for payment
    in, 243
  as long-term incentives, 242–244
  methods of payment for, 242–244
  variable cost and fixed basis for payment
    in, 243–244
  variable cost and variable basis payment
    in, 244
Stock purchases:
  loans for, 163–164
  and margin calls, 163
Stock values, factors affecting, 16
Stress on executives, impact of, 35–36
Structural adjustments, 64–69
  amount of, 65–66
  causing compression of differential, 64–65
  and competitive position of company,
    64–66
  reducing pay incentive, 64–65
  timing of, 65–66
Subordinates, relationships of executives
  with, 34–35
Substantial risk of forfeiture, 273, 276
Superiors, relationships of executives with,
  33–34
Supplemental health care coverage:
  company tax deductions for, 165
  Internal Revenue Service requirements
    for, 166
  as a perquisite, 165–166
  proxy treatment of, 183
  tax effectiveness of, 165, 181
Supplemental pensions:
  advantage to company of, 178
  determining amount of supplement in,
    177–178
  for executives, 176–178
  used to encourage retirement, 179
  value to executive of, 178
  (See also Retirement plan)
Survey community:
  and competitive position of company,
    65–66
  for salary survey, 49
Survey leveling, 51
Survey ratio, 51
Survivor benefits, 100

Survivor protection:
  as employee benefit, 98–109
    company coverage, 100–102
    endowment policies, 99
    life insurance, 98–100
    survivor benefits, 100
    (See also Insurance; Life insurance)
  as perquisite, 166–175
    assignment protection, 166
    business travel protection, 166
    combination term and permanent life in-
      surance, 168–169
    key employee life insurance, 167–168
    kidnap and ransom insurance, 168
    proxy treatment of, 183
    retired lives reserve, 174–175
    Section 79 plans, 168–169
    split dollar insurance, 169–174
    tax effectiveness of, 181

Tasks, 39–40
  listing, in job description, 40
Tax *(see specific taxes)*
Tax assistance:
  company tax deductions for, 151
  as perquisite, 151
  proxy treatment of, 182
  tax effectiveness of, 151, 180
Tax avoidance, 152–153
Tax considerations of compensation elements, 3–6
Tax deductions *(see* Company tax deductions)
Tax effectiveness:
  of airplane use, 148–149, 180
  of apartment or hotel room use, 151, 180
  of assignment protection, 166, 181
  of automobile use, 148, 180
  of business liability insurance, 161, 180
  of chauffeured limousine, 180
  of children's education, 162, 180
  of club membership, 159, 180
  when compensation ruled as unreasona-
    ble, 298
  of conventions and conferences, 180
  of credit cards, 180
  of deferred compensation, 179, 181
  of dividends from stock, 263
  of domestic staff, 160, 180
  of employee benefits, 138
  of employee services, 180

Tax effectiveness *(Cont.):*
of executive dining room, 150, 180
of executive washroom 158, 180
of expense accounts, 158, 180
of financial counseling, 180
of first-class travel, 180
of home entertainment, 160, 180
of job title, 180
of key employee life insurance, 181
of kidnap and ransom insurance, 181
of legal services, 151, 180
of life insurance, 181
of loans, 162–164, 180
measurement of, 5–6
of medical examinations, 165, 181
of nonmarket stock options, 258
normal value of, 5
of office accommodation, 158, 180
of outplacement assistance, 147, 180
of parking facilities, 148, 180
of perquisites, 142, 180–181
of personal escorts, 161, 180
of personal liability insurance, 162, 180
of phyical fitness programs, 150, 180
of product samples, 147, 180
of retirement benefits, 181
of salary, 85
of season tickets, 159, 180
of security systems, 180
of short-term incentives, 216
of spouse travel, 161, 180
of supplemental health care coverage, 165, 181
of survivor protection, 181
of tax assistance, 151, 180
of time off with pay, 142, 180
of yacht use, 180
Tax evasion, 152
Tax-free rollover, 123, 128, 134
Tax impact, company options affecting, 4–6
Tax liability:
on company loans, 164
deferred, 125, 133
on deferred compensation, 269, 270, 272–273, 275
on depreciated properties, 153
and doctrine of constructive receipt, 271
on economic benefit, 271–272
on estates (*see* Estate tax liability)
on exercise of stock option, 220, 222, 224, 226

Tax liability *(Cont.):*
and unreasonable compensation, 298–300
on withdrawals from pension plans, 127–128
Tax penalties, 134
Tax preference income, 226–227
Tax Reform Act of 1969:
deferred compensation plans prior to, 273
and stock options, 226
Tax Reform Act of 1976, 91, 220
and deferred compensation, 274
impact on estate planning, 154
and stock options, 227
Tax shelters, 153, 274
company tax deductions for, 153
margin calls as, 163
risk/reward ratio of, 153
Taxation:
of constructive receipt, 6
of distributions from pension plans, 127–128
of economic benefit, 6
of expenses, 4–5
of imputed income, 6
of insurance income, 101
of life insurance proceeds, 107–108
of pension benefits, 110
rates of, 3–5
rules affecting Tax Reduction Act form of employee stock ownership plan, 132
of short-term incentive awards, 214–215
under 10-year forward averaging rules, 127–128
of withdrawals from pension plans, 127–128
Technical Corrections Act, 131–132
Term insurance, 99–100
Termination of executives:
reasons for, 90
and stock appreciation rights, 240
and stock options, 223, 236
Testamentary trusts, 155–156
Threshold stage of market cycle, 11–12, 15
Time off with pay:
as employee benefit, 88–90
court leave, 88
disability plans, 89

Time off with pay, as employee benefit
(*Cont.*):
funeral leave, 88
paid holidays, 88
severance pay, 89–90
vacation allowance, 88
as perquisite, 142–147
disability pay, 144
liberalized vacation, 143–144
outplacement assistance, 146–147
sabbatical leave, 144
severance pay, 144–146
tax effectiveness of, 142–143, 181
work at home, 144
Total plan participation vesting, 126–127
Travel and entertainment expenses, 94
(*See also* First-class travel; Spouse travel)
Treasury method for evaluating cost of
stock, 222
Trusts, 155–157
Educational Benefit, 162
generation-skipping, 156
insurance, 157
inter vivos, 155–156
irrevocable, 156
living, 156
revocable, 156
testamentary, 155–156

Unemployment compensation, 90
Unified estate and gift tax table, 154–155
Unisex tables and defined contribution
plans, 128

Unreasonable compensation, 298–300
checklist for, 299
taxation of, 6
Updated career earnings plans, 112

Vacation allowance as employee benefit, 88
Vacation time (*see* Liberalized vacation)
Value of house in retirement planning, 136
Vesting:
class year, 126–127
in deferred compensation plans, 269, 270
rules of Employee Retirement Income
Security Act for, 109, 126–127
total plan participation in, 126–127
Vesting formulas for qualified retirement
plans, 109

Wash sale transaction, 219
Whole life insurance, 98–100
Withdrawals from pension plans, 127–128
effect of unisex tables on, 128
taxation of, 127–128
Work at home:
as perquisite, 144
proxy treatment of, 182
tax effectiveness of, 180
Workaholics, 36
Worker's compensation, 88

Yacht:
as perquisite, 149
proxy treatment of, 182
tax effectiveness of, 180